Foreign Policy
for a New Age

Foreign Policy for a New Age

Robert G. Wesson

UNIVERSITY OF CALIFORNIA, SANTA BARBARA

HOUGHTON MIFFLIN COMPANY · Boston

Atlanta Dallas Geneva, Illinois Hopewell, New Jersey
Palo Alto London

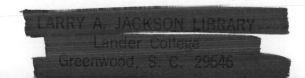

Printed in the U.S.A.

Library of Congress Catalog Card Number: 76–13999

ISBN: 0–395–24652–0

Contents

Preface

The goal of this volume is to convey a broad understanding of American foreign policy—what it has and has not been, the major problems it faces, and the directions it may be taking. This aim implies a forward-looking view, an endeavor to regard the actions of the United States in the world arena, not only in terms of conventional security preoccupations but also in light of the complex global reality of the latter 1970s.

For this purpose, the book traces the interventionist course of the United States, from the Spanish-American War through the Vietnam conflict, and focuses on the ambiguities of American foreign policy making. It then considers both the military and the sometimes neglected nonmilitary aspects of American foreign policy. It investigates the requirements of rational foreign policy in relation to the other advanced industrial states, the communist states, and the nations of the Third World, which include two-thirds of humanity and a large share of the world's problems. Finally, this book places American foreign policy in the context of the new international order that is taking shape.

The approach of the book is neither revisionist nor traditionalist. In such a controversial area, it is impossible to give broad answers that everyone will find acceptable. Divergent opinions are represented by works cited in footnotes and the bibliography. Clear-cut judgments are expressed in many areas, however, in the conviction that an author need not be ashamed of his own ideas; the reader may decide whether these ideas are rational and well founded.

It is a pleasure to acknowledge the valuable assistance of a number of scholars who have read and criticized this work; in some cases

they have lent their help several times and at all stages, from prospec-
tus to finished manuscript. These individuals include Professors Walter
C. Clemens of Boston University; Roy Olton of Western Michigan University; Richard D. Sears of Wake Forest University; Vernon Van
Dyke of the University of Iowa; and Gerald D. Watson of the University of Northern Colorado. Although probably none of them will agree
with everything expressed herein, their general guidance and detailed
comments have substantially improved this work. Thanks also go to
Deborah T. Wesson, whose assistance in innumerable ways has helped
to make the book possible.

R.G.W.

Introduction

The modern world lacks a compass to guide it through the jungle that has sprung up from its technology, and American society lacks direction—as do other societies—both in its internal evolution and in its relation to the broader world, its participation in the community of states. At the beginning of the 1970s, the United States turned from confrontation to dialogue with its adversaries during a generation of cold war, the Soviet Union and China. American foreign policy has since emerged as little more than an incoherent series of ad hoc responses to pressing needs—military withdrawal from Vietnam, defusion of the explosive Near Eastern situation, grappling with the petroleum cartel, negotiation about strategic weapons, and the discovery of means by which to reduce the clamor of the Third World, to name a few. There have been some half-hearted efforts to develop new doctrine, but they have had little impact. For example, the so-called Nixon Doctrine of helping allies only insofar as they would help themselves was little more than a rationalization for turning the fighting in Vietnam over to the Vietnamese (Victnamization) and for the retrenchment mandated by revulsion against the unsuccessful war. There was some idea of working toward a new multipolar balance of power, in which China, Japan, and western Europe would join the present military superpowers, the United States and the Soviet Union, in keeping the peace. But this pentagonal arrangement was only a neat theory based on Secretary of State Henry A. Kissinger's reading of nineteenth-century European diplomatic history and was never operative. *Détente* became a catchword, only to raise new questions.

It is not absolutely essential, of course, that the United States possess any grand concept of foreign policy. During most of its history, the country managed quite as well without much of an overall design as when it formulated a clearer concept of mission. It is certainly better to limit oneself to trying to solve practical difficulties as they arise rather than to march off on ill-conceived crusades. But the anarchic world of today has a more obvious need for leadership than did the world of a half-century or a century ago, and no nation other than the United States is in a position to exert much positive influence. The United States is not only by far the richest and the most industrially powerful nation; it is also the chief fountain of modern technology and ideas, the most creative and freest to lay out new roads. No other nation can lead the industrial world in dealing with the petroleum question or undertake the reconstruction of the world economic and monetary systems. The United States cannot escape a special responsibility that comes not by a conscious design to dominate but mostly by default of the rest of the states of the world. If the United States were suddenly to shrink to powerlessness, another nation would perhaps come forward to assert world leadership; but as long as the United States stands with its industrial weight and technological prowess, no other leader is likely to come forward. Unfortunately, the leadership role is frustrating when one does not know how or whether to lead.

In this situation, the guidelines of the past generation do not seem very helpful. The dominant concern has been security in a political-military sense, and the major question has usually been rather simple in principle: are the safety and vital interests of this country better served by intervention or by noninvolvement? This question has been answered differently according to mood and circumstances, but it has never required such a fundamental rethinking as is now in order. At present the basic problems are quite different: whether the freedom of nations is compatible with the development of a workable world community, and whether international cooperation can be sufficient to enable humanity to surmount the troubles of the technological age. There is now a need for a deeper reorientation than ever before in American history, a reorientation from a basically national approach to a global approach to world affairs.

A major thesis of this book, then, is that the state system has evolved fundamentally and will probably continue to change rapidly, while foreign policy thinking lags seriously behind. The international system is not a mechanical affair, a mere constellation of interacting loci of power, but a set of subtle interactions based on the values of leaders and peoples. These values, the desiderata sought by states in dealing with one another, have altered markedly in the last several decades; insofar as purposes have changed, the state system is essentially transformed. Ways in which the state system has changed (which are elaborated subsequently, mostly in Chapter Nine) include (1) a large growth of nonpolitical interaction and thus of the interdependence of states; (2) increased impingement of external upon domestic affairs, with a consequent merging of foreign and domestic policies; (3) a shift of concern from territorial and security issues to economic matters; (4) a decrease of ideological fixations and a recognition of the need for cooperation across different political philosophies; and (5) the rise of nonmilitary threats to security and well-being, including such issues as energy availability, population growth, resources management, and environmental quality. The structure of the state system has also changed markedly in several ways. American economic dominance has receded sharply; the United States produced about half of world gross national product (GNP) in 1947, 34 percent in 1960, and 27 percent in 1975.[1] The ability of the United States to go its own way has declined correspondingly in other areas. The number of independent nations has grown from somewhat over 50 at the end of World War II to over 140. Many of the new countries, formerly included in colonial empires, are very much poorer than the industrialized states, and the development gap has become a major rift in the system. Alliances have tended to lose firmness. Diplomacy has become less bilateral. Many specialized international organizations have evolved as instruments of multilateral diplomacy.

These facts are all obvious and are well known in high government circles and elsewhere. A recent high-level commission has commented rather extensively on some of the changes.[2] Secretary of State Kissinger himself, although his background is primarily in traditional diplomacy, remarked in January 1975 that issues of energy, resources, environment, and the like now rank with the traditional issues of defense, ideology and territorial rivalry.[3] The thesis of interdependence, long on the agenda, has become popular to the point of modishness and is a regular topic of official declarations on international questions.

Yet this awareness of crucial changes remains largely inchoate and has yet to become an important factor in foreign policy. About 95 per-

---

1. *Commission on the Organization of the Government for the Conduct of Foreign Policy*, Government Printing Office, Washington, 1975, p. 26.
2. Ibid., p. 27.
3. Ibid., p. 25.

cent of appropriations for foreign relations still go to the military. If some policy makers make a greater effort to see humanity as a whole and stress the need for common action to overcome long-range dangers, others still see power as the central issue and focus on interstate conflicts. Scientists are especially prone to the former outlook,[4] politicians to the latter. But even though generals are likely to support their profession, while professors are supposedly pacific and enlightened, the dichotomy is not clear. General Maxwell Taylor, for example, finds that nonmilitary threats have overtaken the military,[5] while many academics analyze foreign relations in terms of rather narrowly conceived power. A recent work states flatly that power, prestige, and security are the goals of foreign policy and suggests no others.[6]

The primary thesis of this book, then, is the need to draw far-reaching conclusions from the alterations of the international scene and to modify the directions and emphases of foreign policy accordingly in hopes of the evolution of a better international order. The book has, however, another and somewhat less obvious thesis. Beginning approximately with the Spanish-American War of 1898 and continuing through the Vietnam war, the United States has gone somewhat astray in the direction of interventionism; the nation has attempted to do things that it was not well prepared to do and has used methods and means that ill suited the national political character. In short, because of its constitutional structure and the pluralistic nature of its society, the United States is poorly equipped for an imperial or semi-imperial role. So far as the country has tried to assume such a role, frequently proceeding contrary to the laws and the spirit of the Constitution, it has generally been disappointed. The happy conclusion is that the basic transformation called for to adapt American foreign policy to the new world is to renounce the interventionist bent and turn back toward the pre-1890s tradition. This shift entails checking the "imperial presidency" and restoring responsibility and openness to the conduct of foreign affairs; it also implies shifting attention from the use of force abroad to the economic and cultural aspects of foreign relations, areas in which the United States excels.

---

4. As expressed, for example, in *The Bulletin of Atomic Scientists.*

5. General Maxwell Taylor, "The Exposed Flank of National Security," *Orbis,* 28 (Winter 1975), 1011–1022.

6. John H. Esterline and Robert B. Black, *American Foreign Policy: The Department of State Political System and its Subsystems,* Mayfield, Palo Alto, 1975, p. 23.

Chapter One traces the penchant for forceful intervention in foreign affairs from the Spanish-American War through two world wars, the cold war, and the involvement in Vietnam, longest and most frustrating of all. Chapters Two, Three, and Four discuss the main dimensions of foreign policy: the overemphasized military aspect, the increasingly prominent economic factors, and the underemphasized psychological or attitudinal elements. Chapter Five describes the institutional mechanisms through which foreign policy is formulated and effected and various checks and balances in the system. The next chapters discuss relations with the broad groups of countries with which the United States must deal: the Western industrial nations (including Japan), with which political frictions are slight (Chapter Six); the ideological adversary communist states (Chapter Seven); and the non-Western, developing or less developed countries, relations with which have historically a novel character (Chapters Eight and Nine). The less developed countries require two chapters because international contentions increasingly revolve around their demands. Chapters Ten and Eleven discuss the ongoing metamorphosis of the state system, with its changing values and dangers, and the movement toward a new order. The final chapter examines briefly the part that this country might be expected to play in the construction of the new order.

Foreign Policy
for a New Age

CHAPTER ONE

From Isolationism
to Interventionism

THE BASIC TRADITIONS

Makers of foreign policy are guided largely by the experience of the past.[1] The world is so complicated and unpredictable, and it is so unclear how national interests are to be defined in new circumstances, that the fallible and finite men in charge of destinies of states analyze the unknown in terms of the known, doing more or less as has been done or seeking to avoid the mistakes of the remembered past. It is trite to say that the generals prepare for the last war, which is the one they know about. The diplomats also try to avoid the last war; much of the diplomacy of the period after World War II was rationalized in terms of shunning the blunders that led to that war. Even the ordeal of Vietnam has led to only a partial mental breakaway from the patterns established in the 1950s based on analogies with the 1930s.

But the American tradition is dual; there are politically isolationist and antimilitarist elements as well as interventionist-militarist elements. Within five years of the crusading fervor of World War I, the United States relapsed into strict noninvolvement in European political affairs. In the latter part of the Vietnam war, repugnance became so strong that officers felt unable to wear uniforms in public. The feeling has never been entirely absent that it is better not to be too much entangled in the affairs of other nations, that if the United States has to step in to set things right it should be for only a limited time. Having done our duty, we should be able to relax and tend our own garden.

This relatively isolationist stance has been the older and long-dominant mood; the backbone of the American character has been a sense of detached superiority. Even before independence, settlers who braved the Atlantic for weeks of turbulent sailing could easily believe that they had reached a New World (a *New* England or *New* Jersey) and that they had left behind the evils of the European system—its balance of power politics, cynical diplomacy, and useless wars of greedy princes.[2] When conflicts with the British monarchy arose, the

---

1. Cf. Ernest R. May, *"Lessons" of the Past: The Use and Misuse of History in American Foreign Policy*, Oxford University Press, New York, 1973. See also Irving L. Janis, *Victims of Groupthink*, Houghton Mifflin, Boston, 1972; John G. Stoessinger, *Nations in Darkness: China, Russia, America*, Random House, New York, 1971; Stanley Hoffman, *Gulliver's Troubles, Or the Setting of American Foreign Policy*, McGraw-Hill, New York, 1968.

2. As argued by Thomas Paine in his famous pamphlet *Common Sense*. For the disinclination of the colonists to participate in European contentions, see Felix Gilbert, *To the Farewell Address*, Princeton University Press, Princeton, N.J., 1961.

colonists were led to renounce loyalty to the metropolis not only by their rather slight grievances but also by their desire to be liberated from European conflicts; the movement of resistance to British rule began during and shortly after the Seven Years War (1756–1763). After the American Revolution, Americans could take pride not only in their victory over a leading European power but also in their ideals and daring republican institutions. These ideals and institutions were a major stimulus for the French Revolution and an inspiration for political liberals of many generations.[3] The young nation went on to virtually unbroken and unexampled success. The original colonial territories were multiplied many times over with minimal difficulty. Even the one war that it cost to round out the continental domain, the conflict with Mexico, was more glorious than it appears today. Although the Mexican army was considerably larger than the American army and the Mexican leaders had hopes of victory, the war turned into a parade of American victories. Never has so rich a domain been put together at so little cost.

Economic success confirmed political virtue. From colonial days, Americans had been better off materially than the people of Europe, largely because of the abundance of land and other resources. With the expansion of agriculture across the plains and the growth of industry, American wealth grew more outstanding. Especially after the Civil War, the economy boomed. By 1890, the United States had surpassed the old leader (Great Britain) in heavy industry, and the American share of world production kept on climbing. By 1900, the United States accounted for nearly 40 percent of the world's output of iron, steel, and coal—a share about twice as large as that of today—and the nation was the leading grain exporter, as it has remained ever since.

Material and political success was made possible by various factors, including the natural advantages of the central part of North America and the protective moat of the oceans, the antagonisms among European powers, and the control of the seas by Britain, a relatively nonaggressive power with shared cultural and political traditions. Success may also have derived partly from institutions that invited men to work to improve their condition and nurtured a strong sense of superiority. With a vision of rational progress deriving from the Enlightenment (the skeptical philosophical movement of the eighteenth century),

---

3. R. R. Palmer, "Social and Psychological Foundations of the Revolutionary Era," in *The New Cambridge Modern History*, Vol. 8, ed. A. Goodwin, University Press, Cambridge, 1968, pp. 441–443.

Americans saw themselves as morally better people who enjoyed rights denied to European masses.

Like remakers of the political order in modern Russia, China, and elsewhere, the leaders of the American independence movement felt that they were fighting for a cause of broad validity, for a new and better form of government and society. History subsequently seemed to confirm the special ("manifest") destiny of the American way. With a representative government unique in the world, unburdened by kings and haughty aristocrats and feudal bonds, the United States had a claim to be, if not mistress of the globe, certainly a good example for all. Thomas Jefferson had said that the revolution in which he shared "was intended for all mankind," [4] and this feeling flourished as the republic expanded and the economy boomed. As John Quincy Adams wrote in 1821, America "is the well-wisher to the freedom and independence of all. . . . She will recommend the general cause by the countenance of her voice and by the benignant sympathy of her example." [5]

This glow, which endured until the Vietnam war, came more easily because the United States was by far the least militaristic of the major powers. At the outset, the Founding Fathers wished to avoid a standing army, preferring to rely upon a popular militia. They inserted into the Constitution several provisions intended to check military power, including not only power of the purse (no appropriation being for longer than two years) but also the reservation to Congress of the right to declare war and the authority to make rules for the army and navy. Until the Civil War there was no compulsory military service even in wartime; a peacetime draft began only as the country drifted toward entry into World War II. Territorial expansion came so easily that it was taken for granted and hardly related to military power.

The hard-fought Civil War led to no militarization; in following decades, the army became little more than a corps of Indian fighters. In 1895, it had 27,495 men; that is, only one person in 1,650 was in the army. Military spending was less than 0.5 percent of the national product, about half the proportion of largely disarmed Japan today. In 1910, after the United States had taken on an imperial role, the army had 79,000 men, compared with Germany's 615,000 and France's

---

4. Quoted by Hans Morgenthau, *Purpose of American Politics*, Knopf, New York, 1960, p. 159.

5. Quoted by Ronald Steel, *Pax Americana*, Viking, New York, 1970, p. xi.

607,000.[6] Successful generals, from Washington through Grant and Eisenhower, became president, but they were even less interventionist than presidents from a civilian background; it was taken for granted that the army stayed clear of politics; nor was the navy a consequential instrument of national purpose. Its chief function through most of the nineteenth century was to protect American shipping from irregular (non-European) threats. In the 1870s the navy had become impotent and run down, with obsolete wooden ships; only in 1883 was a small-scale building program begun out of fear that any confrontation with a major power could prove embarrassing. In 1891 the Chilean navy was still stronger than that of the United States.[7]

Moral superiority and antimilitarism together contributed to a complex of sentiments roughly lumped together as isolationism, which might perhaps better be called continentalism. With terrritorial and economic expansion, the United States came to seem more and more a world to itself, serenely secure, a uniquely free nation on a bounteous continent. With a sense of omnipotence in the blessed New World, Americans saw little reason to become involved in the quarrels of the Old World. Wars were the work of monarchs, and the balance of power was seen as their vice. The power politics of Europe was part of the evil system that the colonists had left behind and demonstrated to be inferior by their success.

By corollary, as it came in the nineteenth century to be the hegemonic power in its hemisphere, the United States lost its feeling for dealing with equals. Friends were (as in Latin America) inferiors.[8] There was little idea of compromising principles in political combinations. Power politics was unnecessary, in the American view, because a single right should prevail—an attitude sustainable only where, as in North America, there was a single unchallengeable great power. It was felt that the normal condition of the world was harmony with respect for law, as prevailed on the American continent; turmoil and political contest could only represent forces of evil. Problems would be solvable if only there were good will or if other nations could be brought to imitate American political virtues.

---

6. *Encyclopedia Britannica*, 11th ed., XXII, 757; XI, 825; X, 795. For a history of United States armed forces, see Walter Millis, *Arms and Men: A Study in American Military History*, Putnam's Sons, New York, 1956.

7. David F. Long, *The Outward View: An Illustrated History of United States Foreign Relations*, Rand McNally, Chicago, 1963, p. 186.

8. As noted by Hoffman, *Gulliver's Troubles*, p. 113.

This attitude implied a moralistic approach to international affairs: actions were to be seen not in terms of legitimate national interests, which might conflict with legitimate interests of others, but in terms of absolute right. Foreign policy became permanently swathed in morality.[9] It became (and remained) customary to state American positions in lofty tones. With faith, as it were, in "the power of positive thinking," it often seemed to be assumed that noble statements, as in the Open Door policy for China, were sufficient and were a substitute for more positive action.[10] Depreciation of power politics, moreover, meant distrust of diplomacy. In practice, American negotiators often reaped advantageous settlements, as in the various transfers of territory to the United States. Nevertheless, diplomacy was regarded as vaguely un-American. It was assumed that in the diplomatic arena the naive nation was likely to lose to the shysters of the European chancelleries. Diplomacy should be unnecessary, as compromise was unnecessary, when the right was clear.

For such reasons the American foreign policy establishment was weak and small; the State Department had only a handful of employees through the nineteenth century, sixty-nine in 1893.[11] American foreign representation was amateurish. Uniquely among great powers, the United States rewarded successful businessmen and campaign contributors with ambassadorships, a practice that has not yet been fully laid to rest. There was a reluctance not only to enter alliances but also to take any kind of joint action. The allergy was not merely a rejection of European bonds; numerous bids for alliances with Latin American nations were rejected without serious consideration. In 1885 a multilateral treaty for the suppression of slavery was refused on the grounds that it might imply excessive involvement. This feeling was hardly overcome until the post–World War II revolution.

Something of this feeling has lived on despite the avidity for alliances manifested in the 1950s (when the United States was spreading bases around the world and holding its protective wing over more than forty countries) and despite the shrinkage of the world and the tendency to assume that any trouble anywhere implies an American re-

---

9. Charles Frankel, *Mortality and Foreign Policy*, Foreign Policy Association, New York, 1975, p. 10.

10. Cf. George F. Kennan, *American Diplomacy 1900–1950*, University of Chicago Press, Chicago, 1951.

11. Graham H. Stuart, *The Department of State: A History of Its Organization, Procedures, and Personnel*, Macmillan, New York, 1949, p. 182.

sponsibility. The State Department has remained low in prestige, distrusted by Congress and usually by the president as well. The diplomatic professionals have been especially deprecated, whether as too conservative (as by Presidents Franklin Roosevelt and John Kennedy) or as too liberal (as in Senator Joseph McCarthy's attack on those who allegedly betrayed China to communism). A civilian-minded, business-oriented, and basically rather pacific people naturally tends to distrust the military arm as something slightly alien to the American way of life. It was with relief that the country saw peacetime conscription ended in 1973; the demurrers were from those who feared that a professional military force might become politically potent. The principle of civilian control of the defense establishment has never been questioned and has recently even been strengthened as the Congress has asserted its rights of oversight and inquiry. It remains an American ideal that the rest of the world should require no more forceful American intervention than the good example of which John Q. Adams spoke, as the nations dedicate themselves to the pursuit of prosperity and mutually beneficial commerce.

This ideal, indeed, comes more to the fore as the United States loses some of the sense of superiority and responsibility engendered in the post–World War II period not only by American power and wealth but by successful leadership. On the one hand, American material superiority has shrunk drastically; American productivity and prosperity are no longer so very exceptional in the world. On the other hand, the country that congratulated itself on its noble enterprises, its generous help first for postwar reconstruction and then for the uplift of the needier nations, its championing of freedom, and its opposition to communism finds itself more reprobated than admired in the world. The American mission obviously went astray, misled by the blindness that often penalizes success; the inadequacy of the cruder types of power has become all too evident. Taking a new look at itself, America must question whether many of its efforts were not ill spent.

THE WARS: ENTRY INTO THE WORLD SCENE

For more than a century, the overwhelming purposes of American foreign policy were the strength and security of the republic at home, and the expansion and fulfillment of dominion across the continent. These goals were usually supported with enthusiasm (except when and where complicated by the slavery question); they were an adequate outlet for the energies Americans wished to dedicate to foreign affairs; and the results were contemplated with general satisfaction.

However, the clarity of American policy should not be overdrawn. Even before the series of wars led to what was often called the globalism of the cold war and the commitment to save Vietnam from communism, the principle of noninvolvement was qualified. It applied chiefly to European power politics, for which the young republic retained a repugnance tinged with fear well after it had much surpassed the great European powers economically. In other areas (Latin America and the Far East), the United States asserted itself occasionally at an early date.

In 1823 President James Monroe asserted a sort of protectorate over the republics of Latin America: the United States would regard as an unfriendly act any effort to reimpose European rule. This ambitious fencing off of the New World, which still colors United States relations with its southern neighbors, was somewhat unrealistic because much of Latin America was closer to continental Europe than to the United States, not only economically and culturally but also in part geographically. The policy was effective mostly because it corresponded to British policy, although Monroe declined to act jointly with the British. It was probably also unnecessary, since there was no real threat to the Latin American states. Thus the Monroe Doctrine was soon virtually forgotten, seldom invoked until after 1890, when it became the lever of pretext for scores of actions, mostly irritating to Latin Americans and of little profit to the United States.

Asians, likewise, were seen as needing American help against predatory European powers. The first interest, however, was commerce. From the time of England's Opium War against China (1839–1842), the United States was pressing for equal access to the fabulous and mostly mythical Chinese market. In 1853 Commodore Matthew C. Perry demanded of Japan good treatment for stranded American sailors and coaling stations for ships. When the Japanese hesitated to end their old seclusion, he forced open the door. Japan became for a time something of an American protégé, because the Japanese regarded the United States as less dangerous than other maritime powers. Perry also took possession of several Pacific islands, including Okinawa; they were, however, rejected by Congress, as was Hawaii, where there had been a predominant American interest since the 1840s. The United States was not ready for expansion far afield.

In the last decades of the nineteenth century, however, the outlook was changing. With the continental frontier closed and Indian resistance ended, the country was ready for new worlds to conquer. More populous and richer than leading European powers, the United States was capable of world primacy if it had cared to assert the claim. At the same time, colonial empire building, which had subsided earlier in the century, came back into fashion in Europe. To have an overseas empire and to share in the civilizing of the non-European world became the badge of national maturity; in the 1880s and 1890s Britain, France, Germany, Russia, Italy, and even Belgium became involved in a scramble for territories in Africa and Asia. The United States followed the mode, albeit somewhat belatedly and hesitantly. A Washington paper stated in 1891, "The taste of Empire is in the mouth of the people even as the taste of blood in the jungle." [12]

American interest naturally centered on Latin America, which for generations had been regarded as the area of particular interest to the United States. In 1889, the Inter-American movement was launched under United States auspices, with a conference of the republics of the hemisphere; at this conference such ambitious projects as a hemispheric customs union and a common currency were considered. The rebuilding of the decayed navy was begun, and in the 1890s the new bumptiousness nearly led to war for insignificant causes with Chile, Italy, and Britain. In 1895, President Grover Cleveland's secretary of state, Richard Olney, demanded that Britain arbitrate its boundary dispute with Venezuela and declared, "Today the United States is practically sovereign on this continent, and its fiat is law upon the subjects to which it confines its interposition. Why? It is because its infinite resources, combined with its isolated position, render it master of the situation and practically invulnerable as against any or all other powers." [13] Cleveland had the satisfaction of pleasing the Irish-Americans, and the British backed down.

A few years later an opportunity to assert this sovereignty presented itself. The country allowed itself to be whipped by sensational journalism into a fit of indignation at the brutal repression of the latest uprising in Spanish-held Cuba. Then the explosion-sinking of the battleship *Maine* at Havana in February 1898, with the loss of 260 lives, raised tempers to boiling. The Spanish government, aware of its weakness, was willing to yield to American demands, but in the excitement, President William McKinley asked for a declaration of war "to secure

---

12. Long, *The Outward View*, p. 186.
13. Ibid., p. 173.

a full and final termination of hostilities between the government of Spain and the people of Cuba." [14] Men volunteered with great enthusiasm, Theodore Roosevelt charged up the hill, and Admiral George Dewey decimated the Spanish ships at Manila as if they were sitting ducks.

At the war's end the nation had to decide what to do with the spoils. Cuba might have been annexed logically because of proximity, but the promise of independence was kept and American forces pulled out in 1901. However, the United States retained a right of intervention through the Platt Amendment (incorporated into the Cuban Constitution) and, several times up to 1920 used force to restore order. Puerto Rico was taken over as a simple possession, eventually to be given the ambiguous status of "Commonwealth."

The Philippines, an archipelago of thousands of islands near the Asian mainland with 7.5 million inhabitants, caused more headaches. Many Americans were opposed to the acquisition of large numbers of people whom they would not welcome as fellow citizens in new states and who showed no desire to become American subjects; the Filipino struggle for independence lasted four years and cost twice as many battle casualties as the war with Spain.

By some the holding of colonies in European style was seen as a betrayal of American traditions, a contradiction of democracy. Others believed it was not only unprofitable and inappropriate for the United States to acquire an empire, but unconstitutional as well.[15] There was and is no basis in the American Constitution for the government of noncitizens. However, the mood shifted in the wake of victory, appetites for dominion grew, and President McKinley decided that it was the American duty to "civilize and Christianize" the already mostly Christian Filipinos. It was claimed (as with sundry other territories) that if the United States did not take the Philippines, Germany or Japan would do so. There were also arguments of economic gain (less for Philippine trade than for the United States, as it gained a stepping stone to Asia), or strategic advantage and national destiny, and of the spread of democracy. Withal, the annexation was accepted by the

---

14. For an account, cf. Kennan, *American Diplomacy, 1900–1950*, pp. 10–11; Long, *The Outward View*, pp. 187–193; Julius Pratt, *Expanionists of 1898*, Johns Hopkins Press, Baltimore, 1936.

15. On the debate, see Thomas G. Paterson, *Imperialism and Anti-Imperialism*, Thomas Y. Crowell, New York, 1973.

Senate only after a bitter struggle, and it was never assumed that American rule was to be permanent.

This was the climax of territorial expansionism. In the heat of war, the United States annexed the Hawaiian Islands, whose American rulers had been knocking on the door for many years. Thereafter, however, the United States acquired only scattered small territories of real or presumptive strategic importance, such as the Panama Canal Zone and Samoa. American imperialism was a feeble imitation of simultaneous European ventures, hesitant and half-hearted and not in proportion with potential American power. Being "essentially an inwardly oriented society," [16] the United States was unprepared to manage and exploit alien peoples in a way that would make empire rewarding. As a Filipino delegate to the United Nations said in 1960, "The Americans are no saints, but . . . as imperialists they proved more inept than their rivals in the game; they allowed us too many liberties." [17]

The United States, however, increasingly asserted itself in the affairs of other states in ways that seemed to itself well intentioned if not altruistic but that others might interpret as imperialistic. Thus, in 1899–1900 the United States called for an "open door" in China—that is, an end to the exclusive concessions that Japan and European powers had been squeezing from the Celestial Empire. The Open Door policy was a rather ineffectual statement that became a sort of moral commitment to maintain the integrity of China and that led to Pearl Harbor and to the exceptional intensity of anti–Chinese communist feeling in the cold war. Other diplomatic interventions multiplied: President Theodore Roosevelt acted as peacemaker between Russia and Japan in 1905 and helped to arrange a conference on Morocco in 1906. More important, he treated Latin America (at least the Caribbean area) as an American back yard. He took the Panama Canal Zone by arbitrary executive action, with cavalier disregard for the rights of Colombia. He inaugurated the Roosevelt Corollary to the Monroe Doctrine, whereby the United States would assume responsibility for states that defaulted their international obligations. Under this patronizing doctrine, the marines attempted for many years to set things right by bayonet in several Caribbean countries, and were finally withdrawn only in the 1930s.

---

16. John Spanier, *American Foreign Policy Since World War II*, 6th ed., Praeger, New York, 1973, p. 271.

17. Long, *The Outward View*, p. 201.

President William Howard Taft was more inclined than his predecessor to promote American aims by financial power rather than by gunboats. But Woodrow Wilson, an idealistic liberal, intervened in Nicaragua and Haiti and became deeply involved in disturbances in Mexico consequent on the revolution begun in 1911. Wilson inaugurated the dubious (but not yet discarded) practice of using nonrecognition to pressure disapproved governments and was determined to harry from power a Mexican president who had murdered his predecessor. The Mexican port of Vera Cruz was bombarded and occupied in reprisal for slight injuries to American sailors; as Wilson said, "I am going to teach the South American [sic] republics to elect good men." [18] Later he sent General John J. Pershing with 12,000 men on a wild goose chase after Mexican revolutionary leader Francisco ("Pancho") Villa, who had been making raids across the border in order to demonstrate anti-Americanism.

Thus, on the eve of World War I, the United States, sensing its enormous power, was becoming rather carefree in the exercise of it, at least where no strong opposition was contemplated. There was, however, a universal and passionate desire in 1914 to stay out of the fray. Nevertheless, events led first to partisanship and then to participation, in a process somewhat like what was later to be called *escalation*.

Many factors brought America into the conflict, including traditionally greater sympathy with England and France than with Germany, fear of the potential consequences of German supremacy, more effective public relations of the Allies, and trade with the Allies and consequent economic interest in their victory. More difficult to weigh but probably no less important was the feeling that this country had a role of leadership to play in world affairs, and this leadership came to mean active involvement in the war. Such a feeling was likely to animate any responsible president; Wilson, a former professor of political science, was especially prone to abstract idealism and wanted to help the less enlightened. The United States, in his view, could serve all nations as no other country could. Wilson's major goal was the establishment of a security system to protect freedom and independence.[19] It is hence possible that persuasive reason for American entry into the war (or at least for the enthusiasm with which participation was

18. Jules David, *America and the World of Our Time*, Random House, New York, 1970, p. 38.

19. Arthur S. Link, *Wilson the Diplomatist: A Look at His Major Foreign Policies*, Johns Hopkins Press, Baltimore, 1957, p. 65.

greeted) was the feeling that the United States was responsible for the new world order being forged in the war. In the universal showdown, it seemed right for America to fight to end militarism, to make the world safe for democracy, and to ensure permanent peace and harmony in the American way. Consequently, when the German sinking of American ships justified entry into the war, this action represented not only a challenge but also an opportunity.

The war was another entry in the record of grand successes. The pacific nation rapidly mobilized enormous military strength, the German military machine was crushed, and America rose to a zenith of prestige and influence. Other countries were weary and impoverished and morally compromised by their territorial claims, whereas the United States was fresh, strong, rich, and at least outwardly unselfish. At the time of the armistice, Wilson proclaimed, "It will now be our fortunate duty to assist by example, by sober and friendly counsel and material aid in the establishment of the just democracy throughout the world." [20] Wilson had enunciated peace aims in his Fourteen Points: a call for freedom, self-determination of peoples, and the rule of law, in the American tradition. The last point was to replace the supposedly outworn balance of power, which had led to the holocaust, with a universal peacekeeping organization, a League of Nations, "not a balance of power but a community of power, not organized rivalries but an organized common peace." [21] In effect, Wilson wished to create a universal legal order in the American image.

This glowing vision was, of course, beyond American political capacities. Hoping to democratize foreign affairs, Wilson had proclaimed "open diplomacy" in the belief that people in general were more reasonable than diplomats; during the peace negotiations in Paris, however, he found that he had to bargain privately and make many concessions in order to buy support for the League. At home, there was at first strong journalistic and popular support for the League of Nations,[22] but the feeling grew that, evil having been defeated, other powers could take care of themselves. In November 1919, when Wilson refused to accept amendments, the Senate rejected the Treaty of Versailles with the Covenant of the League of Nations. The

---

20. Quoted by Jean-Baptiste Duroselle, *From Wilson to Roosevelt,* Harvard University Press, Cambridge, Mass., 1963, p. 87.

21. Quoted by J. William Fulbright, *The Crippled Giant: American Foreign Policy and Its Domestic Consequences,* Random House, New York, 1973, p. 266.

22. Long, *The Outward View,* p. 270.

reversion of sentiment was very rapid. In a few years, America had turned so far from world responsibility that the idea of joining the innocuous World Court, as proposed by four presidents from 1923 to 1935, could be damned by suggesting that it might be a stepping stone toward involvement with the League.

Sensing that participation in World War I might not have been truly necessary, the country turned inward even more emphatically than before. Immigration, which had been swelling to such a point that it threatened to overwhelm the older ethnic stocks, was for the first time severely restricted. Economic nationalism prevailed, and a wall of protective tariffs rose still higher around American industry. There was more antiforeign feeling than for decades past, and isolationism became a conscious policy. The army was quickly and fully demobilized; its ranks continued to decline until by 1927 it had only 125,000 men, compared with 635,000 in the French army.[23] In the early 1920s the government even declined to answer mail from the League or to cooperate with its humanitarian agencies.[24]

Even where the United States had strong feelings, it was hesitant to act. Thus there was a deep repugnance for the Bolshevik government established by Vladimir I. Lenin in Russia in 1917, but there was no disposition to do more than let the supposedly healthy counterforces in Russia assert themselves. While British and French leaders wanted to crush Bolshevism "in its cradle," Wilson in 1919 thought that the problem of Russian extremism would yield to discussion and reform. When the Allies intervened in the Russian civil war, the United States sent a few men to the Murmansk area and a contingent to Siberia, the latter mostly to check the Japanese.[25] The United States held back when other powers recognized the Soviet state and established diplomatic relations in 1924 and the following years; yet businessmen were permitted freely to trade with the Bolsheviks, and the United States soon became a leading source of equipment and technology for the communist state.

Isolationism in the 1920s was slightly tempered by efforts to exert moral leadership, particularly in naval disarmament and in the Kellogg-Briand Pact (1928) outlawing war. But as the depression came

23. *Encyclopedia Britannica*, 14th ed., XXII, 760; IX, 592.

24. Betty Glad, *Charles Evans Hughes and the Illusion of Innocence*, University of Illinois Press, Urbana, 1966, p. 174.

25. George F. Kennan, *The Decision to Intervene: Soviet-American Relations, 1917–1920*, Princeton University Press, Princeton, N.J., 1958, pp. 405–420; also William A. Williams, "American Intervention in Russia, 1917–1920," in *Containment and Revolution*, ed. David Horowitz, Beacon Press, Boston, 1968, pp. 26–71.

on after 1929, introversion deepened. The mood was reflected in an acrimonious debate over why the country had allowed itself to be drawn into the war, a little like the soul-searching over Vietnam in the period 1968 to 1972. The conclusion—that arms dealers and bankers were largely responsible—led to the passage of a series of laws (1934–1937) designed to restrict severely dealings with belligerents in a future conflict.

Meanwhile, however, the dissatisfied chauvinistic states—imperial Japan, Nazi Germany, and fascist Italy—were roiling the international waters; President Franklin D. Roosevelt in his second administration began to turn attention increasingly to the world scene. By October 1937, he seemed to have become convinced that the United States should play a leading part in keeping order. He then suggested that aggressor nations—having in mind chiefly Japan, which had begun a large-scale invasion of central China a few months earlier—should be "quarantined." However, the reaction to his suggestion was strongly negative, and the United States, potentially by far the strongest of nations, took practically no part in the diplomacy leading to the outbreak of World War II in 1939. Even after the Nazis began overrunning Europe, the general feeling was that the outcome of the war was less important to the United States than staying clear of it.

Under the leadership of the popular and activist Roosevelt, however, the country moved toward participation. Neutrality laws were modified to permit arms sales to belligerents. Shocked by the Nazi blitzkrieg and conquest of France in May and June of 1940, the United States began rebuilding the armed forces; in September 1940, the first peacetime conscription in American history was authorized. Fifty overage destroyers were transferred to Britain in exchange for bases in British colonies in this hemisphere. In March 1941, the Lend-Lease Act undertook to supply Britain with munitions. From April on, American naval vessels helped to protect British shipping and occasionally encountered German submarines. After the Nazi attack on the Soviet Union in June 1941, President Roosevelt quickly joined Prime Minister Winston Churchill in offering aid. In August, Roosevelt and Churchill issued the Atlantic Charter, a vague statement of war aims for peace and freedom, including an international security system and utopian freedoms from fear and want.[26] Shortly afterward, the American navy began to take active measures against submarines, and Roosevelt seized on the resulting incidents to arouse the country.

If Japan had not attacked Pearl Harbor, Roosevelt might have

---

26. David, *America and the World of Our Time*, pp. 209–212.

been unable to secure full American participation. In the 1940 presidential campaign, wherein Roosevelt ran for an unprecedented third term on grounds of the emergency, both parties encouraged complacency and promised to keep America out of war. In the summer of 1941, Congress extended the Selective Service Act by a majority of a single vote. Many conservatives, from aviator Charles Lindbergh to former President Herbert Hoover, insisted that the United States need not be overly concerned with Europe. This attitude reflected partly distrust and dislike for the leadership of Franklin Roosevelt, but it owed more to the traditional belief that America could take care of itself in the world. The Japanese, however, coming to a deadlock in negotiations with the United States and facing exhaustion of oil supplies because of the embargo on exports of strategic materials, opted for the military advantages of surprise and thereby ended the great debate.

World War II was America's coming of age in world affairs. Participation in World War I was somewhat like an excursion or a crusade; in World War II, the United States, with more determination than enthusiasm, fully and permanently assumed a world role. The need for entering World War II, unlike that for entering World War I, has seldom been questioned. This attitude exists partly because of Pearl Harbor (possibly the most searing event of modern American history) and partly because of the patent aggression of the principal adversaries.[27] Whether or not it was necessary for security in a physical sense—the Germans probably already had more empire than they could long control—the United States became convinced that it was no longer possible to sit back and hope that the world would remain comfortable, and the response was primarily military.

INTERVENTIONISM TRIUMPHANT: COLD WAR AND VIETNAM

There was still considerable feeling in 1945 that the country, having negated the evil, should return to business as usual. Men were mustered out of the armed forces as rapidly as possible, lend-lease was

---

27. A negative opinion is entered by Bruce M. Russett, *No Clear and Present Danger: A Skeptical View of the United States Entry into World War II,* Harper and Row, New York, 1972. For a somewhat dubious view of the need for the war in Europe, see A. J. P. Taylor, *The Origins of the Second World War,* Atheneum, New York, 1962.

abruptly halted, munitions factories were reconverted (reliance being placed partly on the new-found nuclear weapons), and thoughts turned to the pleasures of peace. However, there could be no rapid disengagement because, having demanded unconditional surrender (although something less was accepted in the cases of Italy and Japan), the United States assumed responsibility for the government of West Germany and Japan. American forces had to stay there, and there they remain more than thirty years later. Moreover, at the end of World War I the United States could go home and leave two basically friendly and respectable powers, Britain and France, in charge. After World War II, there was some hope that Britain could carry a fair share of the burdens of world order, and there was widespread expectation that the United Nations would help to keep the peace. But it soon appeared that American withdrawal would be practically equivalent to allowing most or all of Europe and the rest of the world to fall under the hegemony of the Soviet Union, an alien, tyrannical power overtly dedicated (according to its official ideology of universal class struggle) to the destruction of the traditional "bourgeois" social and international order.

During the war, a great effort was made to overcome the widespread (but by no means universal) antipathy toward the Stalinist, totalitarian Soviet Union. There was genuine appreciation of the fact that the Russians fought energetically and often heroically, inflicting and suffering far greater human losses than the Western powers. Americans were ready, indeed eager, to put out of mind Stalin's past sins, including the 1939–1940 annexation of the Baltic states and the war against Finland. President Roosevelt was so determined to see the Russians in the best light that, when the Russian Division of the State Department reported realistically on Stalin's purges, he ordered the division abolished and its files destroyed.[28] Knowing little about Russia and Marxism-Leninism, he accepted something close to the official Soviet version of affairs and counted on his own ability to manage the Soviet dictator and win his trust and cooperation by friendliness. He remarked with naive faith, "I think that if I give him everything I possibly can and ask for nothing in return, noblesse oblige, he won't try to annex anything and will work with me for a world of democracy and peace." [29] Before his death, he was questioning whether

---

28. Barbara W. Tuchman, "If Mao Had Come to Washington: An Essay in Alternatives," *Foreign Affairs*, 51 (October 1972), 61.

29. Quoted by Julius W. Pratt, *A History of United States Foreign Policy*, Prentice-Hall, Englewood Cliffs, N.J., 1965, p. 416.

friendliness was enough, but the assumption of Soviet cooperation was basic to his hope for a stable postwar world in which the leading powers should act together as world policemen.

But Stalin reciprocated no trust. Even under the pressures of the war emergency, he would not allow Americans to observe the use of Lend-Lease munitions by Soviet armies; thus the Western powers and the Soviets conducted practically separate wars against the common enemy. As soon as victory appeared on the horizon and thoughts turned to the making of the peace, dealings became more difficult; after the Yalta Conference (February 1945), the deterioration of American-Soviet relations was practically continuous. The principal question was the future of the countries that the Soviet Union could occupy or threaten with its armies. Where they were in a position to do so (as in most of eastern Europe), the Russians proceeded to establish regimes dominated by themselves, eventually so dominated as to seem to the West mere puppet states. The United States was prepared to agree that Stalin was entitled to insist on friendly governments along the Soviet Union's western borders, but it was not easy to accept that the result of a war begun to prevent Germany's conquest of eastern Europe should be Soviet rule of the area.

There were other causes of the cold war. President Harry S. Truman was much less hospitable to the Soviet viewpoint than Roosevelt had been, and under him the team that had worked with the Russians to win the war was replaced by men with a more narrowly American focus. When the United States and the Soviet Union were no longer fighting the Nazis, the philosophic and political differences between the two nations became obtrusive again. The Soviet regime, which had muted its Marxist ideology during the war for survival, began to reassert it as a means of controlling its dominions and perhaps of extending further its domain. Both sides came out of the war in a self-assertive mood, and the United States had vague ideas that victory should be translated into the general triumph of American ideals of political and economic freedom. The United States was producing over half of the world's industrial goods because of wartime destruction of other industrial centers, and it had a monopoly on the new superweapon, the power of which was demonstrated by the ruins of Hiroshima and Nagasaki.[30] With these advantages, the nation rapidly lost patience with a power that flaunted its antagonism to all that America stood for.

---

30. For effects of the atomic bomb on American diplomacy, cf. Barton J. Bernstein, "Roosevelt, Truman, and the Atomic Bomb, 1941–1945: A Reinterpreta-

With its usual proclivity to accept the status quo, the United States did little more than protest, less and less vigorously, the establishment of subservient governments in areas where the Soviet army held control. But new frictions and new crises continually arose. For example, Soviet troops along with British troops had entered Iran in 1941 to protect the wartime supply route, promising to withdraw within six months after the end of hostilities. They stayed on into 1946, however, and sponsored a puppet state in northern Iran. Only after a confrontation in the United Nations and a secret threat of force from Truman did they withdraw. The lesson seemed to be clear, although it was not yet so expressed, that a determined stance was necessary to halt Soviet expansionism.

Hostility became the general mode in 1947 as a result of pressures in Greece and Turkey. The British, who were supporting a conservative government in Greece against a communist insurgency, felt unable to continue; unless the United States intervened, the pro-Western regime would be replaced by a presumably Soviet-controlled one. At the same time, Turkey was being pressed by Soviet territorial and military demands. The Truman administration was assailed by the fear that if either Greece or Turkey was "lost," a domino effect might turn much of the Mediterranean area and the Near East into a Soviet sphere [31] and undermine the incipient recovery of morale in Europe. President Truman and his advisers moved rapidly to support those countries and undertook something novel in American history: a peacetime program of political warfare.

Although many people were still reluctant to admit that we were not going to be good friends with the Russians or that it was necessary to assume responsibility for the politics of faraway lands, this was the real onset of the cold war, which was to dominate American foreign policy for a generation afterward. Truman stated the case in his message to Congress in terms of lofty universal ideals, of the American way, and of good and evil worlds in conflict. "Our way of life is based on the will of the majority . . . free elections . . . individual liberty. . . .

---

tion," *Political Science Quarterly*, 90 (Spring 1975), 23–69. See also Robert M. Lawrence, *Arms Control and Disarmament: Practice and Promise*, Burgess Publishers, Minneapolis, 1973, pp. 2–3. The contention that the bomb was used to overawe the Russians is developed by Gar Alperowitz, *Atomic Diplomacy: Hiroshima and Potsdam*, Simon and Schuster, New York, 1965.

31. For a vivid account of the early part of the cold war, as seen from the United States State Department, cf. Dean Acheson, *Present at the Creation*, Norton, New York, 1969.

The second way of life is based upon the will of a minority forcibly imposed upon the majority. It relies upon terror and oppression." In sum, "I believe it must be the policy of the United States to support free peoples who are resisting attempted subjugation by armed minorities," that is, those of pro-Soviet persuasion.[32] Truman thereby made it easy to generalize the commitment to any government that might claim to be fighting communism, although he had no such intention at the time. His administration also undertook a reorganization of its national security apparatus, including the restructuring of propaganda and intelligence agencies. Having structured itself to wage the contest better, the United States came to accept the contest as a fact of life.

Communism was less monolithic than was supposed, and the Greek communists were undercut when Prime Minister Marshal Tito of Yugoslavia, who had established a communist state with little help from the Russians, refused to accept Soviet dictation and split with Stalin in 1948. The Greek rebels thereby lost their chief source of supplies. Stalin, fearful of complications, never did much to help the Greek revolutionaries, and the civil war shortly petered out. Turkey, with American backing, easily resisted Soviet pressures. The Truman Doctrine thus seemed sufficiently successful to be used elsewhere.

Many steps deeper into the cold war followed. The Marshall Plan for the reconstruction of Europe became unequivocally, after communist countries declined to participate, a project for halting communism by building up the battered economies of noncommunist states. In February 1948, the Czech communists ousted the democratic government and put Czechoslovakia behind what had become Stalin's "Iron Curtain." In April, the Russians began a blockade of the Western-held part of Berlin, a city inside the Soviet occupation zone that had been intended as the capital of a united Germany. Refraining from breaking the land blockade by force, the United States resorted to an impressive but expensive airlift, the success of which persuaded the Russians to back down.

Goaded by such challenging or threatening actions, the United States undertook another revolutionary step in foreign policy—permanent "entangling alliances" outside the Western Hemisphere. In April 1949, the North Atlantic Treaty joined the United States, Britain, France, Belgium, the Netherlands, Luxembourg, Italy, Denmark, Norway, Portugal, Iceland, and Canada (and later Greece and Turkey)

---

32. Spanier, *American Foreign Policy Since World War II*, p. 41. For full text, see *The New York Times*, March 13, 1947, p. 2.

into a defensive alliance. The United States had become engaged in world politics as it never had previously and to a degree beyond that to which any other state had been committed.

The cold war was brought to fullness by violence: the attempt of the North Koreans in June 1950 to overrun the southern part of Korea. The two Korean states, set up in the Soviet and American occupation zones, had hardly been envisaged as permanent, and the United States had shown little strategic interest in the area. However, there was bitterness over the recent completion of the conquest of China by the communists; the administration was reluctant to see another country go communist; and there were fears that the attack, apparently sanctioned if not sponsored by the Russians,[33] portended a widespread violent offensive. The State Department saw the assault on South Korea as analogous to Hitler's conquest of Austria, promising further aggression and a new world war if it should be allowed to succeed.[34] President Truman answered the communist aggression immediately by ordering American forces into action; with very little interest in Korea per se, the United States found itself engaged on largely ideological grounds in a new type of conflict, "limited war."

Because of fortuitous Soviet absence from the Security Council (boycotting to protest the exclusion of Communist China), the United States could secure Council endorsement and the fight could be covered by the banner of the United Nations. It was nevertheless almost entirely an American operation. After initial setbacks, the war went well, and the removal of communist rulership in North Korea seemed in prospect in the latter part of 1950 as American troops pressed toward the Chinese border. But Chinese communist forces entered the fray and drove back the Americans in an unaccustomed military defeat, until the front was finally stabilized near the original boundary between North and South Korea. The fighting then became senseless but dragged on until July 1953, after which Stalin's death permitted a softening of the communist position.

Long before the Korean War came to the end of its three years, Americans were questioning it. The effect of the indecisive struggle, however, was a hardening of American attitudes into undifferentiated and militaristic anticommunism. The Chinese communists were portrayed as major world devils, and the loss of China seemed a disaster,

---

33. Adam B. Ulam, *The Rivals*, Viking, New York, 1971, p. 171.
34. George F. Kennan, *Memoirs, 1950–1963*, Little, Brown, Boston, 1972, p. 92.

explicable only by treason.[35] The search for scapegoats led to the era of McCarthyism, a time of uninformed intolerance led by Senator Joseph R. McCarthy of Wisconsin, which not only purged the State Department of Asian experts but cramped American political thought. American foreign policy also became militarized. Previously, chief reliance had been placed on economic and political measures to check the spread of communism, but the military buildup of the Korean War now became permanent. The defense budget had fallen below 5 percent of the gross national product (still up from pre–World War II levels below 2 percent). The Korean conflict lifted defense expenditures to 20 percent of the GNP, and the proportion stayed over 10 percent for many years. In June 1950, Congress was debating a defense budget of $14 billion; a few weeks later, it rushed through one of $45 billion.[36] It was decided virtually without dissent to escalate the nuclear arms race by developing the hydrogen or fusion bomb, which promised to be a thousand times more powerful than the atomic fission bomb dropped on Hiroshima. Before 1950 American armed forces had been stationed in former enemy countries only; by 1959 they had taken up positions in forty-two countries. Emphasis in foreign aid was shifted from economic to military aid and the building up of allies to fight communism. Defense pacts were multiplied, bringing in South Korea, Nationalist China (the Republic of China), Japan, Pakistan, Thailand, and the Philippines. In 1958 the United States seemed prepared to risk nuclear war to prevent the Chinese communists from taking the small, intrinsically valueless, and strategically unimportant islands of Quemoy and Matsu from the Nationalist Chinese.

American foreign policy became more ideological than ever before or after. Soviet communism was seen as something like the Nazi plague, only more dangerous because of its greater power and potential. America could never be secure while such a deeply hostile political form was powerful in the world. Parallels were drawn with the appeasement of Nazi Germany and the 1938 surrender of Czechoslovakia at Munich, without adequate consideration of the difference in circumstances.[37] The imposition of a communist order was regarded as permanent and irreversible. Peace was seen as indivisible, and communism (as a solid hostile movement) must not be allowed to expand directly or indirectly anywhere lest it be energized and the forces of

---

35. Stoessinger, *Nations in Darkness,* p. 167.
36. Lawrence, *Arms Control and Disarmament,* p. 13.
37. As commented by May, *"Lessons" of the Past,* p. 84.

freedom demoralized. There was no doubt as to what freedom was or as to its supreme value for the United States and ultimately for all peoples as they matured to appreciation of it. It was taken for granted that the United States had a special mission, practically that proclaimed nearly forty years earlier: to make the world safe for democracy. Many people thought that merely "containing" communism was immoral.

American foreign policy took on a somewhat messianic cast; the cold war, like earlier shooting wars, became seemingly an end in itself. Agreements with the enemy might be dangerous because the optimistic West might lower its guard. There was little idea of a softening of communist regimes; when Georgi Malenkov, Soviet premier after Stalin's death, made some conciliatory proposals, Secretary of State John Foster Dulles brushed them aside on the ground that acceptance would strengthen the faltering Soviet regime. Dulles also felt that some tension was necessary to sustain American and European support for the anticommunist alliance. Trade with communist powers was seen as only adding to their power to destroy freedom.

Despite the break with Stalin of communist Yugoslavia (which the Truman administration moved to support after two years), the idea of independent communism was rejected in principle. Little account was taken of Sino-Soviet differences as they surfaced toward the end of the 1950s. Leftists were classified as communists. When a left-leaning government gained power in Guatemala in 1954, Secretary Dulles pushed the Latin American states into an arms embargo, and the Central Intelligence Agency (CIA) sponsored an exile invasion that overthrew the regime. The struggle became one not merely against Soviet power but for the maintenance of an approved social and political order; social discontent became equivalent to anti-Americanism, and the latter to procommunism. It seemed necessary to defend American, or at least anticommunist, ideals and economic freedom everywhere.

By the later 1950s, however, the cold war began running down. One reason was that it was becoming dangerous. In 1953, the Soviets produced a hydrogen bomb about the same time as the United States; in 1957, with the launching of the first sputnik, the Soviets seemingly leaped ahead in rocketry. Khrushchev bragged (falsely) about factories turning out intercontinental missiles "like sausages." John Kennedy, becoming president in 1961, felt that he had to replace the Dulles doctrine of massive retaliation (an unrealistic threat of nuclear punishment for local aggression) with flexible response, at the same time overreacting to the supposed missile gap with an overwhelming buildup of American strategic forces.

The boundaries of the contest also lost clarity. The Soviets began courting neutral powers, and it was ridiculous to brand as communists all who were on friendly terms with them. In the Suez crisis of 1956, when Britain and France (with Israel) tried to punish Egypt for nationalizing the Suez Canal, the United States found itself on the Soviet side in opposition to its allies. By the fall of 1959, it was possible to invite Khrushchev to view the United States for himself. Eisenhower proposed to go to Moscow in 1960, but this summit meeting was canceled and the cold war revived by the U-2 incident, when an American reconnaissance plane was shot down over the Soviet Union.

Through these years there were numerous nerve-wracking crises, caused basically either by instability in the Third World (Laos, Congo) or by Khrushchev's threats (Berlin, several times repeated). But the last crisis proved to be the tensest. After the failure of his gambits in Germany and the Third World, Khrushchev tried to win a round by emplacing in Cuba rockets capable of threatening the United States from short range.[38] The Kennedy administration reacted by declaring a partial blockade of the island.[39] For a few days the world envisioned possible Soviet and American measures and countermeasures; nervous Europeans scurried to the supposed safety of Ireland. But the United States was substantially superior both in conventional forces in the Caribbean and in strategic weaponry, and the Soviet leaders were not insane. They pulled out their rockets with a little face saving, and the world was sobered by the fleeting vision of hell.

The temper of the cold war changed. The Soviets drew back, moderated their ideological temper, and went to work on their armory so that they would be able to challenge the United States more effectively at a later date. For other reasons, also, the cold war was fading. Its major premise, bipolarity, was eroding. The Soviet bloc was loosening; not only was China at odds with the Soviet Union, but Russia's eastern European satellites were showing some independent spirit. Western Europe had become prosperous, more secure, and less dependent on the United States; France especially stood opposed to American predominance. A host of new states in the Third World wanted nothing to do with the cold war, but rather wanted to get on with

38. On the Soviet decision, cf. Adam B. Ulam, *Expansion and Coexistence*, Praeger, New York, 1974, pp. 667–671.

39. For a systematic analysis of the American reaction, see Graham T. Allison, *Essence of Decision: Explaining the Cuban Missile Crisis*, Little, Brown, Boston, 1971.

their own development. Americans, too, were tired of the cold war and were prepared to think of communists as human beings; a large sale of wheat to the Soviet Union in 1963 was a breakthrough. Détente seemed well on the way, despite inertia on both sides.[40]

Yet ironically the 1960s saw the climax of interventionism when the reasons for it were wearing out. From the Cuban missile crisis, Americans drew the lesson that it was necessary only to stand firm, and confidence in the American mission soared. Secretary of State Dean Rusk proclaimed (February 13, 1963), "We shall persevere in this worldwide struggle until freedom prevails" and later indicated the American intention to protect any threatened state, whether or not under obligation to do so. He also pointed out that Americans "simply cannot understand the revival of the notion of absolute independence in dealing with affairs within the free world." [41] The House of Representatives resolved (September 23, 1965) that the United States should unilaterally use force against any attempted communist subversion in the Western Hemisphere. President Lyndon B. Johnson gave the impression that American foreign aid (even as it was declining) should cure world poverty, and American power should ensure the rights of all peoples everywhere. In an interview, he said immodestly, "We are going to make life better and more enjoyable for all the three billion people of the world. We've got a moral duty, a Christian duty to help our neighbors."[42]

This carefree globalism was translated into action in the Dominican Republic in April 1965. When a civil war broke out, 21,000 marines and paratroopers were sent in to thwart a supposed communist danger; [43] this ill-considered and exaggerated response, the first military intervention in Latin America since 1925, generated a reaction and led Americans to question seriously the militaristic approach. The crisis of confidence in American foreign policy began; it has hardly yet been overcome.

The bloodless meddling in Santo Domingo (that is, in the Caribbean area where there was most precedent for intervening) was child's

40. Arthur M. Schlesinger, *A Thousand Days: John Kennedy in the White House*, Houghton Mifflin, Boston, 1965, pp. 918–923.

41. *The New York Times*, May 10, 1964, p. 1.

42. *Newsweek*, August 2, 1965, p. 21.

43. On the intervention see Rowland Evans and Robert Novak, *Lyndon B. Johnson: The Exercise of Power*, New American Library, New York, 1966, pp. 515–525.

play compared with the blundering into Vietnam. Reasons for the costly effort to keep a small, alien, rather unimportant Asian country on the right side of the fence were various. They included overconfidence, militarization of policy, the tendency to see any leftist or anti-American force as dangerous and communistic, and the idea that it was necessary to demonstrate that "wars of liberation" could not succeed. Entanglement was also a result of the American character. Because of pride and the conviction of moral right, policies could not be reconsidered when they did not succeed, but rather had to be intensified. Once the commitment had been made, United States leaders feared to admit that it was a mistake and to draw back lest they be branded "soft on communism." [44] The little more needed to turn the trick swelled until half a million Americans were fighting in vain to subdue an Asian guerilla movement.[45]

The first significant American commitment to the anticommunist side in the Vietnamese conflict was provoked by Mao Tse-tung's victory in China in 1949 and the Korean War. When the French gave up the fight to retain control of their former colony in July 1954 at the Geneva conference, the United States assumed sponsorship of an anticommunist South Vietnam.[46] Although things went fairly well for a few years, South Vietnam proved difficult to govern, economic and military aid always had to be increased, and by the beginning of 1963 the American advisers were a small army of 13,000. In August 1964, President Johnson used a trivial encounter of an American destroyer with North Vietnamese torpedo boats to secure from Congress the nearly unanimous passage of a broad enabling (Tonkin Gulf) resolution. This was nearly a declaration of war, authorizing the president "to take all necessary steps, including the use of armed force, to assist

---

44. Bruce Russett, "The Americans Retreat from World Power," *Political Science Quarterly*, 90 (Spring 1975), 10. This is the general thesis of David Halberstam, *The Best and the Brightest*, Random House, New York, 1972.

45. On reasons for involvement, see Leslie H. Gelb, "Vietnam: The System Worked," *Foreign Policy*, 4 (Summer 1971), 140–167; Ralph K. White, *Nobody Wanted War: Misperceptions in Vietnam and Other Wars*, Doubleday, Garden City, N.Y., 1968; Robert L. Gallucci, *Neither Peace nor Honor: Politics of American Military Policy in Viet-Nam*, Johns Hopkins Press, Baltimore, 1975. For a strongly stated case against involvement, see Ralph Stavins, Richard J. Barnet, and Marcus G. Raskin, *Washington Plans an Aggressive War*, Vintage Books, New York, 1971. Documents are given in *The Pentagon Papers as Published by The New York Times*, Quadrangle Books, New York, 1971.

46. Chester L. Cooper, *Lost Crusade*, Dodd, Mead, New York, 1970, Chapter 4.

any member or protocol state of the Southeast Asia Collective Defense Treaty requesting assistance in defense of its freedom." [47]

Johnson said at his 1965 inaugural, "What is at stake is the cause of freedom," but the situation in South Vietnam continued to deteriorate. The ground forces having achieved little, the joint chiefs of staff thought a few weeks of bombing North Vietnam would turn the trick; early in 1965 there began the air attacks on that country which finally ended only at the beginning of 1973. Since the North Vietnamese failed to fall on their knees, there seemed no other course than to flood in American troops, whose numbers swelled steadily to 525,000 in 1968, more than twice as many as were engaged at the height of Korean fighting.

So accustomed were Americans to fighting communism that there was little initial opposition to this massive engagement in a dubious cause. Protesting voices rose to a chorus of dismay and indignation only when costs became painful, especially to youths subject to conscription, and when it became evident that the venture was unsuccessful. A sudden communist offensive at the lunar New Year, Tet, in February 1968 resulted in the temporary capture of many towns in South Vietnam and showed the fragility and perhaps even unpopularity of the American-sponsored government. The Johnson administration was faced with a harsh dilemma: to commit still more forces, at the risk of more violent protest and inflation, or to reconsider and deescalate. On March 31, Johnson, his presidency soured by the war, declined renomination and began the laborious process of disengagement by restricting the bombing of North Vietnam and starting peace talks with the communists in Paris.

The new president, Richard Nixon, by instinct a "hawk" in the assertion of American right and prowess, saw the necessity to pull out of the fruitless war but did so only as gradually as seemed politically permissible.[48] In consequence, withdrawal of American forces was stretched out over the four years of the first Nixon administration to

---

47. See Townsend Hoopes, *The Limits of Intervention*, David McKay, New York, 1969; John Galloway, *The Gulf of Tonkin Resolution*, Associated University Presses, Cranbury, N.J., 1970; and Thomas Halper, *Foreign Policy Crises: Appearance and Reality in Decision Making*, Chas. E. Merrill, Columbus, Ohio, 1971, Chapter 4.

48. For a statement of the purposes of the administration, see Henry A. Kissinger, *American Foreign Policy: Three Essays*, Norton, New York, 1969.

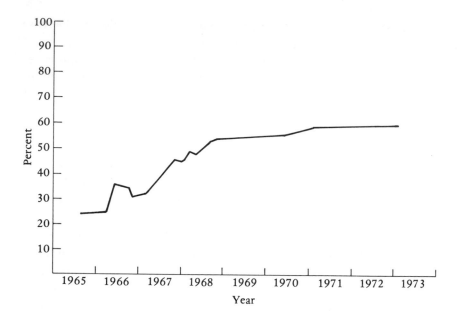

Figure 1 Public Reaction to the Vietnam War
Percentage of persons answering "yes" to the question, "In view of the developments since we entered the fighting in Vietnam, do you think the U.S. made a mistake sending troops to fight in Vietnam?" Other possible responses were "no" and "no opinion." (Results of Gallup Polls used with permission of the American Institute of Public Opinion.)

give maximal time to arm and train South Vietnamese forces. Disengagement was also punctuated by such episodes as the incursion into Cambodia in May 1970, which sparked such an outcry as to put most American universities temporarily out of operation. Rapprochement with the big communist powers, marked by presidential visits to Peking and Moscow in February and May of 1972, deprived the Vietnam war of whatever ideological rationale it may have had; but the United States responded to a North Vietnamese spring offensive in 1972 with more intensive bombing and a blockade (by mining) of North Vietnamese ports. After prolonged negotiations about now forgotten details and a final flurry of bombing at the end of the year (mostly, apparently, to satisfy the hawks in Saigon and Washington),[49] a ceasefire was agreed to on January 27, 1973. The ceasefire brought no cessation

49. Tad Szulc, "How Kissinger Did It: Behind the Vietnam Ceasefire Agreement," *Foreign Policy*, 6 (Summer 1974), 21–69.

of fighting, which continued in South Vietnam more or less as before; but it permitted the removal of American forces. Still, American participation in combat in Indochina dragged on as the United States Air Force tried to help the tottering pro-Western government of Cambodia. Under pressure from Congress, the administration halted this action as of August 15. Military and economic aid to South Vietnam and Cambodia continued.

Through 1974, it seemed possible that the corrupt South Vietnamese government with American materiel might pull itself together to save itself. But in the first part of 1975, the bubbles of illusion began to pop. The insurgents in Cambodia, who held nearly all the countryside, besieged and took the capital. As the communists wound up this victory, President Thieu's forces in South Vietnam wavered, then collapsed; the American president was meanwhile demanding that Congress allocate nearly a billion dollars of additional aid for the South Vietnamese. The curtain fell on the most inglorious episode of American history with the evacuation of the American embassy in Saigon by helicopter on April 30, 1975. Shortly afterward, the least important land of Indochina, Laos, likewise came under the domination of the Pathet Lao, or Communist party.

The defeat of the long American enterprise was shocking to many, although a relief to some; when it was over and the air had cleared, it all seemed to make much less difference than expected. Outside Indochina, no dominoes fell. There was not a blood bath, but rather a "reeducation" program for those who had stood by the American side in South Vietnam (those most engaged having been evacuated to the United States). Indochina came under the rule of neither the Soviet Union nor China. Although American prestige suffered for a short time, within six months it was restored, indeed improved by disencumbrance from the incubus of a senseless war.

THE COST OF INTERVENTION

With Vietnam, the era of generally increasing willingness to reach out and set things right by muscle seemingly came to its end. Interventionism, which represented a reversal of the noninvolvement that has served the country well during most of its history, has usually seemed against the inclinations of the American people. They have hardly been prepared to support forceful action with enthusiasm unless it is provoked by acts of violence—for example, the blowing up of the *Maine* in 1898 (in all probability no fault of the Spanish), the sinking of American ships in 1917, and Pearl Harbor. Even the cold war owed much to violence, beginning with civil war in Greece and intensifying with the North Korean assault. An emotional reaction makes it possible for a large majority of the public to give willing assent, at least for a short time. The sacrifices become acceptable not because of a sober calculation of national interest but because of a figurative slap in the face of America. One reason for dissatisfaction with the Vietnam war was that there was no such sense of injury, although the administration played up alleged attacks on United States naval vessels (Gulf of Tonkin) and guerrilla action against American air bases.

Acceptance of major interventions thus has been in part emotional and so subject to erosion. It is consequently not surprising that each interventionist episode has been followed, after the excitement has waned, by doubts and recriminations, a sort of morning-after reaction. It has been particularly questioned whether the action was in the interests of the majority or of a small but powerful minority. Enthusiasm in World War I was so far reversed that it became the general sentiment by the early 1930s that the United States had been deceived and maneuvered into war by selfish interests. Even in World War II, in which the enemy was morally indefensible, some Americans said that Roosevelt's ambition caused him to guide the country into ever sharper conflict with Germany and Japan. The cold war was subjected to reassessment even before it ended; mounting revisionist literature merged into impassioned criticism of involvement in Vietnam, which had seemed the logical fulfillment of the anticommunist campaign.

In the Vietnam war, the reappraisal went as far as was logically possible: to a total incrimination of American policy as not only misguided but intrinsically evil. Revisionists charged that the pretended concern for freedom and anticommunism was just an effort to use American power for corporate gain—at best the result of the clash of economic systems, at worst a conspiracy to maximize profits at the expense of the people. Gabriel Kolko wrote, "Ultimately, the United States has fought in Vietnam with increasing intensity to extend its hegemony over the world community and to stop every form of the revolutionary movement which refuses to accept the predominant role of the United States in the direction of the affairs of its nation or region." [50] In its milder forms, this reassessment was entirely in the tradi-

---

50. Gabriel Kolko, *The Roots of American Foreign Policy: An Analysis of Power and Purpose,* Beacon Press, Boston, 1969, p. 132.

tion of dissent, going back to the War of 1812 and the Mexican War,[51] with a note of Wilsonian idealism. The premise was that powers would get along pacifically if leaders would hearken to the people. The more extreme views, however, amounted to an interpretation of American foreign policy in terms of Leninist mythology, and this analysis was extended far into the past. Thus, expansion across the nearly empty continent was treated as evidence of an inherently evil nature, and the Open Door policy in China was seen as representing merely "American determination to keep China politically sovereign and whole for purposes of exploitation by the burgeoning United States industrial complex." [52]

Such perceptions seem increasingly unrealistic as the emotional stress of Vietnam recedes. It may well be argued, however, that American military intervention, at least since the end of acquisition of territories suitable for incorporation into the republic, has always been overdone and thus to some degree has been unproductive or counterproductive. When the country flies to arms, it never knows the just measure.

This is certainly true of the Spanish-American War. As noted earlier, everything that the United States wanted for Cuba could have been gained by negotiation with a Spain that was quite aware of its weakness.[53] To extend the war to the Philippines was an absurdity perpetrated by the big-navy men led by Theodore Roosevelt, and the acquisition of Puerto Rico was a complete non sequitur. As early as 1907 even Roosevelt regretted having gotten into the Philippines, seeing no material rewards and a military liability. He also concluded that there was a fundamental contradiction between democratic government and imperial rule.[54]

The various excursions of the United States Marines into Caribbean countries early in this century were equally purposeless and fruitless. The result of the effort to improve Haiti, the Dominican Republic, and Nicaragua led only to reprobation for the United States throughout Latin America and to dictatorship in the countries involved. Theodore Roosevelt's impatient snatching of the Panama Canal Zone was conceded to be a misdeed when the United States paid damages of $25 million to Colombia in 1921.

---

51. As noted by Robert W. Tucker, *The Radical Left and American Foreign Policy*, Johns Hopkins Press, Baltimore, 1971, p. 153.

52. Walter LaFeber, *America, Russia and the Cold War*, John Wiley, New York, 1972, pp. 2–3.

53. Kennan, *American Diplomacy*, pp. 10–11.

54. Howard K. Beale, *Theodore Roosevelt and the Rise of America to World Power*, Johns Hopkins Press, Baltimore, 1956, pp. 455–456.

Woodrow Wilson may deserve credit for having kept the United States out of World War I for two and a half years, but he finally led the country into battle with great enthusiasm. Whether the world and the United States were better off for American belligerency is questionable. While it was certainly in the American interest to prevent the defeat of Britain and France, a compromise peace would have probably been a better outcome than the defeat and humiliation of Germany. In January 1917, Wilson wisely called for "peace without victory." His effort to destroy militarism by armed action was futile, and the peace he helped draft prepared the way for a war of revenge twenty years later. Wilson incidentally saved the Leninist revolution in Russia, giving the world the benefit of the communist movement.

It has been much more difficult to argue that American entry into World War II was misguided, because the Japanese aggression seems adequate cause for intervention, and to doubt the need to fight Nazi Germany seems to condone the gas chambers wherein millions of people (mostly Jews) were murdered. In 1941, however, Japan was cornered by the embargo on oil and other materials, in which the British and the Dutch joined the United States; with only a few months' worth of supplies, Japan had either to seize oil fields in Southeast Asia or to accept American conditions. Hence, from July to December of 1941, the Japanese negotiated rather humbly by the standards of their previous bravado. But the United States, as often, pushed too hard. Realizing that American economic sanctions were hurting Japan, Franklin Roosevelt raised his demands from a halt in Japanese operations in China to prompt withdrawal from all Chinese territory.[55] Having been engaged in China for a decade, the Japanese were not prepared simply to pull out and recognize the government of their enemies. (An America that took nearly five years to disengage from its much smaller commitment in Vietnam may well understand their difficulty.) The American administration knew that the Japanese would probably opt for seizing the raw material–producing European colonies in Southeast Asia, and it expected to go to war if they did. But the Japanese had no idea how difficult it might be for Roosevelt to persuade Congress and the American public of the need to fight to prevent British and Dutch colonies from falling into the hands of Japan. Choosing the advantages of a surprise raid on the American navy, the Japanese solved Roosevelt's problem.

---

55. Russett, *No Clear and Present Danger*, p. 57.

Hitler solved another problem by declaring war on the United States a few days later. However, the decision to enter the war was essentially American; there had long been no pretense of neutrality, and the American navy was virtually at war with Germany well before Pearl Harbor. As in the case of World War I, few will doubt that it was very much in the American interest to prevent a German victory, but it can reasonably be questioned whether American belligerency and the total crushing of the Axis powers were necessary. Material support to Britain and the Soviet Union should have sufficed to prevent their defeat.[56] In any case, little American help had reached the Russians by the turning point of the war, the battle of Stalingrad at the beginning of 1943. The doctrine of unconditional surrender may have been propagandistically useful in underlining the evil of the enemy, but it seemed designed to assure a fight to the bitter end. The result of the total destruction of German power was to save eastern Europe from Hitler by placing it under Stalin. How one weighs this achievement depends mostly upon where one stands on the right–left political spectrum.

The result of total victory, in any case, was the cold war; and if there has been little controversy about World War II, there has been a great deal about the diffuse and multiform conflict that followed. In its genesis, however, it was clearly defensive. Stalin was a cruel, deceitful man, capable of any crime or treachery toward his own people; it may well be supposed that, if there had been no resistance, he would have extended Soviet dominion as far as his resources permitted. American anticommunists, unlike Hitler, did not have to invent provocations; Soviet demands on Turkey, refusal to evacuate northern Iran, threats to Berlin, and other belligerent stances were all too real. The United States, which had left the scene blithely after World War I, cannot be seriously faulted for having stayed around after World War II to prevent a despotic state or a hostile authoritarian political movement from gaining excessively from the impoverishment and disorders created by the cataclysmic war. If the settlement had been left largely to others, it might have been excessively unfavorable to the vital interests of the United States and the sort of society that it had always upheld, these aspects being confused not only in the minds of leaders but also in political reality.

The basic American cold war doctrine was "Containment,"

---

56. Ibid., p. 30.

expounded by Soviet expert George Kennan in an anonymous article in *Foreign Affairs*, July 1947. It was an essentially defensive posture: the Soviet Union must be denied additional invigorating conquests by a patient and prudent use of American strength, "a vigilant application of counterforce at a series of constantly shifting geographic and political points," wherever the Russians threatened the states around their periphery. If thus "contained" politically, the Soviet Union would, it was assumed, gradually lose its truculence and ideological drive, coming to "a far greater degree of moderation and circumspection." American disarmament and withdrawal would be appropriate only when the Soviets became convinced of the futility of attempting to spread their system by force or subversion or lost the will to do so.

Kennan's logic was sound, and his prediction of the eventual loss of expansionist dynamism by the Soviet system has been fairly well confirmed. But this logic was misused and the cold war went astray.[57] Containment was excessively negative and could be taken as an argument for a universal drive not merely to check Soviet imperialism but to make the world safe for the American way and (incidentally) American business. Containment led to interventionism and to possibly chauvinist feelings that America was called upon to keep order around the world. The doctrine could not determine how the United States should meet subversive movements that might be anti-American but that did not represent clear-cut Soviet aggression. It might mean standing on the side of the status quo everywhere—an unfortunate position for a nation that would like to think itself progressive. Since only communism was seen as the enemy of freedom, the United States found itself embracing unprincipled dictators. Containment also made it likely that, in complicated situations, the United States might stumble into a morass of indefinite and bootless intervention.[58] The country did not know how to do without overdoing.

In its old assumption of moral superiority, the United States was frequently careless of the ideas and feelings of others, especially peoples of alien cultures. It was assumed that the United States knew what was best for humanity or the "free world" and should act accord-

---

57. For Kennan's afterthoughts, see George F. Kennan, *Memoirs, 1925–1950*, Little, Brown, Boston, 1967, pp. 363–367; also, "Interview with George F. Kennan," *Foreign Policy*, no. 7, Summer, 1972, pp. 5–21.

58. There was awareness of these pitfalls in the State Department in 1947, but awareness did not prevent falling into them. Cf. Seyom Brown, *The Faces of Power*, Columbia University Press, New York, 1968, p. 43.

ingly, should direct rather than consult; it was as though America was
dealing with clients, not allies. As states usually do, the United States
moralized and simplified, preferring to stand not simply against Soviet
aggrandizement but against a general evil, communism, and for a
vague ideal of freedom, which was assumed to be at issue in local wars
and disturbances. This attitude led to rigidity; American diplomacy
stuck to anti-Stalinism long after Stalin, and its anti–Chinese communist fixation seemed frozen for a decade after it had lost whatever logic
it may once have had.

Moreover, because Soviet ideology and communism were opposed
to private ownership of property, the legitimate purpose of checking
the potential expansion of an authoritarian power became mingled
with the defense of private property (particularly American business
interests) in moralized self-seeking. There was no reason to expect that
American foreign policy should be unselfish, only that it should be enlightened. Much was lost when the richest power took on the image of
an economic imperialist in the eyes of many who did not feel endangered by communism.

The conduct of the cold war also went astray in a reliance on
military power as a means of influence. The simple and obvious way to
oppose communism, and the way most easily explained to the people,
was by making the United States a sort of world policeman. Political
conflicts were put in military terms; NATO (the North Atlantic Treaty
Organization), for example, was a largely military response to a largely
political problem: the providing of stability to governments threatened
more by subversion than by invasion; its Southeast Asian counterpart
was much worse. The United States had hundreds of bases abroad in
the later 1960s; it is doubtful that more than a minor fraction were
rationally necessary. But, as presidential adviser W. W. Rostow
wrote,[59] "There is hardly a diplomatic relationship we conduct in the
world, or move that we make, that does not involve in it the question:
Does the U.S. have the capacity and the will to use military force to
back its play?" In the view of many nationals of other countries, it
seemed obvious that the United States was much more threatening to
their independence than was the distant and weaker Soviet Union.

In becoming militarized, American foreign policy came to look
more like the evil it stood against—dogmatic, intolerant, careless of
independent rights, secretive and deceptive. The CIA, on the model of

59. W. W. Rostow, *View from the Seventh Floor*, Harper and Row, New York,
1964, p. 34.

the Soviet Committee of State Security (KGB), undertook subversion in weak countries, and the American agency became much more widely known and hated than the Soviet. Assuming the rightness of its might, the United States spread its wing over many nations without really asking whether they desired protection. Americans had no idea that the United States might be tempted to misuse or overuse its power. A threat of reduction of American influence appeared as a threat to the security of the United States and was inadmissible.[60] The obligation of leadership was assumed as a duty. President Johnson said in 1965, "We did not choose to be the guardians at the gate, but there is no one else."

The cold war was militarized by the conflict in Korea, which seemed to indicate that the problem was largely military and thus had to be met by force. The American response, as usual, was overdone, both in a broad sense and in Korea itself. What began as an effort generally approved by allies and neutrals to repel the North Korean onslaught was turned into an effort to liberate North Korea. This purpose found little sympathy in the rest of the world. The Chinese warned that they would intervene,[61] but American leaders, pleased with the aroma of victory, paid no heed. The result was a much stiffer, more costly, less justified, and increasingly unpopular war.

It is an exaggeration to claim that the United States was very prone to military action in the cold war; out of more than a hundred significant conflicts, American forces entered only three besides Korea.[62] Each such undertaking, however, was an overreaction. The sending of marines into an unsettled situation in Lebanon in 1958 was a nervous reaction to a nationalistic coup in Iraq. President Dwight D. Eisenhower claimed that the Soviet Union and Egypt were interfering by radio broadcasts and that political instability in Lebanon was related to the communist pattern of conquest. Happily, however, there were few if any communists around, no one started shooting, and the marines were withdrawn, after 102 days, from one of the most purposeless ventures of American diplomatic history.

President Johnson's dispatching of forces to the Dominican Repub-

---

60. Robert W. Tucker, *A New Isolationism: Threat or Promise?*, Universe Books, New York, 1972, p. 89.

61. William Whiting, *China Crosses the Yalu: The Decision to Enter the Korean War*, Macmillan, New York, 1960.

62. As noted by Herbert K. Tillema, *Appeal to Force: American Military Intervention in the Era of Containment*, Thomas Y. Crowell, New York, 1973, p. 5.

lic in April 1965 was less fraught with danger to world peace and more concordant with the United States' traditional role in the Caribbean; unfortunately, it was also hasty, unilateral, based on false premises, and contrary to stated American policies and treaty commitments. The ex post facto sanction of the Organization of American States did not help much. President Johnson said in justification of his action (May 2, 1965): "The American nations cannot, must not, and will not permit the establishment of another Communist government in the Western Hemisphere." But since most Latin Americans regarded the intervention as arrant imperialism, it was a bonanza for extremists and communists. The Dominican president, Juan Bosch, exaggerated pardonably when he wrote that there were 53 communists in his country before the intervention (as American spokesmen had claimed to find communists in the rebel forces), but 53,000 after it.[63] This action also served as an excuse for the Soviet invasion of Czechoslovakia in 1968.[64]

In Vietnam, infatuation with force as a solution for political problems reached its apogee. No substantial national interest was at stake in what was essentially a civil war. There was no real question of expansionism on the part of either China or the Soviet Union, which were already sharply at odds when the United States began large-scale participation. There was a weird unrealism in the effort to support freedom and democracy by napalm and bombs in tonnages dwarfing those rained on Germany in World War II. The technological mentality of destruction triumphed in vegetation-destroying defoliants, "search-and-destroy" missions that seemed devised to alienate the peasantry, and daily body counts that made American assistance seem a macabre cross to bear. President Johnson and Secretary of State Rusk nevertheless permitted themselves to call Vietnam as vital as Europe and lacked the moral courage to admit that an error had been made.

The venture failed, despite all calculations of American capabilities, because repugnance gradually built up—it was the first war to be fought on television, and journalists did not hesitate to report the worst. The technological means of destruction were grossly inappropriate to the real task of nation building, as well as inefficient; the cost was about $300,000 per guerrilla liquidated, a sum equal to the yearly

---

63. Richard J. Barnet, *Intervention and Revolution*, World Publishing, New York, 1968, p. 15. See also Philip Geyelin, *Lyndon B. Johnson and the World*, Praeger, New York, 1966, Chapter 10.

64. Thomas M. Franck and Edward Weisband, *Word Politics*, Oxford University Press, New York, 1971, Chapter 6.

income of about 3,000 Vietnamese. Daily bombing sorties could not
make up for the fact that the United States did not have an effective
government to defend.[65]

The war was more than failure; it was ultimately responsible for
the fact that all Indochina became communist, an outcome made possible by embitterment and destruction of the old social order. Materially,
the war cost 56,000 American lives and about 300,000 wounded; it cost
perhaps a million Vietnamese lives as well as several millions of
wounded or maimed; it made about ten million people refugees; and it
rendered millions of acres in Vietnam temporarily or permanently unproductive. Spilling over, it brought huge loss of life and property to
Cambodia and (to a lesser degree) to Laos. The financial cost to the
United States was at least thirty times what the Russians spent supporting the North Vietnamese. (When all the bills are in, including
veterans' benefits, the cost to American taxpayers may be $300 billion
or more.) The avoidance of new taxes to pay the bills generated inflation. The balance of payments was thrown into severe deficit, and the
American dollar had to be loosed from the gold standard and in effect
devalued. Many a domestic program was deferred or canceled, and the
war contributed greatly to the decay of American urban centers.

If the principal purpose of Vietnam was to discourage communism
and leftist subversion, to show American firmness, and to uphold
American prestige, the effects were contrary. The war caused the enemies of this country to gloat. As Secretary of Defense Robert McNamara
wrote to the president (May 19, 1967) in growing disillusionment:

> The picture of the world's greatest superpower killing or seri-
> ously injuring 1,000 noncombatants a week, while trying to pound
> a tiny backward nation into submission on an issue whose merits
> are hotly disputed, is not a pretty one. It could conceivably pro-
> duce a costly distortion in the American national consciousness
> and in the world image of the U.S.—especially if the damage to
> North Vietnam is complete enough to be "successful." [66]

Repugnance at the methods and dimensions of destruction in Vietnam,
disbelief in the justice of American motives, and the inability of the
big rich country to subdue a brave and determined Asiatic peasantry

---

65. Cf. Hans J. Morgenthau, "The Roots of U.S. Failure in Vietnam," in
Analyzing International Relations: A Multimethod Introduction, ed. William D.
Coplin and Charles W. Kegley, Praeger, New York, 1971, pp. 113–126.
66. *Time,* July 12, 1971, p. 27.

were magnified because the massive and well-supported effort of the communist movement and the Soviet Union to discredit "American imperialism" was joined with the persuasions of American opinion makers.

Previously, an American president traveling abroad could count on a friendly or even enthusiastic popular welcome virtually anywhere; by 1909, there was hardly a country except for those run by dictatorships (like Greece and Spain or, on the other side, Russia and China) where he would not encounter hostile demonstrations. Up to 1965, the United States was something of a model nearly everywhere; afterward, because of the reported behavior of its forces and the breakdown of order in racial and radical violence at home, the United States became an antimodel. The spate of bombing of North Vietnam in December 1972, for example, raised a frenzied outcry wherein intelligent noncommunists did not mind comparing Nixon with Hitler.

The war, which was the center of world attention in 1965–1972, raised the atmosphere of violence everywhere. It probably hindered pacific settlement in the Near East, as Arabs (with Soviet encouragement) equated America with imperialism. The American policy of punishing a land that supported guerrillas encouraged India to strike Pakistan for supporting guerrillas in Kashmir; later India made itself an analogue of North Vietnam by coming to the aid of a rebellion in East Pakistan (Bangladesh). It is not known whether the Soviets might have desisted from invading Czechoslovakia in 1968 if there had been no Vietnam, but the Vietnam war certainly deprived the United States of the capacity to react or to aid the Czechs. Opprobrium for the Soviet transgression was much less than it would otherwise have been. The secretary general of the United Nations noted that Soviet aggression did not involve burning villages.

Beneficiaries of the Vietnam war were radical leftist or communist movements. The war gave them genuine heroes, plausible villains, and a moving and understandable cause. It returned to the extreme leftist parties some of the respectability they had once enjoyed as leaders of the anti-Nazi underground. It held communist parties together in opposition to "American imperialism." Communists in conclave, when they could agree on little else, happily joined in shouting denunciations of American actions in Vietnam. The war raised, or at least helped to maintain, the Soviet ideological temper by providing a specific context for the general thesis of struggle; it encouraged the neo-Stalinists and hawks in the Soviet leadership. The United States ceased to be an acceptable alternative model for Soviet dissidents. What had seemed to be a tendency toward relaxation and liberalization in the

Soviet Union and the Soviet empire was reversed coincidental with escalation in Vietnam if not because of it.

Europeans or Asians did not need to develop their criticisms of the United States or to borrow them from the communist arsenal; it was enough to quote from the American press. Many Americans assured the world that their society was sick, perhaps hopelessly so. A failure of the magnitude of Vietnam was a new and traumatic experience. Since it was inconceivable that failure was due to weakness or to circumstances, it must be the result of immorality; this response paralleled the McCarthyist reaction to loss of China. The intellectuals who identified with the government during the Kennedy years, when Harvard trooped to the Potomac, became detached during the Johnson administration; during the Nixon presidency they became deeply alienated, because of Vietnam as well as the attitudes and style of the administration. Disapproval turned into righteous indignation. Patriotism became "old-fashioned patriotism," a dirty word with the enlightened that recovered its respectability only after American participation in the war had ended.

Since anticommunism was seen as responsible for the Vietnam horror, anticommunism became an evil force. Scholarly and journalistic attitudes became much friendlier to the Soviet Union and especially to Maoist China, which was closer to the Vietnamese. Many a "liberated" intellectual took such absolutist dictators as Mao or Castro as heroes. The United States was correspondingly denigrated; such adjectives as *fascistic, genocidal,* and *racist* were accepted as axiomatic by a considerable sector of opinion.[67] It was not atypical that a columnist of a leading newspaper wrote of America as "the most dangerous and destructive power on earth." [68] To assuage feelings and simplify a complex problem, the apparent nonsense of Vietnam was made intelligible by associating it with capitalist predacity and militarism.[69] "American imperialism" became a standard cliché of the left, in the perception of which the prosperity of the United States and the poverty of the underdeveloped world were due to corporate exploitation. Since the United States was the "leader of the world imperialist forces," defeat in Vietnam was to be welcomed as progress toward a better order.

---

67. Cf. Arnold Beichman, *Nine Lies about America,* Library Press, New York, 1972.

68. *The New York Times,* May 8, 1972, p. 35.

69. Cf. George Wald, in *Issues of the Seventies,* ed. Leonard Freedman, Wadsworth, Belmont, Calif., 1970, pp. 373ff.

Debate over the war served as catalyst for a mass of insurgent emotions and resentments, which were expressed in a multitude of ways from riotous demonstrations to long hair, the burgeoning of the drug culture, and unconventional sexual mores. Some people took the position that America could be saved only by violent revolution, and a large part of the potential leadership of the future became imbued with a more or less Leninist mythology of world and social order.[70] Many more citizens became deeply pessimistic. Although it was incredible to an earlier generation, it was reported that one-third of the nation's student population preferred to live somewhere other than the United States.[71] Such effects began to diminish as American participation in the fighting was limited and then ended, but American society will long remain scarred.

There was another set of consequences within the government. The Johnson administration, sidetracked from its social and reformist purposes, came to dedicate nearly all of its energies to the prosecution and justification of the war. Perhaps worse, the administration found itself driven to falsification both to itself and to the public; *cover-up* and *credibility gap* became the common terms of political discourse. The impatience of interventionist presidents has regularly led to illegalities and the abuse of power ever since Franklin Roosevelt set the Federal Bureau of Investigation onto critics of his anti-Axis course in 1940, but the abuse of power rose to an unholy climax in the Vietnam years, with secret and illegal military operations in Indochina and harassment of oppositionists in the United States. Watergate was one of the many ugly offspring of Vietnam.

FROM PAST TO FUTURE

It seems clear from a survey of American foreign ventures of the past eighty years that the least successful aspect of United States foreign policy has been the exercise of force for causes not directly and manifestly defensive. As a military-imperialist-interventionist power, this country has been a dismal failure. This failure is closely related to the nation's pluralistic-democratic structure. In the absence of authoritarian controls on information and political expression, it is difficult to carry on for long any costly foreign activity without a conviction of

---

70. Steven J. Kelman, "Youth and Foreign Policy," *Foreign Affairs,* 48 (April 1970), 414–426.
71. *The Wall Street Journal,* May 1, 1972, p. 12.

national danger. The American public tolerated three years of escalation in Vietnam only because the costs in blood and money were relatively small—in the range of one-tenth of the fatalities due to traffic accidents and 3 to 4 percent of the national product. Even so, in the absence of a conviction that the war was necessary, it became unbearable for American society and unsustainable for the government. During the Nixon years it was tolerable, to a degree, only because American forces were being steadily (although slowly) withdrawn.

It consequently seems doubtful whether in the future the United States will be able to apply military force abroad, except perhaps on a small scale and for a short time,[72] unless there is a clear-cut attack on the American nation. This seems perhaps the least likely of contingencies; the difficult situations facing the nation will probably be ambiguous and without a clear-cut right or wrong, and will almost certainly not be an unequivocal threat to the national safety. Moreover, these situations are likely to involve complex, nonpolitical problems (from the price of oil to the management of the ocean floor) that do not greatly raise blood pressure. Revulsion from blanket anticommunism was strong enough that President Nixon, much of whose career was built on anticommunism, found it quite suitable to move toward normal, even friendly relations with the leadership of mainland China (People's Republic of China) and the Soviet Union, and detente became the strongest claim of his administration. The relief with which this turn was greeted amounted to virtual admission that much of cold war policy, at least in its later years, had been misguided.

More broadly, the Vietnam debate revolved around the question of intervention, the feeling that the United States had become entrapped by meddling and should meddle less. Most people seemed to agree that this country should be much warier of trying to direct the affairs of other lands. Congress began looking more critically at military aid programs; hints of involvement, such as furnishing a few planes to a beleaguered African government, sufficed to raise protests and start an inquiry. The proposal to station 200 American civilians in the Sinai Peninsula to monitor the Israeli-Egyptian armistice caused the Senate majority leader, Mike Mansfield, to remark, "As far as I am concerned, one Vietnam is one Vietnam too many" (September 1, 1975). The person in the street was very ready to be rid of foreign troubles. According to

---

72. An example of this point is the rescue-reprisal operation against Cambodia after the seizure of an American merchant vessel, the *Mayaguez*, in May 1975. This series of events is discussed in Chapter 11.

a 1972 survey, no less than 73 percent of those asked agreed with the statement: "We shouldn't think so much in international terms but [should] concentrate more on our own national problems and building up our strength and prosperity at home." [73]

There can be no real new isolationism; [74] it is likely that the United States in the future will be not less but more involved in world affairs, but military means seem to have become largely irrelevant to the making of the new world order. Instruments of force, while still fashionable, are not only burdensome and dangerous but are unhelpful for most needs of modern states. Territorial disputes, to which military capacity is relevant, have not entirely ceased to exist, but they have been reduced to a minor concern of a large majority of foreign offices. To the contrary, states are preoccupied with import and export controls, exchange rates, material supplies, world prices, international corporations, and the like. It is increasingly true that economics dominates foreign policy, although discourse (and the thinking of statesmen) often fails to reflect this fact.

Rather less noticed [75] is the cultural and informational integration of the world community. Autonomous cultures and cultural development seem to have been superseded, except perhaps in China and the Soviet Union. Even these nations find it hard to remain outside the global mainstream. The Soviet Union is increasingly permeable to foreign ideas and fashions, and China follows at a distance. This fact is also inherently favorable to the United States—by a wide margin the world's leading exporter of ideas, modes, and information—although there has been very little effort to turn it to advantage.

In consideration of the kind of world order that may be fostered, there is already a model in the interrelations of the advanced industrial countries, a group nearly equivalent to the United States and its allies (the so-called Western countries plus westernized Japan). By historical standards, relations among these states are decidedly harmonious, with virtually no threats of violence. They are linked by a network of cooperative organizations, and their economic intercourse is free and mutually advantageous to an unprecedented degree. Despite their

---

73. *Time,* December 25, 1972, p. 12.

74. For a statement, see Tucker, *A New Isolationism: Threat or Promise?;* and James A. Johnson, "The New Generation of Isolationists," *Foreign Affairs,* 49 (October 1970), 136–146.

75. Although this trend has been discussed by such writers as Zbigniew Brzezinski, *Between Two Ages,* Viking, New York, 1970; and Lester R. Brown, *World without Borders,* Random House, New York, 1972.

bickerings, it is easy to suppose that most problems would become solvable if all the world could be assimilated into similar patterns.

No such assimilation is in prospect. One reason is that roughly a third of the world's population and industrial capacity and an undefinable but large fraction of its military potential are under the governments which subscribe to Marxism-Leninism, shut their societies and economies off from the rest of the world so far as they find feasible, and are (at least in theory) hostile to the social and political systems prevalent in the rest of the world. Whatever the virtues of detente, a gulf separates the fourteen or so communist states from others, especially those of the advanced industrial world.

A somewhat different but perhaps even deeper gulf separates the less developed countries (the states that have not yet gone far toward assimilating the scientific-industrial revolution) from the more developed or richer countries. The problems of the less developed countries, or of the less fortunate among them, are so grave that they may well be regarded as insoluble. Unless, however, the troubles of the majority of humanity can be brought under control, the rest can enjoy neither an easy conscience nor assured prosperity.

Such factors must be taken into consideration as the United States seeks an image of the viable future world society. The United States wants a safe world within which there should be progress toward a more satisfying existence, a world of economic and cultural progress untroubled by threats of political violence. This goal implies a shift of focus in dealings among states away from competitive-security goals (primarily force-related) and toward cooperative and mutually beneficial arrangements to which force does not pertain. Such a shift requires a difficult adjustment: the harmonization of the independence of nation-states (which have a sovereign freedom to do injury to others) with the necessity for subordination of the interests or supposed interests of individual states. How or whether this adjustment may come about remains to be seen, but it will probably entail maximal permeability of national boundaries and the assumption of more and more functions, in an inherently international world, by international or multinational organizations of various kinds; meanwhile, differences among states will tend to decrease in both number and intensity. Such a system could take the form of a loosely bound, slightly competitive, nonviolent world with national sovereignty overlaid by international function—a world, as it happens, that is quite in harmony with the better American tradition, the aspirations of the New World republic, and the spirit of constitutional and democratic government.

CHAPTER TWO

Military Dimensions

NUCLEAR OVERHANG

The ability of the nation to work its will or to influence others depends upon many things, from commercial relations to the skills of its representatives. However, when the American president says, "We must remain strong," he is generally understood to refer to firepower, the capacity to kill and destroy. Military strength, President Gerald R. Ford asserted on October 9, 1975, is the most important program of the government. Foreign policy has traditionally been preoccupied with security, the ability to defend independence or vital interests primarily by force. The ultimate prerogative of sovereign states is the use of force against other states to bend if not destroy them. This aspect of the interactions of sovereignties in the anarchy of the unbridled state system is basically primitive. Nevertheless, force, or the possibility or threat of its use, however uncivilized, is very much alive and represents a major preoccupation of decision makers, an expense beside which everything spent for the improvement of the international system shrinks to microscopic insignificance. National security also entails the gravest dangers to the nation.

Development of technology, from the taming of fire onward, has always implied dangers; and the nuclear threat to civilization is a by-product of the scientific-technical revolution of this century. Nuclear energy provides only one component of the new power of annihilation. Nuclear explosives are made effective by highly developed delivery systems, computers, and guidance mechanisms, rockets, and so forth, and modern conventional warfare can be unspeakably destructive. More persons were killed in the 1945 bombing of Dresden (135,000) than in the nuclear attack on Hiroshima (75,000). Several pounds of nerve gas would suffice to depopulate a large city. It is probably also technically feasible to kill a major part of humanity with bacterial agents.[1] Such weapons, however, have not been brought into the mainstream of military thinking, whereas nuclear explosives seem to be more acceptable—in part, perhaps, because of the precedent set by the United States in 1945.

Modern weapons give great advantages to the offensive. The enhancement of this advantage has been the regular result of advancing military technology; the blitzkrieg of World War II in a sense was

---

1. On the exotic agents, see I. P. Perry Robinson, "The Special Case of Chemical and Bacteriological Weapons," *The Bulletin of Atomic Scientists,* 31 (May 1975), 17–23.

transitional to atomic war. But conventional war is limited by the need to transport huge volumes of shells or bombs. Nuclear explosives are so much more energetic as to raise the brute force of the offensive a thousand or a million times over. Other technical developments further multiply offensive capabilities. Satellites, for example, make it possible to locate exactly objectives anywhere on earth; rockets can be so precisely directed as to land within a quarter of a mile or less of their target after a journey of five thousand miles in half an hour; and warheads gain added effect by conversion to multiple targeting (multiple independently targeted reentry vehicles, or MIRVs). The means of defense, in contrast, hardly advance at all. Virtually nothing is done to protect populations, which are vulnerable as a hermit crab without a shell.

The world, unable to keep worrying about anything for very long, has become inured to the atomic danger hanging over it, especially since no superpower's atmospheric tests (banned by treaty in 1963) raise spectacular and deadly mushroom clouds and infect milk with radioactive strontium. But the facts surpass imagination. The uranium or plutonium of the A-bomb releases about twenty million times as much energy as the best chemical explosive. The material of the H-bomb is about one thousand times again more rich in energy; a megaton bomb weighs only a few hundred pounds. It is also cheap, and the force of H-bombs is limited practically only by the inutility of explosions beyond a certain magnitude. Khrushchev once set off a blockbuster equivalent to 60 million tons of TNT, but no one has subsequently found it worthwhile to make another such monster. A 5- or 10-megaton bomb can destroy a large city. The Hiroshima bomb had the force of a mere 13,000 tons of TNT.

Since nuclear destructiveness comes cheap, the United States and the Soviet Union have tens of thousands of nuclear weapons, amounting, it is estimated, to the equivalent of over 10 tons of explosive power per inhabitant of the planet. Several thousand land-based rockets are tucked into armored underground silos, loaded and ready to start to targeted destinations on a moment's notice. There are scores of submarines, each capable of launching sixteen rockets from oceanic depths. Many hundred strategic bombers are each able to carry several times the total explosive force used in World War II. There is a large panoply of smaller, tactical nuclear weapons designed for battlefield use, all a grand tribute to human ingenuity and technical capacity.

Over nine-tenths of the world's nuclear potency is in the hands of the two countries that, partly for this reason, are called "superpowers."

But others have found the possession of such might attractive. The British collaborated with the United States in the original development of the A-bomb and have benefited since, as a privileged ally, from cooperation with the United States. They consequently have spent only about $5 billion for their deterrent, a small force but one capable of causing damage (with sixty-four launchable missiles in four nuclear submarines) that no nation would willingly take upon itself. The French saw nuclear weapons as a means of regaining great-power status after the war and went to work in the 1950s in the face of American disapproval. They were able to test an A-bomb in 1960 and an H-bomb in 1968, and they continued atmospheric testing in the South Pacific up to 1975, despite a growing clamor of opposition. By 1980 they may have deployed missiles with multiple-targeted warheads. However, for lack of technical assistance from the United States, their three-submarine deterrent has been much more costly than that of the British. The Chinese, who were impelled by pride and fear to develop nuclear weapons, advanced quickly, thanks to Western-trained physicists. Like the French, the Chinese have tested in the atmosphere— their first A-bomb in 1964 and an H-bomb in 1967. The Chinese also have a few intermediate-range missiles operational. In 1974 India joined the club by exploding an underground nuclear device, claiming that it had only peaceful purposes.

The atomic arms race, however, is the responsibility of the super-powers. The United States undertook in World War II to develop the nuclear explosive predicted by physicists; the task was undertaken in some fear that the Germans might develop such a weapon first, as they might have if Hitler had been more open to scientific advice. The destruction of Hiroshima and Nagasaki was not necessary, but both the Russians and the Americans realized at the time that the new super-weapon might be advantageous in the bargaining that became increasingly sharp as alliance turned into cold warfare. The standard Soviet interpretation was that the purpose of bombing Japan was to intimidate the Soviet Union.[2]

After the war, in the face of pressure to "bring the boys home," military planners looked with favor upon arms that required few men yet furnished great power. The means of delivery was the heavy bomber, which implied air bases wherever possible around the

---

2. As contended also by some American historians, such as Gar Alperovitz, *Atomic Diplomacy: Hiroshima and Potsdam,* Simon and Schuster, New York, 1965.

periphery of the Soviet Union and Communist China (The People's Republic of China). This need for bases, in turn, spurred the overblown alliance policy of the cold war years. In the early 1950s, the Soviet Union brought a competitive force into being, but the United States endeavored to remain sufficiently superior to think in terms of "community punishing power" or massive retaliation—the ability credibly to threaten nuclear punishment for communist transgressions.[3] After 1957, with Soviet satellites circling overhead and a growing number of Soviet intercontinental ballistic missiles (ICBMs), the United States became subject to instant destruction like the rest of the world. One response was to bolster conventional forces and thus to avoid a need to initiate a suicidal exchange in response to local aggression. Conventional weapons provided the capacity for flexible response, with forces not only for a ground defense in Europe but for combating the wars of liberation of which Nikita Khrushchev was fond. Another answer to the incipient neutralization of American strategic power was the development of tactical nuclear weapons, although the use of little nuclear devices was obviously likely to lead to bigger ones. Still another response was to increase American strategic forces, thereby to keep a suitable lead over the Soviet forces, although it was not and is not clear how much more utility resides in a thousand weapons than in a hundred if the hundred are enough to pulverize a country.

In reaction to the alleged missile gap of 1960, American nuclear forces were expanded far beyond the need to match the Soviet effort. By 1962 the United States had a sixfold numerical preponderance of nuclear weapons. This fact, together with Soviet humiliation in the Cuban missile crisis of that year, stimulated (or at least was followed by) a steady counterexpansion of Soviet forces. American missile emplacements reached a plateau by the mid-1960s and leveled off with decreased cold war sentiment and concentration of attention on Vietnam; there were then 1,054 launchers on land and 656 launchers on 41 Polaris submarines, and these figures have remained the same. But Soviet strength surged steadily ahead, and American superiority became dubious after 1969. Doctrine was revised correspondingly to require a capacity for assured destruction and an ability to "take out" at least a quarter of the Soviet population and three-quarters of Soviet industry, even in the event of a first strike by the Soviets against

---

3. Robert M. Lawrence, *Arms Control and Disarmament, Practice and Promise*, Burgess Publishers, Minneapolis, 1973, p. 11.

American forces. For safety, each of the three weapons systems (land-based missiles, submarines, and long-range bombers) was to have this capability, perhaps several times over. At the same time the United States sought to achieve crisis stability—that is, to reduce the temptation of the Soviets to strike first and to decrease their fear that the United States might be tempted to do so. In 1970 the president pledged not to develop weapons "which the Soviet Union could construe as having a first-strike potential."

But the strategic race surged on thereafter, concurrent with the movement toward detente. The Russians developed new and larger missiles that were apparently aimed at the American land-based deterrent. They also began work on antiballistic missile (ABM) systems. Having been distracted from strategic weaponry by Vietnam, the United States turned back to it when relieved of Asian combat, accelerated work on its own ABM system, and developed multiple warhead missiles to frustrate any Soviet defenses. The ABM systems, which were technically dubious, were restricted by the agreements reached at the first series of strategic arms limitation talks (SALT I) with the Soviet Union, and the number of launchers was fixed. But the United States continued to multiply the capacities of both land- and sea-based missiles, converting them to multiple targeting—a single submarine carrying the new Poseidon missiles could erase 150 enemy cities. The Soviet Union followed, with a few years' technical lag. Meanwhile, bigger and better submarines and bombers—Trident and B-1 on the American side—were on the way, and technical ingenuity promised such marvels as the cruise missile. This is a cheap little unpiloted plane, about the size of a telephone pole with a nuclear warhead, that skims over the earth with a range of over 1,500 miles and a computerized accuracy of a few feet. Launchable from bombers, submarines, or other vessels, it is practically immune to interception and very promising for first-strike capability; [4] hence it is a menace to the security of both sides. Without excessive cost, the United States could readily deploy tens of thousands of cruise missiles on planes, ships, and submarines.

Presently, the two superpowers do not seem to be very uneven in their military potential. The Soviet military budget is quite as high as (and perhaps somewhat higher than) the American military budget in

---

4. *Science*, February 7, 1975, pp. 416–417; Kosta Tsipis, "The Long-Range Cruise Missile," *The Bulletin of Atomic Scientists*, 31 (April 1975), 15–26.

real terms.[5] The United States has a large lead in total number of warheads (8,500 by mid-1975), but the Soviet Union is closing the gap. The Soviets have somewhat more launchers and, thanks to bigger missiles, they also have several times more "throw weight" in strategic missiles; this lead is compensated for by American superiority in bombers, not to speak of tactical "nukes."

The chief American advantage is in technological superiority, despite the fact that the Soviets spend substantially more on weapons research and development. American technological superiority translates into greater reliability and accuracy of American missiles. Mostly by virtue of accuracy, the American arsenal is calculated [6] to have had, in 1974, 5.6 times the missile kill capacity of the Soviet. Because of this accuracy and more hardening on the American side, the Soviet Union would need twenty times its present capacity to have a 97 percent probability of destroying the entire American land-based system; the United States would require a doubled capacity for assured destruction of the Soviet silos.[7]

It would thus seem that mutual assured destruction (MAD) is a reality, and it is not logically evident why either side should feel the need to generate ever more destructive power. The Soviet purpose is probably mostly prestige. Khrushchev wanted missiles "so that the U.S. would start treating us better." [8] In 1972, the Soviet press gloated over the SALT I agreement as consecrating equality with the United States; it is reasonable to suppose that the Russians (like not a few Americans) would regard clear nuclear superiority as a badge of true greatness.

A half dozen Poseidon submarines, each with sixteen missiles, should be ample to deter attack on the United States. It is widely feared, however, that if the Soviets achieve strategic superiority they may use this advantage for political or psychological purposes, forcing the United States to retreat in a hypothetical crisis as the Soviet Union retreated in 1962. The United States made symbolic use of nuclear force by ordering a worldwide alert (October 25, 1973) to deter the dispatch of Soviet forces to the Near East.[9] This brandishing of nuclear

---

5. *The New York Times*, July 22, 1974, p. 2.

6. Kosta Tsipis, "The Calculus of Nuclear Counterforce," *Technology Review*, 77 (October–November, 1974), 40–41.

7. Kosta Tsipis, "Physics and Calculus of Countercity and Counterforce Nuclear Attacks," *Science*, February 7, 1975, p. 397.

8. Nikita Khrushchev, *Khrushchev Remembers: The Last Testament*, Little, Brown, Boston, 1974, p. 53.

9. There were some doubts as to Soviet intentions, but Kissinger saw the threat

strategic forces (the rationale of which Secretary of State Henry
A. Kissinger promised, but failed, to explain) was a somewhat doubtful substitute for more normal diplomacy; it could not productively be
used often. Nuclear capacity is a very gross political instrument. It did
not help the United States very much during the cold war, nor did it
enable the Soviets to maintain their influence in China when that
country had no nuclear arms and no prospect of assistance from the
United States. That a nation could profit from nuclear blackmail is
entirely hypothetical.

Secretary Kissinger has allowed himself to wonder, "What in God's
name is strategic superiority?" [10] The United States has to take a stance
of readiness to use strategic nuclear weapons if they should be necessary to defeat a major assault, but a desperate nuclear exchange would
be virtually suicidal for both parties, since each has the capacity to
devastate the other many times over. In this situation, the nuclear confrontation is like a poker game in which bluffs cannot be called, and
the utility of adding to arsenals is largely (perhaps entirely) psychological. It is taken to be important for the pride of Americans and the
attitudes of allies and adversaries that the United States maintain a
clear superiority; the military budget tells friends and foes that the
United States is prepared to back up commitments and to play an
active role in world politics. As expressed, for example, by Eugene V.
Rostow, "We are cutting our military strength, at a time when our military and political capabilities in world politics should be increasing. . . .
We are retreating when we should be standing fast. . . .We can hope to
reach [world peace] only by building up and maintaining a stable
balance of power." [11] The psychological value of the Soviet strategic
forces, ironically, derives largely from the publicity given to them by
American authorities.

The most likely physical use of nuclear weapons is of those grace-
fully called tactical on territory of third powers. The United States has
never promised not to be the first to use nuclear arms but holds
about 22,000, scattered in many countries, in battle readiness.[12]

---

as necessary to forestall the risk of the Soviets installing themselves as saviors of
Egypt. Marvin C. and Bernard Kalb, *Kissinger,* Little, Brown, Boston, 1974, pp.
497–499.

10. Cited by Paul H. Nitze, "The Strategic Balance: Between Hope and
Skepticism," *Foreign Policy,* 17 (Winter 1974–1975), 136.

11. *The Alternative: An American Spectator,* 8 (August–September 1975), p. 8.

12. For a survey, see S. T. Cohen and W. C. Lyons, "A Comparison: U.S.–
Allied and Soviet Nuclear Force Capabilities and Policies," *Orbis,* 19 (Spring
1975), 72–92.

In the worried aftermath of the Vietnam debacle (May 1975), North Korea was put on notice that a new invasion would be met by nuclear weapons, despite the superiority of South Korean forces. But tactical nuclear weapons are formidable; they range up to the Pershing missile, which has a range of 450 miles and a payload of up to 400 kilotons. There are believed to be 7,000 tactical "nukes" on the Western side in Europe and several thousand on the Eastern; these numbers are quite adequate to devastate the area of potential exchanges ten times over.[13] How cross-volleys could be kept limited has not been explained.

In the name of security, the superpowers have purchased insecurity.[14] Thanks to the tactical nuclear bridge between conventional arms and doomsday weapons, any serious confrontation between the superpowers might ignite general destruction. In addition, the possibility cannot be excluded that some bold leader may someday feel that it is necessary or wise to threaten to use some of the magnificent power in his armory or may be driven by fear to a desperate gamble. Happily, the submarine arm is still nearly invulnerable; thus no one invoking nuclear arms can be confident of emerging unscathed, although scientists are working on antisubmarine warfare. There is always a finite chance of some mad intrigue setting off a nuclear exchange. Moreover, the bigger the stockpiles, the larger the possibilities of an accident, which would not only be calamitous per se but which could trigger Armageddon. The greater the pile-up of strategic weaponry by the superpowers, the more difficult for other countries to refrain from following, thus complicating the equations and multiplying the dangers.

ARMS CONTROL AND DISARMAMENT

The Soviet-American nuclear arms race has been propelled by fear and by its own momentum.[15] The potency of the weapons is such that it

---

13. Barry Schneider, "Big Bang from Little Bombs," *The Bulletin of Atomic Scientists*, 31 (May 1975), 24.

14. Cf. Barry E. Carter, "Nuclear Strategy and Nuclear Weapons," *Scientific American*, 230 (May 1974), 20–31. A relatively positive assessment of the utility of nuclear weapons is given by G. W. Rathjens, Colin S. Gray, and others in seven articles in *Orbis*, 18 (Fall 1974). See also Paul H. Nitze, "Assuring Strategic Stability in an Era of Detente," *Foreign Affairs*, 54 (January 1976), 207–232.

15. For a general account, see Chalmers M. Roberts, *The Nuclear Years: The Arms Race and Arms Control, 1945–1970*, Praeger, New York, 1970; James Dougherty, *Arms Control and Disarmament: The Central Issues*, Center for Strategic Studies, Washington, 1960.

seems indispensable to counter whatever the opponent may do or be capable of doing. If some nuclear weapons are desirable, more are even better. Uncertainty raises fear; Soviet secrecy feeds hawks in Washington. Still more does doubt about Soviet intentions, which are not aired in public debates, official or unofficial, and which frequently seem quite different as expressed in the Soviet press and by diplomats over vodka glasses. It is only a guess whether the Soviet leaders really believe an American attack to be possible, since there was none when it could have been carried out without risk of retaliation, or whether they hope to achieve political goals through nuclear weapons. It is likewise unclear whether they wish to be perceived by the United States as threatening (in which case they might make dummy rockets as they have made dummy planes) or as unthreatening (in which case they would make every effort to hide or disguise nuclear installations).

Superiority is commonly regarded as intrinsically desirable, aside from any use that might be made of it. Research generates pressures; designers feel that, if a weapons system is possible, we should build it.[16] If we do not build it, the antagonist supposedly will do so anyway; we ought to attain the attainable, as Mount Everest had to be climbed because it was there. A successful antisubmarine system would be disastrously destabilizing, yet the United States must work on it; if it should be developed, this fact would give the Soviet Union the key information that it could be developed. Even if a system is not practicable, we should try to make it so; many hundreds of millions of dollars were spent on the ABM system before it was finally written off as useless.[17] Interservice rivalry helps to push ever forward,[18] and bureaucratic inertia keeps outmoded systems in existence. If land-based missiles become vulnerable, they are not phased out and replaced by less vulnerable submarine launchers. If there is to be a new nuclear submarine, there should be a new supersonic bomber.

Against these forces, pressures for disarmament have been feeble. Nonetheless, since the beginning of the nuclear age there have been countless meetings, conferences, and committees seeking to alleviate the folly and burden of a nuclear arms race. Representatives of the great powers have come together, alone or accompanied by neutral

---

16. F. A. Long, "Arms Control from the Perspective of the 1970's," *Daedalus*, 104 (Summer 1975), 12.

17. *Time*, October 20, 1975, p. 8.

18. Cf. Morton H. Halperin, *Bureaucratic Politics and Foreign Policy*, Brookings Institution, Washington, 1974.

delegates, almost every year, but there has been no caging the atomic devil. The issue has usually boiled down to one of controls over arms and disarmament. Soon after Hiroshima, in 1946, the United States presented in a flourish of generosity the Baruch Plan for turning atomic weapons over to a veto-free (and probably American-dominated) international agency; the Soviets denounced this as an institutionalization of the American monopoly and responded with a call for a good-faith ban on atomic weapons.[19] These remained the directions of American and Soviet disarmament proposals for many years. The Soviet Union regularly urged a general ban on the use of nuclear weapons; the United States feared that such a ban would disarm the West but not the Soviets and stressed control and verification. Sometimes the two sides came closer, as when in negotiations over the banning of underground nuclear tests Khrushchev acquiesced to three on-site inspections yearly; this was a big concession for any Soviet leader, a fact which the United States failed to grasp.[20]

The deadlock seemed complete and the discussions futile as long as cold war tensions prevailed, but in 1959 an agreement was reached on the demilitarization of Antarctica. In 1961, the United States and the Soviet Union formally agreed to work toward "general disarmament, abolishing all military forces under U.N. inspection," and this goal is theoretically still in force. In 1963, concern over fallout led to a ban on nuclear tests in the atmosphere, a sensible halfway measure in view of the inability to agree on control of underground explosions. In 1967, the powers prohibited nuclear weapons in outer space. Subsequent years brought the Nuclear Nonproliferation Treaty, the Ban on the Emplacement of Weapons of Mass Destruction on the Seabeds (against fixed underseas nuclear rockets, mines, or weapons depots), and the Ban on the Production and Stockpiling of Biological (Bacteriological) Agents and Toxins. Each of these agreements was rather symbolic, inhibited the spread of nuclear arms where no one had undertaken to place them (for example, in the Antarctic and in outer space), or was intended mostly to sustain the predominance of the leaders (as were the test ban and nonproliferation treaties).

More serious negotiations got underway as the United States real-

---

19. On the Baruch Plan, see John W. Spanier and Joseph L. Nogee, *The Politics of Disarmament: A Study in Soviet-American Gamesmanship,* Praeger, New York, 1962, pp. 75–82, and Lawrence, *Arms Control and Disarmament,* pp. 4–5.

20. For a general account, see James E. Dougherty, *How to Think About Arms Control,* Crane, Russak, New York, 1973.

ized that the beginning of a Soviet ABM system portended escalation of the arms race. Moreover, the superpowers had undertaken in the Nuclear Nonproliferation Treaty to work toward disarmament; it was feared that if they did nothing in this direction, it would be more difficult to restrain the spread of nuclear weapons. In January 1967, President Lyndon B. Johnson suggested negotiations; because of hesitation and the Soviet invasion of Czechoslovakia, however, discussions were not started until late 1969.

After more than two years of strategic arms limitations talks (SALT) it was possible to reach two accords when President Richard M. Nixon went to Moscow in May 1972. One was a permanent (but explicitly denounceable) treaty restricting ABM systems to two on each side. The other was a temporary (five-year) agreement limiting land- and submarine-based missiles (built or being built). The figures, which were not stated in the text of the agreement or by the Soviet press—presumably because the Soviet leaders do not care to tell their people how many rockets they have—were 1,054 and 1,618 intercontinental missiles for the United States and the Soviet Union, respectively, plus 656 and 710 submarine missiles carried by 41 and 45 submarines, respectively; there were some provisions for replacements and substitutions. The Soviets were permitted more launchers in compensation for American advantages in other categories, especially numbers of warheads. Each country was to use its national means of verification—principally satellites circling the earth at various altitudes with arrays of sensors and cameras, capable of picking up objects less than a foot in diameter.[21]

Outwardly these agreements represented a breakthrough in relations between the superpowers. However, they not only failed to reduce the nuclear overhang but also permitted, and perhaps even encouraged, an acceleration of the arms race. A large part of the nuclear arsenals was omitted; the limitation on launchers said almost nothing about size, accuracy, or multiplicity of the payloads. Both sides continued to press forward with improvements of their destructive capacities. On the Soviet side, this meant progress on MIRVs, new rockets, and new submarines. On the American side, since the original purpose of MIRV (to counter a potential ABM system) had been abandoned, the Department of Defense pushed steadfastly to make MIRVs

---

21. For a survey of the background of SALT, see Lawrence, *Arms Control and Disarmament*, and Robert L. Pfaltzgraff, Jr., *Contrasting Approaches to Strategic Arms Control*, D. C. Heath, Lexington, Mass., 1974.

accurate enough to destroy Soviet missile sites; the department wished
thereby to present a first-strike threat, something widely recognized as
undesirable for the United States because it might make the Soviet
Union feel that it had to risk a preemptive attack. The navy proceeded
with its Trident supersubmarines, due to cost well over a billion dollars
each before the predictable cost overruns; the air force advanced its
new bomber, the B-1, to begin replacing B-52s about 1980; and sundry
new missiles and automated engines of death had their claims.

Subsequent arms control agreements have been no more effective.
The limitation of underground testing to 150,000 kilotons, signed in
July 1974, was peculiarly hollow. Not only was the ceiling very high; a
power could legally test any explosive device by labeling it "peaceful."
The tentative Vladivostok agreement of November 1974, hailed as a
triumph of American diplomacy, limited launchers (missiles plus
bombers) to 2,400 on each side (of which 1,320 might be converted to
multiple targeting) until 1985. Except insofar as the Soviet Union
might otherwise construct more than 2,400 launchers, it seemed rather
an arms expansion than a limitation agreement, since each side was
called upon to build up to the ceiling in the decade given. President
Ford spoke of the American "obligation" to do so,[22] and Secretary of
Defense James Schlesinger stated that the United States would build
more under the agreement than had otherwise been planned, particularly more Trident submarines.[23] It was taken for granted that the
compact would make it harder for Congress to cut the arms budget.[24]
Maxima become minima.

Secretary of State Kissinger stated on March 5, 1974 that détente
did not permit arms reduction; it seems that armaments competition
has a life of its own. The distrust that justifies armaments competition
cripples bargaining to halt it, and there is not sufficient trust between
the United States and the Soviet Union for either nation to stake its
security on a written agreement. Another impediment is the excessive
complexity of the weaponry. There are too many factors to balance to
the general satisfaction: sizes and kinds of weapons, launcher numbers,
megatonnages, multiple warheads, accuracy, geographic advantages
and disadvantages, relations to allies and third parties (especially

---

22. *The New York Times*, December 4, 1974, p. 1.

23. Ibid., December 7, 1974, p. x. A skeptical view of the need for the Trident
is taken by William M. Rose, "Submarine or Anti-Submarine," *The Bulletin of
Atomic Scientists*, 31 (April 1975), 27–30.

24. *Business Week*, December 7, 1974, p. 40.

China), and difficulties of monitoring compliance. A major snag has been whether cruise missiles and certain Soviet bombers should be treated as tactical or strategic. It is practically impossible to achieve equality in all dimensions, or even to define offensive weapons. One can always assert, with factual arguments, that too much was given away, just as one can always argue persuasively that one side or the other is ahead militarily.

The long lead times for planning and constructing weapons systems require negotiations looking far to the future; on the other hand, the consultations and talks are so protracted that the landscape changes while they drag on. Negotiations are tied up in bureaucratic rigidities and power struggles; each branch of the service has to get as much for itself as possible. Most of those who advise about disarmament are necessarily the experts in regard to weaponry, usually military men; not only does military caution—the "worst-case" approach—weigh heavily, but one cannot assume that military men strongly favor undermining the importance of their profession. No one profits directly by disarmament, and not much is spent on it; the 1974 budget included $6.7 million for the Arms Control and Disarmament Agency, $85.5 billion for the Department of Defense. If agreements are reached, there are usually differences of interpretation and accusations of breach of faith to poison the political atmosphere. Thus there have been many charges of Soviet violations of the SALT I accords,[25] and the atmosphere was perhaps worse because the Soviet Union could be accused not only of arms racing but also of bad faith.

The worst feature of arms control negotiations, however, is that they give weapons a value they would not otherwise have. It may be impossible to show that certain devices would add to the security of the United States, but they may well be considered as a bargaining lever. The Soviet Union justifies military power as a means to disarmament.[26] The American administration candidly urges new programs as bargaining chips for talks in progress, but once started the programs become valuable and have to be kept. The cruise missile is a case in point. G.W. Rathjens finds that "it is likely that if negotiations are serious, and especially if they are prolonged, weapons will be procured which otherwise would not be, either to strengthen a nation's hand in international negotiations or to generate support for agreement from

25. *The New York Times,* August 5, 1975, p. 2.
26. Samuel B. Payne, Jr., "The Soviet Debate on Arms Limitation," *Soviet Studies,* 27 (January 1975), 43.

important domestic groups, such as the military establishments." [27] In the logic of negotiations, the limitation of arms, no matter how useless, is a concession to be made only for some payment; more weapons are always useful for a tradeoff. The arms race thus acquires meaning in the context of bargaining. This valuation of arms by the superpowers also helps to persuade other powers of their utility, something for the limitation of which a price can be demanded. Controversy, speculation, and bargaining all stimulate interest in the acquisition of the superweapon.[28]

Thus, ironically, disarmament diplomacy may impede disarmament. As long as talks are going on, it is virtually impossible to cut back on weaponry, even though additional arms may be recognized to be superfluous. Arsenals may be enlarged as a precaution against failure to reach agreements. The antimilitarists are disarmed by the bargaining in process, and they are given something on which to fritter away their energies. By calling for talks on troop withdrawals from Europe, General Secretary Leonid Brezhnev of the Soviet Communist party effectively torpedoed the Mansfield Resolution for the withdrawal of a part of American forces; there is no point in giving away what the adversary may be willing to buy. One may assume he also undercut agitation in eastern Europe for the reduction of Soviet garrisons. The issue remains a dead one at least as long as the talks continue, which may be indefinitely. The idea of negotiated withdrawals, moreover, is to be coupled with compensating improved capabilities. "MBRF [mutual balanced force reduction] talks require that we modernize our hardware, our thinking, and the tactical options available and required at the lower end of the nuclear spectrum." [29] The use of weaponry to secure a concession from the Russians, particularly acceptance of some limitation on arms, suggests that they should seek to minimize or undo that concession in any way possible and that they should develop weapons to exert such pressure in their own right. Bargaining over weapons may even lead where a country would not otherwise consider going. If the United States wants to prohibit mobile ICBMs on land, this desire is reason for the Soviet Union to produce ICBMs or at least make the United States pay for a promise not to do so.

Some have become impatient. "Nothing is more preposterous,"

27. Comment in *Controlling Strategic Nuclear Weapons*, ed. Walter Slocombe, Foreign Policy Association Headline Series, No. 226, June 1975, p. 53.

28. George H. Quester, "Salt II and Potential Nth Countries," in *Contrasting Approaches to Strategic Arms Control*, ed. Pfaltzgraff, pp. 261–263.

29. James K. Polk, "The Realities of Tactical Nuclear Warfare," *Orbis*, 17 (Summer 1973), 447.

Beres exclaims, "than the current character of agreements to limit strategic arms." [30] When the superpowers have 420,000 times the explosive force of the Hiroshima bomb deliverable by missiles alone, it would seem more promising for the United States to consider critically what policies and arms are necessary to its safety and welfare and to act accordingly. Just as it may be beneficial to the United States to lower trade barriers whether or not other countries make counterconcessions, it may be beneficial to restrict weapons systems without specific compensation from the Soviet Union. Thus, the land-based missiles that cause most controversy and threaten nuclear stability might well be phased out in favor of the other less vulnerable systems, despite their advantages of size, accuracy, and cheapness. It would be logical to endeavor to minimize instead of enhancing the psychological significance which is their chief utility.

The nuclear arms race, in which superiority is indefinite and unusable and the only real purpose of weaponry is symbolic terror, is a weird game that one party cannot halt unilaterally; one player, however, can show a lack of enthusiasm and dispirit. Nuclear arms should not be prestigious but rather a subject of shame for the barbarism they imply, the implication of indiscriminate slaughter beyond the mores of Genghis Khan. A high level of military spending is a bad example by the power which contributes most to the world political climate and which, by its historical tradition and political nature, might better stress the disutility of nuclear arms. Since arms control can come only on a voluntary basis, it depends upon the deemphasis of force and violence. Nuclear arms are a sort of political ornament, a type of conspicuous consumption beyond material utility.

The Soviet Union might give little sign of being impressed by more flexible nuclear policies of the United States but it could hardly remain uninfluenced; the Russians are very prone to follow the Western example in material things. Many persons, especially outside the government, have urged that the United States might simply declare it had enough arms and refrain from adding to them or might take small steps toward reduction of more vulnerable and destabilizing weapons and challenge the Soviets to follow. If they did, other steps could follow; if not, the United States could mark up a moral victory.[31] In

---

30. Louis R. Beres, *Transforming World Politics: The National Roots of World Peace,* University of Denver Press, Denver, 1974, p. 43.

31. As advocated, for example, by Charles Osgood and Walter C. Clemens, Jr. and by G. W. Rathjens, *Orbis,* 18 (Fall 1974); Bernard T. Feld, "The Charade

the past, steps away from militarism by one superpower have sometimes been followed by the other, as in the moratoria on atmospheric testing prior to the formal ban in 1963 and the 1968 renunciation of weapons in space. Khrushchev in retirement thought that the Soviet Union should have reduced its useless armaments expenditures even if the United States did not follow, and his successors may be as rational.

For the Soviets, military strength is an important self-vindication, compensating for weaknesses in civilian production and cultural creativity, but they could make better use of the huge amounts of capital currently consumed by trying to keep up with or surpass American strategic capacities. Much of the Soviet desire for nuclear strength is probably mere emulation, the feeling that what is good for America is good for the Soviet Union, which finds it painful always to be behind. If attachment to nuclear force were generally regarded as backward, especially by the United States, it would be much easier for the Soviet leadership to spend their rubles on more positive pursuits. The important thing about nuclear weapons, for all practical purposes, is what people think about them.[32]

The risks of restraint can hardly be greater than the risks of a spiraling arms race. Western civilization faces numerous possibilities of disaster, mostly noncataclysmic; a Soviet attack seems one of the least likely possibilities, provided that the United States maintains the capacity to destroy Soviet cities not twenty or thirty but only several times over. Soviet Russia, after all, has become in practice a settled, rather conservative and undynamic power. The Nixon administration spoke of but did not follow a doctrine of sufficiency, strength adequate to make a challenge unacceptably risky.

Many persons, led by high officials in the Department of Defense, believe that it might be politically disastrous to permit the Soviet Union to gain a lead or even real parity in weapons counts. Their principal fear is that American allies would become demoralized or that the Soviets would be emboldened to more forward and expansionist policies. As one observer put it:

> For the salient problem of the overall U.S.–Soviet relationship is at present the perceived insufficiency of Western military power, and given the constraints which limit the growth of that power in

of Piecemeal Disarmament," *The Bulletin of Atomic Scientists,* 31 (January 1975), 22–29.

32. As observed by Quester, "Salt II and Potential Nth Countries," p. 262.

virtually all other dimensions, it is apparent that strategic policy offers the only avenue for alleviating this insufficiency. Hence, in the strategic realm we need much more than a minimum for deterrence narrowly defined, and we should rather acquire the maximum that is worthwhile to have, especially since the United States retains a comparative advantage in this sector of the overall military competition, and in no other.[33]

The more usual judgment, however, is that the security of the United States may be decreased by evidence of arming beyond clear defensive needs; it would be less helpful for security to build extra megatonnage than to appear to the world pacific and inoffensive. Even if the Soviet Union should achieve apparent superiority where superiority is meaningless, it is not evident that this development would lead the powers to court Moscow or to lose respect for the less militaristic Americans. The arms race is to be halted only by a new realism, as the nations increasingly recognize their interdependence and as the modern world perceives the obsolescence of political violence.

CONVENTIONAL FORCES

Most weapons talk is of nuclear arms and sophisticated delivery systems, but less than a third of American military spending is for nuclear forces, upkeep being a much bigger item than procurement. Even if there were nuclear disarmament, costs might continue to be high for an arsenal of tanks, planes, and ships, plus projectiles for them to deliver and defenses against them.

American military expenditures, however, have been tending to decline as a proportion of the gross national product (GNP) for more than fifteen years. In 1954, defense, spurred by the Korean War, took 12 percent of the GNP. This figure edged downward through the early 1960s, rising only slightly during the Vietnam war. It fell sharply as American forces were pulled out of Vietnam in 1970–1972, although the administration held that savings from ending combat should be applied to rebuilding the rundown strategic forces. The percentage was down to slightly under 6 percent by fiscal 1974. The military slice

---

33. Edward N. Luttwak, comment in *Controlling Strategic Nuclear Weapons,* ed. Slocombe, p. 48.

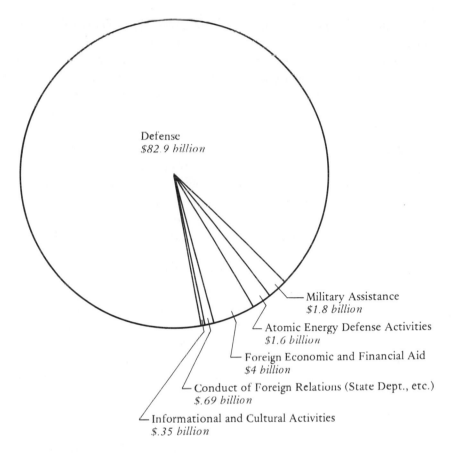

Defense
$82.9 billion

Military Assistance
$1.8 billion

Atomic Energy Defense Activities
$1.6 billion

Foreign Economic and Financial Aid
$4 billion

Conduct of Foreign Relations (State Dept., etc.)
$.69 billion

Informational and Cultural Activities
$.35 billion

Figure 2 Foreign Relations Expenditures by the U.S. in 1975, by Category. (*The Budget of the U.S. Government,* pp. 338–339.)

of the budget, 55 percent in 1955, was 25 percent in 1975. In view of the cold war and the repugnance (acquired in Vietnam) for military intervention, the Department of Defense became more restrained in its proposals; the Congress, formerly very complaisant, turned critical. Support for defense spending dropped most sharply among the young and among the educated, who had formerly been most interventionist.[34]

But the antimilitarism of the later Vietnam years subsided, and arms control negotiations required more refined and more expensive weapons systems. The defeat of American clients in Vietnam and

---

34. Bruce Russett, "The Americans' Retreat from World Power," *Political Science Quarterly,* 90 (Spring 1975), 3–11.

Cambodia sent the doves fluttering to cover. The challenge of the Soviets—who have raised military spending by 3 percent annually since 1960, currently outspend the United States [35] (although estimates are unreliable in terms of both money spent and value received), have nearly twice as many men under arms as does the United States, and continually bring out new instruments of conventional as well as nuclear warfare (as does the United States)—is a powerful argument for the hawks. The Congress is very reluctant to tackle the military experts regarding defense needs unless there is strong public feeling, and appropriations for major weapons systems are rarely denied.[36] Such pruning as is done is likely to be more cosmetic than real.[37] Consequently, although congressmen, diplomats, and editorial writers repeat that the United States is no longer to be the world's policeman, the defense budget is expected to rise by $4 to $6 billion yearly for the next decade, maintaining its approximate share of the GNP.

The pullout from Vietnam and the changed climate permitted the armed forces to shrink from 3.5 million men and women in 1968 to 2.1 million in 1975. Because of general philosophy and the association of the draft with the antiwar protest, the Nixon administration from the beginning worked toward an all-volunteer army. This return to tradition became effective in 1973, to the regret of some who considered professionals readier than conscripts to engage in military intervention.[38] Military pay consequently had to be made competitive with civilian incomes.

The high cost of volunteer armed forces plus the American bent for technology caused increased reliance on sophisticated weaponry, even robotization. Not only are submarines and bombers to have fantastic gadgetry; all manner of futuristic destructive devices are ready or projected. Maneuverable, target-seeking "smart bombs" and probably laser-artillery shells have phenomenal accuracy. Laser "death rays" are on the drawing boards. The air force of the future may replace pilots largely with remotely piloted vehicles—electronically guided

---

35. By as much as 50 percent according to Defense Department estimates; *The New York Times*, October 23, 1975, p. 29. On Soviet forces, see Jeffrey Record, *Sizing Up the Soviet Army*, Brookings Institution, Washington, 1975.

36. Les Aspin, "The Defense Budget and Foreign Policy," *Daedalus*, 104 (Summer 1975), 157.

37. Barry M. Blechman and Edward R. Fried, "Controlling the Defense Budget," *Foreign Affairs*, 54 (January 1976), 240–241.

38. Charles W. Maynes, Jr., "Can We Afford Not to Have It?," *Foreign Policy*, 18 (Spring 1975), 114.

bombers and fighters capable of outperforming manned planes in some respects without risk of life and costing less than a tenth of the $3.6 million tag of the F-4 Phantom. Military conservatism and machismo, however, hold back the automation of the forces. As an officer said, "To be a pilot you have to fly dogfights by the seat of your pants, not from some distant TV screen." [39]

Although the demoralizing effect of Vietnam has been largely surmounted, a peacetime army is difficult as well as expensive to keep in shape, even more so in a climate of detente. Men go through the motions of training according to the book with no belief that they are likely to be called upon to use their skills in combat. With few promotions to work for, and these allocated by seniority, there is little incentive to effort. Under these conditions, the American army may come to occupy a place more like that of Latin American armies, for which an external combat role is almost inconceivable but which frequently seek an internal political role.[40]

In a time when no one imagines any threat of nonnuclear attack on the United States and intervention abroad is rather discredited, one justification for general forces, which take more than two-thirds of the defense budget, is that defense spending has its political momentum. Reductions are painful, eliminating the jobs or reducing the career prospects of many influential men. As military skills become superlatively specialized in technology, it is all the harder to go back to civilian life. The services fight among themselves over shares of the budget for the sake of glory and promotions as well as the safety of the United States, and then they join to defend their budget requests before president and Congress. At budget time Soviet advances are regularly discovered to be putting the United States in second place.[41] Congress is also aware that closing bases and cutting down military orders hurts employment and pocketbooks. The defense budget is a stimulus to the economy. The Nixon administration added $5 billion to the post-Vietnam defense budget as an antirecession measure;[42] Secretary of Defense Schlesinger stated frankly that spending was increased by

---

39. Robert Gillette, *Science*, November 9, 1973, p. 561.

40. It is symptomatic that military personnel and dependents in Europe consume two and one-half times as much alcohol as average United States residents; *Christian Science Monitor*, December 4, 1975, p. 6.

41. On the need for better management, see Blechman and Fried, "Controlling the Defense Budget," 233–249.

42. *Businss Week*, January 19, 1976, p. 51.

more than $1 billion to perk up a lagging domestic economy.[43] However, defense expenditures are also strongly inflationary because they add to the money supply but not to purchasable goods.

A better case for large expenditures on conventional arms rests on the feeling that the United States cannot avoid becoming involved in some of the violent conflicts that may erupt around the world. General Maxwell Taylor stated the argument as follows:

> Any one of our allies—we still have more than forty—may get into trouble and invoke our help. . . . We may become embroiled in political upheavals to be expected in Third World nations suffering from overpopulation, poverty, and bad government. As the leading affluent "have" power we may expect to have to fight for our national valuables against envious "have-nots". . .[44]

In general, American allies would have manpower adequate to defend themselves in a nonnuclear confrontation if they felt it necessary, and an attack massive enough to overwhelm their defenses could be mounted only by the Soviet Union. The argument for or against large American conventional forces to defend allies is, then, the argument for or against large American forces in Europe. To urge that the United States should be resigned to becoming militarily "embroiled in political upheavals to be expected in Third World nations" or should contemplate fending off the armed attacks of envious poor countries suggests that the military department is looking for a use for its shiny tools. But as long as world politics is conceived as a contest of wills for something called power, it is essential for the United States to keep up a stance of strength, if only to keep up self-esteem and faith in its future.

Controversy arises from the fact that no one really knows, or certainly has not explained, just what relation the military establishment bears to foreign policy, just what commitments the nation must sustain, what forces are needed to sustain them, what the true vital interests of the United States are and how they are to be defended. In this uncertainty, the military establishment continues to be a serious burden not simply because of the quite bearable economic costs but primarily because of the tendency to build foreign policy around the biggest department of the government.

---

43. *The New York Times*, February 27, 1974, p. 9.
44. Maxwell Taylor, "The Legitimate Claims of National Security," *Foreign Affairs*, 52 (April 1973), 586.

NAVAL POWER

The role of the navy (except for strategic nuclear submarines) is somewhat like that of land and air forces overseas, the distant projection of American power to support American foreign policy locally or generally. But the navy, requiring no permission to sail into the vicinity of other nations, is more flexible and may be more effective than forces stationed abroad. And the American navy rubs shoulders with the navy of the Soviet Union. American "control" of the oceans is a matter of preponderance over the chief rival.

The surface fleet could hardly play much part in a nuclear war; this kind of war would not be likely to last long enough for a blockade to come into being. It would seem that the surface navies of the superpowers, like their nuclear arsenals, have largely psychological utility; for show as much as for shooting, they are majestic mobile displays of strength and will, glorified and costly flagpole stands. Khrushchev in retirement spoke frankly of the surface fleet as a showpiece.[45] But the American navy would have a large role in any future intervention in the Third World, especially if overseas land and air forces are more or less phased out. Carrier planes did much of the bombing in Vietnam; the navy serves as a mobile air base. It may act as a deterrent to possible hostile actions; if there were no American ships in the Mediterranean, for example, the Soviet Union would feel freer to act there and small states would be more hesitant to oppose it. In September 1970, the United States Sixth Fleet in the Mediterranean was in a position to threaten action unless Syrian tanks pulled back from their incipient invasion of Jordan; and its imposing presence may have had something to do with Syrian withdrawal and the end of the crisis, although the Israeli air force was probably at least equally persuasive. A less successful exercise was the sending of a flotilla, headed by the carrier *Enterprise*, to the Bay of Bengal at the height of the India-Pakistan war late in 1971. This action was unconvincingly presented as a measure to evacuate American citizens; it was intended as a signal to India and the Soviet Union of grave American displeasure. Its effect, however, was to antagonize both India and Bangladesh. To offset American pressure, India proceeded to sign a treaty of friendship and cooperation with the Soviet Union and extended naval facilities to the Soviets.

---

45. Khrushchev, *Khrushchev Remembers: The Last Testament*, p. 33.

During the Vietnam war and into the early 1970s the Soviet Union was outbuilding the United States navy by a wide ratio; the Soviet navy, which had been far behind, reached approximate overall parity with the American navy by 1973. Although the Soviets have built some smaller helicopter carriers, until recently they have shied away from the enormously expensive aircraft carriers of which American admirals are fond. But they have developed numerous new types of vessels, such as small, cheap guided-missile crusiers with the clout of a battle-ship and a much greater range.[46] As troublesome to the United States as the physical growth of the Soviet navy has been Soviet geographic ex-pansion, which has carried the visible projections of Soviet power to areas until recently beyond its shadow. Formerly a small defensive force, divided among the several seas that border the Soviet land mass—the Arctic Ocean, the Baltic Sea, the Black Sea, and the Sea of Japan—the Soviet navy has become practically a worldwide force. In the North Atlantic, its ships outnumber those of NATO. In the Medi-terranean, chief center of naval rivalry, it has surpassed, off and on, the American Sixth Fleet numerically. It has staked out a presence in the Indian Ocean and, with a base at Cienfuegos, Cuba, has made itself at home in the Caribbean.

Soviet competition has required refurbishing the American navy, which was allowed to run down during the Vietnam war. Adding up ships as if they were baseball scores, the naval men used the statistics to persuade Congress to be generous. In 1975, the United States actu-ally had fewer ships than in 1939, and manpower had dropped from the pre-Korean level of 1,460,000 to 785,000. The American navy was not quick to leap into the new age; but it, like the army, is moving toward futuristic weaponry: automated ships with very small crews but immense firepower, speedy air-cushion vessels, and laser beams to destroy aircraft or missiles. Its chief pride is its fleet of nuclear sub-marines, which is to be made bigger and faster with the addition of the Tridents; but it wants more mammoth carriers, the queens of the seas, perhaps the most expensive objects in existence, with a price tag of $2 billion each. It is difficult to compare the two navies, with differ-ent numbers and qualities of many species of vessels. But by 1975 the American navy again was decidedly larger in manpower and tonnage

---

46. For the Soviet view, see E. T. Wooldridge, Jr., "The Gorshkov Papers: Soviet Naval Doctrine for the Nuclear Age," *Orbis*, 18 (Winter 1975), 1153–1175; and Sergei R. Gorshkov, *Red Star Rising at Sea*, Naval Institute Press, Annapolis, Md., 1975.

and was rapidly outbuilding the Soviet navy. The American navy is probably technologically superior,[47] and it may also be better prepared. Soviet naval vessels sit at anchor most of the time, and Soviet pilots put in less than half the flying time of American pilots.[48]

It is not clear what meaning there may be in "control" of a given ocean at a time when navies of superpowers are extremely unlikely to start shooting at each other and are too vulnerable to affect greatly the outcome of hostilities if they did. But if "control" means showing the flag more effectively than does the rival power, it seems to be accepted as intrinsically desirable that the United States navy "control" all major seas outside the immediate Soviet sphere. It is not clear what the Soviets may stand to gain from having a few ships cruising around the Indian Ocean—they cannot effectively coerce any riparian power—but the fact that they are there and have facilities in Somalia calls for a larger American presence. Consequently, it has seemed logical to the Pentagon to build a naval and air base on the small British-held island of Diego Garcia.[49] One argument advanced in favor of the base was to improve the position for bargaining with the Soviets to limit forces in the Indian Ocean.[50] Supposedly a major purpose is to protect the nations of the region, but these have mostly manifested aversion to such protection and the project became a major irritant in relations between the United States and India. The Indian foreign minister, who certainly had no desire to come under Soviet hegemony, called the American presence "sinister," claiming that it posed a real threat to the security of littoral states.[51] The United Nations General Assembly has several times urged in vain that the Indian Ocean be made a "zone of peace" without bases or nuclear weapons.

Real uses, aside from ceremonial visits to friendly states, may be found for cruisers and carriers; and they are innocuous compared with the proliferation of nuclear destructive weapons. If conventional force is to be applied, there is something to be said for the flexibility of the navy. But if warships may conceivably intimidate, they are also likely to anger; and radicals would in most cases only be helped by a few

---

47. Michael T. Klare, "Superpower Rivalry at Sea," *Foreign Policy,* 21 (Winter 1975–1976), 165.

48. *The New York Times,* July 22, 1974, p. 2.

49. Alvin J. Cottrell and R. M. Burrell, "Soviet–U.S. Naval Competition in the Indian Ocean," *Orbis,* 18 (Winter 1975), 1109–1128.

50. *The New York Times,* July 18, 1975, p. 2.

51. *Christian Science Monitor,* March 3, 1975.

American shells or bombs landing in a country that somehow had so provoked the United States as to become subject to naval coercion. It is difficult to envision a naval role in a major war; convoying supply ships to a European theater, for example, surely belongs to the past. Big ships are an expensive and outdated means of upholding the national prestige and can make only a limited contribution to building a better international order free from the use of force. They may be a temptation. If there are gunboats, then why should there not be gunboat diplomacy?

CLANDESTINE OPERATIONS

If the navy makes a show of power with little thought of its being actually exerted, the secret or intelligence service has the opposite assignment of employing force invisibly. Yet the Central Intelligence Agency (CIA) contributes far more to the world's image of the United States than does the navy.

The United States got seriously into the business of intelligence and subversion in World War II; but the CIA was not put together until the beginning of the cold war. By original intention, it was to function mostly as a center for the collation of information gathered by other agencies, such as the Defense and State departments; but it also became a gatherer of intelligence, with 18,000 employees and a budget of about $750 million, discreetly supplied out of the funds of the Department of Defense. The budget is unconstitutionally secret, supposedly because knowledge of it would be useful to foreign intelligence agencies, particularly the Soviet Committee of State Security (KGB); it may be reasonably suspected also that the CIA enjoys its unaccountability. The entire American intelligence community may have spent as much as $10 billion in 1975,[52] a figure that suggests a certain amount of uncontrolled waste. Since domestic police and counterespionage, the province of the Federal Bureau of Investigation (FBI), are separated from foreign operations, the CIA is America's spy center, although perhaps nine-tenths of its information is garnered from impersonal or public sources, such as satellite observations and

52. *The New York Times*, January 27, 1976, p. 1. See also Harry H. Ransom, "Congress and the Intelligence Agencies," in *Congress against the President*, ed. Harvey C. Mansfield, Academy of Political Science, New York, 1975, p. 158.

newspapers. As shown by congressional hearings, it was intended to be an intelligence-gathering agency only.[53] But the CIA, with the propensity of unchecked officials to make their own law, also quickly undertook—contrary to the wishes of President Harry Truman [54]—a variety of operations which may or may not have been legitimate but which it deemed should be kept from the general view.

The intelligence-gathering, information-collating, and future-predicting activities of the CIA have been very important to the president; meetings of the National Security Council were probably opened with a briefing from the CIA. The agency has been fairly successful. It predicted the instant victory of the Israelis in 1967 and gave warning of the Soviet invasion of Czechoslovakia in 1968, although it slipped, like the Israelis, on the 1973 war. Its assessments in Vietnam were generally closer to the mark than those of the military services or the State Department, although it may have lowered its estimates of communist strength to suit political requirements.[55] Some serious misappraisals have also come to light; the CIA misjudged the will and ability of the Chinese to intervene in Korea and of the Soviets to put rockets in Cuba. It misdirected an American rescue mission to an empty North Vietnamese prisoner camp in 1971, guessed incorrectly that a small invader force at the Bay of Pigs could count on an uprising of the Cuban people, and failed to predict the Turkish invasion of Cyprus in 1974 and massive Soviet grain purchases. Its most important estimates, those of Soviet nuclear capacities and intentions, remain untested. The agency would be little noticed and uncontroversial, however, if it were dedicated only to intelligence.

The CIA came to its glory as master of miscellaneous skullduggery in the cold war, whether from the need to compete with Soviet machinations or from a desire to use all available means for the good cause. In the disturbed Europe of the first postwar years, it planted stories in the foreign press, paying as necessary; it bribed statesmen; it subsidized trade unions, newspapers, magazines, and radio stations. The two most important, Radio Free Europe and Radio Liberty, depended almost entirely on CIA financing. It may have influenced the critical Italian election of 1948. It supported anticommunist organizations, especially of refugees. It once plotted to contaminate Cuban sugar, a

---

53. Ibid., p. 156.
54. Roger Hilsman, *The Politics of Policy Making in Defense and Foreign Affairs,* Harper and Row, New York, 1971, p. 59.
55. *The New York Times,* September 19, 1975, p. 7.

project vetoed by President John F. Kennedy.[56] It allegedly schemed to assassinate Fidel Castro in 1961, very likely at the instigation of President Kennedy and with the assistance of the Mafia.[57] With or without presidential authorization it also may have taken aim at various times at Fidel's brother Raul, Che Guevara, Patrice Lumumba of the Congo, Haitian President Duvalier, Dominican President Rafael Trujillo, and President Sukarno of Indonesia.[58] Quaintly, it plotted against Castro's beard, planning to place a depilatory in his boots.[59]

The CIA could not organize coups without the support of the nationals of a country; but on occasion it provided a catalyst, organization, and decisive backing. It was involved in the 1953 overthrow of a nationalistic, pro-Soviet or anti-Western leader in Iran and the return to power of the Shah. It sponsored the toppling of a leftist government in Guatemala in 1954. It sidetracked Soviet money and supplies for Congo rebels in 1961. Without consulting the State Department, it supported and armed the ill-fated attempt to overthrow Castro by a landing of 1,600 Cuban exiles in April 1961.

The CIA was active in, and on the fringes of, the Vietnam war. It intrigued against the Viet Cong, engaging in torture and homicide to root out the subversive infrastructure in "Operation Phoenix," in which 20,000 people were killed (according to former CIA Director William Colby).[60] It has been accused of complicity in the overthrow of Prince Sihanouk of Cambodia in 1970. It carried on a small war in Laos, training, paying, equipping, and practically commanding an army of 95,000 men for a decade. It dropped agents and supplies for sundry groups behind enemy lines, turning local feuds to anticommunist purposes. It allegedly trafficked in drugs.[61]

The standing of the CIA began to decline at the same time the cold war showed signs of easing. It lost face when a U-2 reconnaissance plane was shot down in the Soviet Union in 1960, and more so with the Bay of Pigs fiasco in 1961. President Kennedy took a rather dim view of its activities; he tried to check it by giving the ambassador

56. Harry H. Ransom, *The Intelligence Establishment,* Harvard University Press, Cambridge, Mass., 1970, p. 95.

57. *Time,* June 2, 1975, p. 10.

58. *The New York Times,* November 21, 1975, pp. 50–53, gives the Senate Committee report on assassination plots.

59. *Newsweek,* December 1, 1975, p. 29.

60. *Time,* January 19, 1976, p. 17.

61. Alfred McCoy, *The Politics of Heroin in Southeast Asia,* Harper and Row, New York, 1972.

in each country supervisory authority over all programs, including CIA agents, in his country. The changing atmosphere of the later 1960s, growing American repugnance for the interventionism that led into the Vietnam war, and lessened concern for the politics of the less developed countries turned the CIA away from its more romantic endeavors. It has come to weigh more heavily the costs, presumably to reserve its intervention for important cases. Disclosure of CIA financing for various organizations, such as the National Student Association in its overseas work, brought termination of such programs or their transfer to nonconfidential support. The CIA became more of a gray bureaucratic agency, stressing electronics over espionage and striving to process the mountains of information poured into its limited digestive apparatus. CIA influence in the White House was partly exorcised by the demands of détente, and Secretary Kissinger was said to rely more on the State Department's intelligence bureau. It was a sign of flagging morale that ex-agents have published in the last several years half a dozen derogatory accounts of their agency.

The agency by no means surrendered its romantic mission, however. As revealed by Congressional investigations, it spent some $8 million (equivalent to much more when exchanged on the Chilean black market) to "destabilize" the legitimate Marxist government of Salvador Allende. It provided $350,000 to bribe members of the Chilean Congress to frustrate Allende's minority victory; then subsidies were given to anti-Allende newspapers, strikers, and so forth. These were not small sums for a poor nation of ten million people, whose largest political party spent only $123,000 on the 1973 elections. The generals who overthrew Allende in 1973 did not have to be subsidized, but they were certainly confident of United States approval. This intervention troubled many Americans, but much worse for the CIA was evidence of misdoings in the United States, including surveillance, wiretaps, and break-ins, where the CIA was not legally authorized to operate. The agency was connected with the Watergate affair and other reprehensible actions of the Nixon administration; perhaps more serious, it had engaged in surveillance of thousands of dissidents in the Vietnam years. It even showed itself insubordinate by disobeying a presidential order to destroy stocks of poisons in 1970.

These revelations led to debate, in Congress and elsewhere, on the proper role of the CIA and its clandestine activities. The chief argument in support was that the CIA had frequently been successful, helping to keep western Europe from communist domination in the postwar years, returning Guatemala and Iran to the pro-Western fold, and so forth. Many would agree with the statement allegedly made by Kissinger regarding Chile: "I don't see why we need to stand by and watch a country go communist due to the irresponsibility of its own people." [62] This view assumes a right of intervention on behalf of virtue and American interests as seen by the United States, in violation of international comity and treaty obligations of the United States, such as the Charter of the United Nations and the Charter of the Organization of American States: "No state or group of states has the right to intervene, directly or indirectly, for any reason whatever, in the internal or external affairs of any other state."

The other chief justification of CIA activities was that others do it, in particular the Soviet KGB. President Gerald R. Ford said at a press conference on September 17, 1974, "I am reliably informed that communist nations spend vastly more than we do for the same kind of purpose." [63] It is undeniable that the secret agencies of the Soviet Union and other communist countries spend very large amounts for subversion and operate quite unscrupulously, although they are not known to have attempted murder of heads of state. It may well be argued that the United States should not leave the field to them. In Chile, for example, Allende received, it is generally believed, far more money from communist sources to help him carry through a Marxist revolution than his opponents received from the United States; [64] and he engaged in illegal and repressive acts (mild, to be sure, in comparison with those of the dictatorship that succeeded him). A purist attitude by the United States thus might unduly penalize the democratic forces in contested areas.

For such reasons, the supporters of clandestineness call themselves "realists." They seem, however, to fail to add up real costs. In weighing the value of operations anywhere, it is easy to forget the effects everywhere. These include enormous damage to the American image and prestige. As stated by former Secretary of Defense Clark M. Clifford, "Our reputation has been damaged and our capacity for ethical and moral world leadership has been impaired. . . . Knowledge about

---

62. *The New York Times*, September 11, 1974, p. 14.

63. Ibid., September 18, 1974, p. 1. This argument was also made by the *Commission on the Organization of the Government for the Conduct of Foreign Policy*, Government Printing Office, Washington, 1975, p. 100.

64. Allende obtained sufficient financing abroad to raise Chile's indebtedness by $900 million. Paul E. Sigmund, "Less than Charged," *Foreign Policy*, 16 (Fall 1974), 147.

such operations has become so widespread that our country has been accused of being responsible for practically every internal difficulty that has occurred in every country in the world." [65]

The CIA is the best of scapegoats, especially in the less developed countries, for which it epitomizes their exposure and impotence. Left ists blamed it for bombings in Italy; and the Voice of Palestine, broadcasting from Algiers, called on Arabs to "kill everyone who is American because all of them work for American intelligence." [66] In 1972, the monthly journal of the Algerian armed forces wrote that the CIA had recruited flies as spies, attaching microscopic transmitters to their backs.[67] President Sese Seko Mobutu of Zaïre became convinced that the CIA was plotting to kill him and in reprisal, in June 1975, expelled the American ambassador. When the president of Mexico was stoned by a band of university youths, he credited the CIA; the Mexican foreign minister commented, "One must assume the CIA operates in all Latin American countries unless there is proof to the contrary." [68] Indian politicians blamed the CIA for most of the disturbances that overtook the country after the euphoria of victory over Pakistan died away. Marxist politicians said that the CIA sent letter bombs through the Indian postal system to tarnish the Indian reputation; chief ministers from north to south found the CIA behind extremists of the left as well as of the right.

Evidence was not necessary; as Indira Gandhi, prime minister of India, remarked, "It is not up to us to prove it, but it is up to the CIA to disprove it." [69] She saw her fears confirmed by events in Chile; perhaps the most important factor in her distrust of the United States was her reiterated belief that the CIA was at work in India.[70] Secretary of State Kissinger, who approved the Chilean operation, had to try to convince Prime Minister Gandhi that the United States would dream of no such thing in socialistic and somewhat pro-Soviet India. Greeks were fully convinced that the United States inspired the Cyprus coup of July 15, 1974, and they believed, less realistically, that the CIA arranged the murder of the American ambassador to Cyprus.[71] After

65. *The New York Times*, December 6, 1975, p. 12.
66. *Time*, June 18, 1973, p. 55.
67. *The Manchester Guardian Weekly*, October 14, 1972, p. 17.
68. *The New York Times*, March 18, 1975, p. 7.
69. *The Manchester Guardian Weekly*, November 4, 1972, p. 9.
70. *The New York Times*, September 27, 1974, p. 4.
71. *Newsweek*, September 2, 1974, p. 34.

an abortive minicoup in Portugal in March 1975, crowds in Lisbon chanted, "Down with the CIA." Such is the reputation of the secret agency that some intelligent men suspect that it had to do with the killing of President Kennedy. The Soviets and various leftists help the rumor mongering, but the CIA has supplied the raw material.

As remarked by Arnold Toynbee, "For the whole world, the CIA has now become the bogey that communism has been for America." [72] The agency is at least a psychological presence, an object of paranoid fear in most countries of the world. It has become a suitable and convincing scapegoat because of its history, in which myth fills the gaps of facts; it represents what is most irritating to people of weaker countries, wealth and technological virtuosity applied arrogantly and ruthlessly. Because of the CIA, the conviction has crystallized that the United States is opposed to the freedom of other peoples. Americans who dislike the idea of CIA passive surveillance of some American citizens can well imagine how Third World nations may react to the idea that their politics and government are at the mercy of the intrigue, corruption, and subversion that an agency of the world's richest power can bring to bear. Most of the CIA's work is in less developed nations that can hardly be called a threat to the United States, and its interference may seem to be exploitation of their poverty and backwardness. The United States makes much of the principle of independent sovereignty, but clandestine operations derogate it. The claim, on the part of the strongest power, of the right to intervene is in effect a claim of the right to indefinite dominion.

There are more specific costs. American missionaries, scholars, and others working abroad become suspect and are from time to time charged with being CIA operatives. The Peace Corps has been severely handicapped. Multinational companies are suspect because they are known to have furnished cover for many agents; and American business suffers whenever the United States is perceived as untrustworthy and guileful. Many ambassadors have been unwanted because of alleged CIA connections. The diplomatic image of Secretary Kissinger himself is tarnished by awareness that he was chairman of the committee approving the Chilean operation. Political defenders of the CIA have often cited the necessity of intelligence gathering, which merges into covert operations, as justification for covert operations; CIA

---

72. Quoted by Fletcher Prouty, *The Secret Team: The CIA and Its Allies in Control of the United States and the World*, Prentice-Hall, Englewood Cliffs, N.J., 1973, p. 54.

directors even use the word *intelligence* to mean both things, to cover the dubious with the necessary,[73] but intelligence gathering is hampered by subversive activity. This distracts and may make foreigners more hesitant to cooperate with intelligence work. "Dirty tricks" also presumably alienate potential recruits of high quality. The CIA has been driven to reassuring candidates that the old tricks belonged to the past.[74] More crucial is the fact that amoral or immoral subversive actions blow the cover for essential information gathering. The CIA is plagued by defections, bitter attacks, and exposés because many persons strongly believe it is engaged in evil activities.

Secretary Kissinger was led virtually to lie about the Allende affair to Congress. Because clandestine operations usually become counterproductive if publicized, they require secrecy and deception. There is something attractive about this; espionage is thrilling in life as in fiction, and secrecy is convenient and ego-nourishing.[75] It is exhilarating to call the boys together and dream of clever schemes to clobber the enemy. But secrecy is dangerous, corrupting, and incompatible with the democratic approach. *Secret* means *uncontrolled,* which probably means *illegal.* In unchecked operations it is very difficult to maintain good judgment. It is at best hard to draw the line between prudent and foolish actions, and men dealing in the shadowy realms of highly secret subversion make many errors. The Bay of Pigs affair has often been cited as a misjudgment; it was the best thing that could have happened to Cuban communism. It practically wiped out the previously substantial resistance to Castro.[76] Without such solidification, it is doubtful that Castro could have made Cuba communist. It also raised Castro's prestige in Latin America to its acme. CIA efforts to subvert the Albanian government from 1949 to 1953 fixed Albania in its anti-Western stance.[77] Heavy CIA involvement with the Greek military regime,[78] overthrown in 1974, made most Greeks at least doubtful of American friendship. By contribution to his downfall and failure to

---

73. Ransom, "Congress and the Intelligence Agencies," p. 154.

74. *Time,* March 31, 1975, p. 27.

75. As observed by Victor Marchetti, *The CIA and the Cult of Intelligence,* Knopf, New York, 1974, p. 272.

76. Herbert L. Matthews, *Fidel Castro,* Simon and Schuster, New York, 1969, p. 152.

77. Nicolas C. Pano, "The Albanian Cultural Revolution," *Problems of Communism,* 23 (July–August 1974), 46.

78. Laurence Stern, "How We Failed in Cyprus," *Foreign Policy,* 19 (Summer 1975), 34–78.

reckon the consequences, the CIA turned Chilean President Allende from a failure into a martyr in the eyes of most of the world.

In short, if gains are weighed broadly against costs, it would seem that few CIA "dirty tricks" have paid off. The CIA spends several times more money than the State Department plus the United States Information Agency; and its subversive activities may well have done more harm to the American position in the world than the good that those plus foreign aid could do.

The clandestine actions of the CIA are contrary to the American mentality and traditions and must be understood with reference to the cold war, in which an American agency imitated its adversary. It was more necessary and excusable in the chaotic early postwar world. There was a real ideological contest, and red-blooded Americans wanted to beat the communists at their own dirty game. But as an undercover, largely self-propelling force, the CIA epitomized the shortcomings of American foreign policy in the cold war: a narrow focus on action without making sure that the object was worth the cost or was really in the American interest; short-range awareness; and force-mindedness, putting great technical skills in the service of doubtful projects. The agency became independent enough to build up such an operation as the Bay of Pigs without ever securing the approval of higher authority for the scheme as a whole.[79] It countered dangers as it perceived them; because of its vested interest in tensions, it may have done something to provide appearances of dangers; reportedly, it once subsidized the communist *Daily Worker*.[80]

CIA subversion is another of the several aspects of foreign policy that would not be started today but that continue by momentum from other times. Thus, whatever excuse there may have been for the United States to tamper with French politics in unsettled postwar years has long since disappeared, and the effort would probably be counterproductive today. CIA subversion is immoral according to the American concept of morality, an unsuitable means for an open society and inappropriate for the foreign policy of a democracy, which should be carried out in such a way that citizens can in good conscience support it. There are legitimate actions to be undertaken quietly; for example, the CIA is reported to have organized their internal security for various pro-American foreign rulers. It is hard to draw the line

---

79. Prouty, *The Secret Team,* p. 40.
80. According to Taylor Branch, *Harpers,* 248, (January 1974), 60.

between the legitimate and the illegitimate, and a clandestine service is likely to find work for itself. But it would be sound policy if the United States were to be involved in only the barest minimum of what has to be kept secret. It may be proper to assist friendly democratic forces abroad; many other countries do as much. But this activity should not be undertaken by a paramilitary spy agency.

The operations of the CIA are less likely to be abolished because it, like other agencies, is self-propelling, and thousands of influential people have a stake in it. Presidents, being subject to human weaknesses, naturally like the CIA as a powerful tool, the uses of which have to be justified to no one. Until recently, the Congress, awed by the national security argument, has been incredibly loath to control or check the agency, which draws over itself a blanket of "national security." Congress investigates but draws back from effective measures to end abuses; it even investigates apologetically, lest some usually rather mysterious national security interest be damaged.

But the United States has better tools for building foreign policy— its economic and technical capacities, its cultural abundance, and its example of an unrepressed society. In all of these areas, unlike subversion, the United States is much better qualified than its principal competitors. If there should seem a likelihood of the establishment of a leftist dictatorship in Portugal, for example, American labor unions might assist their Portuguese counterparts, Americans of Portugese background might encourage the democratic parties, the government might offer transitional economic assistance, and so forth. Former Director Colby stated that there would be no "major impact" on the nation's security if the United States ceased all cloak-and-dagger operations against foreign countries.[81] But he also argued for "dirty tricks" as "an option between diplomatic protest and sending in the marines," without considering that there are many better courses of action if it is actually necessary that something be done.[82]

An amendment to the Foreign Assistance Act of December 1974 limited the CIA to its original and basic purpose of intelligence gathering except for such operations as should be found by the president to be important to national security and reported to committees of Congress. If respected, this law would substantially restrict the notorious

81. *The New York Times*, September 14, 1974.
82. Paul C. Warnke, "Apes on a Treadmill," *Foreign Policy*, 18 (Spring 1975), 21.

operations of the American organization that is best known to the world and in the eyes of many people practically stands for the United States. If the president, then, were to announce that the CIA was giving up its tricks, he would not be believed. But after a few years of no more news of CIA skullduggery, the atmosphere would be clarified, relations with many countries would be much easier, and American foreign policy would have taken a big step back from the interventionist aberration.

ARMS AID AND TRADE

A very different means of influence is the supplying of arms, as aid or on a more or less commercial basis. Perfectly legal, it is in many ways an attractive means of implementing foreign policy. A country acquiring American (or Soviet) weapons ipso facto aligns itself to some degree with the United States (or the Soviet Union); one usually goes to a presumed friend for the tools of death and the instruments of power. With arms go instructors and advisers, who are supposedly close to military commanders and are influential people, especially in less developed countries. One looks first to the old supplier for new needs, and spare parts are always required. Recipients of military wares are likely also to seek related nonmilitary goods from the same source. They go to the supplier for training, and they may well absorb political ideas from that source. Influence acquired by arms deals is fairly lasting, because a switch from the American to the Soviet system (or vice versa) is costly and protracted. Military aid may be made conditional on military bases; even without such tradeoffs, such aid gives the supplier privileged status with the receiving state. It is also much easier in case of trouble to assist a country that has been receiving American arms.

It is the American way to send machines rather than men, and it was once naively hoped that the Lend Lease program would suffice to get rid of Adolph Hitler. The habit of arming allies was easily carried into the cold war. In 1947, when Greece seemed threatened by communist-led subversion and Turkey faced a menace of Soviet invasion, it was logical to furnish military equipment and technology. Military aid was continued as a means of giving substance to alliances and strengthening allied and friendly powers. It blossomed with the Korean War and the consequent heated atmosphere. The Eisenhower

administration then stressed aid for allies as a means of economy,
since dollars went further in poorer nations. Military assistance was
only 26 percent of the foreign aid program in 1950, but in the period
1951–1954 it was 70 percent or more, thereafter declining. In 1960,
military aid went to forty-two nations, and in the mid-1970s it continued to flow in driblets to scores of nations and in billions of dollars
to a favored few, such as Israel. Furnishing or denying it was a means
of exerting pressure or inducing action; it induced several countries
to assist the American effort in Vietnam. Promises of large-scale arms
deliveries made it possible for Israel to agree to surrender strategic
positions in the Sinai peninsula in 1975. Military aid has never been
effective in promoting democracy, however; recipients, such as Turkey
and Pakistan, have used American arms for purposes specifically
prohibited by the contracts.

Military aid is a regular accompaniment of American economic
aid, sometimes packaged with it, sometimes separate. The Pentagon
has periodically urged that military aid be included in its budget, but
the Congress and the State Department have resisted. Recently it has
been reduced to under $1 billion yearly (excluding Israel), although
true amounts are in dispute; Congress has talked of terminating it entirely. It has gone in the 1970s mostly to South Korea, the Philippines,
Turkey, and Greece (plus Israel, a special case). Military Assistance
Advisory Groups, attached to embassies, supervise the program on the
spot.

Since 1964, sales of arms have far outdistanced gifts. The dividing
line is not clear, because sales may be on easy credit terms with reduced prices; but sales, mostly for cash, have recently been about
three-fourths of arms exports. Most are taken out of government stores;
private sales must in any case have official approval. Sales have become important for the American balance of payments, spiraling from
$3.6 billion in fiscal 1973 to about $14 billion in 1975, the bulk of the
latter figure being arms sales to the oil-rich Near East. Arms sales mean
jobs, about 47,000 for each billion dollars of annual sales.[83] In addition,
foreign markets increase volume and thus decrease unit costs to the
United States and keep assembly lines operating when Pentagon demand fails.

Growth has been almost entirely in sales to the less developed
countries (LDCs). The United States formerly took the position that

83. *Business Week*, August 11, 1975, p. 20.

they should, unless directly threatened, devote their resources to development. It was also reasoned that military aid might foster military dictatorship, giving the generals more independence of civilian authority, although it is not evident that this has occurred in practice.[84] In the 1960s the United States endeavored to discourage Latin American military spending and severely limited arms sales to the area. The chief result was that buyers went elsewhere. In 1972, the ceiling was lifted, and the current American policy is to sell rather freely to practically any government except communist powers, on the grounds that if the United States does not supply arms others are ready to step in.[85] The world's second largest purveyor of arms is the Soviet Union, which sells to many Third World nations on easy terms, payable in local currency or by barter. Soviet arms are frequently expensive, but they have been an effective means of spreading Soviet influence, especially in the band of countries from Algeria to India. When the United States embargoed arms to India and Pakistan after their 1965 war, India became dependent on the Soviet Union for its military needs. Recently, Soviet arms sales have been growing even more rapidly than American.

The world's third largest supplier is France, which has been broadminded in accepting orders; a French specialty is the excellent Mirage fighter, which is cheaper and is sold on easier terms than competitive American planes. French helicopters and missiles are also very popular. Arms sales, nearly $5 billion annually, are a significant component (8 percent) of French exports and make possible an armaments industry important for French national pride. Next come the British, whose specialty has been naval vessels. West Germany has been promoting sale of high-class arms as an antirecession measure. Israel is also a major exporter. About fifty other nations sell arms to more than a hundred countries. Some Third World countries, such as India and Brazil, have been building up local arms industries and may be expected to enter the field. The purveyors nowadays are almost exclusively governments; the sinister private arms dealers, perhaps intriguing to make a market for their wares, have less than 5 percent of the business.

The world arms trade is one of the leading growth industries. It amounted to only $300 million in 1952, but totaled $5 billion in 1969

84. Edward J. Williams, *The Political Themes of Inter-American Relations*, Duxbury Press, Belmont, Calif., 1971, p. 114.

85. Cf. Colin S. Gray, "Traffic Control for the Arms Trade," *Foreign Policy*, 6 (Spring 1972), 153–169.

and about $18 billion in 1975 (in current dollars). The increase has been consequent upon the independence of many new states from former European empires and the prevalence of military dictatorships in the Third World, where nearly all the tension spots are. Recently the increased price of oil and the flood of money to petroleum exporters has swelled the arms trade; the oil rich countries, hardly knowing what to do with their cash, are easily sold on the need for more and better tanks and planes, while the industrial nations see a chance of recycling some of the money drained from them. Thus, over $5 billion in arms sales to the Near East in 1974 kept the United States balance of payments from going deeply into the red, the lure of cash overcoming any reluctance to arm enemies of Israel. Iran and Saudi Arabia contracted for over $10 and $6 billion worth of arms in 1975 (including the newest and fanciest and some weapons not yet in the American arsenal) and piled them up far beyond the capacity of the proud owners to make them operative.[86]

There is much to be said against the arms trade. It may cause instability and increase tensions; some rulers will probably be tempted to use their shiny weapons, although others may wish to keep the expensive toys intact. It is to be surmised that escalation of the conventional arms race favors proliferation of nuclear weapons. Arms sales, accompanied by advisers and moral commitments to governments, might embroil the United States if wars should occur. The sale of arms involves the United States in supporting military dictatorships. It is also repugnant that the United States should be a merchant of death. The arms business inevitably gives the United States an interest in tensions, although there has been no evidence of stirring up trouble for the sake of sales. Corruption has been involved, since some vendors have spent freely to facilitate sales. For the LDCs, modern arms are something of an addiction. They are wanted partly because of rivalries; Chile has to keep up with Peru, and Iraq arms because Iran does. Armaments are also an example of conspicuous consumption, a mark of power and progress, like a national airline. Their most probable use is to overthrow the government or uphold a dictatorship.

No remedy is at hand. The suppliers are too competitive, even exclusive of the communist states; the desire or need to turn an honest penny seems too strong for them to agree on limitations. It would be high abnegation for a country running a deficit from oil purchases to

---

86. See Edward M. Kennedy, "The Persian Gulf: Arms Race or Arms Control," *Foreign Affairs,* 54 (October 1975), 14–35.

decline to sell arms to a rich oil exporter. The LDCs themselves are averse to controls that would accent their inferiority and decrease their freedom to arm as they see fit, while the industrial nations pile up weapons at will. In December 1974, eight Latin American nations issued a declaration of intention to limit arms and desist from offensive weapons, but the result of this initiative has not yet appeared. The problem is to a large extent the fault of the advanced nations; if they were not so visibly pleased with inordinate arsenals, the LDCs would be less entranced by them. The armaments business is part of the world's general syndrome, to be cured (like various other ills) when or so far as international violence is outmoded.

MILITARY ALLIANCES

The stationing of forces and the furnishing of munitions are commonly interwoven with promises to come to the aid of various countries if they should be attacked; the postwar period was characterized by a proliferation of alliances. Once it would have been almost as heretical to advocate alliance with a European power as to propose repeal of the Constitution, and even the ardor of World War I was insufficient to overcome the allergy—the United States remained only "associated" with the "allies." But the United States, seeking to learn from experience, took the lead in forging the antifascist coalition of World War II into a formal alliance. When Stalin became the enemy in the cold war, it came naturally to revive as much as possible of the wartime grouping against Soviet expansionism.

Principal west European countries led the way, however, in forming a defensive alliance shortly after the communist takeover of Czechoslovakia in 1948. The United States put together the North Atlantic Treaty Organization (NATO) a year later, in April 1949, largely under the stimulus of the Berlin blockade. The Americas had already been joined in the Rio Pact (1947). The success of NATO suggested the formation of other such alliances around the periphery of the Soviet bloc. With the Korean War and what was seen as a growing threat of communist violence, it was believed that American security would be served by clear commitments, with an implied threat of massive reprisal.

Pact building hence rose to its climax in the early 1950s. In 1951, there were defense treaties with the Philippines and with Australia and New Zealand. The signing of peace with Japan was accompanied by a security treaty. This was not precisely an alliance, because there was no Japanese obligation to use armed forces (forbidden by the Japanese constitution); but in effect it was similar to or more far-reaching than American alliances with other countries. In 1953, after the war in Korea, a mutual defense treaty was signed with the Republic of Korea, and another with Nationalist China in the following year. After the Geneva accords on Indochina, the Southeast Asia Treaty Organization (SEATO) was invented to shore up Southeast Asia and protect noncommunist Vietnam. In the face of growing instability in the Near East, the Bagdad Pact (later Central Treaty Organization, CENTO) was put together in 1955 with the American blessing. The United States prudently chose only to become associated, not a full member; but it has participated in CENTO committees and in 1959 made bilateral semialliances with Iran, Pakistan, and Turkey.

The treaties of alliance do not promise very much specifically. Thus, CENTO partners agree merely to "cooperate for their security and defense." A member of SEATO is committed to "act to meet the common danger in accordance with its constitutional processes," the "danger" being restricted by American reservation to a communist one. The same elastic phrase appears in the Australia-New Zealand-United States (ANZUS) pact. NATO has the strongest language: "The Parties agree that an armed attack against one or more of them in Europe or North America shall be considered an attack against them all." Since the American Constitution reserves to Congress the right to declare war, the treaty could hardly go further. However, the president can send American forces into action, and it is assumed that an attack against a treaty partner of the United States by a communist power would elicit an American military response.

There are also understood alliances. With no written obligation, the United States is thoroughly committed to the defense of Israel, and Israel necessarily aligns its foreign policy with that of the United States. American bases in Spain likewise imply a commitment to the defense of that country in the absence of a treaty commitment.

The strongest kind of alliance commitment is the stationing of American forces in an allied country. It is then assumed that an attack on that country would involve an attack on Americans and therefore automatically involve the United States. American troops based abroad are also intended to support friendly governments, to discourage anti-American parties, and generally to support American foreign policy. "U. S. armed forces and particularly those deployed overseas give the

United States a source of general influence." [87] This implication that
the United States gets its way by threat of force is overdrawn; but it
was indeed the aim of much of American diplomacy of the postwar
era to acquire and maintain hundreds of bases (mostly for bombers
and for sites for intelligence activities), until more than a million
Americans were stationed abroad.

There are other reasons for keeping forces abroad. It means having
them near trouble spots where they might be called upon to intervene.
It facilitates realistic exercises. It is no more expensive than keeping
them in the United States, often less so. An unstated reason for foreign
bases is that military men like foreign stations. There is more or less
romance in the exotic; the standard of living is high, with sundry al-
lowances, perquisites, post exchanges, perhaps domestic servants, and
so forth; there is more gravy with less of the bones of hard work. Foreign jobs are also often more prestigious and interesting than the domestic humdrum. For such reasons, United States military authorities
have rarely taken the initiative to close a foreign post.

For over a decade, however, the American forces abroad have been
shrinking. Bomber bases are no longer needed, foreign governments
have demanded their closure, and commitment to the cold war contest has waned. In late 1975, however, there still remained over 400,000
Americans abroad in dozens of nations. Some 300,000 were in Europe
(most of them in Germany), 20,000 in Britain, and a scattering in most
other NATO powers; nearly all the remainder were in Asia, especially
in Japan, South Korea, and the Philippines.

This military presence in foreign lands is a mixed blessing, especially in poorer and weaker countries. It creates an image of power
but also gives an impression of hegemonic militarism; as flagrant evidence of superiority, it is a major irritant in United States relations
with less developed countries. Filipino nationalists point to the American soldiers and sailors who make themselves at home on Filipino soil.
Greeks were offended by the virtual immunity to prosecution of male-
factors in American uniform. Anti-Americanism in Turkey in the early
1970s was more or less proportional to American visibility and diminished as American forces there were pared to a few thousand. The
intrusive American presence was apparently largely responsible for

---

87. Leslie H. Gelb and Arnold M. Kuzmack, "General Purpose Forces," *The
Next Phase in Foreign Policy*, ed. Henry Owen, Brookings Institution, Washington,
1973, p. 217.

giving the communists a share of political power in Iceland. At the same time, governments are less than totally grateful. Spain demands over $1 billion in military assistance as the price for extending for five years the American lease on bases there, at the same time imposing restrictions on their use; for example, the bases could not be used to support Israel in the 1973 war. The Philippines threaten to restrict the operation of the United States Seventh Fleet. The Greeks, resentful of American policy in Cyprus, spoke of closing all American bases but compromised by limiting their use. The Turks would like $1 billion or so yearly rent.

There is much less pressure for Americans to go home, however, than might be expected from the axiom that everyone wants to be master of his own home. If American troops had not been in Europe, Japan, Korea, and elsewhere at the end of the respective wars, it would hardly have occurred to the host countries to beg for them; but since they are there, it seems more comfortable and safer for them to stay. They are part of an accepted status quo; governments become adjusted to them and to some extent rely on them; their departure would mean a leap into the unknown. There are also economic advantages. A host of people and businesses, from bartenders to construction companies, profit by the presence of American troops, and they are a treasured source of foreign exchange.

In some cases, inertia seems to be the chief reason for keeping the forces where they are. It is difficult otherwise to understand why American soldiers should still stand in defense of the freedom of the Republic of Korea more than two decades after the fighting has ended. The North Koreans are bellicose, but the South Koreans are more than twice as numerous, much wealthier, and amply armed by the United States; the South Koreans also showed themselves to be excellent fighters in Vietnam. American officers in Korea have pointed out that American troops are not needed there to fight,[88] and it is embarrassing to have Americans upholding the autocratic regime of President Park Chung Hee. Yet the United States is very hesitant to remove its forces especially after the humiliation of Vietnam, for fear of destabilizing that strategic corner of Asia. In March 1974, the United States turned aside a North Korean suggestion for a formal end to the war because this would presumably entail withdrawal. The South Korean leadership has, of course, a strong vested interest in the status quo and does all it

---

88. *The New York Times,* March 1, 1975, p. 4.

can to keep Americans in Korea, although a reunited Korea might serve American long-term interests.[89] The chief danger is that the dictatorship, relying on American support, may become excessively corrupt and unpopular, opening the way to communist subversion.

There has been the most controversy concerning the possible reduction of American forces stationed in Europe more than thirty years after the end of the war that brought them there.[90] They are, in any case, not much resented. Alliances seem to function best among peoples at similar economic levels, as among the United States, Canada, and the west European NATO partners, and between the United States and Japan. On the contrary, there was never much understanding between the United States and Thailand, and Greece and Turkey do not belong to NATO in quite the same way as countries on an economic level comparable to that of the United States, such as Belgium or Denmark. There has been recurrent friction for years between the United States and Turkey, although no people is more distrustful of the Russians than the Turks. Anti-Americanism surged in Greece under the military dictatorship of 1967–1974; the Greeks viewed the United States as the chief supporter for the colonels and thus as "an instrument of our repression." [91] They perceived the United States as so rich and powerful that the Cyprus coup of August 1974 could have been executed only with American complicity. As a result of that coup and the ensuing Turkish intervention, American relations were spoiled with both Greece and Turkey, each nation believing that the United States owed it more support. Greek forces were withdrawn from NATO. Turkey, infuriated when Congress cut off military aid in reprisal for the use of American arms for offensive purposes, moved to take over American bases, depriving the United States of some of its most precious military posts.

In less developed countries, an alliance raises fears of domination; many see it as a machination of the superpower for a purpose (anticommunism) of little interest to them. It creates dependency and, by opposing leftism and subversion, probably facilitates the retention of power by unpopular and unprogressive elites. On the other hand, small allies, such as the Republic of China or the Philippines, can use some

---

89. Selig Harrison, "One Korea," *Foreign Policy*, 17 (Winter 1974–1975), 35–62; idem, "Reply," *Foreign Policy*, 18 (Spring 1975), 180.
90. This and other matters concerning NATO are discussed in Chapter Six.
91. *The New York Times*, August 20, 1974, p. 3.

of the funds they receive via the alliance to meddle in American politics.[92]

Alliances complicate relations and may raise counteralignments. American affiliation with Pakistan facilitated Soviet influence in India, and CENTO contributed to anti-Westernism in the Arab world. A more important drawback is that alliances make foreign policy rigid. Commitments, once made, become self-perpetuating, although circumstances may have changed. It is easier for all sides to keep things as they have been. There is also organizational momentum. The framework of the alliance is composed of concrete people on the many staffs and committees, who always seem to be doing something useful, and who, if one task is accomplished, will find others. For such reasons, although the essential purpose of American alliance policy—to halt communist or Soviet expansionism—has substantially changed, alliances remain in place. It is the official purpose to maintain NATO "until circumstances permit the introduction of general, complete, and controlled disarmament," [93] that is, until the millennium.

Alliances fitted into the ways of the cold war. Not merely deterrents of hypothetical aggression, they were instruments of a general political security. Alliances supported the forces of order (the conservative forces in the world) and stiffened anticommunism both within and without. They formed a framework for general political cooperation; for example, for a long time NATO made it easier for the United States to dissuade partners from recognition of Communist China and, less successfully, to restrict trade with the communist states.

Since the 1950s, however, alliance building has lapsed into abeyance, and there are no suggestions for new commitments. Insofar as the cold war and its emotions have been left behind, the rationale of alliances fades. In post-Vietnam disillusionment, the American people are very reluctant to consider sending troops to combat anything less than a direct and immediate threat to the United States. Even among a sampling of business executives there was found little support for military intervention to protect allies other than Canada, regardless of treaty obligations.[94] This reluctance to intervene does not mean, of course, that the United States might not rally to the rescue of a nation

---

92. Robert O. Keohane, "The Big Influence of Small Allies," *Foreign Policy*, 2 (Spring 1971), 176–179.

93. "Declaration on Atlantic Relations," *The New York Times*, June 20, 1974.

94. Russett, "The Americans' Retreat from World Power," p. 6.

grossly attacked, especially one obviously important to the American world position; but in order to sustain vigor, alliances require the emotions engendered by confrontation.

Only NATO continues to be relatively vigorous, because there is some residual apprehension of Soviet domination and because NATO represents not only a military group but also a community of like-minded states. Only NATO ever achieved a consequential collective defense effort. But it has less and less implied general conformity with American foreign policy; the capital of an alliance member (Paris) was chosen as a neutral spot for negotiations between the United States and North Vietnam. NATO did nothing toward coordinating foreign policy in the Arab-Israeli war of 1973, the fuel crisis of 1974, or the Angolan problem of 1975–1976.

The other alliances hang together only because they are all tied to the big American peg. The alliance with Japan is taken for granted because it hardly restricts Japanese foreign policy and because the world is still dangerous enough for the Japanese to wish to take shelter under the American nuclear shield. The alliance with Australia and New Zealand lacks a visible enemy, but there seems no great reason to drop it. CENTO maintains an anemic existence, practically out of view. SEATO, discredited by the Vietnam war, passed away in 1975. It never included more than two (the Philippines and Thailand) of the dozen countries of Southeast Asia.

The whole idea of alliances has become somewhat questionable in the nuclear and satellite age. The institution of alliance was devised in simpler days to join military forces in the world where nations balanced one another by armies and navies and certain territories were strategically vital. But nowadays, military cooperation in an inadmissible war having become problematic, an alliance means mostly a guarantee. Nuclear and nonnuclear powers cannot be real allies in the old sense, since they do not share in the ultimate power. It is characteristic that neither the United States nor the Soviet Union is prepared to turn nuclear weapons over to allies. There would also be no point to an alliance between powers, each of which held a first-class deterrent. Although the combination would have more overkill than the powers have separately, this excess could do little to promote their security, whereas it perhaps would increase risks and certainly would reduce freedom of action. In any event, semisuicidal nuclear hostilities will not be undertaken because of any commitment on paper but only because survival as a free nation seems highly imperiled. Alliances are designed to fix in advance the course a state will follow in a foreseeable contingency, but the contingencies are unforeseeable and the course cannot be plotted in advance. Alliances were intended to remove uncertainties, but this goal is no longer possible. Perhaps it is no longer necessary; uncertainty may suffice as a deterrent. Thus the United States is very far from having an alliance with China, but uncertainty about how the United States would react to a Sino-Soviet war deters the Soviet Union from trying to apply the Brezhnev Doctrine to China.[95]

Today probably no one would propose the set of alliances presently centered on the United States if they had not been created in the cold war years. Like much else, they seem to belong more to the past than the future. But they are not likely to be cast aside, because this action would be an unnecessary affront. Instead, it seems likely that these national groupings will gradually have less to do with the conduct of states.

MILITARY INTERVENTIONISM

Most of the foreign policy instruments of the cold war were designed to secure desired results—or to prevent undesirable outcomes—without the use of the military bludgeon. On occasion, however, American forces were ordered into action, and the engagement in Vietnam dominated American thinking for eight years; thus military interventionism seemed to some to be characteristic of postwar American foreign policy.

It has hardly been an American specialty, however. Historically, states have maintained armed forces to use them, and when the United States engaged in scores of operations from the war with Tripoli (1801–1805) to the seizure of Veracruz (1914), it was behaving in the accepted manner of the great powers. The habit, however, has seemed to be declining. Between the world wars, there were few military interventions by anyone until the fascist powers began the march to war.

Since World War II, military intervention has had only a limited scope. The war ended the will as well as the capacity of the losers, Germany, Italy, and Japan, to act forcefully abroad. France, Britain, the Netherlands, and Portugal all tried to use force to save imperial positions, but in each case the results were very bad. The 1956 Suez excursion, the last outburst of European gunboat diplomacy, not only

---

95. Harold C. Hinton, "The United States and the Sino-Soviet Confrontation," *Orbis*, 19 (Spring 1975), 44.

failed to retain the Suez Canal for Britain and France but cost them much of their remaining influence in the Near East.

Only the United States and the Soviet Union still have the capacity for military action abroad. The Soviet state is better prepared than less authoritarian countries to employ force successfully, as it has done in suppressing dissidence in its bloc, especially in Hungary in 1956 and Czechoslovakia in 1968. It can prepare in secret and move by surprise, it is willing to act ruthlessly, and it has no need to account to its citizens for its actions. The major rationale of the American alliance network and defense budget is that, having never been chastened by defeat, the Soviets might be tempted to move again to advance their interests by force. It is noteworthy, however, that they have not employed their armed forces in the postwar period except to reassert control of territories that seemed to be slipping from their grasp. Soviet foreign policy has seemed too cautious to engage in risky adventures, although it might be contended that only American strength and purpose has kept it so. The United States has thus, since 1956 (with the exception of the Soviet disciplining of Czechoslovakia in 1968), seemed to be the only big power with a yen for mixing violently in the affairs of others, and as such has drawn more than its share of the opprobrium of world anti-imperialists, especially the intellectuals.

For the United States, the lesson of Vietnam was not easily learned. Only as it became clear that the war had soured was it possible, in March 1968, for the administration to consider cutting its losses by disengagement. For nearly another year, until the very end of the Johnson administration, American forces in Vietnam continued to grow slightly. Then President Nixon spent four years withdrawing, during which time the number of American casualties was greater than during the years of build-up. Still, the idea of saving face, of showing that America was faithful to its undertakings, and the reluctance to see lost what had been fought for kept the United States involved. Two years after American troops had left, American money, equipment, and advisers were still striving to shore up the hard-pressed governments of South Vietnam and Cambodia; Secretary of Defense James Schlesinger reinvoked the old domino theory, and President Ford asked Congress, "Are we to deliberately abandon a small country in the midst of its life and death struggle? . . . We cannot escape this responsibility." [96]

After Congress failed to vote the monies, which could not have

---

96. *The New York Times*, February 26, 1975, p. 1.

been spent in any case, and the anticommunist regimes in Cambodia and South Vietnam collapsed (in April 1975), the American president and the secretary of state nervously reiterated that United States resolve was not weakened by the alleged loss, although the general relief at the end of the war was stronger than concern over its outcome. Not many outside the adminstration seemed to consider that the failure of the American-sponsored governments in Saigon and Phnom Penh was a tragedy for Western civilization or proof that the United States was no longer strong. American businesses elsewhere in Southeast Asia were not appreciably affected.[97] The Australian prime minister, whose country might be more threatened than the United States, remarked, on April 22, 1975, "Australia's security and long-term interests are not affected by the political color of the rulers in Saigon." India, with far greater reason than the United States to fear a communist wave splashing out of Vietnam across Asia, seemed unworried. In a reaction of rage and frustration, American air and naval power was thrown against the Cambodian navy, but this was only a brief venting of feelings. Similarly, Secretary of State Kissinger angrily broached the idea of military action against the states which had the temerity to quadruple the price of petroleum. His statement was carefully qualified: the use of force might be considered in case of "some actual strangulation of the industrialized world."[98] But it was later backed by the White House; the administration that had flatly ruled out a higher gasoline tax was prepared to toy with the idea of war in the Near East. The idea was, of course, an impractical daydream[99] and was soon forgotten.

Whether the lesson of Vietnam will be ignored, or forgotten by a fickle public remains to be seen. The Congress is evidently wary of new involvements, as shown by its cautious reaction to the stationing of an American civilian team between Israelis and Egyptians and its refusal to provide help for anticommunists in the Angolan civil war. But the game of world politics is engrossing, for Ford as it was for Kennedy, Johnson, and Nixon. Secretary of Defense Schlesinger in 1975 echoed statements of Johnson a decade earlier: "The United States retains the moral responsibility to serve as the guardian of freedom

---

97. *The Wall Street Journal*, July 16, 1975, p. 1.

98. *Business Week*, January 13, 1975, p. 69.

99. The contrary was argued by Robert W. Tucker, "Oil: The Issue of American Intervention," *Commentary*, 59 (January 1975), 21–31; and "Further Reflections on Oil and Force," *Commentary*, 59 (March 1975), 45–56.

around the world. No other nation can do it." [100] Presidents like crises and action wherein they can display leadership, and they think in terms of a "test of wills." They feel that their participation is vital; President Ford insisted on being aroused from sleep to be given bulletins of Turkish deployment on Cyprus, in a quarrel of remote interest to America. It is a game that has to be won, by force if need be. Presidents slide into commitments and then must demonstrate the nation's faithfulness to its undertakings—in effect, a commitment to indiscriminate globalism.[101] Leaders have always found it difficult to recognize the limitations of crudely exercised power. Forceful action is simple and appealing; it promises prompt results and proves maturity. The pleasure of victory comes less from achieving a desired aim than from crushing the enemy. The temptation to shoot may thus be irresistible when there is no other obvious answer.

Almost always, however, restraint probably serves the national interest best. The benefits from intervention invariably diminish in retrospect. The expected gains are immediate and visible in the working of the national will. The disadvantages are less apparent because they are long-term and diffuse. Readiness to intervene makes people everywhere distrustful of American purposes. There is always a chance of escalation of what was intended to be a limited engagement of resources. It is also much easier to become involved than to pull away. The national image may suffer. It was urged in connection with Vietnam that the United States had to stick to the job to reassure its allies, but its allies were for the most part dismayed by the war and were better able to collaborate with the United States when it was over. When this country looked a little less overwhelming, international relations were easier. When the armed forces of a great power are fighting those of a small power or a guerrilla movement, the general presumption, especially on the part of the many weaker states, is that the great power is aggressive and is serving its own interests at the expense of the weaker side. It is a confession of moral and political weakness for a very strong power to resort to such means. Most important of all, the world leader should avoid staking its prestige upon a struggle of doubtful meaning and uncertain outcome. Use of force against any small nation is a potential threat to the independence of all small nations and an affirmation of their helplessness.

---

100. *Time,* December 1, 1975, p. 12.
101. J. L. S. Girling, "Kissingerism: The Enduring Problems," *International Affairs,* 51 (July 1975), 339.

The major debates on American foreign policy in this century have centered on intervention, whether the United States should or should not exert coercive violence in foreign lands. The argument is based more on mood than on logic. One side says: We are big and strong; therefore, we are responsible for world order, since no one else can guard the ramparts of freedom everywhere. The other says: We are big and strong, so we need only hope and work for peace and a better international order without troubling ourselves about political quarrels that do not threaten us. Feelings swing, but at this juncture it seems clear that the United States can no longer afford to permit the issue of intervention to dominate foreign policy; too much else, both at home and abroad, demands attention.

Although it may be impossible to exclude all intervention in principle, it seems to be fairly well agreed that the United States should intervene only in favor of well-organized governments that have broad popular support. Such governments seldom need or want alien armed forces. Likewise, intervention is a bad bargain unless the major allies are prepared fully to support it; however, they have shown little inclination to do so.[102] The excuse for getting involved is that the United States is protecting the weak and serving principles broadly accepted by the world community, but only in the case of Korea has there been broad support. Interventionism has done much to make the United States unpopular in the world, particularly in those parts eligible for intervention; such unpopularity increases the risks and costs of getting into fights. Thus, if security means the ability to manage our affairs as we desire, intervention decreases security. The example of resort to violence is bad in a world where the United States is still the chief model; if the United States were to use force to work its will in the Near East, it would be much easier both for the Soviet Union to coerce Turkey or Iran and for desperate poor nations to consider blackmail against the rich.[103] Just as there are better means of action than subversion, there are better means of action, diplomatic and nonviolent, if it is necessary to step in—a proposition that requires powerful evidence. If the social costs of the Vietnam war are weighed in the balance, it is difficult to conceive a major military action, except for

---

102. For an anti-interventionist argument on somewhat different grounds, cf. Melvin Gurtov, *The United States and the Third World: Antinationalism and Intervention*, Praeger, New York, 1974.

103. As observed by Warnke, "Apes on a Treadmill," pp. 16–17.

national defense, that would be likely to contribute to the strength and well-being of the United States.

The diplomatic costs are seldom weighed in advance, and the domestic costs—least of which is the expenditure of money—seem seldom to be taken into account at all. Vietnam should have taught us that prolonged intervention—and who can be sure that any intervention may not be prolonged—may be ruinous for American society. Moreover, there is a real political cost. Conservatives as well as liberals should bear in mind that any use of force abroad by the United States seems likely, under modern conditions and unless supported by all major sectors of American opinion, to lead to illegalities and abuse of power and so to strain the constitutional system.

CHAPTER THREE

Economic Dimensions

ECONOMIC INTERNATIONAL RELATIONS

The interactions of states fall into two broad areas, usually rather distinct: security affairs, concerned with the threat of some nations to use force against others; and ordinary transactions, dealing mostly with the exchange of goods and services by mutual consent and for mutual advantage. Publicity and debate about foreign policy deal largely with the first area; the actual business of the government, at least below the level of president and secretary of state, is overwhelmingly concerned with the second area.

Security affairs, especially between big powers, are involved with distant or hypothetical dangers; in the nuclear realm, they deal with the unimaginable. Practical and immediate matters of economics, of finance, and of cultural exchange, on the other hand, are on an entirely different level and usually involve current needs. Realistic and banal, they detract from the glamour that military and security issues lend to foreign policy. They are conducted less by diplomats than by thousands or hundreds of thousands of little people, mostly concerned with their own interests. Those who manage international relations among free market economies—bankers, traders, or financial authorities—are of a different mentality from generals and traditional envoys. Even in the case of the communist states, which try to keep all trade within state channels, officials conducting foreign affairs act in a different spirit and in a much more matter-of-fact manner than do the ideological leaders.

Economic affairs and dealings in other areas not involving security also differ from the conventional stuff of international relations in that these matters impinge directly upon the people. Issues of war and peace may ultimately be decisive, but they are mediated through governments. If certain policies are followed, the citizenry may pay higher taxes or become subject to conscription by virtue of political decisions. But in day to day existence people pay more for bread because of foreign purchases of wheat, or they can buy cheaper television sets because of Japanese competition. The external world feels only minimal impact from American nuclear submarines or even American military alliances; but the impact on other people from American corporations, American-originated programs on their television screens, or American tourists in their bazaars is enormous.

Since security affairs become distant, contingent, and less pressing as violent conflict apparently recedes, the United States and other industrial nations are giving an ever larger part of their attention to the more visible problems of the day, such as the price of oil, the instability of currencies, and inflation. Insofar as states cease to fear violent attack, economic goals take priority; these goals are achievable by full participation in the world economic system.[1] Even the most politicized of powers, the Soviet Union and other Marxist-Leninist states, seem to be giving priority to economic affairs. Interest in procurement of technology and credits outweighs considerations of prestige and may be the most important factor in Soviet policy toward the United States.

The importance of economic relations between states is an outgrowth of modern technology. The world has shrunk (it is trite to say) because of ease of travel and instant communication. Businesses learn of supply and demand around the world and hope to profit thereby. An Iowa firm can easily establish and manage a branch in Hong Kong, and the Japanese can tailor products for American requirements almost as readily as can manufacturers in New York. Capital has become fluid, and investment is international. Since 1960, world trade has risen more than twice as rapidly as domestic production, and the internationalization of the world economy grows more rapidly (through foreign investment and technical cooperation) than does world trade. Foreign policy likewise becomes more entwined with domestic policy; farmers, like hotel keepers, are influenced by worldwide market and monetary conditions. Labor unions and steel producers join to avert a strike for fear of stimulating imports. American airlines demand subsidies to compete with foreign subsidized carriers. Domestic inflation affects the balance of payments, which influences the value of the dollar abroad and inflation at home. On the economic front, domestic policy and foreign policy are inseparable.

Whereas the political issues facing the nation are rather few and can usually be stated rather simply, economic issues are multitudinous and usually very complex. This divergence, plus the fact that economic affairs touch private interests directly, means that the two kinds of foreign policy are handled very differently. Political questions are managed by the president and his advisers with the assistance of a few agencies, mostly the State Department and others concerned with national security. Foreign economic questions are the province of more than sixty departments, bureaus, and agencies, and all efforts to

---

1. C. Fred Bergsten et al., "International Economics and International Politics: A Framework for Analysis," *International Organization*, 29 (Winter 1975), 20.

coordinate them have proved ineffective. In political affairs, the executive goes to Congress only so far as it must, usually to get funding; Congress is in the thick of economic matters, partly because private interests speak through it and partly because it must legislate many changes.[2]

Economic questions differ from political matters in spirit. In the latter, the primary issue involves redistribution of power, and the gain of one nation is usually the loss of another. Economics, on the contrary, deals with the production of values, and normally both parties gain from transactions. In economic matters, a state may well make a proposal advantageous to other nations as well as to itself. Economic affairs, however, are mingled with political. The United States, for example, has some expectation of alliance solidarity in major economic policies and would like to use its political position, especially its presence in Europe, as a lever in economic bargaining. The standing of the dollar as a basic world standard has political significance. Trade with controlled economies requires political approval and will undoubtedly continue to respond to the tension barometer. The United States can hardly exert political or military pressure on the Soviet Union, but the granting or withholding of export credits and of Most-Favored-Nation treatment, or the facilitation or restriction of grain sales, is a potential lever on Soviet policy. The Arab nations have taught the world much about the usefulness of an economic weapon in the hands of otherwise weak countries; thanks to oil, Iran and Saudi Arabia have become major powers in terms of their ability to influence world affairs. The less developed countries (LDCs) have striven with much less success to use political means, vocal protests, and clamorous majorities in the United Nations and other governing bodies to extract economic concessions.

The enormous expansion of international intercourse of all kinds is primarily a function of technologies that overcome distance. But this expansion has been made possible by the cooperative policies of nations in the postwar period in contrast to the restrictive modes of the interwar years; and it has come about under the leadership of the United States. One of the charges of revisionism during the cold war was that the United States opened up the world to American business for selfish reasons. The opening of the world has, in fact, been beneficial to many nations besides the United States. The United States,

---

2. Cf. Richard N. Cooper, "Trade Policy Is Foreign Policy," *Foreign Policy,* 9 (Winter 1972–1973), 18–36.

Europe, and Japan all profit from one another's prosperity. Economic benefits include both an improvement of the American standard of living in the partial merging of the American economy into the world economy and the development of a host of opportunities for American enterprises in the world market.[3]

But a liberal economic system, like a liberal political system, is by definition open and nonrepressive; within it, new powers can rise. During the era of strong American economic leadership many countries, especially those in western Europe and Japan, have greatly increased their share of world production and wealth and thereby have greatly reduced American dominance.[4] Economic power derives not from status or military strength but from having goods that others desire; military strength, as the Russians have discovered, can be used for economic ends only to a very limited degree. In the plural world of numerous buyers and sellers of most commodities, economic power has limited coercive value,[5] and it cannot be exercised without a cost to both parties. As American dominance recedes, how well a truly pluralistic world economy will operate remains unclear, but there is no reason to assume that it cannot function well.

Politically, a high level of interchanges means interdependence, hence common interests and probably a reduction of antagonisms. Authoritarian governments that would like to exclude outside ideas cannot entirely shut themselves off from the open world economic order, and they do so partially only at a material sacrifice. Extensive interaction among independent sovereignties nourishes pluralism and some degree of freedom; no despot can control either the world flow of wealth or the international market of ideas. A world of relatively unhampered interchanges should be hospitable to the ideals of toleration, freedom, and rationality to which the United States claims to aspire. A world of economic nationalism would be subject to many more frictions than at present, and would be even more dangerous than the present world.

It has been American policy to encourage mobility of capital and technology and to foster international economic enterprise and the

---

3. For the view of a mercantilist countercurrent, see Gregory Schmid, "Interdependence Has Its Limits," *Foreign Policy*, 21 (Winter 1975–1976), 188–197.
4. Bergsten, "International Economics," p. 16.
5. As noted by Alvin Z. Rubinstein, *Soviet and Chinese Influence in the Third World*, Praeger, New York, 1973, p. 4. See also Klaus Knorr, *Power and Wealth*, Basic Books, New York, Chapter 6.

continued growth of unrestricted trade among nations. This process implies an effort to reduce the artificial barriers to trade and to foster an efficient international monetary system. It means also facilitating the free flow of capital and technology (that is, according to liberal economic theory) to areas where they are needed in the interest of world economic growth. These are policies congenial to the American tradition and political system and in theory, although certainly not always in practice, to the general welfare of the nations.

TRADE BARRIERS

Since the founding of the republic, the United States has sought to foster its own commercial interests abroad. However, foreign policy was decidedly parochial, concerned mostly with promoting American exports and discouraging imports that were competitive with American products. Despite its leadership in world industrial production from about 1890 on and despite its dominance in world trade and finance after World War I, the United States declined to consider broader economic problems. Only after the bursting of the speculative bubble of the 1920s led nations to a competitive effort to export unemployment, causing a disastrous shrinkage of world trade that magnified the Great Depression, did the United States think seriously about improving the international economic system. In 1934, President Franklin Delano Roosevelt's New Deal, seeing freer trade among nations as conducive to better relations, began chipping away at the very high tariff walls by means of bilateral negotiation of reciprocal concessions for particular products. These concessions were extended to a widening circle under the Most-Favored-Nation principle, under which reductions to any nation became reductions to all, an idea harkening back to the Open Door policy. During World War II, lend-lease agreements were used to advance freer trade, with recipients pledging to cooperate toward removal of barriers. Average United States tariffs, 59 percent in 1932, were reduced to 25 percent by 1946.[6]

After World War II, it was easy, in view of the spectacular economic dominance of the United States, to move toward a basically

6. Robert E. Baldwin and Donald A. Kay, "International Trade and International Relations," *International Organization,* 29 (Winter 1975), 100.

freer trading system. At the Bretton Woods Conference (1944) a framework was established for the management of exchange fluctuations, and the International Monetary Fund (IMF) was set up to police this area. The General Agreement on Tariffs and Trade (GATT) in 1947 laid down ground rules, accepted by all but the communist countries, that established nondiscrimination as the basic principle of multilateralism.

The United States became the center of a general movement for the reduction of trade barriers, and world trade grew steadily at an unprecedented rate. The "Kennedy Round" of tariff negotiations (1963–1967) brought reductions averaging 50 percent in the tariffs of all major industrial countries.[7] With this stimulus, the boom in world trade accelerated to 12 percent yearly from 1963 to 1973. Membership of GATT grew from nineteen nations in 1947 to eighty-five in 1973. For international commerce, the postwar period has been a time of unparalleled prosperity, singularly free of tariff wars and competitive devaluations. Industrial protectionism has been left largely to the LDCs and the communist states.

This progress, however, came into question with the passing of the postwar era of overweening American superiority. By 1970 the ability of many countries with rapidly growing economies (from western Europe and Japan to Taiwan and Brazil) to undersell American goods and flood the American market with the products of their modern industries generated protectionist pressures and strained the American balance of payments, already under pressure from the Vietnam war. The devaluation of the dollar in 1971 and its subsequent floating helped, but could not cure, the ill. The quadrupling of petroleum prices after 1973 then threw the balances of most industrial states deeply into deficit, causing severe pressure to conserve currency by barring imports and pushing exports. The possibility of trade wars was much increased by the economic slowdown that began in most of the world in 1974. It is fairly easy to liberalize trade when production is expanding grandly; in times of shrinkage, however, the temptation is strong to try to get the better of other nations. However, even under the pressure of deficits, nations have generally resisted the temptation to raise import barriers; on the contrary, the more affluent nations have generally tried to come to the rescue of the hard-pressed. Whereas the depression of the 1930s caused a collapse of

---

7. Ibid. The average of United States tariffs was less than 10 percent in 1975.

international trade, in the recession of 1974–1975 world trade continued to grow faster than production.

The freeing of trade is to a large degree a matter of good will; it cannot be effectively mandated by written instruments. In time of trouble, many states (including the United States) have disregarded the rules of GATT, and there are no sanctions except loss of standing in the international community. Moreover, if tariffs are held down by agreement, nontariff barriers, such as quotas, discriminatory standards, sanitary requirements, and merchandising restrictions, can easily be erected. Trade barriers are so multiform and complex that they can hardly be abolished by contract. Liberal trade policy is at the mercy of the political climate.

Although the prevailing political climate has been remarkably successful scaling down import barriers, major threats to the fluidity of world trade have arisen in the opposite direction, the control of exports. Here again the United States has played a leading although less liberal role, as efforts to curb inflation have run counter to freedom of trade. When food prices rose sharply in 1973, the administration placed an embargo on the export of several products—most important among them soybeans—with no consideration of the needs of countries dependent on the United States for supplies. Japan's most important food import was thus unceremoniously blocked, and worldwide inflation was spurred. In October 1973 the export of fertilizers was banned, in disregard of the agricultural needs of the LDCs. American shoe manufacturers have been assisted not only by the tariff on imports but also by a ban on the export of hides. For various reasons, other commodities, such as scrap iron and cottonseed, have been withheld from the world market. Grain sales to the Soviet Union have been criticized and held in check lest they raise unduly the price of bread in the United States. Curbs on the sale of uranium to Europe have cast a shadow over American cooperation in energy policy.[8] A novel foreign policy question has come to the fore: the need to decide how potential shortages at home should be weighted against income from sales, the protection of the American reputation as a trade partner, and the American interest in the principles of unhampered trade. Many other countries have similarly interfered with market forces, mostly to benefit local users or to push up world prices. Thailand, Brazil, and Spain, for example, have halted exports of rice, beef,

8. *The New York Times*, April 15, 1975, p. 7.

and olive oil, respectively; the European Economic Community penalized food exports; Canada began phasing out oil exports. Many
LDCs would like to restrict the sale of raw materials in order to
force more processing at home, insofar as they can without turning
the market over to the competition.

More serious has been the effort by some countries to limit exports
by cartel. The giants in this game are the oil producers, the thirteen
states joined in the Organization of Petroleum Exporting Countries
(OPEC), whose success shook the world. (They are discussed in
Chapter Nine.) Producers of bananas, bauxite, coffee, copper, rubber,
tin, zinc, and other materials have tried, or are trying, to emulate the
oil producers. In the past, such efforts have not been markedly successful; it is too hard to keep the front unbroken. Similar attempts
may be more fruitful in the future, in the manner of OPEC, partly
because of a long-term economic trend: manufacturing can more
readily spiral upward than can production of raw materials, which is
ultimately restricted by finite resources and land. More immediately
pertinent, however, is the increased political consciousness and solidarity of the LDCs, which are the chief exporters of raw materials.
The will to maintain a solid front and to avoid being condemned for
selling out to the big rich countries, especially the United States, is
much stronger than it was a decade or so ago; and a political will
seems essential to cartel solidarity.[9] New approaches are evidently in
order, preferably bilateral agreements between consuming and producing countries, to provide both price stability and guaranteed
access to materials.

American trade policy, however, has become confused and contradictory in the era of declining pre-eminence and of new problems.
Although it is widely accepted in principle that the freest flow of
goods is highly desirable, both economically and politically, there is
still a great deal of protectionism; and policy remains subject to
pressures from interest groups. It may be economically advantageous
over the long run to phase out manufacturing in which the United
States is at a disadvantage (such as certain textiles), but the adjustment costs are high. Subsidies and special favors for American shipping are costly luxuries for uncertain purposes. There are many
inconsistencies: in the midst of the struggle to control inflation in

---

9. Cf. Zuhayr Mikdashi, "Collusion Could Work," Stephen D. Kramer, "Oil is
the Exception," and C. Fred Bergsten, "The Threat is Real," *Foreign Policy*, 14
(Spring 1974), 57–90.

1974, the United States objected strongly to the low prices of eggs offered by Canada, and special duties have been laid on shoes and handbags from Brazil, flowers from Colombia, glass from Italy, and steel from Mexico, because the governments of these countries wanted to sell them cheaper than the United States deemed proper. This response is mandated by an eighty-year-old law, a relic of the mercantilist past, which the government has not strongly endeavored to modify. The reluctance to allow the public to benefit from the willingness of foreigners to sell at bargain prices is an American speciality. In the other direction, there is no clear policy regarding the extent and purposes of export controls, which are used for a mixture of economic and political motives. In a different vein, the United States, while warning smokers at home of the dangers to health, spends money to promote tobacco sales abroad.

In the medley of special interests, it is often forgotten that the United States has a general interest in a liberal trading system. On the one hand, American exports must be maintained at a high level to pay for increasingly necessary imports and to provide a surplus on the merchandise account to pay for whatever programs the United States may seek to advance in the world. On the other hand, a world open to trade, with a greater flow of commerce, technology, and investment among nations, will be more prosperous. International trade spurs technology advancement and accelerates adaptation and progress; it is the most obvious hope for improvement in the status of the poorer countries.

MONETARY PROBLEMS

The contradiction between the internationalization of the world economy and the right of sovereign states to raise barriers at their borders has been to some extent overcome by the generally amicable relations among the economically more important nations. The world economy, however, is divided not only by the customhouses; it is also partitioned into as many pieces as there are sovereign states, because each state has its own standard of value. The biggest problems of international economic management are consequently not matters of tariffs or other interferences with trade but of keeping order in exchange rates and international finances.

Before World War I, gold was the standard to which major currencies were tied, and the system served fairly well to finance the much smaller exchanges of the day. Deficits could be settled by movements of gold, which supposedly corrected the imbalances by their inflationary or deflationary effect. World War I transferred a large part of the world's liquid assets to the United States, and in the aftermath of World War II the needs of reconstruction and the unique ability of the United States to supply the world created a severe dollar shortage. This situation could not be permanent. By 1961, there was pressure against the American gold stock, which still backed the dollar in international transactions; gold flowed steadily out while external obligations rose to exceed American reserves. The government consequently embarked on a series of stratagems and maneuvers to halt the gold drain; these efforts were fairly successful for a decade. However, the costs of the Vietnam war plus the decreasing competitiveness of American industry bled the dollar to anemia, and in 1971 it was overtaken by speculation. Such was the torrent that central banks had to buy billions of dollars in a few days, even hours, to sustain the dollar against stronger currencies such as the German mark and the Japanese yen.

Therewith came the end of the American monetary hegemony. In August 1971, President Nixon announced the devaluation of the dollar by about 12 percent and the end of its convertibility, so that the gold value was purely nominal. Afterward, the finance ministers and central bankers of the leading industrial states tried in vain to put together a new monetary system to replace the fixed rates agreed on at Bretton Woods immediately after the war. However, the situation tended to worsen because of accelerating inflation in the United States and elsewhere; the mobility of capital in the hands of international corporations, financial institutions, and speculators; a continuing American payments deficit; and a vast amount of foreign-held dollars looking for safety. Distrust in currencies drove up the free-market price of gold in 1974 to more than four times the official American price (that is, to $150–$180 per ounce). In these unstable conditions, it was necessary to accept fluctuating, or floating, exchange rates instead of the nearly fixed rates that had been maintained throughout the postwar period. Fixed rates, as mandated by the IMF, were feasible only so long as the leading currency was stable enough for other currencies to rest on it. Consequently, in March 1973 the principal currencies were set adrift to find their own levels, and this relaxation was legalized by the IMF in January 1976.

By mid-1973, there was some easing of the monetary difficulties.

The American balance of payments, after a deficit of nearly $10 billion in 1972, showed a surplus in 1973, and the dollar recovered most of the value it had lost since 1971. During and after the Arab-Israeli war of October 1973, however, the oil-producing states struck an overwhelming blow against the world monetary system by quadrupling petroleum prices. They raised their export surplus from $8 billion in 1973 to more than $55 billion in 1974, half the value of all United States foreign investment. This displacement of wealth put the whole non-oil producing world into deficit, to the extent of $35 billion for the advanced industrial nations and of $20 billion for the LDCs, which found it very difficult to pay their oil bills. Some of the oil-rich nations, like Iran and Venezuela, can use their earnings in their own economies; others, such as Saudi Arabia and Kuwait, have much more money than they can rationally apply. It was calculated that, in five years, the OPEC nations might have an accumulated surplus of some $200 billion.[10]

This imbalance, the largest sudden transfer of wealth in history (except perhaps that which has ensued from great wars), aroused fear of instability, enduring and unmanageable deficits, and possible Arab control of a large slice of the economy of the Western world. However, the threat was less overwhelming than first seemed likely, and market forces showed a considerable capacity to compensate for the dislocation. Higher prices, recession, and conservation measures reduced petroleum consumption. The OPEC nations soon found themselves with surplus production and slightly shrinking revenues. Moreover, there are no truly unspendable surpluses, since the human capacity to get rid of easily acquired wealth is infinite. OPEC imports grew much more rapidly than expected, about 75 percent in the single year of 1974. Entrepreneurs from the United States and elsewhere flocked to oil capitals like flies to honey, offering all manner of assistance in getting rid of excess dollars. It was predictable that imports might easily exceed exports and put the oil producers into deficit before 1980. "Petrodollars" were recycled through many channels, and estimates of the accumulation of dollars by OPEC countries were much reduced. By late 1975, in fact, some major oil producers were themselves borrowing in international markets, and the $25 billion emergency fund planned by the industrial nations in April to rescue

---

10. Thomas O. Enders, "OPEC and the Industrial Countries: The Next Ten Years," *Foreign Affairs,* 53 (July 1975), 625.

economies that were threatened by bankruptcy appeared unnecessary. Western economies were not swamped by Arab investments, either short- or long-term, but the oil producers did acquire a bigger stake in the Western economy. Meanwhile, non-OPEC production grew, and strains appeared in the oil cartel.

A new problem, or set of problems, came to the fore, however. Worldwide inflation amounted to 14 percent in the industrial countries in 1974, about a quarter of it caused by the quadrupling of petroleum prices.[11] Nations wish to manipulate money supplies to combat recession and unemployment and usually spend more than they take in; at the same time, currencies have been untied from gold and released from the discipline of fixed exchange rates. But the monetary stock is international; a big borrower denied credit in New York may pick up the telephone and get it in London or Frankfurt. Hence, inflation is international and uncontrollable by any single country, including the United States.[12]

The whole complex of problems of inflation, money supply, exchange rates, reserves, and capital transfers badly needs international coordination lest the global economy be endangered. The crucial question is one of fixed versus uncontrolled exchange rates. The United States has generally preferred maximal freedom and reliance on market mechanisms of supply and demand, with gold playing a minimal role or none at all. This approach seemed to be necessary when the old system of fixed parities proved unable to adjust to the pressures arising from different growth rates and monetary policies and was abandoned between 1971 and 1973.[13] However, floating exchange rates practically invite competitive devaluations whenever a nation wishes to hold in check a trade deficit by making its exports cheaper and its imports dearer (although rate changes require a year or two to produce compensatory changes in trade). Fluctuations in the exchange rates make calculations of international trade difficult. Over a short period the value of the dollar in leading foreign currencies may vary by 5 to 10 percent for little apparent reason, but profit margins in many transactions are much lower than this percentage. Long-term contracts are subject to great uncertainty, for buyers or for sellers or

---

11. Ibid.

12. "Sowing the Seeds of More World Inflation," *Business Week*, September 8, 1975, pp. 66–68.

13. Jack F. Bennett, "A Free Dollar Makes Sense," *Foreign Policy*, 21 (Winter 1975–1976), 63–75.

for both. International organizations and agreements, such as IMF and GATT, are undercut or paralyzed by instability in the value of currencies. The special drawing rights (credits that IMF members can draw upon to cover deficits), which the United States wished to make into a paper substitute for gold as an international reserve, are made more or less inoperable as a result of fluctuations of the currencies in which they are measured.

To overcome some of these difficulties, the United States has proposed contractual arrangements whereby countries with deficits or surpluses would be required to take steps to bring their accounts into balance. Other countries (especially France, with some support from its European partners) would like to go back to something like the old system, with fixed parities and a stabilizing role for gold, although gold, a metal like many others, is really a commodity, and tying one currency to other currencies fails because of varying rates of inflation and capital movements. Possible compromises include managed floating, with central banks regulating movements, and flexible parities, subject to frequent small adjustments.[14]

Monetary relations cannot be brought into order unless or until domestic inflation is overcome in major trading nations. Fortunately, the rate of inflation has usually been somewhat lower in the United States than elsewhere, giving strength to the dollar. The American dollar remains the leading currency in terms of which other currencies are measured and the prices of major commodities, such as oil, are set on world markets. It is no longer possible for the United States to dictate the outlines of the world monetary system, but leadership still rests with this country.

ECONOMIC DEPENDENCE

The monetary problems of the 1970s made clear how domestic developments, inflation, interest rates, and fiscal policies have foreign causes and repercussions. Expansion and heating up of the economy cause problems with the balance of payments; steps to cope with

---

14. Richard N. Cooper, "Choice of a Monetary System," *International Organization,* 29 (Winter 1975), 96; Office of Economic Development, *Toward a New International Economic System: A Joint Japanese-American View,* Committee for Economic Development, New York, 1974, p. 20.

deficits are likely to be painful domestically. The prosperity of the United States goes with the prosperity of the developed world, and American monetary expansion has led to worldwide recession.[15] Smaller nations have urged that the United States and West Germany, as the world's leading trading powers, spur their economies to promote general recovery from recession.[16]

This development is a great novelty; a half lifetime ago, foreign trade seemed rather marginal for the United States, and what went on in the rest of the world was mostly of academic interest. The United States is still more self-sufficient than many other nations, exporting 7.5 percent of its gross national product (GNP), compared with 23 percent for West Germany, 19 percent for Britain, 16 percent for France, and 11 percent for Japan. But the foreign trade component is of vital importance. In the 1974–1975 recession many businesses looked to foreign markets to keep themselves operating, and the impingement of the world market on the pocketbook and way of life of ordinary Americans has become much more direct and powerful. In 1973–1974 the United States became aware of the impact of world demand for foodstuffs, especially cereals. Grocery prices were pushed up by grain sales and by world shortages of various crops, to the benefit of American farmers and the embarrassment of consumers. Food exports became a prime asset of American foreign policy, whereas previously there had been inconvenient surpluses. Since demand outstripped production, reserves were exhausted and the world faced possibly permanent shortages, with the threat of massive famine in a few years. It seemed likely that in the near future the United States would have to choose between witnessing the starvation of millions or changing dietary habits to make more grain available for export.

Before the United States could stabilize the food crisis, it was confronted with the energy crisis. After food, fossil fuel is the most important material for industrial society; a shortage was beginning to pinch well before the 1973 Arab-Israeli war brought the situation to a climax, as the oil-producing nations pressed the oil companies both for more money and for increasing equity participation. The United States still produces more oil than Saudi Arabia; however, United States production peaked in 1971, and more and more American exploratory wells are dry. As a result, American cars, even despite the

---

15. Harold van B. Cleveland and W. H. Bruce Brittain, "A World Depression?," *Foreign Affairs*, 53 (January 1975), 224.
16. *The New York Times*, July 18, 1975, p. 51.

Alaska pipeline, must increasingly run on foreign oil. United States oil imports provided 8 percent of consumption in 1950; by 1975, they were more than a third.

Approximately 60 percent of world petroleum reserves are in Arabia and the Near East; this region also provides nearly all the world trade (with contributions by Venezuela, Nigeria, and others) because the other biggest producers (the United States and the Soviet Union) are major consumers. The United States requires ever more imports to supplement shrinking domestic sources. The situation hence invites producer countries to join to raise prices. The oil-producing countries were able to achieve only gradual improvements—such as a 50/50 profit split, a 70/30 profit split—until the Arab-Israeli war of 1973. The Arabs were then able to unite to embargo briefly oil shipments to the United States and to cut their overall production by 5 percent per month in order to exert pressure on the entire Western world. In the consequent shortage oil producers got together and raised prices by rapid steps from somewhat over $2 per barrel to about $10, despite the fact that there was and is no shortage of capacity. Airlines were pushed toward bankruptcy by fuel prices; many homes were chilly in the winter; and lowered demand for automobiles helped thrust the United States into a recessionary spiral.

There was no riposte for this new economic weapon. Some attempts were made to bring importers together for bargaining purposes, but these nations lacked unity. The American administration for the short term could only impose some modest conservation measures and an import tax (subsequently removed) on petroleum. For the longer term, the United States sought to achieve energy independence by development of native resources. This solution was not promising. Much more energetic exploitation of American oil fields would result in their earlier exhaustion—known United States resources being good for about fifteen years at the present rate of consumption. Solar, wind, and geothermal energy require much development and promise only partially to substitute for petroleum. Nuclear energy has many drawbacks. Coal is convertible into oil and gas only at excessive cost. Probably more promising but less in the American entrepreneurial spirit would be to modify American life styles to use less energy. Europeans maintain a standard of living about as gracious as the American and in some ways more so, while consuming only about half the per capita energy that Americans do. It does not seem permanently sustainable for 6 percent of the world's population to consume a third of the world's energy.

This situation raises a fundamental question of priorities in the relations of the United States with the rest of the world: the extent to which it is necessary or desirable to seek autarky, or independence of foreign suppliers. Stung by the 1973 oil embargo (although it actually affected United States supplies very little), the administration and much of the public reacted by saying that the nation must never again be vulnerable to the caprices of a foreign cartel. It was particularly feared that an Arab stranglehold on a vital commodity might prevent the United States from coming to the assistance of Israel in a future crisis. However, the cost of energy independence must be reckoned as very high, and it would be an economic absurdity for the United States to rely on domestic production of oil for the equivalent of $12 or more per barrel when the Near Eastern cost of production is in the range of 15 to 50 cents per barrel. Autarky would mean imposing a heavy tax on the American economy.

If the Near East achieves greater stability or if other areas increasingly come into the market—China particularly has great promise[17]—the achievement of energy independence will seem less desirable. However, in the next few decades the United States will have to decide how to live with or to fight against dependence on foreign sources. Along with the Soviet Union and China, the United States is extraordinarily well endowed with mineral resources; it is especially fortunate in coal, which represents the bulk of fossil fuel on earth and of which the United States may have half the world's supplies (an estimated 1.5 trillion tons down to 3,000 feet).[18] But the United States became a net importer of minerals in the 1920s, and dependence grows. Using around 30 percent of world's mineral output, the United States relies entirely or almost entirely on imports of chromium, bauxite, nickel, manganese, and a dozen or more lesser but still essential minerals. In very few cases can the United States count on long-term self-sufficiency; by the end of the century the United States will depend on foreign supplies of all of the most important minerals except coal and phosphate. American industry will face more of the problems that the Europeans and the Japanese had to meet long ago.

It is possible to substitute, recycle, and use minerals more efficiently, but one must foresee increasing competition among the

---

17. Selig S. Harrison, "Time Bomb in East Asia," *Foreign Policy*, 20 (Fall 1975), 3–27.

18. Richard Anderson et al., "Alternative Energy Sources for the United States," *The Atlantic Community Quarterly*, 13 (Summer 1975), 177.

industrial powers for access to supplies located largely in the Third World. There is no real problem of worldwide exhaustion of deposits in the near future, but questions of dependence, monopoly, and fair prices for buyers and sellers will become acute. Equity and the general welfare will probably demand more and more international understanding, from which no nation will be able to hold itself apart except at great cost.

FOREIGN INVESTMENT AND MULTINATIONAL CORPORATIONS

In a relatively tranquil world drawn together by reliable instantaneous communications and rapid travel, people, especially those juridical persons called corporations, are prone to ignore boundaries and extend their activities and investments to foreign lands as they never have before. The United States, as the wealthiest country, has the most invested abroad—about $120 billion—and 30 percent of all United States corporate profits are made abroad.[19] But foreign investment is characteristic of all countries that have funds to spare and, to some extent, of many countries that do not. Non–United States foreign investment is half the world total and is growing more rapidly than American investment abroad; Britain in 1974 had about $35 billion in foreign investment; West Germany, $13 billion; Switzerland, $16 billion; and Japan, $12 billion.[20] Businesses of European countries and Japan have been rapidly extending themselves into many areas, including the United States, in billion-dollar amounts. More than a hundred foreign banks, with assets totaling over $35 billion, operate in the United States, making nearly a tenth of all commercial and industrial loans.[21] Total foreign portfolio investment in the United States amounts to about $80 billion. Foreign investment is not only for capitalists; the Soviet Union invests in scores of profit-making businesses abroad, from petroleum refining in western Europe to bauxite mining in Guinea.

---

19. *Business Week,* May 12, 1975, p. 72.
20. *Business Week,* July 14, 1975, p. 65.
21. Frank R. Edwards and Jack Zwick, "Foreign Banks in the U.S.," *Columbia Journal of World Business,* 10 (January–February 1975), 58.

Most foreign investment is by large corporations. The biggest agent of economic integration in the world and the fastest growing sector of the world economy is the multinational corporation (MNC). Since World War II (and especially since about 1960), with jet transportation, satellite telephone, and low tariffs, global movement of capital and technology has expanded with great rapidity. Foreign investment has also changed in character. Corporations formerly went mostly into the LDCs to exploit natural resources, minerals, or tropical agriculture. In recent years, direct foreign investment has gone increasingly into manufacturing and concurrently has shifted toward the already developed countries, which offer more security, better operating conditions, and larger markets. Of American corporate investment abroad, three-fourths is in industrial countries, the bulk of it in Europe and Canada.[22]

An expanding and ambitious company probably feels that it must go international because the market is worldwide. There is not much more sense in limiting operations to the United States than in limiting them to California, whereas enterprises of smaller countries *must* operate internationally in order to survive. Several thousand American firms have at least one overseas plant; a large majority of the hundred biggest have production facilities in several countries. About 30 percent of all United States foreign trade is intracompany, representing not a purchase but a transfer from the foreign affiliate to the home company or vice versa. The production of American MNCs abroad is over five times the volume of United States exports and exceeds all world exports, amounting to about $450 billion annually as early as 1971.[23] This figure represented 22 percent of free world industrial production, and the proportion rises steadily.[24] Banking has also gone international; all but a few of the world's biggest banks have joined consortia or have established branches abroad. Other businesses in which MNCs are prominent are hotel and restaurant chains and financial services.

A large corporation, pressed to reduce costs, may examine its

22. For a history, see Mira Wilkins, *The Maturing of International Enterprise: American Business Abroad from 1914 to 1970*, Harvard University Press, Cambridge, Mass., 1974.

23. Lester R. Brown, *World without Borders*, Random House, New York, 1972, p. 211.

24. For a strong statement of the potentials of the MNCs, see Richard J. Barnet and Ronald E. Muller, *Global Reach: The Power of the Multinational Corporations*, Simon and Schuster, New York, 1974.

A

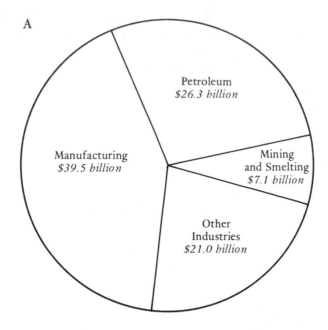

Figure 3 U.S. Long-Term Private Investment Abroad, by Type of Industry (A) and by Location (B). (*Statistical Abstract of the United States,* 1974 ed.)

production to see what may be advantageously done abroad. When a company expands its sales facilities abroad, it may be led to ship parts for assembly instead of finished goods, or license local production of components; subsequently, the international firm buys the licensee. An American corporation may acquire an interest, preferably controlling, in a weaker foreign manufacturer in order to gain quick entree to the market. Anyone wishing to sell much in Brazil, for example, is practically constrained to associate himself with a Brazilian enterprise or set up his own operations in that country. Also, foreign firms may seek affiliation with American firms in order to gain access to the most modern techniques. For this reason European companies have preferred mergers with American competitors. Frequently, Europeans have been willing to put up much or most of the capital for American-affiliated enterprises.

Most of the great multinational corporations have headquarters in the United States and are dominated by American capital. But the proportion of British, German, Dutch, Swiss, Japanese, and other nationalities is growing; there are even some Mexican and Brazilian MNCs. Together, the capital invested by these countries in MNCs may total about as much as the United States capital in such corporations.

B

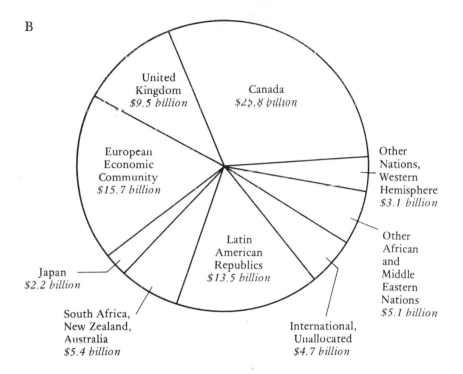

United
Kingdom
$9.5 billion

Canada
$25.8 billion

European
Economic
Community
$15.7 billion

Other
Nations,
Western
Hemisphere
$3.1 billion

Latin
American
Republics
$13.5 billion

Other
African
and
Middle
Eastern
Nations
$5.1 billion

Japan
$2.2 billion

South Africa,
New Zealand,
Australia
$5.4 billion

International,
Unallocated
$4.7 billion

Some corporations have no real national identity, (for example, those incorporated in a tax shelter, such as Liechtenstein or the Bahamas). Where there are appropriate skills, a large home base is not necessary, as in the case of Phillips Electric of the Netherlands and the Swiss pharmaceutical giants. There are also some governmental or semi-official organizations, such as the French and Italian petroleum monopolies, that operate in the same manner as private corporations.

The MNCs are becoming more international. American companies frequently raise capital abroad, a circumstance that probably leads to associating foreigners with directorship. For economic as well as political reasons, it is sought to minimize the number of citizens sent abroad, hiring locally as much as possible. Usually the Americans abroad make up much less than 1 percent of those employed; even managers in Europe and Japan are commonly European or Japanese. Many American firms in Japan have taken in Japanese partners for their local expertise and access to Far Eastern markets. Localization proceeds more rapidly than multinationalization at headquarters. However, as foreign operations become more important, American corporations place more foreigners on their boards; of thirty-five big chemical companies, twelve have given such representation to their foreign interests, and seven out of thirty petroleum giants have also done so.[25]

In an age when it is feasible to coordinate worldwide operations from a single center, when transportation is swift and relatively cheap ($50,000 of integrated circuits can be air-freighted from California to Singapore for about $100), and when trade barriers are at a historic low, companies can plan globally the optimal utilization of resources. An American seller of TV sets buys electronic components in Japan, assembles them with low-cost labor in Taiwan, and has them mounted in cabinets in the United States to save shipping costs.[26] Ford makes tractor engines in England, transmissions in Belgium, and gears in Detroit. Massey-Ferguson sells in the United States tractors with British engines, French transmissions, and Mexican axles. International Business Machines (IBM) assembles computers in many lands with components not only from the United States but also from Britain, France, Germany, and Italy. Many MNCs have at least simpler components built in such low-wage places as Taiwan or Singapore; this procedure may represent a large saving of labor costs since Asian workers are as capable as American workers. Products may be developed especially for foreign markets; both Ford and General Motors made cheap small trucks ($1,100–$1,300) to be assembled in the LDCs from components made mostly in Africa, South America, or the Philippines.[27]

It would thus seem that foreign enterprise, as represented by MNCs, has a great deal to offer, especially to less developed countries badly needing capital and technology. In fact, they usually welcome foreign investment, frequently with enthusiasm. Africans complain of the failure of American companies to take advantage of the opportunities that Africa presents.[28] The Nigerian government advertises, "People are making huge profits in Nigeria, why don't you?"[29] Prima facie, inviting foreign capital to produce something means letting the foreigners do the planning, hire the experts, put up the money, take the risks, and probably pay taxes if not contributions to the personal fortunes of political leaders. If such collaboration results in letting

---

25. *Business Week*, August 19, 1972, p. 60.

26. James E. McLinden, "World Outlook for Electronics," *Columbia Journal of World Business*, 7 (May–June 1972); 70.

27. *Business Week*, May 27, 1972, p. 15.

28. Cf. *African Progress*, July–August, 1972, p. 7.

29. *The Manchester Guardian Weekly*, May 13, 1972.

foreigners have much of the benefit of the LDC's natural resources and of the productivity of its labor, this eventuality seems unimportant at a time when these assets are not being exploited. Having little political tinge, private investment may be more acceptable than official aid. A spokesman of radical-revolutionary Algeria explained deals with American corporations on the ground that "The American people are one thing, and what the American government does in the Mideast and Vietnam is another." [30] Even the Soviet Union, which (in accord with Leninist theory) has poured endless scorn and wrath on the international monopolies, has become somewhat ambivalent because of its desire to harvest the economic benefits of cooperation with monopolies. [31]

If the foreign enterprise is successful, it may give entree to foreign markets, build a variety of contacts with the industrialized world, bring in technology and modern ideas of management and production, furnish the local rich an example of enterprise and organization for production, and share profits with the local government by paying taxes. The MNC creates jobs, ordinarily paying much better wages than local enterprises. It probably helps the balance of payments by producing goods for export (as in extractive industries) or goods that would otherwise be imported, although it may raise the demand for imported materials. In many cases, MNCs generate 15 to 30 percent of a country's exports. The Brazilian branch of Volkswagen energized Brazil's massive boom as it developed subproducers to make more and more (eventually all) components and laid the foundation for a whole new industry. Foreign companies are the most important starters of new production. In the liberal vision of the future, they are the principal vehicle for the transfer of capital and technology to the areas most in need of it. [32]

The MNCs carry to a higher level the classic benefits of international trade and specialization and so make the world more productive. They universalize management and capital, leaping over tariff and nontariff barriers. They raise world productivity by organization, technology, and utilization of resources and manpower; in the LDCs they are almost synonymous with modernization. A Colombian going to work for IBM enters the technological universe as he could hardly

---

30. *Time*, May 29, 1972, p. 34.

31. *The Interdependent*, 2 (April 1975), 3.

32. Robert Gilpin, "Three Models of the Future," *International Organization*, 29 (Winter 1975), 42.

do otherwise without going to an industrial country. By employing highly trained persons the MNC counteracts the brain drain. Although they are frequently branded "monopolies," the MNCs ordinarily increase the amount of competition in any given market. Cheap labor is not usually the chief asset sought, as is shown by the preference for investment in advanced countries; but if Malaysia, for example, offers stability with labor at a small fraction of European or American costs, corporations rush in to assemble labor-intensive products, such as small appliances. Countries are happy to be host to the "sourcing plants."

Of the tens of thousands of businesses operating in alien lands, the vast majority, especially the small ones, cause no special problems and receive little notice.[33] But a foreign-owned and foreign-directed enterprise, especially if large and powerful compared with native businesses, is inherently irritating and injurious to national pride. This reaction occurs not only with American corporations; the Japanese have encountered serious friction both in Southeast Asia, where they are more at home than persons of European descent, and in Brazil. It occurs not only in sensitive less developed countries; Canada and Australia have been annoyed to see so much of their economies, especially extractive branches, subject to foreign ownership. Even the self-confident United States, with a massive economy in which foreign control cuts no figure, is bothered. Resentment has been expressed against aggressive Japanese acquisition of profitable businesses and the construction of new ones competitive with established American producers, and there have been strong fears that Arab oil interests might gain control of American firms. Despite the theoretical American interest in freedom of investment, Congress in 1974 considered outlawing foreign control of American corporations. It was especially disturbed by foreign buying up of natural resources, and some congressmen claimed that American business and labor would suffer from the new competition.

It is not surprising that MNCs cause many problems in less developed countries—many more, indeed, than in the developed countries, where about three-fourths of their activity is. For Germans, a big American corporation is not extremely different from a big German corporation; it represents a roughly similar way of life and economic

---

33. Thomas Aitken, *The Multinational Man,* Geo. Allen and Unwin, London, 1973, pp. 25–35.

and cultural level. For the African or South Asian country, the American corporation stands for something quite alien and at least potentially menacing; moreover, in many less developed countries the multinational corporation is not an incidental supplement to native industry but a dominant giant.

Hence, especially after the foreign business has been operating for a few years, the original benefits of the capital investment fade from sight; the corporation becomes more of an intrusion, an injury to the nationals who seem incapable of running their own economy, whether on a small scale (as Asian merchants in Africa) or a large one (as American copper giants in Chile). If the foreign holding is successful (that is, profitable), it remits royalties and profits, which are a conspicuous burden on the exchange balance. This outflow is as painful as the initial capital inflow was pleasant; such outflows in time exceed net capital inflow. Statistics showing that profits and withdrawals of United States capital in Latin America are about $1 billion yearly in excess of new investments are cited to show that the Latin Americans are being bled or exploited in the Marxist sense, although the profits should be balanced against what the foreign-owned enterprises produce for the country to export, the employment they provide, and the taxes they pay.[34] That capitalism is associated with foreigners gives much impetus to Marxist thinking, a convenient explanation for backwardness in any case. Foreign capital is more vulnerable to criticism when it is concentrated either in extractive industries, thereby profiting unduly (in the opinion of many) from plunder of the natural wealth of the host country, or in plantation agriculture, which is widely unpopular. Foreign capital is easily criticized as an antipatriotic force devouring the people. Even payment of higher than average wages is resented by local businessmen, who are pressed to meet the competition. It is widely agreed that the multinational corporation usually raises the national product and probably has a positive foreign exchange impact,[35] but these advantages do not make it beloved.

---

34. The Soviet press has charged the corporations with injuring Portugal by declining to invest there. *Pravda*, March 15, 1975, p. 3; *Current Digest of the Soviet Press*, April 9, 1975, p. 13.

35. United Nations Department of Economic and Social Affairs, *Multinational Corporations in World Development*, Praeger, New York, 1974, p. 62. For a discussion of utilities and disutilities of the operations of MNCs, see Robert O. Keohane and Van Doorn Ooms, "The Multinational Firm and International Regulation," *International Organization*, 29 (Winter 1975), 170–185.

There are many difficulties of understanding; the broadminded, sensitive, internationalist business executive is not common. Bosses back home frequently forget the problems of managers abroad.[36] Foreign managers are often tactless and supercilious; they are culturally and usually racially different from their hosts. The advanced foreign corporation increases inequality and creates a labor elite.[37]

There are many conflicts of interest. The MNC keeps its top management centralized in the home base and probably carries on all or nearly all of its research and development there; the foreign branches are mere appendages.[38] The MNC may evade or seem to evade taxation and currency controls by juggling transactions among its branches; when local firms do the same, the effect is less injurious. If nothing else, the MNC is too big, too visible, and too foreign, the most obvious intrusion of the dominant powers of the modern world —although the American government has been able to make little direct use of American corporations abroad. If such a corporation does too well, it either remits excess profits or expands locally and becomes still more intrusive. The offense is less exploitation than insult, perhaps less economic than cultural.[39]

There are infinite potential frictions between the MNC and the government of the host country. For example, a foreign-owned utility desires rate increases, which a popular government sees good reason to deny. When service deteriorates, the two sides blame each other, but the government's case is more broadly appealing. Although workers are less hostile to their foreign employers than politicians are,[40] wage disputes arise, and the government is practically obligated to side with its own people against the foreign interest. As the outlook

---

36. Aitken, *The Multinational Man*, pp. 36–40. For problems of the foreign manager, cf. Ashook Kapoor and J. J. Boddewyn, *International Business-Government Relations*, American Management Associates, New York, 1973.

37. Denis Goulet, "The Paradox of Technology Transfer," *The Bulletin of Atomic Scientists*, 31 (June 1975), 42; Keohane and Ooms, "The Multinational Firm," p. 179.

38. Gilpin, "Three Models of the Future," p. 42.

39. Howe Martyn, "Development of the MNC," in *The New Sovereigns: Multinational Corporations as World Power*, ed. Abdul A Said and Luiz R. Simmons, Prentice-Hall, Englewood Cliffs, N.J., 1975, p. 40.

40. George C. Lodge, *Engines of Change: United States Interests and Revolution in Latin America*, Knopf, New York, 1970, p. 262. Workers in the Venezuelan oil and iron ore industries strongly opposed nationalization for fear of losing benefits. Normal Gall, "The Challenge of Venezuelan Oil," *Foreign Policy*, 18 (Spring 1975), 63.

grows darker, the corporation may try to salvage as much capital as possible, openly or indirectly; it thereby further worsens relations and weakens its own position.

For the most part, however, the host government is likely to desire simply to improve its own position and that of its nationals, as increasingly self assertive states take advantage of the decreased will or ability of the United States and other Western countries to protect the interests of their nationals abroad. Many and diverse measures are taken. For example, Malaysia plans to reduce the percentage of foreign ownership in industry and commerce from 60 percent to 30 percent by 1990 and to raise that of ethnic Malay ownership from 3 percent to 30 percent (the remainder staying with ethnic Chinese); there are also threats of nationalization.[41]

Particularly in Latin America, where United States capital has been dominant, there are numerous pressures. Nationalization, usually with compensation which the victims regard as very inadequate, has become frequent. Foreign investment is often prohibited in such areas as banking, insurance, utilities, and communications media (press and broadcasting), which are reserved for nationals because of the potential influence or the expected profitability of these enterprises. Foreign enterprises are likely to be forbidden to raise capital locally. Manufacturers are required to use locally produced materials and parts and are compelled to export as much as possible. Producers of raw materials are required to process domestically. Companies are pressed or legally required to sell a majority interest to Mexicans, for example. Employment of aliens is severely limited. In the extractive industries, the host countries' share of profits has been pushed up from 10 to 15 percent before 1930 to 80 percent or more at present. New concessions in minerals or petroleum uniformly call for government participation. Even in small investments, the host government often demands a half-and-half share for itself, or majority control, while making a minority investment. Currently, American corporations are not liquidating Latin American holdings; but they have few plans for expansion.[42]

In any contest between the host country and the foreign corporation, the former holds the most trumps in the contemporary world. The corporation may have an income much larger than the country;

---

41. *Business Week*, July 7, 1975, p. 32; *The Wall Street Journal*, September 22, 1975, p. 24.

42. For some demands, cf. "Multinationals Find the Going Rougher," *Business Week*, July 14, 1975, pp. 64–66.

Exxon or General Motors has sales larger than the GNP of nine-tenths of the nations of the world. But the sovereign nation holds police power to do what it decrees with persons and property within its domain. Small, weak countries, such as Jamaica or Sri Lanka (Ceylon), are, in fact, more likely to enact discriminatory measures against a foreign corporation than are big, powerful countries, such as Brazil or Japan. In past decades powerful companies could dominate countries such as Liberia (Firestone) or Honduras (United Fruit). But the political leaders of the 1970s have become much more aware of their rights and powers. Host governments may turn the tables by using their control of the properties of the MNC as a diplomatic lever.[43]

When foreign enterprises run into trouble or need to forestall difficulties, they may meddle in local politics. There have been reports from time to time of MNCs backing rightist or conservative elements or governments, as in the coup which overthrew a leftist regime in Brazil in 1964. However, as outsiders, MNCs are less capable than local businessmen of exerting political influence and seem generally to have taken the prudent course of avoiding political involvement.[44] They may contribute to political parties, as local corporations do. They may try bribery, and a few cases have come to light recently—Gulf Oil in Korea, United Brands in Honduras—where large sums were paid to government officials to secure favorable treatment. Such payments are not sound practice, however, since they leave the company open to escalating demands and exposure, especially if there is a change of government. The American Congress, which exposed the cases cited, has considered outlawing such payments. It is defended on the ground that firms of other nationalities engage in the practice and so Americans must do so in order to be competitive; it is difficult, in fact, to draw a sharp line between proper legal or agency fees and the suborning of politicians. Such payments are already in effect illegal, because they are not deductible from taxable income as business expenses under United States law.

The MNC in trouble may also appeal to the home government, which is usually sympathetic, and properly so from the point of view of material national interests. But the home government may not be able to do much aside from quiet representation. If the issue becomes an international confrontation, the host government may feel the more

---

43. Joseph S. Nye, Jr., "Multinational Corporations in World Politics," *Foreign Affairs*, 53 (October 1974), 158.

44. Louis Turner, *Multinational Companies and the Third World*, Wang and Hill, New York, 1973, p. 41.

compelled to take a firm stand for the sake of prestige. American intervention also associates the American government with a probably unpopular corporate interest; the superpower may be seen as the instrument of the great monopoly corporations bent on exploitation of the weak. When the United States ambassador to Argentina expressed opposition in August 1973 to a proposed law restricting foreign investment, nationalists used the fact to make support for the bill by Argentine patriots mandatory.

The United States government has shown most willingness to intervene on behalf of a threatened corporation when it has other reasons to oppose the government in question. Thus, International Telephone and Telegraph (ITT), facing loss of several hundred million dollars of properties in Chile after the election of Marxist Salvador Allende to the presidency in 1970, begged for help; the Central Intelligence Agency (CIA) went into action not to save ITT but to get rid of what was seen as a hostile regime. In this case, ITT failed to prevent the inauguration of Allende; in contrast, its influence, as disclosed by American journalism, was a political bonanza for him.

It is also possible for the American government to take economic reprisals against powers that nationalize United States properties. If there is an economic aid program, it is likely to be terminated, although this action implies a sacrifice of any good will the aid program may have been designed to garner. The United States may also make it difficult for an offending nation to secure credit from international institutions, such as the World Bank, in which the United States has a large share. The United States took this course in the case of Chile. However, in the modern world there are many sources of credit, and the leftist government of Allende was in fact able to compensate for the difficulty in securing credit from American-influenced institutions by borrowing from various other countries, including those in the Soviet bloc, that were eager to help him stay afloat to the discomfiture of the United States.

If the corporation really comes into collision with the host government, it can threaten to pull out, taking with it its expertise, market access, and other advantages. The chief enforcer of international contracts and the reason that countries seldom default their obligations is the need to maintain a good credit rating. If a country is very inhospitable, and particularly if it becomes known as arbitrary and unrealiable, it will not get foreign investment. The chief plea of the American government is that states create a climate conducive to the flow of capital to lands where it is needed.

In practice, expropriation is uncommon, when the enormous

number of companies operating is considered. Failures, mostly for non-political reasons, are much more frequent; from 1967 to 1971, 204 big corporations made 561 foreign divestments while suffering only 21 nationalizations.[45] On the contrary, there are many forms of accommodation. United States firms going into business in the LDCs nowa-days usually share ownership with nationals, although most ventures in the less sensitive advanced countries are wholly owned. There may be arrangements for the host country or its citizens to acquire majority control after a period of years; this procedure is often advisable because the need and utility of foreign control will probably diminish. The corporations may justify themselves by developmental or export projects.[46] Many more or less complicated schemes can be worked out to protect both sides (for example, separating production and marketing, with primarily local control of production).[47]

The hallmark of the modern MNC is the transfer of skills and technology rather than of capital; [48] as the financial director of Sears, Venezuela, said, "We have to work out a way to sell or transfer technology; we no longer can just sell merchandise. The world is becoming more complicated." [49] Instead of seeking ownership the foreign firm may contract to manage an enterprise for a fixed period in return for a fee based on sales or profits. Goodyear thus undertook to manage Indonesian state tire companies.[50] Many countries have contracted with corporations to come in and develop agricultural and other resources.[51] The international petroleum companies have been compelled to relinquish ownership of the oilfields but they remain to operate and distribute by agreement with the sovereign states. Such arrangements may be less profitable than full ownership but are also much less risky.

The sophisticated big corporation may be able to take advantage of the ignorance and passivity of a less developed country. However, if the leaders of a country know how to bargain for what they need,

45. Roger L. Tornedon and J. J. Boddewyn, "Foreign Divestments: Too Many Mistakes," *Columbia Journal of World Business*, 9 (Fall 1974), 87.

46. André van Dam, "A Hearing Aid," *Columbia Journal of World Business*, 9 (Winter 1974), 108.

47. Harold Crookell, "Investing in Development—A Corporate View," *Columbia Journal of World Business*, 10 (Spring 1975), 86.

48. Keohane and Ooms, "The Multinational Firm," p. 207.

49. *Business Week*, October 13, 1975, p. 60.

50. See Wolfgang G. Friedman, "The Contractual Joint Venture," *Columbia Journal of World Business*, 7 (January–February 1972), 57–63.

51. *The Wall Street Journal*, March 18, 1975, p. 1.

they should be able to profit by association with MNCs. The corporation has technology, managerial and other skills, and capital, and it can contribute strongly to economic development while being remunerative to shareholders. Even communist countries have become eager to buy the services of many Western firms.

Although it is widely assumed that the MNCs draw excessive profits out of the lands into which they intrude, it is not always recognized that they add to the wealth of their home country. However, American opinion is divided. Some people argue that the corporations damage the American economy by exporting technology and jobs; public opinion polls indicate a prevalent belief that expansion abroad should be discouraged.[52] It is charged that, insofar as a company transfers manufacturing to a foreign market, it detracts from exports or increases the import of products that would otherwise be made in the United States. MNCs are accused of contributing to the balance of payments deficit and evading taxation. But a 1972 survey by the Department of Commerce indicated that employment in the United States by the MNCs had grown much more than employment in general, and that their trade surplus had expanded from 1966 to 1970, while that of the United States as a whole shrank.[53] Exported jobs are probably replaced with better jobs. Labor unions, however, supported legislation aimed to reduce tax advantages of the MNCs and otherwise to encourage companies to stay home. The executive, more concerned than Congress with the overall American world position and less subject to group pressures, has usually championed the MNC. To squeeze American corporations very much would merely open the field to their European and Japanese rivals or cause American corporations to respond by transferring their center for international operations elsewhere.

There is, consequently, a call for international regulation, a universal code to define the rights and the obligations of businesses and host countries, including questions of monopolistic practices, foreign exchange transactions, taxation, issuance of securities, export controls, and so forth.[54] It is difficult to achieve agreement on such an advance in international law, but it might protect host countries and provide security and predictability for MNCs. These corporations might be wise to adopt at least a voluntary code, calling for noninvolvement in

---

52. *Business Week,* June 9, 1973, p. 42.
53. *The New York Times,* November 20, 1972, p. 59.
54. Keohane and Ooms, "The Multinational Firm," p. 196.

local politics, responsiveness to the host country's desire for participation, reinvestment of a reasonable share of profits, and promotion of local personnel.

Whether or not the MNCs are internationally institutionalized, they are an important and growing part of the world system. They are probably becoming more truly international; there is no reason for great modern productive combines that are drawing materials from various lands, have scattered production facilities, and are selling to the world to be tied to any particular nation. They must have headquarters somewhere, but they have a "global reach," as Barnet and Müller put it, and there is no reason that ownership and management should not be as international as sales. The MNCs are the most effective agencies for integrating and organizing production on a broad scale, and they exert a strong force for the freer movement and more effective application of skills, technology, and capital. Perhaps the best hope of the LDCs for rapid modernization,[55] the MNCs may bring a dramatic shift of manufacturing to countries that have a surplus of labor, especially those in Latin America and Southeast Asia.[56] Many kinds of work more cheaply performed abroad will possibly become extinct in the United States, which will have to keep advancing in technology to maintain its position.

The MNCs, standing above the nation states, must be considered a force for peace; they probably contribute, or could contribute, to a liberal and progressive world order. They represent to some extent an extension of American society and ways; indeed, the virulent protest of such critics of the MNCs as Barnet and Müller is to a large extent a protest against the consumer society, modernization, and Americanization. The MNCs are no longer usable as a direct instrument of state policy—efforts to control their sales to communist countries were resented and have practically been given up. Although management, ideas, and broad policies flow out of the American center, the corporations act for themselves. However, the American-based multinational enterprise is American in orientation, and its purposes seldom clash fundamentally with the interests of the United States. So far as the MNCs forward economic integration, they are serving a fundamental American interest.

---

55. Peter F. Drucker, "Multinationals and Developing Countries: Myths and Realities," *Foreign Affairs,* 53 (October 1974), 134.
56. *Business Week,* August 18, 1975, pp. 118–122.

ECONOMIC STRENGTH

The American share of world industrial output has eased from more than half at the end of World War II to slightly less than 30 percent. The United States has been the leader in productive innovation since the later decades of the nineteenth century, but this lead has been seriously undercut, especially by Germany and Japan. In the mid-1960s, much was made of Europe's technology lag; by now, fears have been partly reversed. The United States was long comfortably the richest country; by now, not only some oil-enriched Arab sheikdoms but various leading European countries (including Switzerland, Sweden, Denmark, West Germany, and France) have comparable or even higher per capita incomes than has the United States. Japan also may catch up in a very few years unless its growth is curtailed.

Yet the American position remains uniquely strong. In 1974, the United States, although exporting a smaller fraction of its GNP than other major powers, was the leading exporter, with 13 percent of the global total; Germany was second with 12 percent, Japan third with 7.4 percent, France fourth with 6.2 percent, and Britain fifth with 5.2 percent. The United States has a sound material base and is still the technological front runner. In computer technology, with its many global applications, the United States is unrivaled. The United States supplies 92 percent of the (noncommunist) world aircraft market and produces 85 percent of the world's integrated circuits. In the late 1960s, the Japanese made cheaper calculators by assembling United States–made circuits, but the integrated circuits of the 1970s vastly reduced the labor content of the calculators and brought the business back to the United States. Similarly, electronic watches have restored to the United States an industry long ago almost totally lost to Switzerland and other countries; the Swiss and Japanese buy components in the United States. Boeing has made more than 400 B–737 aircraft, while its French competitor could sell only ten of a comparable model.

It is slightly paradoxical that the United States is also very strong in agriculture, the specialty of the less developed countries. In grain production, United States farmers are more than a hundred times more productive than farmers in India, and ten times more so than those in the Soviet Union. Agricultural exports were $21.6 billion in 1974–1975, soybeans having surpassed computers and jet planes as the leading export. The American position in world grain exports is much stronger than the Arab position in oil; the United States provides nearly three-quarters of global net food exports, the only other big grain exporters being Canada and Australia. Good prices for American food exports fully compensated for the OPEC's cartel pricing of oil. The Soviet need for grain is also a trump card for American diplomacy, substantially strengthening the American position in contested areas such as the Near East. It may also be a deterrent to war; if the Soviet Union should destroy the United States without a single casualty, Soviet citizens would go hungry. In all probability, world demand will continue to grow, and with it the strength of the American position. Agricultural sales made it possible for the United States to pile up a trade surplus of $11 billion in 1975 despite the high cost of petroleum.

The United States is the world's biggest buyer and seller, with whom it is useful to be on good terms. By comparison, the Soviet Union is an economic pygmy; again and again, states that have turned to the Soviets for support because of resentment against American policies have turned back to the United States because of its ability to supply their needs. The desire to profit from American technology moved many Arabs to put the long history of American support for Israel out of consideration in 1974, to cheer President Nixon from the housetops, and to give a red-carpet welcome to hundreds of American businessmen. Without the promise of American economic cooperation, Egypt would never have agreed to partial settlements with Israel. The United States, not the Soviet Union, was engaged to clear the Suez Canal. The distrust generated in the LDCs by the more militaristic aspects of American foreign policy is at least partly negated by the attractions of doing business with the United States.

It is difficult to use economic power coercively, and attempts to do so are likely to be counterproductive. Food power has been called a great new weapon in the American diplomatic arsenal, but this weapon, like control of access to the American market, is less suitable as a punishment than as a general means of influence and broad pressure. In any case, economic diplomacy is much more harmonious with the older American traditions; it is more in accord with American institutions than military or subversive action, in that it excites less indignation, requires neither secrecy nor illegality, and threatens no mass destruction.

Consequently, concern for the American position in the world might turn much more on productivity, creativity, and economic health than on the superfluity of nuclear warheads. The former are basic and continually operative; the latter are contingent and terminal.

Today, the most rewarding conquests are those of improved technology and management in a competitively modernizing world; in this field the United States has historically shown its best performance as well as its better side. But more needs to be done. During nearly all of the postwar period, the growth rate of the American economy has been below that of western Europe, Japan, and many other countries, and the productivity of labor has risen more slowly in the United States than in most industrial countries, at an average yearly rate of 3.3 percent from 1960 to 1973, as compared with the Japanese 10.5 percent, the French 6.0 percent, and so forth. The percentage of the American product going into investment (that is, spent on future productivity) was also the lowest of major industrial powers except Britain. Private investment in the United States from 1960 to 1973 was 19.2 percent of the GNP; in Japan, 33.4 percent; in West Germany, 26.2 percent.[57] The share of the American GNP spent on research and development has likewise been shrinking (from 3.0 percent in 1964 to 2.3 percent in 1974),[58] while other industrial countries have increased their outlays for these purposes. Even worse, nearly half of United States research and development is for military purposes.[59]

A healthy economy is the precondition for success abroad, and the American world position is much more subject to erosion by American failures than by communist attack. What the Congress does about capital formation and economic growth is more important for United States foreign policy in the long run than are a dozen diplomatic conferences.

---

57. *The New York Times,* June 21, 1971, p. 27.

58. Sherman Gee, "Foreign Technology and the United States Economy," *Science,* February 21, 1975, p. 623.

59. F. A. Long, "Arms Control from the Perspective of the 1970s," *Daedalus,* 104 (Summer 1975), 11.

CHAPTER FOUR

Intangible Power

THE AMERICAN INFLUENCE

Not only is the world on the way to becoming a single marketplace, it is also moving toward the formation of a single cultural sphere; the torrent of information and ideas flowing into the farthest corners of the earth is quite as important to the complexion of the international system as the exchange of goods. Something like a world public opinion is developing.[1]

The world has been overrun not only by the scientific-industrial revolution and the material way of life it entails but also by Western styles and the ideas and attitudes of modernity. In the Middle Ages, every nation, and in fact almost every province, of Europe had distinctive styles of dress; now men and women of the upper classes dress almost identically around the globe. Nations once had their own weights and measures; now the United States is almost alone in still partly holding out against the metric system. Skyscrapers in a hundred countries echo the universal American way of building, and new apartment buildings look much alike in Rio, Novosibirsk, and Detroit. Increasingly the intellectual community shares similar patterns of thought.

Since World War II the leading component of homogenized Western-industrial culture has been the American component. Paris is still the (diminished) capital of *haute couture*, but everywhere one meets styles and ideas imported from or via the United States. Cuban culture remains permeated with Americanisms. The countries of the Soviet sphere have practically ceased trying to exclude American modes and develop their own competitive jazz and fashion shows. Only the poorest and most authoritarian of the communist countries, such as China and Albania, can fairly well keep their people untainted by American-led Western influence. Any easy-going, loose-jointed, popular culture is typically American; the Portuguese, for example, knew that the leftist coup in November 1975 had been turned back when their television screens showed Danny Kaye instead of Soviet heroes of labor. If imitation is a sign of empire, there is truly an American cultural empire. It is clear that American influence in the world derives much more from economic than from military capacities, and it is also arguable that the impact of the United States upon the world's thinking and ideas is even more significant than its economic impact.

---

1. *United States Advisory Commission on Information: The 26th Report,* Government Printing Office, Washington, 1973, p. 6.

Means of cultural influence are many. Trade is important; styles travel with goods, especially consumption goods; and a country's products transport something of its ways. Commerce also means travel and blends with tourism. Instructional programs for foreigners offered by American firms teach not only business practices but American ways of thinking; for example, an aircraft company selling to Iraq brings hundreds of Iraqis to America for management training.[2] The multinational corporations are major conduits of global Westernization or Americanization.

The United States exports its attitudes and lifestyles, while molding an incomplete image of itself through entertainment. Japan and India produce more full-length films than does the United States, but their products are not much viewed abroad; Hollywood has created a universal folk culture. American fare dominates television screens around the world. Even in Egypt during the honeymoon with the Soviet Union, it was the American films that packed in audiences, not the overly serious and usually dull Soviet shows. Reruns of "Bonanza" have been seen by over 350 million people. About a third of Latin American TV is of United States provenance. Over 60 percent of Canadian urban TV viewers subscribe to cable TV relaying United States programs.[3] Only the Soviet, Japanese, and Chinese peoples go largely or entirely without American violence and culture on their screens. The defensive reaction in many countries requires the showing of native productions, but viewers tend to brand these home products as inferior.[4]

Before World War II, the United States exported more graphic artists than art; since the war, our country has given the world most of its new styles.[5] In both popular and sophisticated music, America is the chief trend setter. Until early in this century, the United States was predominantly a literary borrower and imitator, but it has been the world's leading literary producer since the 1930s and has been dominant since World War II, conquering because "the United States seems to sum up the miseries, ironies, and aspirations of modern

---

2. *Business Week,* August 4, 1975, p. 35.

3. *The New York Times,* April 19, 1975, p. 6.

4. On cultural homogenization through United States and United States–style commercial TV, cf. Herbert I. Schiller, *Mass Communications and the American Empire,* Augustus M. Kelley, New York, 1970, pp. 112 ff.

5. Roy McMullen, "America's Impact on the Arts: The Visual Arts," *Saturday Review,* December 13, 1975, p. 98.

man." [6] Translations from American fiction, often subliterary but usually more exciting than the competition, amuse hundreds of millions from Capetown to Bangkok.

National political leaders everywhere keep up with events through *Time* and *Newsweek*, which have no real competitors. The only all all-European newspaper is the Paris-based, American-run *International Herald Tribune*. Although American magazines nowhere dominate the market (except in Canada, where they have come under legislative attack), they largely set the style that national publications follow.[7] Such a thoroughly American journal as *Reader's Digest* has a worldwide circulation of thirty million in twenty-six editions and thirteen languages. The Watergate investigations echoed around the world, giving journalists from Japan and Italy in particular an enhanced conception of their role. The bulk of the world's news is American-processed; Germany's chief window on the world is New York. *The New York Times* provides copy for 136 major foreign papers; Hong Kong newspapers get commentaries on stirrings in China from New York. United Press International (UPI) goes to 113 countries.[8]

United States brands, from shirts to breakfast cereals, are likely to be preferred wherever allowed and competitively priced. Blue jeans have become a badge of modern youth around the world, even in European communist countries. Fast-food chains have taken over from Stockholm to Tokyo. Mexicans prefer hamburgers to tacos, and Third World youths shouting against the latest "imperialist plot" sport American-type T-shirts and hair styles. United States methods are copied in merchandising, management, and techniques of production; American ways permeate big business circles around the world. Most new ideas about social problems as well as technology come to other nations from or at least via the world's chief center of innovation. When other countries pioneer, as in high-speed railroads, the initiative is striking because it is an exception. A wave of concern about pollution and environment surged out of the United States across the world. Dissent and rebellion are an American export, too. The student disorders of 1965–1970 began with the Berkeley Free Speech Movement in late 1964. Even anti-Americanism has been adopted from the United States,

---

6. Marcus Cunliffe, "America's Impact on the Arts: Literature," *Saturday Review*, December 13, 1975, p. 86.

7. William H. Mead, "Multinational Media," *Foreign Policy*, 18 (Spring 1975), 165.

8. Ibid., pp. 155–156, 163.

as people abroad take up the criticisms that Americans make of their own society.

One reason for the popularity of American styles and products is the common disposition of people to imitate the rich and powerful. Hence comes the snob appeal, for example, of American cigarettes or Coca Cola, an appeal probably extending beyond any intrinsic superiority of their flavor. America is modern and a pacesetter; thus it is joy for Russian urchins to get chewing gum and for their elders to acquire American shoes. The fact that the United States is the world's communications center is also important. But American predominance exists also because of American creativity and skills. There is urgent and unceasing competition of products in the huge American home market and more than anywhere else a massive effort to please tastes, fill real or cultivated needs, and persuade the consumer to open his wallet. A flexible and innovative society, the United States is also the world's greatest and most competitive market for all manner of knowledge, entertainment, and edification.

Very likely owing basic discoveries to other nations but striding forward in applying them, the United States has long been in the vanguard of modernity—developing the conveyor belt, the automobile for mass transportation, skyscrapers, telephones, packaged foods, airplanes, refrigerators, television sets, computers, and most of what makes this era different, for better or worse. In a sense, Americanization has little to do with any particular culture but represents modernization. The United States itself eagerly borrows from abroad (for example, Scandinavian furniture styles); other countries take over American inventions and outstrip the United States, as the Japanese have swamped world markets with dynamic transistor radios. But the march of urbanization and modernization in its broad outlines is in the American image.[9] However much European intellectuals love to snipe at the United States and its materialistic culture, they almost universally look to it as the model of technological civilization.

A share of the American impact also derives from leadership in education, an achievement that greatly affects the American position however far it may be from the field of vision of foreign policy architects. This country has the greatest number, and usually the finest, of

---

9. For the American influence in Europe before Vietnam, see Edward A. McCreary, *The Americanization of Europe: The Impact of Americans and American Business on the Uncommon Market,* Doubleday, Garden City, N.Y., 1964.

institutions in almost every branch of learning, the humanities and professional training as well as the natural sciences. Those who want the
best in education look to the United States, although they usually receive little official help beyond some information, probably through
the Institute of International Education, a private agency supported
by the State Department. But foreign students flock into the United
States; there were 150,000 in 1973, approximately ten times as many as
were lured to the Soviet Union. About half of the foreign students are
graduate students and presumably purposeful. They come despite national antagonisms; in 1974, when Libya's relations with the United
States were at a low ebb, more than a thousand Libyans came to the
United States for graduate study, their expenses being paid by the
Libyan government.[10] India is politically close to the Soviet Union, but
tens of thousands of Indians go to the United States to study, only a
handful to the Soviet Union.[11]

Foreign students, like tourists, contribute to the American balance of payments; much more important, they provide a massive export of knowledge and technology. To restrict the brain drain, it is
made difficult for them to settle in the United States, the rule being that
those who come as students must remain outside the United States for
at least two years before applying for immigrant visas. No one knows
how their attitudes are affected, and practically no attention has been
given to the question; but it is usually assumed that those exposed to
the openness of life and discourse in the United States, relatively free
of political pressures, will be unlikely to favor authoritarian ways at
home and will continue to be basically friendly to the United States,
even if they are critical of its policies. The petroleum minister of Saudi
Arabia in the fuel crisis, Sheik Ahmad Zaki Yamani, who was a Harvard man, led the fight within the Organization of Petroleum Exporting Countries (OPEC) for moderation in price increases. Fortunately
for American foreign policy as well as for American business, very
many if not most persons in responsible positions in the Mideast are
American trained.

American students also go abroad in growing numbers. Several
dozen American universities have campuses abroad, the large majority
in Europe, although no foreign university has extended itself to the
United States. There are also a few American colleges abroad, privately operated but more or less subsidized from Washington. Such

10. *The New York Times*, September 9, 1974, p. 2.
11. William P. Bundy, "Dictatorships and Foreign Policy," *Foreign Affairs*,
54 (October 1975), 59.

are the American universities in the Near East, particularly in Istanbul, Beirut, and Cairo. They have been remarkably immune to nationalistic resentments, functioning unimpaired even when diplomatic relations with the United States have been cut. The American University in Beirut has turned out scores of Near Eastern political and economic leaders and operates the biggest and best hospital in the Near East.

The rapidity of growth of knowledge, speed of change, dominance of technology, and expansion of the world stage have brought about a vast enlargement of educational needs. The ability of the United States to satisfy these needs will probably be an even greater asset of American foreign policy in the future than it has been in the past.

Like education, science serves America in many ways beyond the obvious industrial and military applications. The United States does best in the sale of those wares that require the largest input of technology relative to labor, and it does still better with knowledge itself. Sales abroad of United States design and technology in 1970 amounted to $2.2 billion, half of total world exports of this commodity and ten times American imports. Like education, science is also a token of national achievement that does much to make America respected, and the American lead is incontestable. As many as 80 percent of recent scientific and technical discoveries have been made in the United States [12] (thanks in part to scientists of European origin). Half of the world's engineering literature is United States–generated.[13] United States openness contrasts with Soviet secrecy; the latter much reduces the return (both in production and in prestige) [14] from the large Soviet investment in science.

Science, being essentially universal, is a force for international order. It is nonconflictual and cooperative by nature and crosses national boundaries. Scientists revel in international conferences and enterprises, such as the International Geophysical Year. Perceiving world realities and dangers on a global scale, scientists are usually an influence for peace, opposed as they are to coercion, censorship, and dogmatism. Science provides common ground with political antagonists such as the Soviets, as testified by numerous and increasingly successful agreements for exchange and joint work in many fields, especially pollution control and medicine. In the exchange, the Soviets profit

12. Zbigniew Brzezinski, *Between Two Ages: America's Role in the Technetronic Age*, Viking, New York, 1971, p. 27.

13. *Technology: Sputnik, Economic Chauvinism, and World Peace*, Gould, Chicago, 1975, p. 3.

14. Cf. Zhores A. Medvedev, *The Medvedev Papers*, Macmillan, London, 1971.

directly far more than the United States; but the United States reaps the benefit of contacts with the Soviet scientific elite, which has high prestige, is resistant to ideological and party control, and is the sector of Soviet society most open to foreign ideas. American scientists have also done much to ameliorate punitive treatment of dissident Soviet scientists.

Scientific and technological achievements are a source of prestige. The Soviets made the most of their early space successes; it was fortunate for the United States to have the triumphant moon landing of July 1969 and subsequent Apollo missions to offset the discredit of Vietnam. Medicine is perhaps a worthier source of prestige. Just as the fame of acupuncture brightened the Chinese image in the United States in 1972, medical discoveries have improved world opinion of the United States; for example, President Dwight D. Eisenhower in 1955 made a point of announcing a new vaccine for poliomyelitis. It has been Soviet policy to offer treatment in Moscow to ailing leaders of the Third World; but these leaders commonly prefer, as do the less celebrated who can afford it, to resort to western European or (still better) American doctors and hospitals. In January 1973, a surgeon of the Houston Medical Center was summoned to Moscow to operate on the president of the Soviet Academy of Sciences.

America is much better qualified to lead the world technologically than to lead it politically. Insofar as information is centralized, no other country is so well prepared to act as the main storehouse of useful knowledge available for all and as the center of a world information grid.[15] No other is so ready to look for solutions to the problems pressing upon all in the technologically revolutionized universe. Rich and possessing an innovative structure, the United States can do more than any other nation can to attack the problems of the developed and less developed countries and thereby contribute to a more promising international order. But science, like cultural affairs and the formation of attitudes in general, is a neglected area of foreign policy.

THE LINGUA FRANCA

It is an important but hardly mentioned aspect of the American world position that practically anywhere Americans may travel, they will

---

15. As noted by Brzezinski, *Between Two Ages,* p. 299.

find at least a few people who can communicate in their language, and in a hundred countries English is at least the second language. English is the working language of more than eighty delegations at the United Nations, and the language of 90 percent of United Nations documents; it is the official language of twenty-six countries and is used unofficially in at least eighteen others.[16] Most world leaders, from the king of Nepal to Fidel Castro, speak at least fair English. In a large part of the less developed world, the American engineer is under little pressure to learn a native language. The Soviet purveyor of aid, on the other hand, has to communicate in the language of the leading imperialists, and Cuban schools teach English if for no other reason than to facilitate communication with Soviet technicians. A large part of Soviet propaganda is published in English, and Soviet cultural centers abroad lure customers by teaching English.

The enormous growth of world communications, travel, and trade has brought a corresponding increase of the only feasible language, and in an increasingly integrated world, English stands to become ever more the means of international communication. If a Thai wishes to speak to a Bolivian, or even with a Burmese next door, he must almost inevitably use English. There is no real competition. No other language has an equally modern vocabulary; most languages, even the languages of great cultures such as Arabic and Hindi, strikingly lack means of technical expression. Thousands of technical terms exist only in English. French was the medium of diplomacy in the eighteenth and nineteenth centuries, but its base of native speakers is narrow. Spanish prevails throughout the greater part of Latin America, but its economic and technical importance is secondary. German has been largely restricted to central Europe by Germany's loss of two great wars. Russian is used where it has been imposed, especially in eastern Europe, but even there English is increasingly the lingua franca. Russian also suffers from being very difficult, as do Chinese and Japanese in somewhat different ways. Part of the reopening of China was the great boom in the study of English by all kinds of people from pedicab drivers to Chairman Mao Tse-tung.

English is the native language of many more people than any other language except Chinese. Most of the world's communications are in English, including at least 60 percent of scientific publications.

---

16. Lester R. Brown, *World without Borders*, Random House, New York, 1972, p. 271.

Everywhere scientists must read English in order to keep up with their specialties, and scientific journals in other languages ordinarily provide article summaries in English. Higher education practically requires facility in English; in few subjects are there adequate texts in other languages. In Saudi Arabia, for example, higher education is conducted in English, and university students from Japan to Sweden use books in English predominantly. It is the working language of multinational corporations, including most of those based in non–English-speaking lands. Japanese firms use English in correspondence with overseas branches to avoid the appearance of secrecy.

The store of literature in English is by far the world's largest, whether or not it is judged to be the richest. Books in English are published in significant numbers in dozens of countries, including the Soviet Union (1,390 titles in 1970). In India, four times as many books are published in English as in Hindi.[17] Nationalism to the contrary, the use of English has spread since Indian independence. It is effectively the language of government, and the principal newspapers are in English. The globetrotter in dozens of capitals finds that the English-language paper is one of the leading dailies, such as the *Bangkok Post,* the *Karachi Dawn,* the *Ceylon Daily News,* and the *Jerusalem Post.* More irritating to many people has been the infiltration of English into other modern languages. Frenchmen take "le weekend" in "le country," German mothers take "das Baby" to "das Shopping Center," and so on. Japanese keep "uppatodatu" by sprinkling English words in their speech; and the Japanese, unlike the French, do not seem to mind the infiltration. Even the party-managed Soviet press admits thousands of anglicisms, such as *container, credit, jeans, meeting,* and *stewardess.*

It might be better to have a world lingua franca not associated with a particular nation, such as Esperanto. But aside from the fact that English belongs to many nations, the trend has apparently gone too far to be reversed. The more people learn and use English, the more important it becomes to learn it and use it. It is generally to little avail that many nations legislate in favor of their own languages. Almost everywhere English is the second language studied in school, except in some former French colonies and in the sphere of Soviet domination. English is gaining on French in the former French colonies because it is more broadly useful for business, science, and technology. English is more than a school subject; it is an accessory to

---

17. *UNESCO Statistical Yearbook,* 1973, p. 662.

being modern and getting ahead. To reach the broadest audience, scientists must write in English, compelling other scientists to read English. The use of English snowballs as the world draws closer together.

The United States has not done much purposefully to promote the use of its language, and it probably cannot do much directly without causing negative reactions. But the prevalence of English is fortunate for the United States. Learning English does not automatically make people friends of America, but it is convenient for the secretary of state to be able to communicate directly with a majority of the world's foreign ministers. The fact that most of the new Soviet managerial elite have at least a smattering of English means something for détente. The flow of ideas without a linguistic barrier makes difficult the cultivation of xenophobia and extreme nationalism.[18] The prevalence of English should also help Americans to learn about and appreciate the rest of the world.

PROMOTING THE AMERICAN IMAGE

The American influence around the world—influence on people rather than on governments as such—is almost entirely the work of private persons and groups, outside the purview of official policy. President Richard M. Nixon at his second inaugural spoke of building a world "in which those who would influence others will do so by the strength of their ideas, not by the force of their arms." However, if it were made an important official purpose to try to influence the world by ideas, this development would mark a revolution in American foreign policy. The effect on opinion abroad of foreign policy decisions has been considered only irregularly and incidentally. The purposeful wielding of ideas abroad has not been the American way; about four hundred times as much money has regularly been spent on instruments of violence as on more abstract means of influence.

The reluctance to influence opinion abroad is partly due to a sensible aversion to propaganda. For the Soviet Union, *propaganda* is a good word, like *crusade*, and disseminating propaganda is a necessary

---

18. John H. Esterline and Robert B. Black, *Inside Foreign Policy*, Mayfield Publishing Co., Palo Alto, Calif., 1975, p. 156.

and proper activity of the state at home and abroad. In the United States view, propaganda is somewhat deceptive, the big-lie policy of dictators, in which the United States properly indulges only as a last resort. Propaganda may be suitable for selling detergents but it is hardly an appropriate method for the government to employ unless the dirty game must be played because the competition plays it.

To sell the United States and its policies abroad became a recognized official function only in response to emergencies. In World War I, the American Committee on Public Information carried on psychological warfare, but this activity lapsed with victory. In the later 1930s the United States began feebly countering the propaganda efforts of the fascist powers, especially in the American-protected sphere of Latin America. With its entrance into World War II, the United States began serious cultural-psychological operations, seeking to persuade neutrals and to hold friends as well as to demoralize the enemy. A new Office of War Information was set up, and the Voice of America (VOA) began its transmissions in February 1942. Just as the nation did not fully disarm after World War II (as it had after World War I) and for the same reasons, the propaganda organization was never disbanded but was continued through the reeducation program in Germany and Japan into the increasing competition with the Soviet Union for the allegiance of the undecided peoples both of Europe and of the rest of the world. The Truman administration was convinced of the need for the "anticommunist campaign of truth," but the effort was modest until it was invigorated, like the military budget, by the Korean War.

Since the mid-1950s the tendency has been toward a slackening of activities. The budget has edged downward. The exaggerations and eccentricities of McCarthyism were as hurtful to the United States Information Agency (USIA) as to the State Department. The agency's energies after 1965 were concentrated on Vietnam, as it tried to win the backing of the Vietnamese people for South Vietnamese and American policy. This limitation entailed neglect of the American image in the rest of the world at a time when it was most in need of defense. But psychological warfare proved ineffective wherever political policies were defective; after 1969, activities in Vietnam were scaled down. The USIA budget came under increasing pressure, leveling off at around $200 million a year and gradually declining in real terms because of inflation.

An autonomous agency under the guidance of the secretary of state, the USIA carries on a broad range of activities. It makes twenty to thirty documentary films yearly, which are viewed by hundreds of millions of persons abroad. It organizes a few fairs and exhibits. It publishes slick magazines for circulation in the Soviet Union and Poland by reciprocal arrangements with these countries. It subsidizes the translation and publication abroad of a few books deemed suitable. Through cultural affairs officers attached to embassies, it cultivates academic and cultural contacts.[19] In an effort to improve its standing with Congress, which is more sympathetic to the promotion of American material interests than to global enlightenment, the USIA in 1973 began advertising American tourist attractions and exports, bringing new products (from electronic watches to breath analyzers) to the attention of the world.[20]

Notably successful are the more than 200 USIA libraries and reading rooms, some with mobile units to reach the backwoods, and 130 binational centers, mostly in Latin America. Some, like the Amerika-Häuser in Germany, have played a vital role in making American culture available to the local population. In many towns, the American library is among the best available, certainly containing the best collection of works in English. In the Third World, the chief business of the centers, which are usually run cooperatively with local leaders, has been the teaching of the English language. It has been estimated that the centers attract over 25 million readers yearly and have a quarter of a million students of English.[21]

The biggest thrust of the information program is the VOA, which beams news, commentaries, background programs, and American music to millions of listeners, in a usually bland, fairly objective, and lofty manner. It has its own news bureau, twenty-odd full-time correspondents abroad, and numerous stringers. The VOA broadcasts to inhabitants of the communist or Soviet-dominated world (the Chinese hardly have private receivers) the news of a world screened from them by censorship and propaganda, trying to give some of the benefits of the American press. It directs to the Soviet Union nineteen broadcast hours daily in Russian and minority languages as well as in English. The Soviets attested to the importance of these broadcasts by jamming

19. Thomas C. Sorenson, *The Word War: The Story of American Propaganda*, Harper and Row, New York, 1963.

20. *USIA Authorization for Fiscal 1975, Hearings Committee on Foreign Affairs*, Government Printing Office, Washington, D.C., 1974, p. 36.

21. W. Wendell Blanke, *The Foreign Service of the United States*, Praeger, New York, 1969, pp. 163–164.

them with some 3,000 transmitters until September 1973, after which they relaxed their disruptive tactics to some extent.[22]

The VOA is less jammed (and apparently less effective) than the more loosely controlled Radio Free Europe (which broadcasts to the Soviet sphere in eastern Europe) and Radio Liberty (which broadcasts to the Soviet Union). The VOA speaks for the American government; for this reason, it is somewhat inhibited by its responsibility as official spokesman. Frank Shakespeare, appointed director in 1969, took a rather sharp anticommunist line; his successor after 1973, James Keogh, shied away from controversial anti-Soviet material. In his words, VOA "policy is that we do not interfere in the internal affairs of other countries." [23] The VOA might well be strengthened if it were given more autonomy under a board of citizens. Radio Liberty and Radio Free Europe, with substantial contingents of refugees among their 2,400 personnel, are closer to the news and the problems of the peoples of the Soviet sphere. They broadcast a thousand hours weekly in twenty-five languages from Munich, West Germany; Radio Liberty also reaches the Soviet East by transmitters in Taiwan. Radio Liberty is a major medium for the underground press in the Soviet Union, publicizing reports of protest movements with the Soviet Union, political trials, and the like. It also makes available to Soviet listeners forbidden literary works, such as those of Alexander Solzhenitsyn, providing a channel of communication for Soviet nonconformists.

The cost of a single Trident submarine would finance Radio Liberty for a hundred years.[24] Yet Congress is not happy about supporting the information program and talks of reorganizing it out of existence. The USIA has little standing in the government, it has had many directors, and its morale has not been high. In theory, its basic purposes include not only influencing world opinion but also advising the president and State Department on the effects of foreign policies; by the recommendation of a high-level commission, it should be in at the genesis of foreign policy.[25] But the USIA has been omitted from high

---

22. On the Voice of America, see George N. Gordon and Irving A. Falk, *The War of Ideas*, Hastings House, New York, 1973.

23. *Time*, December 16, 1974, p. 85.

24. A Soviet intellectual was quoted as saying, "If they only knew how we count on these broadcasts to tell us what is going on, they would not think about the cost. That is the best gift the United States can give us" (*Christian Science Monitor*, May 12, 1972).

25. *United States Advisory Commission on Information: The 26th Report*, pp. 1, 25.

councils. Supposedly, the impact of American actions upon the feelings and attitudes of the world should be a major consideration in decision making, but the professionals in the field have not been consulted, nor have they usually even been given advance information of actions that they are called upon to justify. The USIA has little to say even about information policy.[26] It also suffers uncertainty in its message: To what extent is it the mouthpiece of the government or the representative of the nation and how far should it be an advocate of causes and an apologist for policies or a straightforward purveyor of news and American reality? To preserve credibility, the VOA gives the bad news as well as the good; it broadcast the Senate report on Central Intelligence Agency (CIA) assassination plots in thirty-five languages.[27]

But the USIA fills a real need. Only one-fifth of the nations of the world have what might be truly called freedom of information, and for many people the American service is the best window on the outside world. In 1972, radicals regularly stoned the United States Information Service (USIS) center in Calcutta during the day, only to come around to chat with the American cultural officer in the evening.[28] The USIA engenders respect for the United States, makes American cultural achievements more widely available, and can further understanding of American purposes. It carries on a modern activity concordant with the age of popular awareness.

Many other countries, not only Marxist-Leninist but democratic, devote more effort than the United States does to presenting their message to the world. For example, the British Council has been a successful link between Britain and the cultivated people of many lands, making books and other publications widely available, organizing countless cultural events and visits; and the BBC overseas service has shone not only in its news service but in the high quality of the television films that it furnishes to many countries. The French have been still more dedicated to their *mission civilisatrice*; as former President Georges Pompidou said, "Of all countries France is the one most deeply attached to exporting its language and culture." [29] France has a cultural affairs budget more than twice as large as the American budget for cultural affairs. In 1973 France spent 1 percent of the state budget on informational activities abroad; the United States spent

26. Esterline and Black, *Inside Foreign Policy*, p. 147.
27. *The New York Times*, November 21, 1975, p. 54.
28. *Newsweek*, May 15, 1972, p. 63.
29. *Time*, August 7, 1964, p. 67.

one-tenth of 1 percent.[30] Some 20,000 teachers are sent out to *lycées* around the world, where many future leaders and aristocrats learn to think French, while scholarships, exchanges, exhibits, artistic tours, and television programs do their best to create a climate favorable for France. The West German effort is of the same order of magnitude as the French. The Soviets, of course, have the broadest program of all; they spend four to five times as much as the United States for activities ranging from education for promising youth from the less developed countries at Lumumba University in Moscow to reading rooms like those maintained by the USIS. The Soviet Union publishes at least ten times as many books abroad as does the United States, or about 160 million yearly.[31] The Soviet Union and its satellites broadcast internationally twice as many hours weekly as do American stations, and in three times as many languages. The United States is several hundred times as concerned to keep ahead of the Soviets in nuclear overkill as to match their efforts in speaking to the world.

Other ways in which the United States promotes understanding and the spread of ideas include educational, scientific, and artistic exchanges, which are handled mostly by or under the guidance of the State Department. These programs are of special importance in communist countries, which do not permit unofficial exchanges. Under the Fulbright program, thousands of professors, lecturers, and researchers have gone to many countries and have achieved generally excellent results. There are government-assisted binational schools in important cities around the world (especially in Latin America) for the benefit not only of American nationals abroad but also of local children, generally those of the elite. It is assumed that students educated in the United States or in American-run schools abroad gain some understanding of the character and ideals of the United States, and it is likely that they will grow up to take leadership roles in their communities. Expenditures for the entire exchange-of-persons program in fiscal 1974 were $35.6 million; for assistance to binational schools abroad, $1.85 million. The Agency for International Development (AID) allots $17–25 million yearly to help about eighty educational and medical institutions abroad, led by the American universities in the Near East and University of the Americas in Mexico City.

Cultural relations are simplest with friendly advanced countries,

---

30. *USIA Authorization for Fiscal Year 1975*, p. 175.
31. Ibid., pp. 5, 28.

with which there can be an easy and uninhibited interchange; the official role is least needed there. With the Soviet sphere, cultural exchanges have to be carefully negotiated. The Soviet aims have been the display of Soviet achievements and the maximal acquisition of useful knowledge at a minimal cost in personal communication. Soviet students and scientists are sent to study the latest advances in American physics or chemistry, and Americans going to the Soviet Union emphasize social sciences and humanities; the principal presumed gain is in the widening of cracks in Soviet exclusiveness and the development of contacts with influential people. The chief purpose of exchanges with the less developed countries is the transfer of technology and skills as a supplement to, or in part a substitute for, economic aid. Such programs must be handled with tact, lest they be branded "cultural imperialism," and they depend for their success largely upon the cooperation of intellectuals who are likely to be anti-American. Not infrequently, leaders of the less developed countries have viewed American scholars as suspicious or menacing and have placed many obstacles in their way. The Peace Corps, an extraordinary program for the teaching of self-help and democracy along with useful skills, has also run into serious friction and has had to give up its original goals of remaking the life and ways of the less fortunate peoples. It has had to learn to work more with national authorities and less directly with the people. The chief value of the mature Peace Corps may be the experience gathered by Americans intimately exposed to another culture.

IMAGE AND INFLUENCE

The American cultural program—using *cultural* in its broadest sense—is a tiny, almost trivial proportion of the official action of the United States in the world, underfinanced and neglected, of largely unrealized potential. It is paltry not only in monetary terms (especially in comparison with United States expenditures on instruments of force), but also in terms of the attention that it receives from leadership. If it is ever debated in official circles how American creativity can be turned to making a better world atmosphere and so a better world, or how military intervention might affect receptivity to American ideas, the deliberations do not come to light. On the contrary, there is frequently a narrow, one might say thoughtless, approach. The cost of a new submarine could finance a college education in the United States for

50,000–100,000 promising youths, many of whom would undoubtedly attain important positions in their own countries. Yet next to nothing is done to help students come to the United States; even though American colleges are striving to fill their classrooms, it is required that the foreign applicants show in advance their ability to finance four years of education. It is also made difficult or impossible for the ambitious but not wealthy young foreigner to take a summer job, not only reducing the number able to study here but giving a poor impression of American hospitality and concern for the less affluent. Instead of encouraging the publication abroad of books in English (under copyright law), the United States limits importation of books in order to protect American publishers. Financial troubles threaten the existence of the American University in Beirut, which since 1866 has been among the most important channels of American influence in the Arab world; the United States, through AID, recently supplied $6.3 million in support, but that amount is only about a quarter of the budget. In the face of mounting costs, the American University has been driven to raising tuition and selling its assets. The American Hospital in Paris, founded in 1910, has served as an embassy for American medicine but survives on charity.

In brief, in this crucial area of interaction of American and foreign societies, the United States government leaves the field almost entirely to the uncoordinated actions of private parties who are motivated to some extent by idealism but much more by desire for financial gain and who frequently act contrary to the best interests of the United States and the world. This reluctance of government to interfere is in accordance with the American way, yet to fail to place major emphasis on the impact of information is to operate in the past. The world has become more and more like a single village, in which everyone is aware of the deeds and especially the misdeeds of everyone else. Bedouins of the Sahara and Indians of the Amazon region listen to speeches and news on their transistor radios, and a forest of television antennas bring riots in Birmingham or moon walks into living rooms from Caracas to Karachi. Several hundred million viewers saw Americans land on the moon in 1969, and television has become more and more international as exigencies of programming lead national networks to borrow abundantly to keep screens filled. Within a few years, it should be possible for satellites to send television programs directly into homes from anywhere on earth; in this case, the whole of mankind, or at least those able and permitted to have the necessary apparatus, will be able to view the same entertainment and to absorb through this potent medium many of the same images of world affairs. This prospect causes Soviet leaders to shudder, but it would probably be advantageous for the United States to make satellite transmission available for all nations.[32]

There is no reason in this circumstance for what may be loosely called "cultural imperialism." It is legitimate and probably desirable, however, that nations pacifically promote their ideas and ideals. Those which are able to do so have long done so without apology, especially the Marxist-Leninist states, which make a real effort to give the world the benefit of their rather narrow and dogmatic ideology. The United States is in any case continually intervening massively without design or purpose; it might be better to be more purposeful in ways beneficial to the United States and the world. Unfortunately, it is impossible to have free movement of people and information and at the same time to shelter differences. By no one's choice, the homogenization of the world proceeds of itself; although unesthetic, it may be essential for the solution of the world's problems.

The traffic should be two-way. Not only do Americans have much to learn from other peoples, but programs will be more effective insofar as they can be made reciprocal and cooperative. The American television industry, for example, while filling foreign viewing hours (often with what might be called trash) might well be encouraged to import many more programs, for quality as well as variety. Currently only 1–2 percent of American programming is imported. The TV export business may well be much more internationalized, as the movie industry has been, making TV imports less controversial, less subject to nationalistic barriers, and more effective in promoting understanding among peoples.[33] The United States should pay more attention not only to its own image, but also to the opinions and feelings of others.

Only lack of imagination limits the number of suggestions of the measures that might be taken at relatively small cost to give the world more of the better side of American creativity. American-supported (but binationally controlled) secondary and technical schools and universities should be both welcome and beneficial for the less developed countries; the present slender network could be multiplied many times. The United States might give major support to the worldwide struggle against illiteracy—the number of illiterates in the world is probably

32. As suggested by *U.S. Advisory Commission on Information: The 26th Report*, p. 22.
33. Mead, "Multinational Media," pp. 162–163.

still growing. It is much easier and sounder to furnish means of acquiring training and skills to the less developed countries than to try to furnish money; cultural borrowing does not have to be repaid. The receptivity of Marxist-Leninist countries is growing, and exchanges are promising; by furnishing technical assistance—which itself has psychological effects—the United States buys a little opening of their societies. The United States does little for international cultural and scientific get-togethers; Romania is said to sponsor more such congresses than the United States.[34] Many steps could be taken, without interference with the free market, to make available the better productions of American literature, cinema, art, and thought at reduced cost. Official bureaucratic agencies operate under a handicap, but the United States, like other countries, could do much more through subsidized or publicly assisted private groups and organizations. There is a good case in this connection for working more with the United Nations and other organizations; the United States need ask no special privileges.

It is in the general American interest both that foreigners know about America and that the people of this country know about the world outside. The better informed people are and the greater the variety of their sources of information, the more pressure there is on governments (it may be hoped) to act rationally. The better informed leaders are, the more they measure themselves in global terms. In a modern, open world, political relations rest ultimately on the images people form of the United States and other countries. Foreign policy becomes, even though not so recognized, in large degree a matter of opinion formation. It has to do with establishing the climate for the nation and its purposes in the overcoming of enmity as well as the cementing of trust and friendship, the modern equivalent of alliance. In a world of independent sovereignties, international cooperation must come through education and persuasion. Philosophers of the eighteenth century looked to reason or enlightenment to overcome tyranny. This hope has only partially been fulfilled, but in this century we can look only to enlightenment to surmount international disorder.[35]

The United States is best prepared to promote a world cultural and

---

34. Radu R. Florescu, "Ceaucescuism: Romania's Road to Communism," *Current History*, 64 (May 1974), 215.

35. That the making of a new world order is primarily a question of attitudinal evolution is contended by David V. Edwards, *Creating a New World Politics*, David McKay, New York, 1973.

scientific-technical community, which would not exclude conflict but in which conflict would become more tractable and for which national sovereignty would be only a partial mode of cohesion. The modernization of American foreign policy consequently entails greatly increased attention to its psychological-cultural dimensions in order to keep livable and perhaps to improve a tensely changing world.

It may be, as has been foreseen by eminent futurists,[36] that in the 1980s we can expect to have worldwide Americanized cultural patterns, characterized above all by the mass-consumption ethos, with only a few countries or areas holding out. The general trend of easier communications might of itself bring about this development, because the United States is the strongest of world centers. It is in the interest of this country, however, to promote not a specific Americanization but an open, freely communicating world order, wherein there should be room for the universal values of freedom and self-determination to which virtually all states, with varying enthusiasm, subscribe.

For this purpose, American leaders might bear in mind that the United States is the chief model for the world (even for communist states to a much greater extent than is commonly realized) and that the influence of America resides overwhelmingly in its example.[37] The yearning for freedom and the general respect for truth and decency are forgotten weapons in the American arsenal. People know that they can learn more of the truth from American sources, especially unofficial, than from any others; critical attitudes and independence of mind of the effervescent, pluralistic American society go far toward offsetting the offenses of intervention and subversion, making American ways and thought broadly acceptable. Indira Gandhi, while blaming the CIA for (she supposed) trying to destabilize her government, praised the United States for its wealth of ideas.

Much concern for the American image in the world is officially expressed, but it is largely a concern that this country should not appear "chicken" in games of power. There is no visible worry, in contrast, that foreigners might have doubts about a nation that is prepared to engage in criminal activities for purposes of foreign policy. The United States would like to see democracy prosper in the world, but the best assistance that can be given to the democratic ideal would be for the world's

---

36. Herman Kahn and B. Bruce-Briggs, *Things To Come: Thinking about the Seventies and Eighties,* Macmillan, New York, 1972, p. 19.

37. Bundy, "Dictatorships and Foreign Policy," p. 59.

leading democratic power to behave as completely as possible like a democracy, engaging in nothing that is not generally acceptable to enlightened opinion.

It is entirely in the American tradition to stress the influence of the republic in the world. John Adams, Patrick Henry, Thomas Jefferson, and many others felt that in making the American Revolution they were lighting a beacon for mankind; theirs was a great creation, with government based on popular consent and limited under a written constitution.[38] For European intellectuals of the end of the eighteenth century, America was a land of virtuous yeomen and limitless prospects, and the American and French revolutions merged in the incarnation of the ideals of liberty and equality based on constitutional representative government and civil rights. America was the shining example for European reformers and revolutionaries of 1848. The Civil War and the triumph of industrial democracy over the semifeudal, slave-holding South again raised American prestige, and the United States became the glowing mecca of the oppressed people of Europe in the later decades of the century. Victory in World War I and idealistic Wilsonian peacemaking raised the United States to a pinnacle of prestige.

The defeat of fascism in World War II made this country again the model of democracy and success for a discouraged and impoverished world seeking to build a new life. This time, however, the Soviets claimed their share as builders of a new social order and victors over Nazi power. The over-waging and mismanagement of the cold war gradually dimmed the American image, and Vietnam turned much admiration into execration. In the mid-1970s, American support for Israel continued to grate on many nations, while many young states liked to indulge their new-found sovereignty in deprecation of the most powerful, and therefore (as they saw it) the most oppressive nation.

The ideals of democracy and freedom are still powerful, however; the most authoritarian states, such as the Soviet Union, feel compelled to claim to be the most democratic. Democracy is not much more prevalent in the world than it was two centuries ago, and the United States is or could be an example of freedom now as it was when the republic was born. With a few years of enlightened behavior, the United States should be able to make itself again, as it was during the better part of its history, the model not only of material modernization

---

38. Henry Steele Commager, "The Revolution as a World Ideal," *Saturday Review*, December 13, 1975, pp. 13–14.

but of freedom, invention, civilized progress, and respect for norms of international comity. As World War II was threatening to engulf the United States, Henry Luce saw this country gloriously leading the world by productivity, education, charity, and ideals of freedom and justice.[39] He was too sanguine, but the ideal was not unworthy.

---

39. *The Ideas of Henry Luce,* ed. John K. Jessup, Atheneum, New York, 1969, p. 120.

CHAPTER FIVE

The American Capacity

PRESIDENTIAL LEADERSHIP

Whatever prescriptions may be put forward for the directions of American foreign policy, its wisdom and effectiveness depend upon the institutions of the republic, the personalities in command, and the temper and sanity of its people, who are the ultimate deciders. Two somewhat contradictory essentials are necessary: the ability of the apparatus to formulate and carry out policies for the national well-being, and the restraint of the natural inclination of high leadership to assert itself beyond the national needs. The first essential implies chiefly the ability of the president to view broadly and take appropriate action either in defense against foreign threats or in the promotion of national goals. The second implies chiefly the ability of the Congress to examine, criticize, and check the programs of the executive.

American foreign policy making is correspondingly ambivalent. On the one side, the president has broad discretionary powers that have at times seemed to verge on the autocratic. This independence of action has usually been considered necessary to enable the United States to compete in a lawless international universe. The other is the democratic side of foreign policy, which comes to a focus in Congress but which includes many institutions, persons, and groups that have some say in the direction of the nation. Behind this machinery of policy making is that amorphous something called public opinion, which, although it contributes little action and much debate and challenge, is hardly less necessary than executive leadership. The strength of public opinion is the essence of the American political system. Altogether, the American system is an immensely complex foreign policy–making machine, the most complex in the world and the despair of all who would fully understand it. Some would also call it anarchic and self-defeating, but it has the virtues of effectiveness and rationality, at least as compared with other foreign policy apparatuses.

As foreign policy is ordinarily viewed, the presidential side is overwhelmingly dominant. In practice, only the president can take action in relation with other nations. These nations and the public see him as the representative of the United States, head of government and head of state. American ambassadors are his personal representatives.

The presidential role rests mostly on the fact that the president is acting on behalf of a nation in the concourse of nations.[1] Except in

---

1. As stated by Paul Seabury, *The United States in World Affairs*, McGraw-Hill, New York, 1973, p. 35.

areas restricted by law or the Constitution, he exercises the preroga-tives of sovereignty, and the courts have been very reluctant to hinder him.[2] The Constitution endows him with only a few specific powers. He is authorized "to receive Ambassadors" and to name American envoys (with approval of the Senate), and from this authorization may be inferred general authority to conduct negotiations. He may negotiate on his own, although John F. Kennedy was the last presi-dent to do so extensively. He may make treaties, subject to senatorial ratification. Since the beginning of the republic, the president has also assumed that his power to negotiate included the power to make binding "executive agreements"; these have come to outnumber treaties by far and have dealt with important matters (such as Amer-ican bases in foreign lands) that imply a commitment in effect as strong as an alliance. The president is also chief of all the multitude of executive agencies that deal with foreign affairs, the focus and center, the only person who can claim to have the whole picture and all the information.

Most signally, the president is "Commander in Chief of the Army and Navy," and the command has long been taken to include author-ization to send troops into action. On scores of occasions since the infancy of the republic, American forces have gone shooting into foreign countries, mostly in Latin America. Franklin D. Roosevelt made war in the Atlantic on his own initiative, and Harry S. Truman in Korea and Lyndon B. Johnson in Vietnam took the position that they needed no congressional authorization (beyond the necessity of coming to Congress for funding) for large-scale combat. President Richard M. Nixon even carried on warfare secretly in Laos and Cam-bodia. The War Powers Act of 1973, passed over the presidential veto by a congress weary of Vietnam, required congressional approval for any commitment of American troops for longer than sixty days. But the gesture may have served to strengthen the president's hand by giving what he had not previously had—explicit authority to engage American forces for up to sixty days with no congressional sanction; in addition, congressional approval would almost certainly be easily obtained. In an emergency, or even a putative emergency, there is little to prevent the president's doing almost whatever he pleases, and he can probably place American forces in a situation where Congress

---

2. Louis Hankin, *Foreign Affairs and the Constitution*, Foundation Press, Mineola, N.Y., 1972, p. 273.

feels it has little choice but to support them. In May of 1975, President Gerald R. Ford claimed a constitutional power "to protect the lives and property of American citizens," although no words of the Constitution suggest such a power, and ordered attacks on Cambodian forces and territory to secure the recovery of the S. S. *Mayaguez* (and, incidentally, to punish the Cambodian communists).

The president is usually much more effective in foreign than in domestic affairs. In the former, no one can compete with his authority, and ordinarily his critics soften their attacks; to oppose him may mean giving aid and comfort to a foreign antagonist. Thus, in the past a large majority of presidential proposals in the foreign sphere have been passed by Congress, while a substantial majority of proposals for domestic legislation have been rejected.[3] Moreover, the president has even more latitude in the execution of the law in foreign than in domestic affairs. For example, he has recently been able to spend modest sums—a few tens of millions of dollars taken from unclearly defined appropriations—without the knowledge of Congress or contrary to its wishes, as for aid to anticommunists in Angola or for construction of a base on Diego Garcia in the Indian Ocean.

Being relatively unhampered in the conduct of foreign affairs, the active and self-assertive president—no one lacking these qualities is likely to become president—probably enjoys the exercise of his office as leader of the sovereign state. As R. S. Cline observed, "Our leaders like to take action because it is masterful and is usually applauded by the media and the public."[4] From Theodore Roosevelt (or at least Franklin Roosevelt) on, presidents have written their name large in history mostly by their actions on the world stage.[5] Franklin Roosevelt was the architect of victory, and Truman was immortalized by the Truman Doctrine and the policy of containment. Kennedy, who was especially interested in the Third World, fathered the Alliance for Progress and shone in the missile crisis, and Johnson hoped to be vindicated by success in Vietnam. Nixon, even more than Kennedy, regarded himself as an expert in foreign affairs and seems to have

3. As compiled for 1948–1965 by Aron Wildavsky, "The Two Presidencies," in *The Politics of U.S. Foreign Policy Making*, ed. Douglas M. Fox, Goodyear Publishing Co., Pacific Palisades, Calif., 1971, p. 176.

4. R. S. Cline, "Policy without Intelligence," *Foreign Policy*, 17 (Winter 1974–1975), 126.

5. John H. Esterline and Robert B. Black, *Inside Foreign Policy*, Mayfield Publishing Co., Palo Alto, Calif., 1975, p. ix; I. M. Destler, *Presidents, Bureaucrats, and Foreign Policy: The Politics of Organization Reform*, Princeton University Press, Princeton, 1972, p. 88.

hoped to build a new world order by high diplomacy. He harvested great political gains by summitry, especially with his dramatic trips to Peking and Moscow, although these trips were little more than symbolic. In the summer of Watergate, partisans of the accused president pointed to his talks with foreign heads of government as proof that he stood above petty affairs.

For such reasons, the president ordinarily devotes primary attention to foreign policy.[6] In crises or supposed crises, foreign troubles preempt presidential energies. From early 1965, the activities of the Johnson administration were concentrated on Vietnam. Kennedy in his first two months spent more time on Laos than on anything else.[7] The question of whether left-wingers should be permitted to enter the government of a small, primitive, economically insignificant country on the Chinese border took precedence over pressing problems of the organization of a new administration in the United States. The fascination is not, of course, with broad economic or social problems of the world, but with the power game and security (defense) issues. In 1961 Kennedy proceeded with the Bay of Pigs excursion, in part because it was glamorous and (he was assured) could be kept secret.[8] Most foreign policy managers, including top advisers of the president, have been preoccupied with the world as a chessboard, with power plays, maneuvers, and diplomatic tactics, in which they can see themselves as experts; grubby economic problems are for the specialists.[9]

In playing the power game, the president is not only the chief tactician but also the coach and boss of the team. He may formulate decisions or leave them to others; he chooses the players and chooses to hear them or not. All presidents have faced something of the same problems of wanting persons who are at once intensely loyal, highly competent, and frank in their opinions, but each has developed his own style and organizational patterns.[10] Franklin Roosevelt rather unsystematically leaned on different advisers at different times and

---

6. John Spanier and Eric M. Uslaner, *How Foreign Policy Is Made*, Praeger, New York, 1974, pp. 26–28.

7. Wildavsky, "Two Presidencies," p. 177.

8. Martin B. Travis, Jr., "John F. Kennedy: Experiments with Power," in *Powers of the President in Foreign Affairs*, eds. Edgar E. Robinson et al., Commonwealth Club of California, San Francisco, 1966, pp. 152–153.

9. Harold B. Malmgren, "Managing Foreign Economic Policy," *Foreign Policy*, 6 (Spring 1972), 56.

10. Discussed in *The Politics of U.S. Foreign Policy Making*, ed. Fox; Laurence I. Radway, *The Liberal Democracy in World Affairs: Foreign Policy and National Defense*, Scott, Foresman, Glenview, Ill. 1969, Chapter 3; Roger Hilsman, *The Politics of Policy Making in Defense and Foreign Affairs*, Harper and Row, New York, 1971.

for different purposes, while keeping the reins firmly in his own hands. Truman picked competent men, such as George Marshall and Dean Acheson, and gave them considerable leeway; at times he was accused of cronyism. As a good military man, Dwight D. Eisenhower tried to follow more systematic procedures, relying on his secretary of state and a committee system around the National Security Council. Kennedy, in more freewheeling fashion, went to various experts and encouraged subordinates to communicate their views directly to him. After the Bay of Pigs fiasco, he turned more to personal, nonprofessional advisers, including his attorney general and brother Robert Kennedy. He also built up the White House staff. In the Cuban missile crisis, as presidents commonly do in tense situations, he put together a special committee of trusted advisers.[11]

Becoming president by assassination, Johnson felt unsure of himself in foreign affairs and so leaned on the Kennedy team. In the Vietnam war, policy lines were largely laid out in consultation with the "Tuesday Lunch" group, including the secretaries of state and defense and the president's national security assistant; the group was kept small to preserve the secrecy that became a fetish of the administration. Johnson to a considerable extent predetermined the color of the advice given him on the war, to which he felt committed, by withdrawing confidence from those afflicted by doubts and placing next to himself such a firm believer as Walt W. Rostow.

Nixon wished to set up a well-designed mechanism for maximizing his authority. Instead of advice about courses to follow, he wanted to receive clear and concise statements of options available, among which he would choose. The options were drawn up by National Security Assistant (later Secretary of State) Henry Kissinger, one of the very few persons permitted ready access to the president. Nixon was the boss and was prepared to go contrary, for reasons he did not have to explain, to the views of his national security assistant and others, as he did in "tilting" toward Pakistan in the war of 1971 between India and Pakistan. But in practice great authority devolved on Kissinger as the person chiefly responsible for informing the president.[12] Subse-

---

11. On Kennedy foreign policy making, see Roger Hilsman, *To Move a Nation: The Politics of Foreign Policy in the Administration of John F. Kennedy*, Doubleday, Garden City, N.Y., 1967; also, Destler, *Presidents, Bureaucrats, and Foreign Policy*, Chapter 5.

12. For an analysis of Nixon-Kissinger policy making in terms of various models, see Wilfrid L. Kohl, "The Nixon-Kissinger Foreign Policy System and U.S.–European Relations: Patterns of Policy Making," *World Politics*, 28 (October 1975), 1–43.

quently, Nixon (preoccupied by Watergate matters, to be sure) delegated to Kissinger the handling of a Soviet threat of possible unilateral action in the Near Eastern war of October 1973. Kissinger called a rump meeting of the National Security Council and, with presidential approval, called a worldwide alert of strategic forces.[13] The Nixon-Kissinger style placed great emphasis on secrecy and maneuver, often to the neglect of broader consultation or at least forewarning of concerned allies, as in the dramatic opening to Peking and the measures taken to defend the dollar in August 1971. However, the tight lid over decision making enabled the White House to mislead friends, enemies, and the American public alike in the Vietnam peace negotiations.[14] It also harmonized with Nixon's intentions of letting the Soviet leadership think that the United States was capable of irrational or unpredictable action, as in the September 1970 Jordanian crisis.[15] Under the pressure of the Cambodian crisis in the spring of 1970, Nixon, like other presidents, abandoned orderly procedure and relied on rump meetings and irregular consultations.[16]

President Ford, as a homegrown politician with no claim to expertise in the ethereal realms of foreign affairs, at first surrendered foreign policy more completely to Secretary of State Henry Kissinger than had any previous president to his secretary of state. Gradually, however, he seemed to feel that he was missing a good thing. Kissinger was relieved of his post as national security assistant (November 1975) and was somewhat restricted in his entree to the Oval Office, while the president talked and acted more like the leader of the United States in foreign as well as domestic matters.

A recurrent question is how much the president trusts his legally constituted lieutenant for foreign affairs, the secretary of state. The secretary is a prestigious representative of the nation, its primary representative (after his boss) in foreign affairs, and chief of the department which is particularly supposed to study and execute foreign policy. Tradition and good practice seem to require that he be the president's right hand in foreign affairs.[17] However, activist presidents have tended to prefer their own staffers or irregular advisers, who are less in the public view and less subject to congressional scrutiny and

---

13. Cline, "Policy without Intelligence," pp. 127–129.
14. Tad Szulc, "How Kissinger Did It," *Foreign Policy*, 15 (Summer 1974), 24.
15. David Schoenbaum, "Or Lucky?," *Foreign Policy*, 10 (Spring 1973), 172.
16. Hedrick Smith, "Nixon's Decision to Invade Cambodia," in *The Politics of U.S. Foreign Policy Making*, ed. Fox, p. 345.
17. Destler, *Presidents, Bureaucrats, and Foreign Policy*, p. 2.

the need to spend hours before committees of Congress, and whom the president can set aside more readily than the senior member of his cabinet.[18] Franklin Roosevelt, having named Senator Cordell Hull as secretary of state for reasons of domestic politics, proceeded respectfully to ignore him, relying on Undersecretary Sumner Welles, his personal adviser Harry Hopkins, and others. Truman, in contrast, gave his trust to outstanding secretaries—James Byrnes, George Marshall, Dean Acheson. Eisenhower relied fully on John Foster Dulles,[19] only occasionally overruling him; for example, Eisenhower insisted that any rollback of Soviet power in eastern Europe had to be pacific.

Kennedy and Johnson had little confidence in the professionals of the State Department and accorded Secretary Dean Rusk only middling status, paying more attention to their confidential advisers in the White House. Under Nixon, the secretary of state (William Rogers) and his department reached their nadir of significance, since information and recommendations from various sources were channeled through the national security assistant to the president. Kissinger even built up a little State Department with a staff of 120 in the White House basement. He also became the chief negotiator in the extrication of the United States from Vietnam, in the turn toward détente with Russia and Communist China, and in the effort to find a settlement of the Arab-Israeli conflict, while the secretary sat humbly in the shadows. This incongruity was ended by giving Kissinger the secretary's title in September 1973.

The position of a mortal, sometimes rather ordinary, figure is thus formidably strong. The character of American foreign policy depends in the first instance upon what seems at times nearly a matter of chance: the character and predilections of the person elected to the "imperial presidency," [20] particularly his susceptibility or imperviousness to the itch to seek glory abroad. The desirability of such concentration of power has usually been accepted. Liberals generally favored a strong presidency from the time of Franklin Roosevelt's New Deal, seeing in it a potential for action for the national welfare, overriding

---

18. Dean Acheson, "The Eclipse of the State Department," *Foreign Affairs,* 49 (July 1971), 593–606; also Charles W. Yost, "The Instruments of American Foreign Policy," *Foreign Affairs,* 50 (October 1971), 59–68.

19. For secretaries of state through the Eisenhower administration, see *An Uncertain Tradition: American Secretaries of State in the Twentieth Century,* ed. Norman A. Graebner, McGraw-Hill, New York, 1961.

20. As Arthur Schlesinger put it, *The Imperial Presidency,* Houghton Mifflin, Boston, 1973, especially Chapter 9, "Democracy and Foreign Policy."

vested and particularistic interests such as those that find expression in Congress. In the cold war, the necessity for unhampered leadership was usually taken for granted. The advent of nuclear missiles, with a half-hour warning time before the cataclysm, further strengthened the idea that we must have a powerful chief at the ready in charge of the national defense. Many have continued to fear that the president might lack authority to act to defend the national interest.[21]

The Vietnam war, a sorry misadventure by executive fiat, aroused mistrust in most liberals, a majority of Congress, and the public; this response was heightened by dubious actions of the Nixon administration, such as the invasion of Cambodia and the Christmas bombing of North Vietnam just when peace was supposedly in prospect. Watergate and post-Watergate revelations of amorality and abuse of power by the White House, not only under Nixon but in previous administrations as well, affirmed the feeling that the presidency had more than its due share of power. There was growing fear of the isolation of the presidency, wherein someone like Nixon could be wrapped in a cocoon in the White House by a loyal staff protecting him from dissenting views.[22] Among courtiers there are no long-range analyses of problems and no policy debates, only a competition for favor. The Ford administration was ostensibly more open, but policy continued to be made in a very narrow circle. It might then be questioned whether the vision of bombs raining down or of communists seizing control somewhere really required the degree of authority vested in the president. Historians have yet to cite a clear instance in postwar history when American interests have suffered in the long term because of failure to act forcefully. On the contrary, there have been a host of unnecessary and damaging actions.

BUREAUCRACY OF FOREIGN POLICY

As a solitary person, the president can know much about only a very few of the multitude of questions coming up for decision. Where he takes a special interest, and especially in crisis diplomacy, he is decisive. However, he must judge largely on the basis of information and ideas that percolate up to him, and in a sense the providers of memo-

---

21. Spanier and Uslaner, *How American Foreign Policy Is Made*, p. 14.
22. Destler, *Presidents, Bureaucrats and Foreign Policy*, p. 86.

randa and reports, those who generate and filter the information, are the real deciders. Moreover, the president can attend closely to only a small fraction of the mass of responses that ultimately constitute foreign policy. It is the bureaucracy that develops most ideas and that shapes, or reshapes, decisions into effective policy.[23]

The principal agencies dealing with matters of foreign policy are the Departments of State and Defense, the United States Information Agency (USIA) (discussed in Chapter Four), the Central Intelligence Agency (CIA), and the Agency for International Development (AID). Many others, however, have important roles. The Atomic Energy Commission is concerned with nuclear questions; the Department of Commerce promotes trade; the Department of the Treasury worries about the balance of payments; the Department of Agriculture wants markets for farmers; the Bureau of the Budget looks at the cost of international operations; and a host of other agencies clamor for a hearing on matters within their purview. There are, in addition, a legion of coordinating interdepartmental groups and committees, mostly very little publicized.

The Department of State remains primary, however, despite neglect, because it is in charge of most direct relations with foreign governments. It has an apparatus of political officers, from ambassadors on down, stationed abroad to report and communicate, and it receives a thousand or so cables daily and sends back about as many instructions. It has a highly selected, knowledgeable, and well-trained staff both in Washington and overseas. Yet the State Department has had little to do with major foreign policy formation for many years, except insofar as its head personally enjoys the respect of the president. In this case, the secretary of state is likely not to pay much attention to the department under him—John Foster Dulles, for example, did not. Kissinger's assumption of the post of secretary raised the department's morale, but he was more over the department than of it. Carrying on diplomacy as artistry, a contest of powers and personalities, he managed primarily with a small group of intimates who had served him when he was national security assistant, largely shutting out the professionals and specialists and on occasion ignoring their opinions, as he did, for example, with regard to the Angolan civil war in 1975–1976. It may be too much, in any case, to expect

---

23. Cf. Graham T. Allison, *Essence of Decision: Explaining the Cuban Missile Crisis,* Little, Brown, Boston, 1971, for complexities of decision making and the bureaucratic model.

any one person both to head the department and to advise the president.

There are several reasons that the State Department is not called upon more often to help set directions. One is that most presidents since Franklin Roosevelt have tended to think poorly of it as a conservative, inert bureaucracy filled with men in striped pants and cookie pushers. Perhaps more important, the department officials have permanent tenure and are not the president's own people; they serve a sequence of presidents and can be as independent-minded as they please, with no penalty except possibly delayed promotions. The first loyalty of officials is probably to the immediate superior rather than to the distant chief of state. The president cannot, moreover, prevent their letting congressmen or journalists know about policies of which they disapprove.

The State Department is also politically weak. It has a smallish force of some 12,000, divided about equally between Washington and abroad. It lacks any particular constituency, fails to appeal to the public, seems to be (as in many cases it must in effect be) the representative for foreigners, and is critically regarded by Congress.[24] Morale has usually been low since the department was kicked around by the anticommunist demagoguery of the 1950s.

The department is also less than a model of efficiency. It is bound by tradition and probably the most hierarchic of government departments; typically, status is measured by the number of the floor on which offices are located.[25] The least action requires perhaps dozens of signatures, as papers pass through a complex setup whereby officials make work for one another with labyrinthine procedures to assure thorough review if not ponderous triviality.[26] It is an encrusted, some-

---

24. William N. Turpin, "Foreign Relations, Yes; Foreign Policy, No," *Foreign Policy*, 8 (Fall 1972), 53; Charles W. Yost, *The Conduct and Misconduct of Foreign Affairs*, Random House, New York, 1972, p. 154.

25. David H. Davis, *How the Bureaucracy Makes Foreign Policy*, D. C. Heath, Lexington, Mass., 1972, p. 139; John H. Esterline and Robert B. Black, *Inside Foreign Policy: The Department of State Political System and Its Subsystems*, Mayfield Publishing Co., Palo Alto, Calif. p. 40.

26. For organization of the State Department and other foreign policy agencies, with proposals for reform, see Richard A. Johnson, *The Administration of United States Foreign Policy*, University of Texas Press, Austin, 1971; also, Smith Simpson, *Anatomy of the State Department*, Houghton Mifflin, Boston, 1967; Charles Frankel, *High on Foggy Bottom*, Harper and Row, New York, 1969; John F. Campbell, *The Foreign Affairs Fudge Factory*, Basic Books, New York, 1971; William I. Bacchus, *Foreign Policy and the Bureaucratic Process*, Princeton University Press, Princeton, 1974.

what calcified bureaucracy which neither the secretary nor the president can take in hand and reshuffle; schemes for reform are perennially brought forward but seldom applied, and they never work. There are many incentives to avoid responsibility, write innocuous memos, and play the rules of the bureaucratic game. The department is organized both on an old-line political basis (with geographic bureaus and country desks handling relations with particular states) and also with functional bureaus (including those dealing with more modern concerns, such as science, culture, economic problems, environment, and international organization). Prestige and authority still rest mostly, of course, with the political divisions.[27]

It is an incredible piece of irresponsibility, a leftover from simpler days, that ambassadors, especially to the desirable posts, are still named for political considerations; career men go to Gambia and Nicaragua, whereas big campaign contributors (at least until very recently) went to major European capitals; it must be recognized that presidents have also tapped outstanding scholars, such as Edwin Reischauer, John Kenneth Galbraith, and Daniel Moynihan. Envoys sometimes make policy, as did the ambassador to the Dominican Republic who in April 1965 reported to Johnson that it was necessary to rush the marines in to save the situation and the ambassador to South Vietnam who in 1975 sought to shore up the Thieu government in its dying agonies.[28] For the most part, however, the ambassador's position is decorative and administrative. The traditional conduct of diplomacy is worn out, but there is no new concept or pattern to replace it.[29]

It is typical of the difficulties of the State Department that, of the army of employees that the ambassador nominally commands—five hundred to one thousand in principal countries—a small minority, probably about one-seventh, are State Department personnel. The bulk owe loyalty to sundry agencies, including not only the obvious, such as the CIA and the Commerce Department, but also the Departments of Health, Education, and Welfare, Interior, and so on. The largest number are of the military. The Department of Defense over-

---

27. Lincoln P. Bloomfield and Iriangi C. Bloomfield, *The U.S., Interdependence, and World Order,* Foreign Policy Association (Headline Series), New York, 1975, p. 4.

28. For the experience of an ambassador in combat with the bureaucracy, see John W. Tuthill, "Operation Topsy," *Foreign Policy,* 8 (Fall 1972), 62–85.

29. William I. Bacchus, *Foreign Policy and the Bureaucratic Process,* p. 301.

shadows the Department of State abroad and at home. The budget and staff of the former are hundreds of times larger, and it carries comparably more political weight. It has for more sources of information than the State Department; it is typical that in 1973 the navy spent nearly a hundred times as much for intelligence as did the State Department.[30] Congress is as favorable to the military as it is unfavorable to the State Department, partly because of the power which the Pentagon represents, and partly no doubt because simple strength appeals more to many congressmen than subtler aspects of dealing with the world. Presidents from Franklin Roosevelt on have also found military men to be congenial advisers on political as well as military matters and frequently preferred them to civilians during the cold war and the Vietnam war.

The military influence on American foreign policy has been obvious, and many persons in the United States, Europe, and the Third World have seen the United States as a military-dominated society. The cold war certainly made the military a regular part of policy making, with the joint chiefs of staff legally designated as advisers to the president and the National Security Council acting as a forum for military views. Brass hats often outnumbered fedoras around the White House. At that time naval officers were continually perceiving a dire menace from the Soviet fleet, and strategic commanders were pointing to the strength of Soviet rocket forces and their dangerous expansion, especially when budgets were under consideration.[31]

Yet reality is complicated. The American tradition of distrust of the professional military survives in an essentially civilian-oriented society with no militaristic class or caste.[32] When wars were engaged in in Korea and Vietnam, American military men complained bitterly

---

30. Harry Howe Ransom, "Congress and the Intelligence Agencies," in *Congress against the President*, ed. Harvey C. Mansfield, Academy of Political Science, New York, 1975, p. 158.

31. On the military influence see Charles W. Ackley, *The Modern Military in American Society: A Study in the Nature of Military Power*, Westminster Press, Philadelphia, 1972; Stephen E. Ambrose, "The Military Impact on Foreign Policy," in *The Military and American Society*, ed. Stephen E. Ambrose and James A. Barber, Free Press, New York, 1972; David Owen, *The Politics of Defense*, Taplinger Publishing Co., New York, 1972; Adam Yarmolinsky, *The Military Establishment: Its Impact on American Society*, Harper and Row, New York, 1971; Morton L. Halperin, "The President and the Military," *Foreign Affairs*, 50 (January 1972), 310–324.

32. Donald F. Bletz, *The Role of the Military Professional in U.S. Foreign Policy*, Praeger, New York, 1972, Chapter 1.

that they were not allowed to achieve their objectives—the insistence of General Douglas MacArthur on voicing his disagreement was the chief recent exception to the ordinarily complete acceptance by the military of civilian rule. Interventions in Korea, Lebanon, the Dominican Republic, and Vietnam were the responsibility of the civilian leadership. Pessimistic estimates of costs, on the contrary, contributed to decisions not to intervene in Vietnam in 1954 and Laos in 1961. Military men likewise seem to have recoiled in 1975 from the idea of possible action in the Near East to secure oil supplies.[33] The generals often counsel restraint because they are aware of the military requirements engendered by particular policies,[34] and military measures may have resulted less from the officers pushing their views than from civilians seeking military answers to political problems. The military lobby loses effectiveness also because of differences among the branches of the service and between senior officers and civilian heads. Oddly, in 1966 and 1967, Secretary of Defense Robert McNamara advocated a negotiated settlement while Secretary of State Dean Rusk stood for a stern military approach.

Yet the generals' influence in foreign policy decision making is much greater than might seem logically justified when military power is at best a residual and negative means of action. Officers of high rank can freely lobby their viewpoints, mostly for defense spending, with the Congress, which is disposed to accept their professional verdict.[35] There may be some self-reinforcing drive in the piling up of weaponry and the appropriate foreign policies to accompany it.[36] Organizational rivalries and bureaucratic politics within the Defense Department help propel programs.[37] In the country at large, taxpayers' money is spent, in indeterminable sums, to influence taxpayers to spend more money on defense, while defense contractors can charge to the taxpayers the costs of entertaining bigwigs. It seemingly remains true, moreover, that the military mind inclines to conservatism and a simplistic approach to political problems. Those whose life and career are concerned with the use of force seem more ready to assume

33. *The New York Times,* January 10, 1975, p. 3.

34. Esterline and Black, *Inside Foreign Policy,* pp. 29–31.

35. On pressures for defense spending, see Les Aspin, "Games the Pentagon Plays," *Foreign Policy,* 11 (Summer 1973), 80–92.

36. Cf. Sam C. Sarkesian, *The Military-Industrial Complex, a Reassessment,* Sage Publications, Beverly Hills, Calif., 1972.

37. Morton H. Halperin, *Bureaucratic Politics and Foreign Policy,* Brookings Institution, Washington, 1974, Chapter 3.

that foreign policy problems are basically of a military nature—the securing of adequate strength, measured largely in firepower—and are to be solved by augmenting and, so far as necessary, applying force.

The CIA, because of its penchant for operations along with information gathering, is closely allied with the military—almost nine-tenths of the intelligence dollar is spent by the armed forces—and akin to it in spirit. The foreign policy role of the CIA is potentially very large, as it winnows from the mountains of incoming data a few facts to enlighten the president and other high officials.[38] To some extent, the CIA may be an invisible government, as outlined in Chapter Two, dangerous because of its irresponsibility and truculent mentality. Its importance and prestige have suffered from the fading of the cold war, the decline of world fever, and many damaging exposés; the apparent inability of the Congress really to restrict it, however, evidences the limits of rationality in American foreign policy.

The political and military agencies of foreign policy meet in the National Security Council, whose chief is the national security assistant. This body was set up in the reordering of the foreign policy apparatus at the beginning of the cold war to advise the president on security questions. It was and is basically a cabinet committee to coordinate the ideas and planning of the military with the State Department, the CIA, and other agencies and groups concerned with the entangled military and political issues of a trying world. However, the National Security Council never seems to have fulfilled expectations, as presidents have consulted it irregularly if at all. It has added to the weight of the military, and it may have been an additional complicating wheel in the machinery.[39] Its staff, however, has grown continually, rising to its zenith under Nixon[40] and declining after Kissinger was appointed secretary of state. On its margins are a welter of secret committees, including the 40 Committee (to pass on subversive actions), the Defense Program Review Committee, the Special Action Group (for crises), the Senior Review Group, and the Intelligence Committee (to set guidelines).

In the absence of broad understanding within the government, there is virtually no means of effectively coordinating the multitude

---

38. Chester L. Cooper, "The CIA and Decision Making," *Foreign Affairs*, 50 (January 1972), 223–236; see also references in Chapter Two.

39. Yost, *The Conduct and Misconduct of Foreign Affairs*, p. 143.

40. Cf. John P. Leacacos, "Kissinger's Apparat," *Foreign Policy*, 5 (Winter 1971–1972), 3–24.

of agencies influencing foreign policy, short of presidential action. Each agency sees itself as fulfilling an important aspect of the national interest and thinks in its own terms with its own priorities; as a rule each favors courses that give it a greater role. Each clamors to be consulted on anything conceivably in its sphere or affecting its interests. Each tries to justify its own budget by emphasizing its role, possibly as much concerned to vindicate its authority as to achieve the goals of the republic. Each views from a different perspective. For example, in the 1962 controversy over the Skybolt missile—a proposed medium-range rocket for launching nuclear warheads from bombers—the air force wanted to maintain a rationale for manned bombers; the defense comptroller saw the missile as a budget problem; for Secretary of Defense McNamara, it was a demonstration of the correctness of his cost-effectiveness approach; and the State Department looked upon the Skybolt as a means of satisfying certain defense needs of the British. The secretary of state was worried that cancellation might be a shock to relations with Britain. The president was concerned with these considerations plus the need to keep the budget within bounds. In the end, the British were offered Polaris weapons instead.[41]

There are many distortions in the process of governmental decision making, as in large organizations everywhere. Information must pass a dozen hurdles to reach the president; it is shaped on its upward route to fit the prejudices and wishes of the higher-ups, and these people listen to those whose thinking is close to their own. There is a bargaining relation between superior and subordinate from which truth seldom emerges unbruised. It is safest to be conventional; it profits more to be wrong with the authorities than to be right against them; to be noncommittal means never to be proved in error. After the Bay of Pigs affair, Chester Bowles was fired for his tactlessness in having been right in his opposition to it.[42] "Agreed recommendations" mean compromises and generalities based on mutually reinforced self-confidence protected by psychological walls against discomfiting information, pressure against deviations, and the self-censorship of doubters. Foreign affairs are at best unbearably complicated, too

---

41. Morton H. Halperin, "Why Bureaucrats Play Games," *Foreign Policy*, 2 (Spring 1971), 71. Cf. also Morton H. Halperin, "The Decision to Deploy the ABM: Bureaucratic and Domestic Politics in the Johnson Administration," *World Politics*, 25 (October 1972), 62–95.

42. Irving L. Janis, *Victims of Groupthink*, Houghton Mifflin, Boston, 1972, p. 45.

complicated for the policy makers to take all facets into account; one simplifies at the risk of misrepresentation.[43]

If the permanent bureaucracy is inefficient, it acts as a restraint on the foreign policy of its boss. Unable to control the president's decisions, it can make it easy for him to go in one direction, hard to go in another.[44] If a bureaucracy does not like a decision, it probably appeals for reconsideration or postpones implementation; for example, military authorities simply sat on President Kennedy's order to remove Jupiter missiles from Turkey.[45] The agencies jealously guard the partial independence that permits them to resist or possibly even sabotage policies; as much as they desire large budgets, autonomy is even more precious.[46] Those who disagree with a particular course of action may follow it like good soldiers, but in the American milieu of self-assertiveness, some, fortified by their expertise and sense of right, are likely to try to do something. They may, if deeply aroused, resign ostentatiously, making a public statement of their dissent; more likely, they will talk to sympathetic congressmen or leak damaging stories to the press, giving an impression of disarray damaging to the administration. The president can hardly afford to let it be known that he goes against the advice of the experts and professionals. Thus, beginning in 1967 unhappy officials were undercutting the Vietnam war, and Kissinger once said that to prevent disclosures bureaucrats must be kept ignorant of policies that they were supposed to execute.[47]

CONGRESS: THE BALANCE WHEEL

The American government is unique among major powers, in that the legislative branch, which may well be controlled by a party other than the president's and which is never subject to close party discipline, participates directly and indirectly in the conduct of foreign

43. For a survey of types of irrationality entering the advice given the president, see Alexander M. George, "The Case of Multiple Advocacy in Making Foreign Policy," *American Political Science Review,* 66 (September 1972), 751–785; Janis, *Victims of Groupthink,* gives a detailed analysis of the triumph of concurrence over objectivity.

44. Stephen D. Krasner, "Are Bureaucracies Important?," *Foreign Policy,* 7 (Summer 1972), 159–179.

45. Destler, *Presidents, Bureaucrats, and Foreign Policy,* p. 3.

46. Halperin, "Why Bureaucrats Play Games," pp. 75–76.

47. Cline, "Policy without Intelligence," p. 123.

relations. In the 1970s the Congress has come to exercise this role as never before in American history. One reason has been the lesson of Vietnam and the feeling that we would have been better served if the president had been less free to act and if the Congress had investigated and criticized presidential policy earlier and more vigorously. In addition, the Congress happened to be Democratic while the president was Republican; it is perhaps remarkable that the congressional majority did not snipe more truculently at the president. Less familiar is the fact that congressmen provided themselves with larger staffs and more means of information gathering and so were less dependent on what the administration was pleased to divulge.

The Congress participates directly in foreign policy to a greater extent than is commonly realized. Senators and representatives travel widely and present their views to foreign statesmen, chatting as individuals and as delegates with presidents and dictators around the world. Legislators, in Congress and out, let their views be known on almost anything that the president may undertake, and foreign governments watch Congress carefully for indications of United States attitudes.[48] Foreign dignitaries visit congressional leaders and groups and often hear them express ideas different from those of the executive. From time to time leaders are invited to address the Congress; many, from Soviet leader Brezhnev to Israeli Prime Minister Itzak Rabin, have lobbied with Congress for their views. In 1975 King Hussein of Jordan wrote personally to one hundred senators and fifty congressmen about the purchase of antiaircraft missiles.

The major impact of Congress on foreign affairs, however, derives from constitutional powers that are greater and more numerous than those given to the president, reflecting the strong desire of the framers of the Constitution to check executive power in this area. Congressional powers broadly overlap the powers of the president. The conduct of foreign policy is hence always a potential battleground on which at any time it may be contended that the Congress is infringing on the legitimate authority of the president or, more usually, that it is failing to exercise its constitutional mandate and is abandoning the field to the executive.

In theory, the Congress might reduce the president to a puppet in foreign affairs if it were united and purposeful. It can decree just

---

48. Alton Frye, "Congress: The Virtues of Its Vices," *Foreign Policy*, 3 (Summer 1971), 115–116.

what funds are to be spent for what purposes, and it can mandate the organization and procedures of the Executive branch. The Congress can control foreign commerce and the movement of persons across international borders. The Senate can ratify treaties and confirm appointments or decline to do so. The declaration of war is up to the Congress, which also can "make rules for the government of the land and naval forces," a proviso that could potentially negate presidential command; it was evidently intended for Congress to have broad powers over the military.

In practice, however, the Congress is neither united nor purposeful and is usually satisfied to let the president manage. Senatorial advice and consent has left the president free not only to negotiate quite on his own but also to enter into executive agreements if these are more convenient than the formality of a treaty. The Congress has largely abdicated to the president its power to control foreign commerce by the Trade Agreements Act of 1934 and its successors. Even the power of the purse, the most jealously guarded of congressional prerogatives, is slackly used. Congress seldom (as noted in Chapter Two) tries seriously to cut the defense budget or to deny the executive the monies demanded even for secret operations; until 1969 the Congress was fearful of grappling seriously with these decisions lest it appear "soft on communism." For a long time the chief concern of the Senate Armed Forces Committee was which states were to get bases.[49] As for the war power, Congress has invariably backed the president in emergencies. Even those members who disapproved of the Vietnam war were very reluctant to pull the rug out by withholding funds. For many years Congress (and a large share of the public) has disliked foreign aid, but it has regularly voted several billion dollars yearly at the behest of the executive.

The effective powers of Congress are at best negative and restraining. It can rarely frame alternative policies.[50] Because of numbers, cumbersome procedures, a structure based on committees and seniority, sectionalism, and interest representation, Congress may be unable to act effectively even when there is a majority will. The executive still has a battery of experts whom congressional committees seldom try to challenge. Unable to check details, the Congress can

49. Wildavsky, "Two Presidencies," p. 180.

50. On congressional limits, see Barber B. Conable, "Our Limits Are Real," *Foreign Policy*, 11 (Summer 1973), 73–79.

hardly do more than push in broad directions reflecting public opinion.

The Congress does like to be consulted about major moves, but the executive, wishing to make decisions with minimal interference, has rarely consulted. The chief exception of the postwar period was in the drawing up of the United Nations charter; congressional leaders were brought into the negotiations, and thus acceptance and ratification were smoothed. A president may work with a few members of Congress whom he finds congenial, as Johnson did with Senator Richard Russell and Nixon at one time did with Senator Henry Jackson. But the executive ordinarily desires to consult only to the extent of informing congressional leaders after decisions have been made (frequently after actions have been taken) and wants least to bring Congress into the sensitive matters where its scrutiny might be embarrassing.[51] Johnson explained ex post facto to congressional leaders his reasons for intervention in the Dominican Republic, assuring them that at least two communist agents had been found in the rebel leadership.[52] President Nixon did not see fit to bring congressional leaders into discussions of any of his crises but kept policy formation even more secretive than did previous administrations.

The willingness and ability of Congress to assert itself regarding foreign policy has, of course, varied widely. It may be a broad rule that when there is a general consensus, the Congress gives the president free rein. When the consensus breaks down, the Congress presses its views. From the rejection of the Treaty of Versailles in 1919 through the passage of the Neutrality Acts of the mid-1930s, the Congress was self-assertive. In World War II, it turned around to give its full support and remained generally amenable to executive initiatives (despite some acrid debates as cold war policies were being fixed) until the country was divided by Vietnam. It seems likely to continue questioning and limiting executive action until there arises a new basis of unity.

Congress can also influence foreign policy broadly and indirectly through its informational role. It can make its feelings known through resolutions that have no legal effect but that declare American positions to the world. The floor of Congress provides a forum almost as

---

51. Francis O. Wilcox, *Congress, the Executive, and Foreign Policy*, Harper and Row, New York, 1971, pp. 41–42.

52. Rowland Evans and Robert Novak, *Lyndon B. Johnson: The Exercise of Power*, New American Library, New York, 1966, p. 517.

good as the White House from which to make pronouncements that may resonate through the country and give expression to refreshingly varied views. Statements in Congress have been educational regarding a host of issues, such as détente, multinational corporations, and racial oppression in South Africa. In a different vein, congressional sniping undercut the position of Secretary of State Acheson and has been damaging to Secretary Kissinger, who has received much less general approbation in Congress than in the country at large.

Congress not only reflects public opinion but helps greatly to inform it. The Congress can investigate and publicize practically anything, as its committees, aided by competent staffs, seek background for legislative action or simply illuminate national policy. For several years, hearings held by the Senate Foreign Relations Committee under its chairman, J. William Fulbright, laid out facts and opinions regarding the Vietnam war. Congressional hearings provide platforms from which private persons may present their views with nationwide press coverage. The president is not required to inform Congress about either negotiations or deliberations within the government, and he may invoke executive privilege to prevent officials from testifying or to withhold documents, as Nixon frequently did. But refusal to answer indicates that there is something to hide, and the Congress has sought, perhaps imprudently, to question subordinates regarding the advice they gave to their superiors. Congress can go far if it desires. If officials hold back information, even at orders of the president, it can theoretically coerce by the threat of contempt citation and possible imprisonment. The secretary of state and his aides spend a great deal of time testifying and even more preparing for hearings, an exercise possibly beneficial to character. Dean Rusk claimed that he spent half his time justifying foreign policy to the country (mostly, that is, to Congress).[53]

Inquiries may be general (into the broad purposes and execution of foreign policy) or specific (into details of diplomacy around, say, the Cyprus question). Formerly the Congress—or its responsible committees—was very loath to look into the CIA, but since Vietnam and Watergate Congress has brought out and washed publicly much of the dirty linen of this organization, an airing of the sanctum sanctorum of official secrecy unexampled in political annals. Much more information doubtless comes out because of awareness that it may

---

53. Wilcox, *Congress, the Executive, and Foreign Policy,* pp. 66–67.

otherwise be brought out by congressional interrogators. The CIA is far more open about itself than any foreign counterpart.[54] Congress is the potent enemy of executive secrecy; even if documents and testimony are not frankly published, they are probably leaked to the press.

Whether observers approve or disapprove of congressional interference in foreign policy commonly depends on their disapproval or approval of presidential policies. In the course of the Vietnam war, liberal opinion looked to Congress for salvation, but a leading critic, Senator Fulbright, had earlier wished that the president were less hampered by a "decentralized, independent-minded, and largely parochial-minded body of legislators." [55] In the past the Congress has frequently shown itself to be more nationalistic (in a sense) than the executive, more parochial, less disposed to support international endeavors, less generous to poorer countries, and more representative of special interests. Antiforeignism in Congressional attitudes carries over to distrust of diplomacy and negativism toward the State Department and the USIA. In the cold war, Congress was less willing to distinguish shades of communism and more determined to close the doors against Communist China, although voices in Congress spoke for an opening to that country years before the executive moved. The position was not consistent; in 1961 Congress was hostile to allowing communists to participate in the Laotian coalition government but strongly opposed to sending American troops to Laos.[56]

Congress has sought special protection for many interests. For example, it long held up tariff preferences for the less developed countries. Both houses have vehemently protested in advance any concessions regarding United States sovereignty over the Panama Canal Zone, despite the executive conviction that concessions are indispensable. Prior to 1968, the usual congressional action on the defense budget was to restore cuts made by the president in requests by the armed services. Some actions seem inexplicably narrow, such as the long-time refusal of the Senate to ratify a harmless United Nations convention against genocide. Some congressional forays into diplomacy may have been ill advised, such as the Jackson Amendment, placing conditions on Most-Favored-Nation status for communist countries

---

54. C. L. Sulzberger, in *The New York Times*, May 10, 1975, p. 29.

55. Quoted by Barry M. Goldwater, "Additional Views," *Foreign Policy*, 8 (Fall 1972), 33.

56. Halperin, *Bureaucratic Politics*, p. 69.

in regard to freedom of emigration, The Congress is hardly wiser than the people at large; it, too, cheered the president's violation of the War Powers Act in the *Mayaguez* incident.

The Congress, however, has earned the approval of liberal intellectuals in the 1970s[57] for its part in halting the Vietnam war, for its investigations into subversive activities, and for its hostility to new foreign adventures. These actions are only an extreme manifestation of a tendency as old as American history. The Congress through the nineteenth century was, as has been mentioned, almost invariably less willing than the executive to annex new territories. Exceptionally, it was Congress that pushed the president to war in 1898. Yet the Congress precluded the annexation of Cuba by the Teller Amendment, which was passed just before the declaration of war. It was the executive that decided on the acquisition of the Philippines. The Congress has otherwise, and particularly since World War I, almost always been more cautious than the executive. In the 1930s it tried to legislate noninvolvement; it had to be pulled into World War II by Franklin Roosevelt and the Japanese. It rapidly lost enthusiasm for the Korean War. Congressional doubts kept the United States from entering the Vietnam war in 1954 to save the French position. The congressional role in ending the Vietnam war is familiar, and fear of congressional reaction doubtless inhibits thoughts of new interventions.

Congressional insistence on applying to Turkey the law prohibiting the use of United States–furnished arms except for defensive purposes caused horror in the administration because of the threat to useful bases, but it was conceivably salutary to give meaning to the law. Rather remarkably, Congress has become a champion of human rights, decrying official indifference to violations in many dictatorial countries.[58] Most important, the ordeal of investigation has dampened the capers of the CIA. In 1975, the Senate displayed considerable irritation that the administration had stepped covertly into the Angolan civil war without consultation and confined Secretary of State Kissinger to diplomacy and the denunciation of the Cubans for sending in their forces, letting others be the interventionists. Although Congress seems at times to be a bumbling impediment to action, this hazard is much less significant than the fact that Congress can act at least as a potential check on abuse of power.

---

57. As maintained by Frye, "Congress: The Virtues of Its Vices," 108–125.
58. *The New York Times,* March 28, 1974, p. 17.

It is not necessary that Congress impede positive foreign programs. Something of a bipartisan tradition in foreign policy has existed since the days when President Truman worked closely with Congress in the establishment of the United Nations and the beginnings of the policy of containment and was rewarded by its cooperation.[59] Positions are seldom taken in Congress for purely partisan reasons; the electorate is not much concerned with the voting record in foreign affairs in any case.[60] In no instance since World War II has Congress divided along strictly partisan lines over a foreign policy issue.[61] Congress, dependent on the executive for information, loath to risk national security, and unable itself to act, is usually quite ready to give the president the benefit of the doubt. The president may have to present the case in detail, and Congress may ask questions, but if the case is a good one Congress will probably accede. Thus it demanded all the facts relating to the 1975 accord for an American presence in the Sinai; having heard the testimony, it concurred, and the agreement was thereby affirmed.

Occasionally, the Congress originates ideas that do not seem to have occurred to the experts of the executive branch. These ideas include the exchange-of-persons program, the use of agricultural surpluses in foreign aid, and the Arms Control and Disarmament Agency.[62] It has shown good will, effective or not, by regularly favoring disarmament initiatives. The Senate took the initiative for the most useful arms control agreement of the postwar period, the ban on nuclear testing in the atmosphere in 1963, when outlawing underground testing proved difficult.[63]

The Congress contributes, too, by putting forward another aspect of America from that presented by the administration. It is convenient for negotiators to be able to promise freely, but it is actually advantageous that congressional approval may be needed for agreements.[64] Congressional expression makes positions more understandable, explaining and rationalizing American policies or objectives to negotiations here and abroad. Congress, with all its shortcomings, is a unique asset in the conduct of foreign policy.

---

59. Halperin, *Bureaucratic Politics*, pp. 63–64.
60. Spanier and Uslaner, *How American Foreign Policy Is Made*, p. 79.
61. Wilcox, *Congress, the Executive, and Foreign Policy*, pp. 14–15, 99.
62. Ibid., p. 14.
63. Frye, "Congress: The Virtues of Its Vices," pp. 112–113.
64. Ibid., p. 110.

INTEREST GROUPS

Congress is supposed to represent the people, and the executive branch is responsible ultimately to them; however, "the people" consist of a multitude of groups with their own interests and outlooks. They cannot be easily defined. They are usually thought of as pressing Congress because this body is more subject to electoral concerns, but they also work through executive agencies. Farmers' organizations, for example, seek favorable treatment in foreign as well as domestic matters through the Department of Agriculture. The executive agencies are usually understood as acting officially, but in practice they are among the most important pressure groups seeking to influence Congress. For example, the military services establish liaison with Congress and lobby extensively (without having to register) for their particular branch of the service or projects.

Interest groups are not usually consulted but have to project themselves. Probably a majority are economic, led by such organizations as the National Association of Manufacturers and labor's AFL-CIO (American Federation of Labor–Congress of Industrial Organizations). Shipping interests, Canal Zone employees, and others joined to oppose relinquishment of rights in the Panama Canal Zone.[65] The farmers have acquired a strong new interest in foreign policy because of big sales abroad; they are effective enough that it is politically difficult to entertain an embargo on grain sales to the Soviet Union. The longshoremen, on the contrary, decided that grain should not be exported to the Soviet Union and in August 1975 held up shipments for a few weeks. The so-called military-industrial complex no doubt makes it at least a little harder to cut military budgets. Military contractors lobby, entertain, and hire hundreds of retired high officers, perhaps as much for their connections as for their expertise. They are joined by nationalistic veterans' organizations.

The business interests most attentive to foreign policy are the multinational corporations. Their influence usually does not appear to be overwhelming; a big corporation is probably less potent in Congress than the union of its workers, and dairy farmers can exert more pressure than can banks.[66] The multinational corporations can hardly swing the government to the defense of their foreign interests unless

---

65. Thomas M. Franck and Edward Weisband, "Panama Paralysis," *Foreign Policy*, 21 (Winter 1975–1976), 174.

66. Malmgren, "Managing Foreign Economic Policy," p. 44.

the economic motive is supported by a political one, and there is no big program of economic imperialism (if only for the reason that the American government is too disorganized to carry one out). Lacking any broad economic policy, the government only carries on a sort of bargaining between miscellaneous and often conflicting domestic interests and foreign interests.[67]

Very different are ethnic groups, which are among the most influential on foreign policy.[68] For many years, Irish-Americans promoted anti-British measures. Polish-Americans and others of east European origin kept up anticommunist feelings during the cold war. In deference to people of Baltic background, the United States still declines to recognize the annexation of the Baltic states in 1940 by the Soviet Union. The Jewish community has been an effective determinant in United States support for Israel since the Jewish sector is large, influential, committed, and organized. There are other potentialities; for example, Americans of African descent, the most numerous of the minorities in the United States, might virtually dictate policy toward Africa. They have not done so for lack of organization and political purpose.[69]

There are also a great many institutes or societies for the study of foreign policy and defense questions that furnish intellectual input for foreign policy through governmental agencies and through the formation of informed public opinion. For example, the RAND Corporation and the Hudson Institute, military-civilian organizations, mostly provide expertise to the armed forces on contract, making carefully researched and relatively objective studies without the constraints of the bureaucracy. There are numerous foundations and policy-study institutes at major universities, with which the State Department tries to keep in touch. Such organizations as the Brookings Institution and the Overseas Development Council sponsor and publish a great number of more or less learned studies on international issues, contributing to the world of ideas in which the government operates. Not least, the Foreign Policy Association seems influential, mostly through contacts with decision makers and through its publications. Still more influential is the Council on Foreign Relations, an

---

67. Ibid., p. 56.
68. Spanier and Uslaner, *How American Foreign Policy Is Made*, p. 87.
69. Martin Weil, "Can the Blacks Do for Africa What the Jews Did for Israel?," *Foreign Policy*, 15 (Summer 1974), 109–125.

exclusive society of a few hundred members, which publishes the respected journal *Foreign Affairs.*

The Council on Foreign Relations is of special interest because it is sometimes viewed as nearly synonymous with the foreign policy establishment and so is credited with enormous, perhaps sinister influence. Whether there really exists a foreign policy establishment is a matter of taste and definition, but it seems clear that there is or has been an elite of very influential persons with the best business, legal, academic, and governmental connections, who were again and again called upon to give foreign policy directions.[70] So far as there was an elite, it consisted of a loose set of gifted and successful men (mostly from the Boston–New York–Washington area, many of Ivy League background) who were drawn together by a sense of the American mission in the cold war. A focus of their tenuous unity was the Council on Foreign Relations. Of both political parties, they were united only in a foreign policy of democratic capitalism and the desire to see America succeed Britain as the military and economic guarantor of an enlightened world order. Leading and typical members included Dean Acheson, John J. McCloy, Dean Rusk, McGeorge Bundy, George Ball, and Adlai Stevenson. They and a few dozen others who more or less knew one another agreed on the need for active intervention where necessary to uphold the "free world" and particularly to keep South Vietnam anticommunist, as they advised the Johnson administration.

The establishment, so far as it was a reality, was broken on the rock of Vietnam. Its leaders turned away from the war and in March 1968 counseled against escalation. Few of its figures went into or stayed in the Nixon White House; Kissinger, although a Harvard academic by origin, declined establishment advice. Its members or former members fell into disagreement over the extent of their rejection of Vietnam, and they and the younger men who might have replenished its ranks became divided over détente, the size of the military budget, United States responsibilities in the Third World, and many other complex issues. If there is no agreement, there is no establishment.

Another type of group is the political parties. As mentioned in

---

70. Geoffrey Hodgson, "The Establishment," *Foreign Policy,* 10 (Spring 1973), 3–40. For an interpretation of a capitalist elite governing foreign policy, see Richard J. Barnet, *Roots of War,* Penguin Books, Baltimore, 1972.

1 SHORT

relation to Congress, there was remarkably little real partisanship regarding foreign policy even after the breakdown of the bipartisanship of the cold war. Both major American parties consist of broad coalitions, and within each there is a broad spectrum of views on America's relationship with the world. There has seldom been a strong ideological difference between the parties in presidential elections since 1920; the sharpest recent division was in 1972 when Senator George S. McGovern led the forces passionately bent on immediate disengagement from Southeast Asia. The center of gravity of the Democratic party has stood somewhat to the liberal left, that of the Republican party somewhat to the conservative right; just as the former appeals to labor, the latter appeals more to a business constituency. It is probable, but by no means certain, that a Republican administration will be more favorable to defense spending and to support of anticommunist governments without worrying much because they are dictatorial; a Democratic administration is more likely to reduce defense spending while favoring foreign aid and to ask for democratic credentials of allies. There is probably not much difference between the parties in their disposition to intervention, but it may be guessed that the Republicans would be readier to intervene on simple strategic grounds, the Democrats to save supposedly menaced freedom.

In sum, the existence of many groups with a claim—economic, electoral, or intellectual—to be heard by the executive or especially the Congress is a fundamental restraining influence on the government. The claims of such groups may be selfish or shortsighted; they may also be idealistic or farsighted. On balance, they operate to restrain the power-bred impulses that often mislead foreign policy.

PUBLIC OPINION AND THE PRESS

Behind the many groups and organizations that press their views stands a formless something called public opinion, a concept that would be abandoned as hopelessly vague if it were not so useful. There is no single opinion of the public but as many opinions as there are opinionated publics, and a majority as registered by polls may be less influential than the more articulate or committed minorities. The press and broadcasting media to some extent reflect public opinion, or at least the atmosphere as they feel it; they also lead opinion, not only gathering news but selecting, shaping, and interpreting it. Leading papers, broadcast commentators, and even columnists are powers in the land.

Public opinion tends to be critical. Americans generally consider themselves qualified to pass judgment on their elected or appointed leaders. Newsmen are especially critical and may find more satisfaction in pointing out faults and failures than in commending excellence and good judgment. The American press, particularly a few leading newspapers, delves assiduously into governmental actions, foreign and domestic, and pounces eagerly upon the sins of the mighty. In no other nation is there such an adversary relation between government and the fourth estate.[71] The media look for action and tend to play up conflict and find news by probing, denouncing, and reporting differences between the administration and its critics in Congress and elsewhere.[72] It has seemed at times that the press is manageable and amenable to the official version of truth; for example, it refrained from publicizing the preparations for the Bay of Pigs invasion although rumors were rife and Castro was adequately informed. All presidents from Washington and Jefferson on, however, have come into conflict with a press that they wish was more inhibited.[73] The hostility of press and government reached its height during the latter part of the Vietnam war and its aftermath, when the press felt that it had been used to deceive the public, and the government thought that uncooperative journalism was responsible for many of its troubles.

The importance of public opinion for foreign policy is as vague as the idea of what constitutes it. Public opinion is often feeble or nonexistent and may be disregarded in connection with countless issues about which the public does not concern itself.[74] Nevertheless, presidents have to bow to the theory of popular sovereignty, and writers commonly assume that public opinion constitutes at least a limit to what they can do about major questions; public opinion is to a large extent the willingness of the public to tolerate. Nixon did not follow public opinion regarding Vietnam, but it is fair to assume that

---

71. Thomas M. Franck and Edward Weisband, "Executive Secrecy in Three Democracies," in Secrecy and Foreign Policy, ed. Thomas M. Franck and Edward Weisband, Oxford University Press, New York, 1974, p. 9.

72. Wilcox, Congress, the Executive, and Foreign Policy, p. 111.

73. Haynes Johnson, "The Irrespressible Conflict between Press and Government," in Secrecy and Foreign Policy, p. 166.

74. Bernard Cohen, The Public's Impact on Foreign Policy, Little, Brown, Boston, 1973, pp. 186–189.

he would have taken a still stronger line if he had felt public opinion would permit. In his détente policy, he undertook a course at odds with his previous long-term philosophy on the correct assumption that his new approach would win public approval.

Presidents read the papers, view the newscasts, and follow the polls, inadequate as all these may be as indicators of national sentiment. Polls were Johnson's standby as he was escalating the Vietnam war. Kennedy, feeling insecure in public esteem, was especially sensitive to them; the biggest factor in his foreign policy was probably the desire to build public support.[75] Underlings, too, are responsive to what they feel is the climate of opinion, especially what their friends and family are saying.[76] Foreign policy cannot possibly be carried on in isolation from domestic pressures.[77] Ambassador George F. Kennan even felt that those who give instructions to diplomats are primarily concerned with the effect at home.[78]

So far as congressmen and presidents are concerned with reelection, they are reluctant to go counter to the wishes of their constituents, although attitudes evinced at election time may be forgotten later. Foreign policy has figured prominently in nearly all elections since 1936, in part because candidates (like presidents) are apt to be fond of it even though it may be detrimental to them, as it was to Adlai Stevenson in 1956.[79] The elections of 1940 and 1944 were dominated first by the wish to stay out of the war and then by the hope for a rapid end to the war; the election of 1952 was affected by weariness with the Korean War. In 1956, the issues stressed were keeping the peace and nuclear testing. In 1960, Kennedy made much of the "missile gap," and this issue may have given him his tiny winning margin,[80] although Nixon played up his own foreign policy expertise. The elections of 1964, 1968, and 1972 were overshadowed by Vietnam. It has seemed essential that candidates appear on the world scene and show themselves to be competent in world affairs; to confess ignorance is to disqualify oneself.

75. Travis, "John F. Kennedy: Experiment with Power," in *Powers of the President in Foreign Affairs*, p. 193.

76. Cohen, *The Public's Impact on Foreign Policy*, pp. 80–81.

77. Stanley Hoffmann, "Will the Balance Balance at Home?," *Foreign Policy*, 7 (Summer 1972), 60–86.

78. George F. Kennan, *Memoirs, 1950–1969*, Little, Brown, Boston, 1972, pp. 320–321.

79. Stephen Hess, "Foreign Policy and Presidential Campaigns," *Foreign Policy*, 8 (Fall 1972), 13.

80. Ibid., p. 16.

The president quite properly seeks to shape public opinion in his favor by persuasion. He is the great newsmaker and national spokesman; his statements always receive attention, and he can preempt the airways at will; opponents who receive time for rebuttal are less heard. He can draw upon the enormous information resources of the government to plead his case; President Johnson thus used data furnished by the CIA and others in a campaign to sell intervention in the Dominican Republic in 1965.[81] The administration also feeds to the press (through briefings, purposeful leaks, and official and unofficial declarations) the kind of news it wants published. Many newsmen feel somewhat constrained to docility because they may be cut off from government news sources if they offend.

More controversial is the effort of the government to prevent disclosures.[82] There are legitimate reasons for secrecy beyond the obvious desirability of concealing military-strategic matters. Confidentiality is essential for negotiations and for candor within the government and in communications with other governments. Strategic arms limitation talks (SALT) can be better conducted without publicity. Yet it seems clear that the veil of secrecy is often drawn too tightly. There was, for example, no obvious need to keep under wraps the fact that there were negotiations with China preceding the announcement of the Nixon journey; drama was probably the chief motive. The effort to deceive the people regarding the course of the war in Vietnam ultimately helped defeat the purposes of the administration. Even in the Cuban crisis, it is not clear what would have been lost by letting the Soviets know that we knew the missiles were there.

The government has an inordinate passion for secrecy, whether it be to safeguard secrets or to cover up possible embarrassments. In 1971, the Department of Defense had about a million cubic feet of secret materials; the State Department held about 35 million classified documents; and the National Archives guarded some 470 million pages of classified material. Some 55,000 government officials were empowered to classify documents. Although administrative penalties for overclassifying were written into the law, in four years there was not a single case of sanctions for this offense.[83] Despite the Freedom of

---

81. Evans and Novak, *Lyndon B. Johnson, The Exercise of Power*, p. 520.
82. Anthony Lake, "Lying around Washington," *Foreign Policy*, 2 (Spring 1971), 91–113.
83. William S. Moorehead, "Operation and Reform of the Classification System in the United States," in *Secrecy and Foreign Policy*, pp. 100–101.

Information Act (1967; amended and strengthened, 1975), which provided that agencies must release all documents the withholding of which cannot be specifically justified, this situation does not seem to have greatly changed; the bureaucracy inevitably seeks to select the information to be given out, and those on the outside can do little.

Those on the inside can do something, however. When the administration is disunited, and particularly when there are indignant feelings, any piece of interesting or embarrassing information circulated beyond a handful of persons is likely to be leaked,[84] and a large part of the abuses of executive power of recent years—wiretaps, surveillance, and break-ins—have been efforts to stop such breaches of official secrecy. In 1971 the Nixon administration tried in vain to prevent publication of *The Pentagon Papers* on grounds of national security; criminal prosecution was begun (unsuccessfully) against the leaker, Daniel Ellsberg. There have also been recurrent struggles between the executive and Congress over the escape of classified reports, to the detriment of reputations and good relations.

The maintenance of secrecy is characteristic of the authoritarian system, which needs secrecy and imposes it to a maximum; the communists, Soviet and Chinese, have a mania for it. For the democratic state, however, secrecy is burdensome, since it permits the hiding of errors and misdeeds on the one hand and undermines public confidence on the other. It should not be a great problem, however, if the administration has done nothing it is ashamed of. Where actions are proper and the need for secrecy is real, there are rarely leaks. The National Security Agency, which deals with secret communications, is untroubled; the CIA, with its bagful of dirty tricks, is continually suffering breaches of security. The passion for secrecy makes the inquisitive press into an enemy and thus damages good communications.[85] Moreover, the kind of foreign policy dependent on secrecy is that least appropriate for a democratic state in the new age. Secrecy goes with diplomatic game playing and the contest for the advantages of power, which have become largely unreal or irrelevant. It has nothing to do with solving modern problems. Secrecy is a denial of democracy that curtails the ability of the public to know about and judge its government and so blindfolds the nation.

Too much must not be expected of public opinion. Only a very

---

84. Hilsman, *The Politics of Policy Making*, p. 8.
85. Charles W. Bray, "The Media and Foreign Policy," *Foreign Policy*, 16 (Fall 1974), p. 111.

small fraction of the public has any real knowledge of any single issue, much less a reasonable mastery of such questions as the unification of Europe or the role of the United Nations. Most matters are too complex and remote; confusion creates indifference. Only groups directly touched are much interested, and the mass public is indifferent unless it perceives a threat to the United States. Complex issues are simplistically viewed. For example, there is considerable distrust of what may seem to be a giveaway of American interests for uncomprehended reasons; it was hence impossible to proceed toward accommodation with Panama in the election year of 1976. Media coverage of foreign events concentrates on violence and neglects the chronic diseases of the world; détente means less foreign news. In a Louis Harris poll, only 4 percent gave a foreign matter as the subject of their greatest concern, while 64 percent pointed to inflation.[86]

America has always suffered from emotionalism, reacting less with an appreciation of national interests in a complex world than with anger, enthusiasm, or disillusionment. After turning (under presidential leadership) from isolationism to engagement in World War II, the country embraced unconditional surrender, and as soon as the fighting was done it demobilized. Americans want their world clear-cut and simple, and they call for single answers—a fault encouraged by leaders who oversell the evil and the mission. When the Soviet Union appeared as an enemy, it was taken as practically the sole cause of evil; few Americans ventured to suggest balancing containment with bridge building. There was a hunt for scapegoats after the "loss" of China, and some seized upon the logic of the cold war to boycott Polish hams. McCarthyist witch hunting was widely acceptable in the 1950s. A few years later, the public showed itself capable of a rapid turn from unquestioning repugnance toward the totalitarianism of Communist China to rather uncritical admiration of its equalitarianism and neatness. Volatility increases as culture becomes more homogenized and dependent upon a few sources for most of its news.

One theme, however, has remained nearly constant through American history. The public is less interventionist than the leadership. Except in 1898, when people saw no need to count the consequences of an exercise in what has become known as machismo, Americans have usually wished above all to live in peace and have

---

86. *Newsweek,* December 10, 1973, p. 40.

been persuaded to take up arms only when they have felt greatly affronted or endangered. Large and vocal minorities have protested wars that seemed unnecessary for the safety of the nation, such as the War of 1812, the Mexican War, the Spanish War, and in our day the Korean War and the Vietnam war. The electorate has been predominantly pacific, and candidates have appealed to it by promising to keep the country out of war (as in 1916, 1940, and 1964) or to end a war (as in 1952). The only acceptable excuse for attempting to propagate the American way abroad has been that all peoples should enjoy peace.

The public seems to want to trust the national leader, and it will back him in an emergency if he can give any cogent basis for his actions. The president's ratings as measured by pollsters go up or down most markedly as a result of actions taken in the foreign field. The beginning of the Korean War, the Suez crisis, and the Lebanon crisis all saw the people rally behind their leader.[87] Kennedy's popularity increased after the Bay of Pigs failure as it did after the more successful missile crisis, as Johnson's did after his sharp response to the Tonkin Gulf incident, as Nixon's did after the mining of North Vietnamese waters in 1972, and as Ford's did after the *Mayaguez* incident. People like action and want the president to seem to be doing something.[88]

But the public likes a cocky stand only as long as the cost is not apparent. When the excitement fades, the bills start coming in, and emotion is overtaken by reflection, the public becomes impatient, as it did over Korea, although this war was both more justified and more successful than the Vietnam war. At least from the point of view of the pacifist, the public has probably been right on the big issues more often than those charged with leadership. The banning of nuclear testing in the atmosphere came, after many years of negotiations, from pressures from outside the government; if anything is done about disarmament, it is for the same reason. The informed public was right about Vietnam well before the Congress, which in turn was readier than the administration to negotiate a way out from 1965 on;[89] the executive never advanced beyond recognizing the impossibility of carrying on a widely opposed war. President Johnson feared electoral

---

87. Kenneth N. Waltz, "Opinion and Crisis in American Foreign Policy," in *The Politics of U.S. Foreign Policy Making*, pp. 47–48.

88. Doris A. Graber, *Public Opinion, the President, and Foreign Policy*, Holt, Rinehart and Winston, New York, 1968, pp. 342–343.

89. Waltz, "Opinion and Crisis in American Foreign Policy," p. 51.

troubles from pulling back in Vietnam,[90] but he probably feared most having to admit error. As involvement was coming to an end, a poll on March 9, 1975 showed a majority of 70 percent against and only 12 percent for additional military aid to Indochina, a result that made it difficult for Congress to support the administration's requests.

In November 1973, Americans in general were much more strongly in favor of curtailing the president's power to make war than was the Congress. Public opinion was apparently favorable to rapprochement with Cuba long before the administration could bring itself to budge. Over a long period, while the administration has been displeased with the United Nations, the public (as assessed by pollsters) has been more patient. Despite that organization's taking many positions contrary to the American view, the Gallup poll found in a survey published March 16, 1975 that 75 percent of Americans still favored American membership, approximately the same proportion as one dozen and two dozen years earlier. According to pollster Louis Harris, the public has consistently been ahead of the administration on a range of issues dear to liberals, such as global interdependence and opposition to military aid programs and military dictatorships.[91]

There is some confusion in this regard as to whether the mood of the mid-1970s can properly be called isolationist. Skepticism of the administration's actions and professions (the so-called credibility gap) began with extravagant statements made to justify the Dominican incursion of 1965 and grew with repeatedly falsified claims of progress in Vietnam. In 1964, the nation was ready to believe Johnson's tendentious version of the Tonkin Gulf affair; by 1970 Nixon's explanation of the invasion of Cambodia evoked derisive hoots. In 1974 and 1975, various investigations exposed deceits and illegalities in the highest places on a shocking scale. In this loss of faith, few wished to follow the administration into new adventures abroad. The percentage agreeing that "the United States should maintain its dominant position at all costs, even going to the brink of war if necessary" decreased from 56 percent in 1964 to 42 percent in 1974, while those who believed that "we shouldn't think so much in international terms but concentrate more on our national problems and building up our strength and prosperity at home" increased in the same period from

90. Robert L. Gallucci, *Neither Peace nor Honor: Politics of American Military Policy in Vietnam*, Johns Hopkins University Press, Baltimore, 1975, p. 2.
91. *The New York Times*, September 11, 1975, p. 18.

55 to 77 percent.[92] Only a minority would come to the assistance militarily of any attacked nation outside the Western Hemisphere, according to several polls—a feeling that might easily be brushed away by hostilities. From a 1974 survey of six hundred business leaders, it appeared that 57 percent saw domestic problems as the most serious threat to the United States, 18 percent pointed to world ecological troubles, 15 percent indicated difficulties in the less developed countries, and only 9 percent were most concerned with Soviet/Chinese advances; there was no support at all for military intervention against native communist insurgencies.[93] According to a Gallup poll of February 6, 1976, defense stood in public priorities below health care, education, law enforcement, aid for the poor, public housing, pollution control, and mass transport.

The opposition to foreign involvements is based upon a combination of antimilitarism on the part of the well-educated and distrust of leadership and impatience with distant causes on the part of the less-educated. The well-educated, who had formerly been more in favor of intervention, have turned more sharply away from it than the less-educated.[94] In the old consensus led by the intellectual elite, the liberals favored the American world role to do good, the conservatives to stop communism; this shattered consensus cannot soon be restored or replaced.

On the other hand, the public accepts interdependence; asked in 1974 whether it would be better for the United States to take an active part in world affairs or to stay out, 66 percent opted for activity and 24 percent opposed it, almost exactly the percentages of 1964.[95] Foreign aid is unpopular, economic aid only slightly less so than military—a position not surprising in view of the lack of apparent good results in the less developed countries—but 82 percent of the public agreed that "problems like food, energy, and inflation" defied national solutions. No less than 74 percent were willing to give up meat one day a week to alleviate hunger abroad. From the point of view of "establishment" liberals from 1919 to 1965, the public was to

---

92. Lloyd Free, "A Nation Observed," in *A Nation Observed, Perspectives on America's World Role*, ed. Donald R. Lesh, Potomac Association, Washington, D.C., 1974, pp. 141, 144.

93. Bruce Russett, "The Americans' Retreat from World Power," *Political Science Quarterly*, 90 (Spring 1975), 6–8.

94. William Schneider, "Public Opinion: The Beginnings of Ideology?," *Foreign Policy*, 17 (Winter 1974–1975), 111–113.

95. *The Interdependent*, 2 (April 1975), 4.

be educated to the international responsibilities of the United States.[96] This education seems to have been retained, even as the public has turned away from the coercive aspects of responsibility.

Like Congress, then, public opinion usually acts as a brake on the president; at least, it has to be manipulated. Public opinion helps, with the assistance of Congress, to keep the executive branch more or less honest. Publicity favors rationality; if the Bay of Pigs excursion had been publicized, it might well have been halted; if the people had been better informed about Vietnam, escalation might have seemed less necessary. There is no reason to suppose that Americans are basically more pacific than any other people, but in the United States more than in any other major power, the media can and do inform the people about what the government is doing. In Britain, one of the freer of the few democracies in the world, not only are there no parliamentary probes: the Official Secrets Act of 1911 makes it a crime to publish any government information without official permission. It is a token of the American advantage that almost all the world's writing about secret services is American.

Whatever the shortcomings of American public opinion, it is probably more serious, better informed, and more critical of the nation's leaders than public opinion in any other major power. Presidents like to argue that the country should support their initiatives to make the United States more effective in the world; it might be better to ask that the president promote policies that the public can and will support in the long run.

THE QUALITY OF AMERICAN FOREIGN POLICY

It has been often assumed that the freedom and openness of democratic or representative government involves a loss of effectiveness, and that the loss of liberties under a dictatorial or perhaps totalitarian regime is compensated for by more efficient and purposeful government. However, although authoritarian governments can push through ruthless programs for change, it is not evident that they are best capable in the long run of economic and social development. Indeed, the virtues attributed to authoritarian states derive less from strength of

---

96. Cohen, *The Public's Impact on Foreign Policy*, p. 23.

authority than from vigor of revolution. Authoritarian governments inevitably become conservative and corrupt in a few decades.

It is more cogently argued that the constraints of a democratic state, the necessity for consultation and securing consent, the difficulty of maintaining secrecy, and inconstancy of purpose disqualify the government for the effective pursuit of foreign goals. Can a team without an authoritative boss, planning strategy more or less in public view and listening to bystanders' shouts and objections, compete with a team fully under the orders of a decisive leader able to devise and prepare its moves in secrecy, with no interference from the crowd? The Nazis thought not, and events of the 1930s seemed evidence enough that they could outmaneuver the slacker democratic powers of Europe. Long ago, in the 1830s, a good friend of the United States, Alexis de Tocqueville, saw foreign affairs as a principal area of weakness in the young democratic state. In a much-cited passage of *Democracy in America*, he averred that the democracy is unable "to persevere in a design, and to work out its execution in the presence of serious obstacles. It cannot combine its measures with secrecy, and it cannot await their consequences with patience."

Although the CIA could plot assassinations and carry on a semi-secret war in Laos and Cambodia, it is surely true that the United States could not have planned and executed a successful secret strike like that of the Japanese on Pearl Harbor or the surprise Soviet occupation of Czechoslovakia. It would likewise have been unable to mount a campaign of pressure and intimidation like that which gave Hitler control of Austria and Czechoslovakia in 1938 and 1939. Khrushchev could carry on a magnificent bluff concerning Soviet nuclear capabilities in the later 1950s, far beyond the capacity of a less hermetic state. Recently the Soviet Union has been able to devote a much larger part of its resources to military and paramilitary programs than has the United States, since Soviet citizens have little to say about priorities. Likewise, the Soviet leadership did not have to consult or even inform its public about costly military aid programs in the Near East and elsewhere.

Yet the actions that the strong state can prepare and execute in secrecy may turn out to be basically foolish. The attack on Pearl Harbor was brilliantly successful, but it guaranteed the defeat of Japan. If the Japanese had avoided a direct blow at the United States, they might well have been able to take over the European colonies of Southeast Asia without major resistance. Khrushchev's nuclear bluff and bluster brought some trepidation to the West but no real or lasting gains to the Soviet Union. Its effect was a massive American rearmament program, which for a time placed the Soviet Union in a position of marked inferiority. American foreign policy has suffered many follies, but it has never committed madness comparable to Hit ler's attack on the Soviet Union or his gratuitous declaration of war against the United States. It has never been so shortsighted as was Stalinist Russia in the 1939 attack on Finland or in the failure to prepare for the Nazi attack in 1941.

Insofar as the authoritarian state has advantages in international affairs, these advantages are for offensive action. The more loosely structured state finds it difficult to carry on any long-term program of expansion or aggrandizement unless costs are minimal.[97] When questions can be asked and costs counted, an aggressive policy is never popular in the modern age, and it may be surmised that the more popular the government, the more open and more discussed its initiatives, the less likely a nation is to be seriously aggressive.

Quite possibly the United States has failed, by virtue of democratic openness, to gain things it might have gained, although it is doubtful how much of value has been lost. It is surely fortunate for the world that the United States has not been much inclined to crusading and has never exerted anything like its full strength except in what it felt were contests for the national safety.[98] In the wake of such an armageddon as either world war, the most powerful state might well pick up the pieces and subdue its rivals in the name of permanent peace and security. The United States had the overwhelming materiel and technical resources to do so; some people, including the philosopher Bertrand Russell, argued that it was a duty thus to prevent an atomic arms race and the likelihood of an eventual nuclear holocaust.

But it is not in the American way to execute a grand imperial design. If the world is better off ruled by independent powers than it would be under American dominion, it must be thankful for the peculiar political structure of the United States, which has favored extraordinary productivity but has inhibited the use of power abroad.

---

97. As was the case with what was seen as a steady course to empire by revisionist historians, as in *From Colony to Empire: Essays in the History of American Foreign Relations*, ed. William A. Williams, John Wiley, New York, 1972.

98. On the restrictedness of American foreign policy, cf. Stanley Hoffmann, *Gulliver's Troubles, Or the Setting of American Foreign Policy*, McGraw-Hill, New York, 1968, Chapters 8, 9.

The temptation to indulge in the use of force and sundry deviltry has been strong, because of American technical and material capacities, but it has never been given free rein. It is easy for a secondary state virtuously to decry the employment of force in the world; it is very difficult for the state that has the most physical power to refrain from using and misusing it. The United States has not fully refrained, to the indignation of many of its citizens, but it is hard to imagine that any other country with such material superiority would have made less selfish use of it. The wisdom of foreign policy must be measured against the temptations of power.

American foreign policy, of course, is made behind closed doors, but it is the essence of candor compared with decision making in Moscow or Peking. Even democratic countries such as Britain, France, and West Germany retain much of the old tradition that foreign relations belong to the sovereign and are beyond the ken of ordinary folk. In no other major power are means of limiting executive foreign policy built into the political structure. In no other nation is consensus so requisite for action. Nowhere but in the United States would it be accepted that individuals had the right, perhaps the moral duty, to publicize erstwhile secret documents, such as *The Pentagon Papers,* for the general enlightenment or to uncover the efforts of the CIA to advance supposed national interests by unacknowledgeable methods.

The general problem of politics is too much power in the hands of too few. For all its checks, the United States has more obviously erred not by hesitant bumbling or impotence of leadership but ill-considered actions like those that a dictatorial power might undertake. Many of these episodes have been mentioned in preceding pages. They include such deviations as a confused and untempered spirit of anticommunist crusading in the cold war, which viewed a construct, *communism,* as responsible for nearly all the disorder in the world [99] and fantasized about the menace of Communist China. In the latter part of the cold war, the United States was getting out of touch with the real world and living in its own slogans. There have been ample pride and self-righteousness, and an inability to perceive the needs and rights of other peoples. The belief that losses must be due to treason made intelligence and integrity a liability in part of the State Department in the 1950s and prepared the way into Vietnam. There has been an odd rigidity in some positions, such as the disinclination to normalize

---

99. Halperin, *Bureaucratic Politics,* p. 11.

relations with Mongolia or to permit trade with Cuba and the reluctance to perceive that withdrawal from an untenable position (as
in Vietnam) does not weaken but strengthens the American position
elsewhere. The United States has set numerous precedents of negative
value for world order, including operational use of nuclear explosives,
a buildup of nuclear arms, economic discrimination for political pressure (against communist states), export restrictions (of soybeans and
other products), annexation of offshore resources (the continental
shelf), and military intervention abroad (although this practice is old
as history).

The Vietnam war, however, brought out most impressively the
sins and faults of an autocratic-style foreign policy. There were mis-
perception, self-deception, narrow pride, overreliance on force, and
negligent superiority to alien peoples. The administration falsified the
facts to itself and to the people. There were subversive operations
and terrorism. There were secret bombings of nominally neutral Laos
and Cambodia (some 3,600 missions in fourteen months). There was
even such a gaffe as initiating the bombing of North Vietnam while
the Soviet premier was touring there, perhaps on a peace mission.

Unhappily, the painful lessons of Indochina only partly sank into
the administration. Nixon had to be dragged away from the war in
Cambodia, all the while shouting that peace was jeopardized by restricting American bombing. He also promised President Nguyen Van
Thieu that the United States would come to the rescue of the Saigon
government if (as was to be expected) the communists proceeded
to harvest the fruits of their successful struggle. Early in 1975, administration spokesmen were bewailing the prospective "loss" of Cambodia. President Ford at his March 17 press conference seriously
lamented that Thailand no longer considered American protection
necessary. In an interview on April 21, he chafed at the legal prohibition against sending American forces back into South Vietnam.

The final "loss" of Indochina brought a striking demonstration of
emotionalism. When an American freighter, the *Mayaguez*, was de-
tained while passing near a Cambodian island on May 12, 1975, the
administration made a perfunctory effort to communicate with the
Cambodians and then, in quick reaction time, about twenty hours
after the seizure, launched an attack on the Cambodian navy, landed
marines on an island, and bombed the mainland.[100] The United States

---

100. For an account, see Roy Rowan, *The Four Days of Mayaguez*, W. W.
Norton, New York, 1975.

routinely takes in tow ships believed to have violated American regulations, and American ships are routinely arrested by such countries as Ecuador, with the result that the State Department meekly pays the fines. Americans were stung and angry in frustration at the liquidation of the client regimes, and the seizure of the *Mayaguez* was a happy chance to relieve feelings. Bombing went on after the Cambodians offered to release the vessel and crew, and Henry Kissinger proposed B-52 raids. The military operation was not glorious; forty-one men died in the unsuccessful invasion of the island (the crew of the *Mayaguez* being thirty-nine). The operation was also offensive to Thailand, which was used as a base for the marines against the wishes of the Thai government. But it was, as *The Wall Street Journal* [101] and many other newspapers put it, a "thrilling success" for the United States to slap down the Cambodian navy. President Ford (and with him the American public) was happy to see the flag upheld; his approval rating jumped (according to a Gallup poll) from 40 percent to 51 percent. It was inexpensive drama. Congress, including anti–Vietnam war liberals, cheered the violation of the unequivocal law prohibiting use of any funds for military actions "in or over or off the shores of North Vietnam, South Vietnam, Laos, or Cambodia."

The catharsis and the sense of retribution against the Cambodian communists for having had the temerity to beat down an American-sponsored regime were salutary in helping America to cast off the gloom of defeat and to cease worrying that everyone might think that the United States was weak and cowardly. The preference in this case for violence was, however, an aberration like the fury of the wounded buffalo. With reason, severe critics of the Vietnam war had looked forward to liberation from that entanglement as a liberation of America and the emergence of a new community.[102] After the country recovered its balance and saw the world as no more menacing after than before the fall of Saigon, the United States could be itself again, as it had not been since before World War II. The country is not likely soon to undertake another military mission in ideological spirit. Unless the United States suffers a new traumatic experience, the effects of Vietnam will remain in American thinking for a generation.

---

101. *The Wall Street Journal,* May 16, 1975, p. 10.
102. Gabriel Kolko, *The Roots of American Foreign Policy: An Analysis of Power and Purpose,* Beacon Press, Boston, 1969, pp. 137–138; Williams, *From Colony to Empire,* p. 487.

Rational answers may be found. It is probably true, as Waltz put it, that "American institutions facilitate rather than discourage the quick identification of problems, the pragmatic quest for solutions, the ready confrontation of dangers, the willing expenditure of energies, and the open criticism of policies." [103] In the view of Lowi, "Since our record of response to crises is good, then the men in official positions have been acting and are able to act rationally." [104] Many sensible things have been done; the embracing of a policy of nearly free trade, for example, against myriad special interests showed the ability of the confused bargaining system to rise to the opportunity of advancing the general welfare. The United States has both an effective presidency and the means of assuring that it remains within bounds. And the executive branch can learn and change directions to a new course, as signaled by the statement of Secretary Kissinger in January 1975 that issues of energy, resources, environment, and population, rank with those in which he was educated and which made his career (that is, those of military security and political rivalry).[105]

The mulitiple influences of pluralistic American society tend to offset one another and to reduce the ability of the government to take action. But they do not have to immobilize the government. American foreign policy makers need to recognize how much diversity really represents the strength of the nation. The interactions of the nation with the world become increasingly diverse and multifarious; foreign policy deals, or should deal, not merely with the unrewarding contest for power but also with a host of less galvanizing things. Foreign policy is not only alliances and enmities, arms races and disarmament talks, but economic conferences, efforts to alleviate problems of the Third World, management of the oceans, disease control, population imbalances, the spread of American and other cultures, and many other matters that may shape the world of tomorrow and America's place in it. Many of these issues must be met partly or largely by diverse, pluralistic, unofficial America.

It is the American strength in foreign affairs not only that the need for persuasion and compromise blocks (albeit imperfectly) the over-

103. Kenneth N. Waltz, *Foreign Policy and Democratic Politics*, Little, Brown, Boston, 1967, pp. 307–308.

104. Theodore J. Lowi, "Making Democracy Safe for the World," in *The Politics of U.S. Foreign Policy Making*, p. 26.

105. *Commission on the Organization of the Government for the Conduct of Foreign Policy*, Government Printing Office, Washington, D.C., 1975, p. 25.

use and abuse of power but also that the loose society is productive, innovative, and diverse and impinges on the world through its productivity, innovativeness, and diversity. Foreign relations are furthered not only by the government but by thousands of organizations and millions of persons expressing themselves and carrying on their affairs in their own way. Millions of Americans are in countless ways ambassadors or agents of their country abroad; although often at cross-purposes, they represent an unparalleled strength.

The American political system is thus propitious, not for a single grand foreign policy design but for a bundle of many foreign policies, official and semiofficial, joined (it may be hoped) by a broad philosophic agreement on the kind of world desired. The need and the opportunity are new and urgent, yet this broad agreement is an ideal to which many leaders of the nineteenth century would have subscribed. In the already distant day before the agony of Vietnam overtook America, a youthful president was looking in this direction. Before his life was ended, John Kennedy, recognizing some of the complexity and diversity in the world and the fruitlessness of straight hard-line cold war leadership, was looking toward a new kind of American leadership by example in education, social justice, and civil rights.[106]

---

106. Travis, "John F. Kennedy: Experiments with Power," in *Powers of the President in Foreign Affairs,* p. 195.

CHAPTER SIX

The Affluent Societies

ALLIANCE POLITICS: THE NORTH ATLANTIC TREATY ORGANIZATION

The historically derived independent units that make up the international community are all unique in background, outlook, and problems. From the point of view of foreign policy, however, they may be usefully categorized in three fairly well-defined groups. One group is composed of states rather like the United States: the relatively rich and industrially developed nations, which have more or less constitutional and democratic governments and basically private-enterprise economies. Besides the United States, this group includes primarily the western European countries and Japan, Canada, Australia, and New Zealand. Another category includes nations charaterized by adherence to Marxism-Leninism and the maintenance of relatively tightly controlled and closed societies under the rule of a communist party. This group includes the Soviet Union and its satellites plus a few other countries (principally the People's Republic of China), which maintain generally similar forms and ideological commitments. A third group consists of the noncommunist states, which have not as yet become industrially developed and which are hence called developing or less developed countries, or sometimes the Third World. This group includes most of the countries of Asia, Africa, and Latin America.

United States relations with each of these three groups are different. Security questions are commonly predominant with regard to the Marxist-Leninist states, although these countries are by no means so bent on the destruction of what they call bourgeois society as ideology would dictate. The non-Western noncommunist states, whose chief common denominator is poverty (except for a few countries fortuitously enriched by oil exports), have only a secondary capacity to help or hurt the United States except perhaps by withholding natural resources, especially oil. Chronic frictions with these nations derive from differences of economic level and resultant power. With the advanced industrial states, on the other hand, relations are generally friendly, mostly economic, with no serious political issues and little potential for conflict. Dealings with them fit easily in the framework of American institutions and political ideals, being mostly open and unofficial, and require little bureaucratic intervention.

Security questions still figure prominently, however. Except for a few small states (Sweden, Finland, Switzerland, and Austria) the noncommunist industrial states are American allies, and those of the Atlantic area are joined in the North Atlantic Treaty Organization (NATO). The cold war was fought mostly over Third World countries, but the chief fear of the United States was that advanced industrial countries would fall under international communism or simply Soviet domination, thereby adding decisively to the power of the principal antagonist of the United States. Moreover, because it was easier to justify coming to the defense of countries with more or less democratic governments, and because understanding is easier with the likeminded, the United States has promoted alliances above all with the advanced countries; since 1949 the North Atlantic Treaty has been the center of American alliance policy.

NATO, the organization implementing the North Atlantic Treaty, represents a new kind of supranational organization—imitated by the Soviets in the Warsaw Treaty Organization (WTO)—with a unified command and supply system and myriad planning and study agencies, including an advisory semiofficial parliament, the North Atlantic Assembly, and a nuclear planning group. Large naval and military exercises are held from time to time, but no NATO armed force exists; rather, military contingents under national command are designated for NATO control by the respective governments in case of war. Only Germany has committed all of its forces to NATO. Standardization of weaponry, although much advocated for economy, has made little progress.[1] A nation's territory can be used for bases and maneuvers only by consent. Decision making is theoretically unanimous, and NATO ministers meet frequently to talk over affairs. The difficulty of getting fifteen countries to agree on anything is met in practice by seeking a perhaps informal or general consensus; when the ministers fail to reach agreement, problems are customarily turned over to experts for recommendations. European members have formed a suborganization, the Eurogroup, to express their common interests.

The North Atlantic Treaty pledges the members to settle disputes among themselves peacefully, but NATO has shown no great ability to resolve differences. In 1956, for example, Britain and France undertook to recapture the Suez Canal despite American disapproval. In August 1974, NATO could do nothing when Turkey, under considerable provocation, occupied the most desirable part of Cyprus; when the Cyprus

---

1. *The New York Times,* September 26, 1975, p. 8; Thomas A. Callaghan, Jr., "A Common Market for Atlantic Defense," *The Atlantic Community Quarterly,* 13 (Summer 1975), 161.

problem led to a cutoff of United States military assistance to Turkey, to Turkish pressure on American bases, and to fiery anti-Americanism in Greece, NATO could only lament.

The various members are diverse. Britain has always felt itself a bit apart from the continental powers and more closely linked to the United States, enjoying the status of a nuclear power largely by virtue of that association. West Germany occupies the most exposed position, and NATO is more important for it. At one time the Germans were hesitant because they saw affiliation with NATO as impeding reunification; now West Germany has become, with the United States, the chief supporter of the alliance. With increasing reluctance, the Germans have covered much of the foreign exchange cost of United States forces in Europe by buying United States bonds and arms; they have been outstandingly cooperative with regard to détente, trade, and currency matters. The Scandinavian partners, Denmark and Norway, are less involved. The Low Countries, Belgium and the Netherlands, in contrast, are among the most enthusiastic adherents of NATO. Belgium offered quarters for NATO headquarters when France evicted the organization. Canadian participation in NATO amounts principally to defense collaboration with the United States. Greece and Turkey are more protected than participating powers, especially since both were alienated by the failure of the United States and NATO to support them in the Cyprus controversy.

The most difficult member of the alliance has usually been France. A once very proud power that has felt the bitterness of defeat in World War II and the humiliation of the American domination of Europe, France spent many years trying to play a role for which it lacked strength, fighting to retain first Indochina and then Algeria and (under Charles De Gaulle in the 1960s) seeking to play an independent role alongside the superpowers. In this spirit, De Gaulle in 1966 withdrew from the military organization of NATO but remained in the alliance, keeping the guarantee but largely desisting from the cooperative effort to make it effective. France has also tried to provide its own nuclear deterrent, with a few short-range bombers, intermediate-range missiles, and nuclear submarines. The United States has been very unsympathetic to the French effort toward strategic self-reliance, going so far at one time as to refuse to sell computers on the ground that they would contribute to the program. The difficulties may be traced in part to the personal animus of Franklin Roosevelt against De Gaulle during World War II, but they stem principally from the desire of the French for some kind of leadership in Europe and their unwillingness to accept an inferior status to Britain, with its special relation to the United States.[2]

The French have been the leaders of the European doubters of NATO and the value of the American commitment. As the Soviets achieved (in the later 1950s and subsequently) a capacity for inflicting what is politely called unacceptable damage on the United States (that is, killing a considerable fraction of the American people), the question was raised whether the United States would risk its existence for the safety of Europe. NATO strategic thinking has been pulled uncertainly in two directions. From the European point of view, possible Soviet aggression would be best deterred by a nuclear retaliatory threat; American forces in Europe should serve primarily to ensure that America would be engaged from the outset, and there would be no need for NATO to match Soviet or WTO forces on the ground. From the American point of view, it would be better to be able to hold off Soviet forces with NATO conventional forces, at least to afford time to consider before leaping into armageddon. To Europeans, however, this approach means not only that they would be expected to contribute more to the military effort on the lower level but also that a new war might again be fought over the body of Europe, perhaps for the third time sparing the American homeland. With the United States retaining sole control of the ultimate weapons and of the decision to use them, Europeans could not be satisfied when the immediate threat was to them but the transatlantic power held the keys (literally) to the means of their defense. A conventional buildup, however, is costly and would concentrate dangers of destruction in the European theater. The European powers have consequently preferred the cheaper defense of reliance on American strategic power; they spend about 4 percent of their national product for defense, compared to the American 6 percent. Local resistance is difficult and threatening, but massive retaliation is unreliable. In this dilemma, Europeans are worried by the tactical nuclear weapons in the theater (five thousand in West Germany, two thousand in other NATO countries) and also worried by a move to reduce the number of nuclear weapons. They mostly prefer simply to assume that there will be no Soviet attack.

Such questions are entwined with the multiple obscurities of nuclear prospects. No one has any idea whether the Soviet Union and its

---

2. For alliance problems, cf. Henry A. Kissinger, *The Troubled Partnership: A Reappraisal of the Atlantic Alliance*, McGraw-Hill, New York, 1965.

allies might conceivably launch a westward attack, what strength is necessary to persuade them that it would be too dangerous, or how the Western peoples might react to such an emergency. If there seemed a real threat that the Soviets were moving to "sovietize" and appropriate the heartland of the Western world by force, the NATO countries would get to work to build up forces powerful enough to make Soviet aggression impossible. Since nobody is sure whether the Soviets really still desire expansion, it is impossible to define what is needed to counter a threat that might hypothetically develop if they should become more aggressive. It becomes more difficult, also, to separate military and political considerations. In its inception, NATO was intended perhaps less to fend off potential Soviet aggression than to stiffen demoralized European powers against communist subversion. Now the threat of communist subversion strikes less terror. The two biggest communist parties, the French and Italian, have become bureaucratized, staid, and almost accepted parts of the political system. The party with best chances of acquiring national political power, the Italian, has displayed most independence of Moscow and has tried hardest to look democratic.

There is a different fear: that without a powerful shield western Europe would not be overrun but would become putty for Soviet designs—would be "Finlandized" or deprived of independence in foreign policy, like that Soviet neighbor. But to suppose that the Soviet Union is sufficiently strong and dynamic to bend to its will big, rich western Europe as it did little Finland is very flattering to the Soviets. In any case, the military balance in Europe is ambiguous. NATO had roughly (as of 1975) twenty-six divisions, six thousand tanks, and twenty-seven hundred combat planes facing fifty-eight divisions, sixteen thousand tanks, and twenty-nine hundred planes; however, the quantitative superiority of WTO forces is offset by qualitative superiority of NATO. WTO forces certainly do not have the overwhelming strength necessary to launch an offensive with confidence.[3]

It is then asked why it should still be necessary for the United States to keep approximately three hundred thousand troops in Europe to defend allies who, taken together, are more populous and wealthier

---

3. J. I. Coffey, "Arms Control and the Military Balance in Europe," *Orbis*, 17 (Spring 1973), 132–154. Alain C. Enthoven, in "U.S. Forces in Europe: How Many? Doing What?," *Foreign Affairs*, 53 (April 1975), 515, sees NATO ground forces superior to the adversary.

than the Soviet Union.[4] After Vietnam, pullback everywhere was under consideration; in particular there was strong sentiment in Congress for bringing a sizable part of the American army home from Europe. A large fraction of the Senate, sometimes a majority, has expressed itself in favor of the proposal sponsored by Senate Majority Leader Mike Mansfield to withdraw perhaps half of the troops. The administration has always been strongly opposed to this course of action, on the ground that Europe's will vis-á-vis the Soviet Union could be seriously weakened, or that withdrawal would represent a concession to the Soviets and so should be used to get a counterconcession, presumably withdrawal of some Soviet forces.

A possible but unstated reason for opposing withdrawal is that American military authorities like to have forces and bases in Europe. A better reason is that the present situation seems sustainable, hurts nobody very much, and may be a guarantee against unpleasant surprises. Europeans seem generally to agree, despite some rankling at the indefinite presence of foreign troops. In July 1971, a leftist-oriented premier took office in Iceland with a call for the Americans' departure, but when the slogan appeared about to become a reality, Icelanders thought again of jobs and a comfortable security and invited the guests to stay. The French do not want Americans out of the continent even as part of an agreement with the Soviets providing for mutual withdrawal. It is possible that the Soviets, too, are happier to see American forces remaining in Europe, chiefly in Germany, as an impediment to European unity, as a check on possible German ambitions, and as an excuse for keeping Soviet troops in satellite countries. In any case, neither side in the drawn-out negotiations on mutual balanced force reductions (MBFR) has shown much disposition to cut through the quibbling about types of weapons, distance of withdrawal, verification, and so forth. Force levels have seemingly been frozen by disarmament discussions.

Hardly anyone nowadays calls for the abolition of NATO, although most people on both sides of the ocean usually ignore it. In détente, NATO inevitably loses steam. Khrushchev periodically revived it by some crisis or rocket rattling; his successors have not performed this service since the invasion of Czechoslovakia in 1968, although in 1975 fear that Portugal might acquire a communist gov-

---

4. Enthoven, "U.S. Forces in Europe," pp. 513–532.

ernment was a tonic for the alliance. France from the days of De Gaulle and West Germany since 1970 have cultivated amicable relations with the chief NATO antagonist. But whereas Europeans were once apprehensive lest American cold war intransigence involve them in unnecessary difficulties, they have become suspicious of détente lest it include deals at their expense. At best, they feel left out when the superpowers get together to settle world problems.

The United States for its part has recently paid rather little attention to its most important allies. Vietnam was a long distraction, and thereafter priority was given to putting relations with Communist China and the Soviet Union into a better frame. In 1973, the United States urged a new Atlantic Charter to redefine relations of the NATO community in the post–cold war era; other countries, however, did not appear as eager as the United States to formulate the undefinable relations of the United States and its European allies. In fact, the two sides have many divergent interests beneath their agreement on fundamentals. The experience of Vietnam induced less isolationism than unilateralism in American foreign policy, and the United States has repeatedly taken actions affecting its allies without consulting them. Some Europeans, on the other hand, especially the French, seemed happy to take any opportunity to protest American domination or a shadow of it.

The limits of friendship came strikingly to the fore in the fuel crisis of 1973–1974. The United States gave first priority to the safety of Israel, which did not greatly concern the Europeans. The latter, seeing themselves likely to suffer more than the United States from Arab production cutbacks, wished no part of the fight and generally opposed the shipment of arms from Europe to Israel. Of the NATO allies only Portugal was cooperative. Americans made little effort to explain their policy to the allies, even when President Nixon ordered a worldwide strategic alert in October 1973 to deter possible Soviet intervention. When the United States tried to bring other major oil consumers into a common front, the European nations rather scrambled to make the best deals they could individually. In March 1974, it was even reported that the French were urging the Arabs to keep up their boycott of the United States. There was so much irritation that Kissinger said that he found it easier to deal with enemies than with friends and that America's biggest problems were with its "self-assertive" allies.[5]

---

5. *Time*, April 1, 1974, p. 26.

It was apparently neater and more satisfying to deal with decisive authoritarian bosses than to try to find a consensus with cautious leaders of democracies.

The easing of the fuel crisis removed the biggest immediate strain on United States–European relations, and in 1974 the French president, Valéry Giscard d'Estaing, steered France closer to the United States. But the problems of reconciling firm alliance with substantial détente were insoluble. There were two basic difficulties: divergence of material interests and the perennial psychological strain of relations between stronger and weaker parties. The differences of interests included political matters, such as defense strategy and the relation of American and European contributions, but the problems were mostly economic, such as the question of freer entry of United States agricultural products into the European Economic Community (EEC) and fear of American countervailing duties against European steel and autos.

Material differences are generally subject to rational compromise; the strains resulting from inequality are harder to manage. They result not only from the superior wealth and military power of the United States but also from its more favorable situation. Europe needs the United States even more than the United States needs Europe. The two sides consequently see each other differently. From the European point of view, the United States denies Europe an independent role, itself defines the supposed common interest that Europeans should support, goes it alone, and expects the allies to follow. From the American point of view, the allies want American support without offering much cooperation in return. The Europeans, being relatively strong economically, want to keep economic issues separate from political lest they be disadvantaged. The United States, having political leverage by virtue of Europe's need for the nuclear umbrella and desire to see American troops on the frontiers of the Soviet sphere, would use this leverage. To Europeans, talk of American withdrawal sounds something like blackmail.

The gratitude for American aid, which once helped solidify the alliance, has passed with the postwar generation, and the Europeans can be suspicious and sensitive. Although they preceded the United States in their separate approaches to the Soviet Union, the French and the Germans spoke of United States–Soviet collaboration in the Near East to stop the 1973 war as though the superpowers were allotting themselves Near Eastern oil; French Foreign Minister Michel Jobert decried their "dividing up the world." Kissinger attributed to the

Europeans "a certain peevishness" because of "the sense of impotence."[6] It is also doubted, with some reason, that the United States is really interested in European unity, and this skepticism could be detrimental to the American power position. There is little pretense of advance consultation by the United States with Europe or vice versa.

Yet the alliance hangs together indefinitely. It does no particular harm, and its breakup might be dangerously unsettling. Peace depends on the acceptance of a status quo of which NATO is part. Even communist parties in western Europe at least ostensibly accept NATO. Moreover, the members (with the partial exception of fringe members, Greece and Turkey) have much in common: similar values to defend in the world and shared interests to promote. Whatever their squabbles, they prefer to remain friends.[7]

SEMIUNITED EUROPE

Europe cannot treat the United States as an equal unless or until the Europeans achieve sufficient unity to speak with one voice and to act with one will. This potential unity is for Europe the question of questions and a matter of extreme importance for the future of the international order. An effectively united western Europe would fundamentally alter the power configuration of the world.

The EEC, which has already been achieved, is something of a political miracle, without precedent or example as a voluntary renunciation of sovereignty by equal, proud nations. It was made possible because the world wars discredited nationalist rivalries and because of the fear of a new war. Stalinism and the cold war split off the less advanced countries of eastern Europe, leaving a more homogeneous western Europe, and led the United States to promote the unification of the countries it pledged to defend.

The unification of Europe began with wartime anti-Nazi solidarity. It took shape with the Marshall Plan and the necessity of cooperation for recovery. Rebuilding Europe required liberalization of intra-European trade, coordination through the Organization for European Economic Cooperation (OEEC), and a payments union to manage the

---

6. *Business Week,* January 13, 1975, p. 74.

7. Richard H. Sinnreich, "NATO's Doctrinal Dilemma," *Orbis,* 19 (Summer 1975), 461–476, considers the developing strengths and weaknesses.

convertibility of the then still very weak European currencies. NATO forwarded the idea of common action; its founding in 1949 was accompanied by the establishment of a consultative group, the Council of Europe. In 1952 West Germany, France, Italy, the Netherlands, Belgium, and Luxembourg (Benelux) were joined in the European Coal and Steel Community (ECSC), with authority to make binding decisions, an executive power, and a court. A European defense community was proposed but failed because of French rejection. Defense was left to NATO, but long negotiations led to the 378-page Treaty of Rome (effective January 1, 1959) for a customs union and common market of the six countries, with virtually the same organs as the ECSC. After an adjustment period, a full customs union was inaugurated in 1968; free movement of capital and labor and common monetary and taxation policies have also been largely achieved.

The British declined to enter the EEC when it was formed because they dimly visualized that Britain would retain a world economic and financial role, though not a political role. Poor but proud, they were victors, while the continental lands had all been defeated. The British also had special extra-European ties with the British Commonwealth and the United States. The EEC showed a magnificent growth of trade and production, however, and Britain lagged. Through the 1960s Britain knocked on the EEC door, but negotiations foundered on De Gaulle's distrust of the Anglo-Saxons. Eventually, the special relation of Great Britain with the United States became frayed, and after De Gaulle's death France ceased to bar Britain's way. Britain entered the EEC formally on January 1, 1973, along with Denmark and Ireland, converting the Six to the Nine, and ratified its membership by plebiscite in 1975.

The organizational backbone of the EEC is a multinational bureaucracy, centered at Brussels, which handles a budget of about $5 billion; most of this budget goes to agricultural price support. An advisory "parliament" composed of 142 delegates of member parliaments meets at Strasbourg; there is a movement to give this body power to set broad policies and scrutinize the budget. A court of justice has authority to assess fines for violations of EEC rules. There are many consultative and coordinating commissions; ministers and heads of government meet often.

The principal achievement of the EEC has been the removal of most hindrances to the flow of goods, capital, and labor; it has also worked out an agricultural policy considerably more extensive than the agriculture support system familiar in the United States. There has been progress toward control of exchange rates, and it is hoped that in about a decade Europe may have a single currency and a central bank. As of the beginning of 1973, members of the EEC undertook to make trade treaties only as a bloc. The EEC has an adjunct for nuclear energy, Euratom. The EEC is also the center of a large constellation. Greece and Turkey are associate members, and the EEC has special arrangements with Spain, Yugoslavia, twenty-two countries of Africa (formerly French and British colonies), and some small states in the Caribbean. In 1973 a free trade area in industrial products was formed with Iceland and Portugal plus the European neutrals (Austria, Finland, Sweden, and Switzerland). Lands from Poland to India have expressed interest in some sort of affiliation with the EEC.

Progress toward an integrated defense of Europe has been practically nil. Even within the NATO framework, there is a lack of coordination, as sundry countries continue to manufacture their own ammunition sizes, missiles, and so forth, at considerable cost, both financial and in terms of military effectiveness. There has been some thought of merging the separately rather unimpressive British and French strategic forces. Merger would be technically easy, but it is inhibited both by nationalism and by American concern over the sharing of American nuclear secrets plus dislike for independent strategic forces. The problem of Germany is a bar to an all-European deterrent, because the Soviet Union retains residual control rights, along with the United States, Britain, and France; the idea of German hands on nuclear triggers would still raise apprehension. For the British, it is far cheaper to rely on the United States for modern weapons than to develop their own. Shortage of space in western Europe makes it difficult to compete strategically with the more spacious powers. In any case, there is not much drive toward military integration because the Europeans are not very worried and find the present situation tolerable even while they grumble about it.

Whether Europe can continue to advance toward the goals it has set for itself—a thoroughly integrated economy and some sort of federal system—seems doubtful. The international climate is not favorable; if there are starts, there are stops; and severe economic troubles might even tear apart the present customs union. There are numerous frictions. The Germans, who provide the largest share of the funds, are reluctant to pay more unless there is more central control of spending; this the other members resist. Any member nation in trouble acts for its interest with little regard for the EEC or even contractual obligations.[8] The economies tend to grow together, but when Italy faced a large payments deficit in 1974, it promptly erected steep trade barriers. In 1975 the French, in facing a wine surplus, imposed a tax on Italian wines. There is bickering over the price of butter and eggs, the allocation of resources, and exchange rates. Enthusiasm has waned, especially among the youth; what was a bright dream seems to many to represent little more than a superbureaucracy for the benefit of industrialists. Europe has achieved what was easiest and most rewarding: sufficient removal of trade barriers to permit a remarkable economic expansion. The supranationalism to be achieved is at once more difficult and less materially rewarding. It represents a considerable victory that people use a common European passport instead of national passports. More promising, it has been agreed that in 1978 the European parliament should be elected by the people; direct election may give it moral authority to assert political power, but progress is sluggish.

It would be most inconvenient for the Soviet Union if Europe should achieve any real political unity; thus the Soviets have fought relentlessly and bitterly, through communist parties and in their own name, against this outcome, treating unification as a sinister capitalist plot. The Soviets long refused to deal with the EEC or to take note of its existence, although recently they have been compelled to bend. A major reason for the Soviet willingness for détente is probably the well-based hope that it will stall or reverse progress toward the amalgamation of Europe. Not only is it desirable for the Soviet Union to deal separately with the European countries; a prosperous and strong European union would also be a dangerous attraction for the eastern European countries, perhaps bringing Soviet hegemony into question. It would in a remote sense squeeze the Soviet Union against China. The Chinese have shown themselves eager to see western Europe strengthened as their natural ally against the Soviets, who are horrified by any hint of a European-Chinese rapprochement.

American policy favored the EEC as a means of making Europe stronger and more prosperous and supported British entry in the hope of easing the burden of defense. European union was to be the basis of a sounder Atlantic partnership. However, there have been reservations.

---

8. Cf. Theo Sommer, "The Community Is Working," *Foreign Affairs*, 51 (July 1973), 747–760; and Roger D. Hansen, "European Integration: Forward March, Parade Rest, or Dismissed?," *International Organization*, 27 (Spring 1973), 225–254.

The State and Defense departments have been skeptical even of the British nuclear force and have worked hard to block the French *force de frappe*. There have also been doubts over economic matters; the EEC places United States exports, especially American agricultural products, at some disadvantage. But the improvement of demand in the new European prosperity has more than compensated; and the united market offers broader opportunities for branches or subsidiaries of American producers. In sum, the EEC is probably advantageous for American business, but since 1971 the United States has become much aware of allies as competitors. The United States is also disturbed by the EEC's building of a preferential trading bloc by special arrangements with other states, especially former European colonies.

For such reasons and because of friction during the Arab-Israeli war of October 1973 and the subsequent fuel crisis, the Nixon administration came to regard the Europeans as unreliable, to fear that European unity meant more power to act in ways contrary to American interests, and to emphasize bilateral contacts in which Washington would hold a greater advantage. One American demand was for a consultative voice in EEC decision making, a proposal which underlined the junior status of Europe. When the EEC undertook a joint approach to Arab oil producers in June 1974, Secretary of State Henry Kissinger was much vexed. Nevertheless, the long-term effect of the fuel crisis and of the end of United States involvement in Indochina was to make Europeans and Americans more aware of their common interests.

The real barrier to the deepening of European unity is the persistent strength of the supposedly outmoded nation-state. The Germans, the Italians, and the French think of themselves as such, speak a national language, use a national currency, serve in national armed forces, and vote for national leaders. The nation-state is still a mighty structure that only a major revolution could break up and sweep out. Supranationalism is mostly functional, a device for specific purposes requiring enlargement of the sphere of action.

Like many much less viable and effective states of Africa or Asia, the European nation-states are not eager to cast away any large part of their sovereignty. However, unity in the world of today is primarily cultural and economic. For Europe, as for Japan, there may be no real need for a major military capacity as long as the American forces stand behind them. The EEC, then, may function as a new sort of half-power, economic giant, political fumbler, and military lightweight.

Yet it is probably in the fundamental American interest that the

European allies come together as much as possible. American economic interests and Kissingerian realpolitik might prefer a weak rival, but world stability and order would benefit from a firmly welded Europe able to speak and act for itself. Europe looks to its own interests and will do so increasingly if it can overcome divisiveness, but European interests are basically close to American. Europe has no aggressive purposes as a whole, and it can act as a superpower only defensively and commercially. Its basic interests coincide with those of the United States: a stable, nonthreatening, cooperative world order. It would also be salutary if Third World states did not feel that they had to choose between the United States and the Soviet Union for support. European unification would also, of course, largely relieve the United States of the burden of Europe's defense.

JAPAN: ALLY AND RIVAL

Japan stands out as a triumph of rationality, a state that has achieved a leading place for itself by working more effectively than other countries and producing more of the goods that people desire. Like western Europe, Japan has developed great economic strength without being politically aggressive. In the Japanese case industrial growth has been even more robust, while Japanese armament is minimal.

Japan is also remarkable in that it is the only sizable part of the non-Western world that has achieved high industrialization; so successful has the nation been that the Japanese produce as much industrial goods as all the other brown-, yellow-, or black-skinned peoples together (whose total numbers are more than twenty times as great as Japan's). Japan probably has the best-educated work force and the most modern industrial equipment in the world.[9] Japan demonstrates that modernization is no secret of one race or culture. The Japanese example may be more relevant to the underdeveloped world than that of more evangelistic powers (Communist China and the Soviet Union) or that of the more powerful, more resource-rich, and more alien United States.

With few raw materials on its crowded islands, Japan has social

---

9. Norman Macrae, "Pacific Century, 1975–2025," *The Atlantic Community Quarterly*, 13 (Summer 1975), 224.

and historic advantages. It has had for centuries a strong national awareness, exceptional cultural and racial homogeneity, and a coherent social structure capable of realizing the purposes of the leadership. When Japan was opened to the world in the mid–nineteenth century, what might be called capitalism was well developed on a base of feudal institutions parallel to those of pre-modern Europe.

The Japanese set out to strengthen their community by sending men abroad to study, by establishing schools, and by importing knowledge while excluding foreign capital. Around the turn of the century, Japan was sufficiently advanced to compete in the imperialist race, acquiring Taiwan and Korea. Japan adopted a European-style constitution in 1889, because parliamentary government seemed an intrinsic part of Western civilization and thus necessary for progress. Universal suffrage was instituted, political parties functioned, and the Diet (parliament) won some control over the cabinet despite the traditional powers of the deified emperor.

When the economic depression of the 1930s began closing markets to their goods, the Japanese turned to imperialism, first taking Manchuria and then plunging into China proper. Conflict with the United States gradually built up as the Americans became more concerned over Japanese expansion and insisted on Japan's withdrawal from China; this retreat was impossible for the Japanese militarists not only because they had to save Oriental face but also because they had invested so much in the adventure. Fear and pride, coupled with misunderstanding resulting from differences of culture, led to war and loss of the Japanese empire.

The Japanese learned a lesson from defeat and undertook to remold their nation as dictated by the unexpectedly mild American conquerors. The principal antidemocratic forces, the army and the navy, having been removed, a democratic government was set up under a constitution drafted at General Douglas MacArthur's headquarters, including the remarkable Article 9:

> Aspiring sincerely to an international peace based on justice and order, the Japanese people forever renounce war as a sovereign right of the nation and the threat or use of force as a means of settling international disputes.
>
> In order to accomplish the aim of the preceding paragraph, land, sea, and air forces, as well as other war potential, will never be recognized.

Much as West Germany did at the same time with the same success,

Japan obediently adopted other adjuncts of the democratic society as conceived by the occupiers, such as land reform, trade unions, local government with substantial powers, and decentralized education. Japan thereafter functioned as a parliamentary democracy under a figure-head emperor, with freely competing political parties and a remarkably free and well-informed press.

Under the American umbrella, Japan made the most spectacular economic advance of history. The lesson of defeat was not resignation, but struggle for national greatness by pacific means. Japanese industry, which was almost nonfunctional at the end of the war, began rebuilding. The Korean War, for which the American forces procured much of their requirements from Japan, was a big boost to the Japanese economy; thereafter, success fed on success. For many years, the Japanese gross national product (GNP) grew at almost unheard-of rates of 12 to 15 percent yearly. Productivity of labor grew more than 10 percent yearly. Japan became the world's third industrial power, after the United States and the Soviet Union; it possesses a civilian industry much superior to that of the Soviet Union, which is more than 2.4 times as populous. Its GNP is triple that of China, which has about eight times the population. Although Japan has to import virtually all of its raw materials and fuel, productivity has given it a large trade surplus, and it has become a major capital exporter; big borrowers have begun to head for Tokyo instead of New York. Japanese investment abroad has emerged as a major factor on the world financial scene, much of it going to Latin America (especially to booming Brazil), to the United States, and especially to Southeast Asia, for the development of raw materials, which are contracted for long periods.

Behind economic productivity lie good morale and an extremely effective social order. Workers identify with the firm for which they work and expect to remain with it for their entire career;[10] a man belongs to the tribe of Mitsubishi industries rather than to an economic class or social group.[11] Wages are geared to corporate performance, while employers assume paternalistic responsibility for their workers. There are few strikes, and there is little need for checkouts to prevent pilfering. Unions strive to increase productivity, believing that what helps the company helps the worker. Both managers and workers see

---

10. On the loyalty factor, see William M. Wallace, "The Secret Weapon of Japanese Business," *Columbia Journal of World Business,* (November–December 1972), 43–52.

11. Macrae, "Pacific Century," p. 222.

themselves as contributing to Japanese greatness as though they were soldiers and generals at war. It has even been found necessary to fine white-collar employees for working instead of taking their allotted one-week-per-year vacations. Something remains of the old discipline expressed in the kamikaze sentiments such as, "Please congratulate me, I have been given a splendid opportunity to die."[12] There is still a feeling that the Japanese are a single family under the emperor. Japan's economic success is also in large part organizational; the Japanese seemed to have found a better balance between fraternity and competition than other peoples. America may well learn something from the Japanese style of group decision.[13]

Not all is well, however. The growth of production with urbanization has multiplied problems of congestion, poor sanitation, inadequate transport and housing, and air and water pollution. The energy crisis showed the vulnerability of the economy, which is almost entirely dependent on imported fuel. There is a spirit of rebellion among many of the young, as cosmopolitan ideas of freedom and equality conflict with traditional ideals of loyalty and obedience, and labor has become more demanding. Inflation and recession have struck hard. Yet of all major nations, Japan may have the best prospects for continued rapid growth.

It is consequently fortunate that Japanese-American relations have been remarkably good. After the American forces, upon the signing of the 1951 peace treaty, changed from occupiers to allies stationed in Japan under the Japanese-American security treaty, friction continued to be marginal. Some anti-American sentiment grew up on the left, especially among radical students, and the Vietnam war shook American prestige and turned sympathies toward fellow Asians. Throughout the 1960s, however, the Japanese government was decidedly complaisant and deferred to the United States both as victor and as model of economic success.

Problems at issue have been mostly economic. The United States market is essential to Japan both for sale of manufactures and as a

12. In the East Asian-Confucianist tradition, the Japanese spirit of devotion to work is akin to that which makes the North Vietnamese superb soldiers and leads the Chinese to labor uncomplainingly for the people, the Revolution, and Chairman Mao. In the same vein, a Korean prostitute, speaking of the flood of Japanese clients, said, "It's hard for us to accept some—but we must work hard not only for ourselves and our families but for our country's future. Our country needs more money for its economic development." *Time*, June 4, 1973, p. 45.

13. S. Prakesh Sethi, "Japanese Management Practice," *Columbia Journal of World Business*, 9 (Winter 1974), 94–104.

source of materials; this market accounts for over a quarter of Japanese trade. The large Japanese export surplus contributed to the severe pressure on the American balance of payments in the early 1970s, and Japan was faced with a series of demands for the limitation of exports and the facilitation of imports. The Japanese obeyed sufficiently (while United States trade was helped by devaluation of the dollar and other measures) that the imbalance lost importance, while Japanese-American trade rose to $25 billion annually. No other country has been more cooperative on trade and monetary matters, more open to trade and investment.[14]

American security responsibilities in Japan are similar to those in Europe, and the resulting problems are parallel. The security pact, which has been twice renewed for ten-year periods, can be terminated on one year's notice, but neither party has shown any desire to end it. For Japan, the pact has permitted saving that which it might otherwise have seemed necessary to spend for defense; this saving has been an important factor for the level of investment, which is the highest in the world. For the United States, Japan was not only an important country to be preserved but a forward position, the "unsinkable aircraft carrier," against the Asian enemy, Communist China. But as Japan has grown stronger and more self-confident, it has, like Europe, felt somewhat restive under the American nuclear umbrella. The American bases are chronic irritants, although they have been much reduced. Both sides still seem to assume that the American nuclear umbrella is a good thing, but its necessity has become less compelling in the more relaxed world atmosphere. The Japanese position is also strengthened by the seemingly unbridgeable quarrel between the other two sides of the Asian triangle; it is inconceivable that either China or the Soviet Union would launch an assault upon Japan, even if there were no American protection, without attacking or neutralizing the other.

Furthermore, it is not likely that the Soviet Union will gain much influence in Japan by political methods, subversive or otherwise. The Russians and Japanese have usually been at odds since they came into serious contact toward the end of the nineteenth century. The Japanese may have felt guilty toward the Americans because of Pearl Harbor, but they have not forgiven the Russians for refusing to help them end the war in the spring of 1945 and then attacking Japan in violation of

14. Kohi Taira, "Japan after the Oil Shock," *Current History*, 69 (April 1975), 147.

their nonaggression treaty after the United States dropped the atomic bomb on Hiroshima. The Japanese, even communists, unanimously demand return of four small islands occupied by the Soviets just above the northern Japanese island of Hokkaido. Since the Soviet Union adamantly refuses to consider such a cession, there is still no peace treaty between the two powers. For these reasons, the Soviet press long displayed much hostility to Japan as an "imperialist" power. Only with the American approach to China in 1971 was Soviet hostility largely replaced by the strong desire to secure Japanese investment, perhaps of billions of dollars, to aid the exploitation of Siberian resources. The Japanese, however, have been cautious about commitments to the Soviet Union; trade between the two countries is less than a tenth of that between Japan and the United States.

Toward China, Japanese feelings are infused with a sense of guilt for the years of military action against that country and with a sense of community with the motherland of Japanese culture. As admiration for the United States has lessened, most Japanese consider China their favorite foreign country. Japanese industry and Chinese raw materials are economically complementary, and the Japanese, like the Americans, have allowed themselves to daydream about the Chinese market. However, the Japanese and the Chinese are natural rivals for influence in eastern and Southeast Asia, and their mentality and institutions are antithetical.

The United States would vaguely like to see Japan as balancer of both China and the Soviet Union, an offset to the power of these two nations and a check on any potential expansion by either. The idea of a rearmed Japan, however, is regarded with horror, to some extent in the United States and more so in Asia, which has not forgotten the bitter taste of Japanese imperialism. Rearmament is also rejected by most of the Japanese, who have done very well without arms and who have the memory of the only two atomic bombs ever put to use.

It is questionable, however, whether Japan will remain permanently satisfied to be economically strong but militarily weak. In the changing of generations, the nuclear aversion wears off and nationalism resurges. Self-reliance implies possession of whatever forces are essential for defense or for backing of national policy without having to look to Washington; nuclear weapons are cheapest in terms of effectiveness, require least manpower, and best accord with the high technological level of Japan. Moreover, Japan is one of the leading nations in the application of atomic power, a resource that is especially attractive for a nation without domestic fuel supplies. As a byproduct of atomic energy production, Japan should soon have enough plutonium to make several thousand A-bombs yearly, along with the capacity to manufacture at least medium-range missiles. Inevitably, there have been voices in favor of Japan's joining the nuclear club, and Japan has thus far declined to ratify the Nuclear Non-Proliferation Treaty.

Japan has resisted, however, intermittent American pressures to ignore or abrogate the constitutional prohibition and expand its armed forces. The defense forces are now limited to 237,000 men and cost less than 1 percent of Japan's GNP: $3.5 billion in 1973,[15] or $33 per capita as against $404 in the United States. A case for armaments must always be stated in terms of defense requirements, but the Japanese hardly feel threatened by anyone, and it is not clear that a home-based nuclear force would really contribute to the security of the vulnerable islands—a half-dozen H-bombs could practically annihilate the nation. It seems a better gamble to hope for a peaceful world than to rely on a nuclear force, which might be a deterrent but might also be provocative, hurtful to the Japanese position with buyers and sellers, and alarming to China and much of the rest of Asia.

There is little temptation to aggression. Japan does not feel itself a present or potential political superpower; the key of its foreign policy is the low profile. Japanese diplomacy is overwhelmingly oriented toward economic concerns. Its posture, under the American umbrella, is of defenselessness.[16] Its most flourishing trade is with the industrial nations that it cannot possibly dominate, and any signs of militarism would be harmful to business with them. China is no longer a temptation, as it was in the 1930s; there are no European overseas empires to emulate and no European colonies in Asia to be "Asianized." Most of the smaller states of Asia are growing fairly rapidly; already somewhat resentful of Japanese economic domination, they are not likely to submit readily to Japanese hegemony. But the Japanese have done very well commercially in Southeast Asia without a military presence, and their large investments abroad could only be endangered by an adventurous policy. Unless the Japanese become disillusioned with their peaceful approach and come to feel that they are scorned, bullied, or discriminated against because of their lack of military muscle, they may be expected to continue thinking in terms of a nonmilitary future. As a Japanese sees it, "The capacity to serve other nations is the foun-

---

15. *The Military Balance*, International Institute for Strategic Studies, London, 1973.
16. Taira, "Japan after the Oil Shock," p. 184.

dation of our survival"; for example, the Arabs relented on oil cut-backs because they needed Japanese fertilizer.[17]

It becomes increasingly important for the United States to retain the friendship of this new giant. Japan is politically the outpost of the Western world in eastern Asia, and it has a key role in relations of the United States and China. Economically, Japan is already far stronger relative to the United States than at the time of Pearl Harbor. In a few years, Japanese foreign trade may well exceed that of the United States as it has that of the Soviet Union since 1965. If, as some prognosticate, Japan can continue to expand at recent rates, it will be the world's leading economic power in the 1980s.[18] The future course of Japan will have much to do with the future shape of the world. In a sense, Japan is more important than all the rest of Asia, including China. For the Japanese, too, America is the chief partner, both commercially and politically; security means good relations with China and the Soviet Union and close relations with the United States.

There are difficulties. Language is a barrier; Japanese is perhaps the world's most difficult written language. Very few foreigners learn it well, while relatively few Japanese learn foreign languages. Japan culturally resembles China and economically resembles the United States, but its ways are its own. It is said to be much harder for an American to plunge into business in Tokyo than in Karachi, and certainly than in Hamburg or Paris. There is also a racial tinge in American attitudes. Early in this century there was anti-Japanese legislation in California, and after Pearl Harbor Americans of Japanese origin were interned; no one suggested similar treatment for German-Americans. In recent years, it has seemed difficult or perhaps impossible to show intelligent Japanese the same respect as that shown to intelligent Europeans. Americans fail to penetrate the Japanese mentality and seldom make much effort to do so. Officials seem to expect more humility and docility from the Asians.

There has consequently been some arrogance in American treatment of Japan and some resentment of its economic success as somehow unfairly gained; this resentment has been manifested in peremptory demands for limitations of exports such as would hardly be ad-

---

17. Matasaka Kosaka, "The Nature of the Trial Facing Japan," *The Atlantic Community Quarterly,* 13 (Summer 1975), 201.

18. Martin Beresford, "And Now, le Defi Japonais," *The Atlantic Community Quarterly,* 13 (Summer 1975), 220–225. See also Solomon B. Levine, "Japan's Economy: End of the Miracle?," *Current History,* 68 (April 1975), 148–154.

dressed to Europeans. The chief American fault, however, has been more of style than substance: a failure to consider Japanese feelings. While the United States is careless about doing Europeans the courtesy of consulting them regarding policies that affect them, it quite neglects the Japanese, even in Asian affairs. For example, no effort was made to take the Japanese into account in the Vietnam settlement, where they might have played a positive role; they were not even invited to the Paris conference in 1973 to underwrite the ceasefire. In another sphere, the sale of soybeans (far more important to the Japanese than the American diet) was abruptly halted with no effort to soften the blow.

The Japanese are engaged in a singular experiment in unarmed greatness, indifferent to ideology and unburdened by poltical ambitions. It may well be that they represent the style of the future in international relations. American understanding and cooperation will have much to do with the success or failure of the Japanese experiment and so with the shape of the world of the future.

CIVILIZED INTERNATIONAL RELATIONS

The general style of United States relations with its European allies and Japan prevails in dealings with other advanced industrial states: a substantial community of interest, freedom from major political antagonisms, and usually a de facto but diffuse American leadership in a multitude of formal and informal groupings. Such international relations are new in character. Before World War II, the biggest issues were territorial claims—the urge to increase power by acquiring real estate—and the strongest antipathies were between neighboring and kindred states. As a result of wars, nuclear weapons, and the maturation of industrial civilization, outlooks have changed profoundly. There is no longer any important territorial issue between industrialized countries. Among modern nations of roughly similar political and economic development, those that have attained industrial prosperity and play a strong role in the world trading community (excluding the Soviet Union and other states controlled by Marxist-Leninist parties), there are no big political issues at all, no emotionally potent differences that could conceivably lead to risking bloodshed. The great impetus to transcending narrow nationalist positions was given by World War II (driving home the lessons of World War I), which showed that the

enmities that historically tore Europe apart had lost whatever significance they might once have had, and many wartime combined boards
set the stage for postwar international cooperation. Europeans resolved
that there must never again be an intra-European war. Through the
postwar years, the growth in exchanges of goods and people, the vast
increase of communications among nations, and the need for common
action in many areas made traditional nationalism more and more
parochial. A leader such as De Gaulle might still use nationalist feeling
as a morale builder, but it is hardly a cause for serious quarrels in the
Western world, much less for threats of probably suicidal war. On the
other side of the world, Japan gave up the idea of aggrandizement
through arms in favor of progress through work. Nationalism is much
more conspicuous as a force among the less developed, historically nonnational states.

For all developed nations, trade and other advantages of international intercourse are more important than the possibility of a marginal
addition to the national territory (which would probably be disadvan-
tageous because of opposition of the inhabitants, even if it did not reap
worldwide reprobation) or a slight improvement of prestige, a climb
in the pecking order of nations. Hence the largest subjects of diplomacy among these nations are typically questions of mercantile content, such as trade barriers, tariffs, quotas, and the like. Innumerable
practical matters, such as treatment of foreign enterprises and allocation of airline routes, require resolution. Monetary matters, such as exchange rates and their management, have caused many problems.
Occasionally emotions have become fairly hot. An example is the "cod
war" of the early 1970s between Britain and Iceland, arising from the
effort of Iceland to exclude foreign fishing from Icelandic waters to a
distance of first fifty and then two hundred miles and the refusal of
Britain to acquiesce. There have been threats and protests, chiefly on
the Icelandic side, but the "war" has remained at a low level, with zero
casualties. Another example might be the "chicken war" of 1963, when
the United States took umbrage at European duties on American frozen chickens and attacked brandy imports in reprisal.[19] Another typical
conflict of interests came with the reluctance in 1976 of the United
States to permit the Anglo-French supersonic Concorde to land at
New York or Washington.

It has been possible to confront issues between developed nations

---

19. Finn B. Jensen and Ingo Walter, *The Common Market: Integration in
Europe,* Lippincott, Philadelphia, 1965, p. 230.

with little excitement. Officials of the American administration were irate that Europeans made their own approaches to the Arabs in the fuel crisis of 1973–1974, but the country at large took no note of the affront. There is usually a desire for compromise, and issues are resolved or forgotten. To a degree unprecedented in history, the developed nations form an international family, not a very affectionate but a sufficiently compatible one, with no apparent threats of divorce or murder.

They live in reasonable concord because common interests outweigh divisive ones, and they are generally at pains to play down whatever disagreements there may be. Trade and multifarious international exchanges of resources and technology are mutually advantageous, and the advantages are real. In a purely political struggle, the winnings for the people in general are largely illusory. Political standing is a seesaw, and one goes up by pushing others down. However, the economies of the United States, Japan, and Europe move up or down together, and it is taken for granted that the representatives of these nations should meet to coordinate anti-inflationary or antirecession strategies. The governments are sufficiently sophisticated to recognize their profound interdependence and to avoid making political capital of their economic differences. In United Nations debates, the fiery speeches come first from representatives of the less developed world and second from the communist states; it is they who are aroused and wish to arouse others over countless issues of power, race, territorial claims, real or alleged injuries, political interference, and ideological demands.

Common interests make community; despite cultural and racial difference from the occidental majority, Japan is a leading member of the community of advanced nations. The principal qualifications are economic maturity, a large stake in world trade, and the desire to participate; there is no reason to suppose that any advanced Asian, African, or Latin American country would not be welcome.

It seems to be essential, however, to have a liberal political system—one in which an opposition can freely organize and express itself—in order to qualify fully. Dictatorships, such as Spain under the rule of Franco and Greece until 1974, are hardly acceptable as equal partners with western Europe despite rapid economic growth. Much less is it possible to welcome the Soviet Union into the family unless or until it greatly relaxes its economic and political controls. Dictatorships require too much secrecy and are free to act arbitrarily, and negotiations with controlled economies are quite different from those with market economies.

With no major political demands upon one another, the advanced industrial countries have some feeling of community as against the less developed nations, whose problems and claims are different. The two groups stand on opposite sides of a great divide in human affairs; they come more or less into opposition as the poorer countries press for special consideration and favors that the more developed are seldom eager to grant. The two sectors inevitably have different priorities and values. The advanced industrial nations also feel themselves apart from the Marxist-Leninist states, however much they may desire improved relations. It is impossible to feel confident of the intentions of the Soviet Union when its leaders act as a closed corporation that might conceivably swerve from détente to confrontation overnight with no need to account to its own people, and that at the same time maintains a goal of spreading "socialism" and arrogates to itself the right to intervene in other countries in the name of proletarian internationalism. Even with China, where there is less undercurrent of fear, relations are held back by the hermeticism of Chinese society. Trade is limited, foreign businesses and organizations cannot operate, the flow of information is halted at the border, and movement of people is minimal.

For these reasons, the relations of the United States with the industrialized and liberal countries have a different character from those with either the less developed world or the communist countries. With the former, the main problems are questions of development and frictions arising from insufficiency; with the latter, questions of security and the resolution of conflicts are critical. With other developed industrial nations there are concrete disagreements but there is no background of anxiety. With Canada, for example, the United States shares the world's longest unfortified boundary; neither power is to the slightest degree armed against the other. It is assumed that in any threat to the security of North America the two must cooperate, as they do in air defense. Trade between them is approximately equal to United States trade with all of Latin America. Citizens of the two countries freely cross the border.

Yet Canada has shown growing independence in foreign policy; it opened diplomatic relations with Peking far ahead of the United States and became a leading supplier of goods to Communist China while the United States was still boycotting that country. Canadians bristle at slights by American diplomats, fret over United States "cultural imperialism," and act to favor Canadian publications and television programs over those from south of the border. They are even more troubled by the ownership of a large part of their economy by

Americans. American investment in Canadian enterprises totaled $35 billion in 1973; United States companies own nine-tenths of all large Canadian plants—that is, those employing more than five thousand workers—and 60 percent of all Canadian corporate assets. There is agitation for more restrictions and controls, and there is fear of Canada becoming a raw materials–producing appendix of the United States.[20]

Similar principles apply to American relations with other developed countries—Australia, New Zealand, Britain and other countries of western Europe, and Japan. All share a fundamental harmony of interests; the weaker of them, even those outside the American-led alliances, rely ultimately upon the United States for security. Yet there is independence of views on all sides and more than a little friction over many usually complex and often obscure economic issues. The basic cause for uneasiness, tending to aggravate confrontations over specific differences, is that the United States is overly conspicuous (if not overbearing) culturally and economically. Like Canada, Australia turned more independent-minded under former Labour Prime Minister Gough Whitlam. In reprisal for forceful criticism of American policy in the last months of the Vietnam war, the Australian leader was not received at the White House at about the time when Leonid Brezhnev was being embraced as an old friend. The Australians, however, desire to maintain their security affiliation with the United States and thus tolerate the continued presence of secret American communications and satellite-tracking stations whereas they deny similar facilities to the Soviet Union.

Since they have much in common, it has been suggested by foreign policy expert Zbigniew Brzezinski (among others) that the affluent countries should form a sort of league, a "trilateral" association, to promote their interests. But they are likely to unite only in realms of thought. No military threat drives them into closer association; they are all to some extent already under the American nuclear umbrella. Their relations go on in myriad daily doings in many institutional frameworks developed ad hoc; it is the essence of their relations that they are mostly private and spontaneous. Various members of the community have their special relations with parts of the Third World: the United States with Latin America, France and England with parts of Africa, and Japan with eastern Asia. It would be undesirable, more-

---

20. Canadian investment in the United States is approximately equal in volume but causes no comment.

over, to set the more developed nations further apart from the less developed, certain of which (such as Brazil) climb toward the more privileged category. The group of the modernized states is open, and the countries involved cannot go their own separate ways.

They may be pointing to the direction that the world will take in the future. Almost everywhere, territorial claims and ambitions seem to be receding; the exceptions, although conspicuous, are very few in view of the large number of sovereignties that are in contact. Spheres of influence apparently are weakening, perhaps including even Soviet dominion in eastern Europe. The network of interdependency enmeshes everyone. Even for communist states, the necessity for trade outweighs ideology. It is not impossible—although it is still a very distant hope—that relations among states everywhere will come to resemble those prevalent among those most advanced in the application of material knowledge. If so, many problems will become more soluble.

CHAPTER SEVEN

The Communist World

THE ANTITHESIS

Sixteen nations, with about a third of the population of the globe and approximately the same share of world industrial production, stand somewhat apart from the rest of the world. The reasons are not economic or cultural but basically political and historical. These states have undergone a revolution under the banner of a distinctive movement of radical change (Lenin's development of, or deviation from, Marxism) or have been brought by external force (the Soviet army) under this banner. The revolutionary ideology claims specialness and total superiority for the new "socialist" state as part of a universal movement of historical transformation.

Insofar as Marxist-Leninist, or communist, states continue to take seriously their ideology, with its emphasis on class struggle, they must consider themselves theoretically more or less at war with "class-hostile," "capitalist," or "bourgeois" states, chief of which is the United States. (This antagonism against capitalism does not, of course, preclude hostility for other Marxist-Leninist states.) Consequently, communist nations inspire some fear in other peoples because of stated or implied intentions of spreading their form of government, intentions supported by military strength as well as by actions such as Soviet intervention and repression in Hungary and Czechoslovakia. Security considerations are thus prominent in dealing with these authoritarian states.

The communist states are distinct, however, not only in their ideology of conflict and the distrust which tinges their relations with capitalist states. They lay great stress upon the differences of their "socialist" societies from others less "progressive," and the differences are real. To a degree far beyond such dictatorships as are familiar in Latin America and elsewhere, the communists maintain total management of society. The economy is state-run and managed (so far as is feasible) from top to bottom. Means of information are not only censored to prevent undesired opposition but also harnessed to promote correct thinking. The ruling group, the "party," maintains a monopoly of legal organization in the name of the official ideology. In sum, they are markedly closed societies, much more fully integrated than the societies of the industrial West or than the preindustrial societies of the Third World.

To maintain their control of the economy and public opinion, they minimize flows across the borders. Foreign trade and travel are managed by official agencies and are allowed to the extent that the state finds necessary. The communist states, even counting exchanges among themselves, contribute only a little over 10 percent of world trade. Travel across their borders is practically limited to closely controlled tourism, and the flow of information is kept as restricted as is feasible. In many international bodies, especially those dealing with economic matters, they do not participate at all; in others they participate only marginally. By their own design, they form a world somewhat apart.

Hence American contacts with communist states, even when détente is on the agenda, lack breadth and depth. With the Soviet Union, however, there is another, deeper cause of friction. Insofar as diplomacy is concerned with power and prestige, the two strongest states are inevitably rivals. They are the superpowers and possess at least 90 percent of the nuclear capability of the world. They alone have a global reach, while the field of action of others is essentially local. Although events are no longer judged primarily in relation to a bipolar world struggle, an advance of Soviet influence probably means a retreat of American influence, and vice versa. The Soviets encouraged many countries to expropriate American investments and promised to replace Western economic support. The competitors with whom Americans shared the glories of space exploration were the Soviets, and it is with the expansive Soviet navy that the American navy must divide the oceans. The big antagonisms in world relations focus on the Soviet-American confrontation.

The ideological element cannot be neglected. The Soviet Union at one time took the communist movement and its revolutionary mission very seriously; the Bolsheviks who made the revolution in 1917 regarded themselves as exponents of an international movement of the working class, not the heirs of the tsarist state. Lenin, like Woodrow Wilson, wanted to establish a new world order, however different were the Russian leader's means and philosophy. For a few years, the young Soviet state was dedicated to the propagation of its revolution abroad, especially in Germany.[1] Interest in making world revolution waned as Europe settled down after World War I, but the Soviets still pay much attention to communist parties (whose goals are supposedly revolutionary), support them if they are loyal, and try to hold them under Soviet control.

Although the Soviet Union has become a rather immobile state run

---

1. For a general account, see Adam B. Ulam, *Expansion and Coexistence: Soviet Foreign Policy, 1917–1973,* 2nd ed., Praeger, New York, 1974; and George F. Kennan, *Russia and the West under Lenin and Stalin,* Little, Brown, Boston, 1961.

by a stable elite, it still tries to indoctrinate its citizens from kindergarten on with the idea of class struggle as the mover of history, the falsity of nationalism and bourgeois democracy, the essential unity of the workers, the viciousness and evil of the old bourgeois or capitalist order, the destiny of the proletariat as the bringer of a new and better socialist order, and the right of the Communist party to govern as the vanguard of the working class. The Marxist-Leninist faith, including these and related ideas woven into a fairly consistent intellectual edifice, has been propagated so intensively that the thinking of nearly everyone in the Soviet Union, even the cynics, is much affected by it. It is most of all drilled into the rising members of the party and the directing cadres; in all probability the leaders believe in the special destiny that this faith assigns to their land and to them.

A postrevolutionary state thus clings to a revolutionary ideology much more suited to 1917 and 1918 than to the 1970s. There are a number of reasons. One is that the permanent rule by a narrow self-selected group, with only formal concessions to the political rights of the people, requires in this age a special justification, some better mission than the selfish desires of the elite. The claim to absolute truth is needed to justify repression of philosophic or political dissent. Another and no less important utility of Marxism-Leninism is its rationalization for the very existence of the Soviet Union. This, like the Russian empire before it, is no national state but a conglomerate of peoples, most of whom would probably prefer much more self-rule. The Soviet state is held together by military force, by the controlled media and propaganda, and by the strong organizational unity of the centrally directed Communist party; but the whole complicated system would probably not be workable without the ideology exalting the union of the workers and denigrating national separatism as bourgeois.

The result is that the Soviet state is deeply ambiguous (as to a less marked degree its tsarist predecessor was). It is revolutionary and conservative. It is equalitarian and elitist, universalist and self-centered. It is guided by ideology and by realpolitik—the former being mostly rationalization, the latter operational. It is verbally internationalist yet thoroughly Russian-oriented in action. It looks to useful though hardly actually friendly relations with Western capitalist powers, the overthrow of which is supposedly the prime objective of the communist movement which it heads. It stands overtly for peaceful coexistence, yet it ceaselessly warns its citizens that coexistence means no compromise, only struggle by nonviolent means.

If Soviet leaders believed their dogmas fully and literally and drew the logical consequences, the world would be either Soviet-led and communized or a very dangerous place. The men of the Kremlin would view all nonsovietized states as inevitably and totally hostile. Soviet expansion would be dictated by the expectation that bourgeois states must sooner or later attack the Soviet socialist state, as well as by the duty to liberate the masses from the tyranny of capitalism. The Soviet Union would not necessarily reject a truce in the class war of socialism against capitalism, but it would at all times do everything in its power, by propaganda, subversion, and the support of communist parties, to destroy the old governments and their evil and menacing societies.

The Soviet Union has never behaved in quite this way, even when the revolution was freshest and most passionate. Lenin was determined to make peace with Germany early in 1918, when more consistent comrades argued that there could be no peace between ideological opposites. From that time onward, the Soviet Union has been prepared to deal with supposedly incorrigible enemies, and practical interests of state have always overridden the ideal interests of the international working class and its projected world revolution. Above all, the Soviets have been interested in commercial relations with the outside world and in the importation of modern technology—relations that in principle are inconsistent with class warfare.

Yet there has undoubtedly been considerable ideological content in Soviet behavior. Internally, the Soviets have almost always upheld strongly the picture of a virtuous Soviet socialism surrounded by vicious and dangerous capitalist powers. Interpretations of foreign affairs in the Soviet press have usually been quite Leninist, often unrealistically so. Thus, in recent years, Israel has been treated as an American instrument for getting control of Arab oil, and the British effort to keep order in Northern Ireland has been seen as merely the action of colonial capitalists against the people.

Stalin, who was in control from the death of Lenin in 1924 until his own demise in 1953, was much more nationalistic than Lenin and was not disposed to promote revolution except where he could control it. He paid most attention to the building up of Soviet industry (especially heavy industry), to bringing the peasantry under control through the socialization of agriculture, and to purging all potential opposition to himself. But he was happy to expand also. In August 1939, he signed a pact with Adolf Hitler which opened the gates of war, presumably because he wanted to stay out of the fray while seeing the Western powers tear each other to pieces and because he coveted the loot Hitler offered. In 1939–1940 he picked up the three Baltic republics of Estonia, Latvia, and Lithuania (with all of which the Soviets had nonaggression and friendship treaties) and a stretch of Romania. These were nearly all territories that had once belonged to the tsars, but they were all non-Russian. Stalin also made war on Finland when it refused to give up strategic positions, loss of which would have compromised its independence. He seemingly wanted to take the whole country, and he settled for limited gains only because the Finns resisted fiercely and earned so much sympathy in the West that the war became dangerous to his power. After World War II, Stalin staked out something like a Soviet empire in eastern Europe and, as though this were not enough, went prowling around the Soviet periphery for more land at the expense of Iran, Turkey, China, and other countries. Finally, he permitted or encouraged his Korean dependents to try to seize the southern half of Korea.[2]

Expansionist Soviet policy was the cause or (as the revisionists would have it) the excuse for the cold war and for the antisovietism and anticommunism that dominated American foreign policy for a generation and are still much alive. The rationale was containment, which was only an extension of the approach followed with little change since the birth of the Soviet Union: the policy of waiting for internal evolution to normalize and make the Soviets easier to deal with. But the overt containment program, with its militaristic overtones, was in some ways helpful to the Soviet regime. The two-part, bipolar image of the world perfectly suited Soviet dogma and gave credibility to the picture of the worldwide struggle between socialism and capitalism. The widespread American presence, especially the network of military bases around the periphery of the Sino-Soviet bloc, could be and was depicted as an enormous and ominous American empire; insofar as insensitive American leaders permitted this nework to take on imperialistic traits, the Soviet case was strengthened and the Soviet empire was provided with needed justification. If America could be denounced as a colonial ruler, Soviet expansionism could be excused as defensive, while American rhetoric helped to maintain the image of the fierce hostility of capitalism to Soviet socialism. Whenever American policy became militaristic and dogmatic, this turn of affairs suited the Soviet version of world affairs.

It became difficult, however, for the United States to sustain its stance of uncompromising opposition to communism and the Soviet

---

2. On Soviet expansionism, see Ulam, *Expansion and Coexistence.*

Union. The Korean War, which was responsible for much of the militarization of Soviet policy, represented the last forceful outward thrust for which Soviet expansionism could reasonably be blamed. The Soviet push since then has amounted to little more than encouragement and support for communist parties sponsored by and supposedly loyal to the Soviet Union, the securing of naval bases by political deals, and so forth. There have been no blatant attacks on innocent small nations (except police actions to hold the Soviet bloc together), no provocations like those of hysterical dictators.

American policy makers have not been much relieved, however. It had been assumed that if a procommunist party came to power anywhere, it would probably be dependent upon the Soviets and so would be constrained to cooperate politically and militarily with them. The United States might have no means of preventing an expanding communist league from becoming so powerful as to dominate an indefinite part of the world—an outcome which, in the Soviet ideological scheme, was not only possible but predictable. The future, as Khrushchev painted and probably pictured it in the later 1950s, should go about as follows: The Soviet Union would continue to gain, economically and militarily, relative to the United States, surpassing it by perhaps 1970; encouraged by the Soviet example of economic, cultural, and social development, and with the direct help of the Soviet Union, pro-Soviet or national liberation movements would take power in more and more countries, tear them from the imperialist camp, and line them up with the Soviet Union, until the remnants of capitalism collapsed and the world entered the era of communism under Soviet leadership.[3]

In the 1950s, events seemed to be going according to this scheme. The Soviet growth rate was high, while that of the United States lagged, and if one projected graphs of production of basic commodities in the two countries, it appeared that they would soon cross and American economic preponderance would become a melancholy memory. Soviet prestige rose enormously with the first intercontinental ballistic missiles (ICBMs) and the first satellite (1957). The Soviets inaugurated a program of foreign and military aid to swing less developed countries to their side, and friendship for the Soviet Union rose rapidly

---

3. As Khrushchev said in 1959, "We are confident that we shall conquer capitalism. We shall conquer it not by war, but by demonstrating practically to all that the working class has a great truth—the teaching of Marxism-Leninism." *Conquest without War*, ed. N. H. Mager and Jacques Katel, Simon and Schuster, New York, 1961, p. 52.

in many countries. In several (for example, Algeria, Ghana, and Guinea), anti-Western, socialistically inclined leaders came to power and edged their nations close to the Soviet bloc.

For the United States, priding itself on openness and tolerance of divergent philosophies, it was not easy to war against a political creed that claimed to stand for progress, justice, peace, equality, and the ultimate happiness of humanity. Yet it seemed necessary to combat the creed and corresponding political organization that sought to undermine the strength of the West and its potential for resistance to Soviet power. By permitting the contest to be stated at least partly in terms of socialism versus capitalism instead of national independence versus Soviet domination, allowing fictions of class conflict to become political realities, the United States involved itself in something that it was not prepared to judge and handle—the internal composition and social problems of strange peoples. The United States lacked the means to democratize in the way that the Russians could sovietize.

The United States, confused and uncertain in its purposes, thus found itself in an unpromising contest with a huge, purposefully organized, and power-bent Soviet Union; Khrushchev's postsputnik optimism did not seem ridiculous. But the looser, more democratic state can hope to come out well if it can hold out; the dictatorial state must be victorious rather soon or else find its dynamism and strength decaying. The Soviet growth rates declined in the early 1960s, and the Soviet Union seemed in some ways to be losing ground rather than gaining with respect to the West. Khrushchev's ventures in diplomacy brought no big returns, and the West failed to crack up. Worse for the Soviet vision of the future, instead of expanding indefinitely the Soviet sphere contracted sharply with the splitting away (after Yugoslavia) of Albania and China (the latter accounting for two-thirds of the population of the socialist camp).

By the time Khrushchev was overthrown in October 1964, it seemed that the Soviet offensive had been turned back; this feeling contributed to the American overconfidence of the middle 1960s. The post-Khrushchev collective leadership in effect pulled in its horns for several years. The quiet, methodical new Soviet leaders gave up Khrushchev's flamboyance and his hurry for big triumphs, seeking to build more slowly but more solidly. Soviet diplomats and diplomacy left behind their earlier crudity and became more polished and civilized. There was no more bragging about soon surpassing the United States economically, and there was less talk of the proximate worldwide victory of socialism and the utopia it would bring. Soviet foreign

aid was cut back. There was less emphasis on subversion; communist
parties instead tried to gain respectability and to come to power by
legal means, even while remaining verbally loyal to Marxism-Leninism
and theoretically to the Soviet state. At the same time, the Soviet Union
in its dealings abroad shifted emphasis from communist parties to governments. It was quite willing to sacrifice local parties to political advantage; if Nasser repressed Egyptian communists, this action was a
matter of indifference as long as he was amenable to Soviet diplomacy.

But the post-Khrushchev leadership continued and intensified the
confrontation in military terms. Instead of rattling mostly fake rockets
as Khrushchev had done, it set about making real ones. Soviet military
spending by 1972 was estimated to be somewhat higher than American, and Soviet hardware procurement was substantially greater because payment of personnel bulked much larger for American forces.[4]
In 1962, the United States had five times as many ICBMs as the Soviet
Union; a decade later, the Soviets had half again as many as the United
States and had come level with the United States in the number of
nuclear submarines. From 1965 to 1970, the Soviet armed forces grew
from 3.1 to 3.4 million men, while the American forces were shrinking
from 3.5 to 2.7 million. The Soviet army acquired a formidable array
of improved weaponry, including new tanks and missiles and nuclear
battlefield equipment. The Soviet air force and air transport fleet expanded rapidly, with many new types of planes. Coming from near the
starting line, the Soviet navy expanded greatly and spread its presence
not only across the Mediterranean and the Red Sea but to all the
oceans of the world.

It was questionable how far this multisided program was defensively motivated, how far it sprang from the old urge to keep up with
the West, how much it represented ambition for greater power, and to
what extent it may have corresponded to ideological imperatives,
which the Soviets claim to maintain unchanged. When the United
States enjoyed very large strategic superiority, the Soviets showed
much confidence that they were in no real danger. There is little defensive justification for the swelling Soviet navy or for the upward
spiraling of Soviet forces in all categories beyond visible defensive
needs and political commitments; this fact suggests that military expansion may be designed to support a forward foreign policy or at

---

4. Accurate estimates are impossible not only because of Soviet secrecy but
because of problems of pricing, Soviet military goods being relatively very cheap.

least to permit taking advantage of disorderly situations. There is no evidence in Soviet or Russian history or in our knowledge of Soviet politics to suggest that Soviet leaders would hesitate to apply force wherever they might find it advantageous to do so.

FROM CONFRONTATION TO ACCOMMODATION

Despite the built-in hositility of the antithetical superpowers, there was a growing inclination, as the cold war dragged on, to seek agreement. But negotiations were difficult, and both sides held to rigid positions. It was not practical to draw boundaries of spheres of influence, a solution that contravened both Soviet and American principles. There were proposals from time to time for disengagement in Europe, but the United States felt that Soviet forces could easily return, while American forces (for political as well as logistical reasons), could not. The Soviets, on the other hand, could not afford to remove their armies from the satellite countries lest these escape control.

Reciprocity was frequently hard to attain in dealings with the Soviets. For example, the Soviets severely restricted movement of American (and other) diplomats; for bargaining purposes, the United States restricted Soviet diplomats less severely and was not in a position really to enforce even this restriction, since travel in the United States is practically uncontrolled. Disarmament negotiations caused more friction than disarmament. There was some question as to whether concessions to the Soviets generated good will or were regarded as manifestations of weakness, an invitation to press for more. In the Soviet press, at least, concessions to the Soviet view were usually described as something forced out of the unwilling bourgeoisie by the strength of the socialist countries or the force of an aroused public opinion. Americans rightly recognized that a major difficulty was the sense of insecurity of the Soviet leadership, but the insecurity could not be easily removed because it was primarily internal.

By the early 1960s, the cold war was abating. In 1959, Khrushchev announced the intention to promote Soviet industrialization by buying Western factories; the proportion of Soviet foreign trade going to the West has been growing ever since.[5] De-Stalinization resulted in some

---

5. Marshall Goldman, *Détente and Dollars*, Basic Books, New York, 1975, p. 27.

change in the Soviet system. It seemed clear that communism was not about to sweep the world. It had turned out to be much less monolithic and avalanchelike than had been supposed. Not only had Yugoslavia long maintained its independence, but the divergence of China and the Soviet Union was an increasingly evident reality, and there were fissiparous tendencies nearly everywhere in the communist movement. The Cuban missile crisis of 1962 brought increased sobriety. There was no more desire on either side to seek confrontation.

Habits of hostility gradually eased. A large sale of American wheat to the Soviet Union represented a breakthrough in 1963; thereafter, trade with the communists became fairly respectable. In 1963 it was finally possible to ban atmosphere-polluting nuclear testing. A year after the Cuban crisis Khrushchev and the Soviet world seemed genuinely grieved by the death of John F. Kennedy. By 1964, President Johnson was speaking not of rollback but of improving relations with communist states, the desire to "build bridges across the gulf which separates us from eastern Europe." In 1965 and 1966 several small steps were taken toward improvement of relations, including the inauguration of direct air service between New York and Moscow and relaxation of controls on exports to communist countries.

Although the habit of simple anticommunism persisted, the American intellectual community was revising its estimate of the Soviet Union, partly because of the evolution of that state, but equally because of the changing mood of America.[6] The Soviet Union was no longer seen as a demonic model of totalitarianism but as a state gradually becoming more orderly and pluralistic, less repressive and less able to mobilize energies for economic growth; it was not only failing to fulfill Khrushchev's boasts but actually falling farther behind the United States in key areas. The Soviet Union seemed to be becoming, like the United States, more desirous of peace than of spreading its power. Years of stability, during which neither side made unbalancing gains, led to mutual acceptance.

Not only did the Sino-Soviet bloc come apart, but the neutralist world grew up. New states proliferated: twenty-five in the period 1954–1960 and scores more thereafter. The United Nations, instead of being split between Soviet bloc and pro-Western states, was increasingly dominated by the Third World nations, which were much more

---

6. For American perceptions, cf. William Welch, *American Images of Soviet Foreign Policy*, Yale University Press, New Haven, 1970; and John Stoessinger, *Nations in Darkness*, Random House, New York, 1975.

interested in anticolonialism and development than in the Soviet-American duel. It was no longer feasible to deprecate neutralism. Concern over the political alignment of the many unstable Third World countries (aside from Indochina) ebbed; if they were leftist or near-communist, this did not mean Soviet control or any great harm to the United States. Secretary of State John Foster Dulles was thunderstruck in 1955 by the news that Egypt was receiving Soviet arms; by 1963 the United States looked on fairly calmly as the Soviets furnished arms to twenty nations of Asia and Africa. De Gaulle was about as annoying to the State Department as Khrushchev.

Movement toward détente was halted by escalation of the war in Vietnam in 1965, and the aftermath of the June 1967 Six Day War placed the United States and the Soviet Union on opposite sides of the bitter Arab-Israeli quarrel. Nonetheless, they agreed on the Nuclear Non-Proliferation Treaty (1968), expressing their common interest in nuclear monopoly against neutrals and allies. The two powers also expanded consular relations. Year by year, cultural exchanges were continued and tended to increase even as the Soviet press was daily excoriating American imperialism in Vietnam and elsewhere.

Meanwhile, widespread American disgust with the war became repugnance for the anticommunism used to rationalize it. By the time American troops were leaving Vietnam, Americans were coming to recognize that the nightmare of a totalitarian giant purposefully disciplined by police controls and brainwashing to expand its power indefinitely was no more realistic than Khrushchev's vision of burying capitalism by Soviet economic growth. Soviet dynamism was obviously ebbing; it would have been inconceivable for Lenin and degrading for Khrushchev to confess that the hope of bringing the new world order rested on more and better guns instead of the appeal of Marxism-Leninism and the attraction of Soviet society. Revolutionary inspiration was left far behind. The Soviet Union had become less and less either the shining hope of mankind or a fearful monster; it reverted toward what tsarist Russia had been: a dull and inefficient authoritarian society. American public opinion moved also; the Gallup poll found that only 5 percent of Americans had a favorable view of the Soviet Union in 1954, compared with 34 percent in 1973.[7]

For some years the Soviets also had been moving toward a more

---

7. *Gallup Opinion Index*, 96 (June 1973), 24.

realistic view of the world scene,[8] and the solidification of their hegemony over eastern Europe in 1968 and afterward made them more confident in easing tensions with the West.[9] They took a sharp turn toward détente in 1970, when they negotiated an agreement for renunciation of force and recognition of the European status quo with West Germany, which had been a very useful bogey to help keep east Europeans in line. Earlier, they had become very friendly with a capitalistic Western power, France; now Germany was treated as a respectable friend. In the next years the Soviet government began courting Japan (previously much berated like Germany) to secure Japanese cooperation in the development of eastern Siberia—a high-priority project because of Chinese claims on the region. There had been brief thaws in Soviet-American relations in 1955, 1959, 1963, and 1968, but the United States remained the last big capitalist enemy. The American rapprochement with Communist China, marked by President Richard M. Nixon's trip to Peking in February 1972, made it both easier and imperative for the Soviets to extend détente to the United States. The first visit ever by an American president to Moscow followed three months later. The importance the Soviets attached to the visit was shown by their passive reaction to the increased bombing of North Vietnam and to the blockade by mining of its harbors. Despite some opposition within the Soviet hierarchy, a jovial Leonid Brezhnev duly welcomed the archenemy to the Kremlin.

The 1972 summit meeting was marked by an impressive number of agreements. Arms limitation talks had progressed sufficiently to permit agreements limiting antiballistic missile (ABM) installations and the number of missile launchers, the latter for five years. Among nonmilitary agreements were several for cooperation in medical and scientific research. Agreement on a joint space venture reflected the permanent Soviet need for technological import from the West and the recognition that the two biggest powers had a joint responsibility to help solve the global problems of mankind. These agreements also underlined the desirability of cooperation in common interests. A detailed follow-up agreement provided for thirty joint studies to benefit the air, waters, and cities of the two countries. The Moscow meetings also produced a

8. Cf. William Zimmerman, *Soviet Perspectives on International Relations, 1956–1967*, Princeton University Press, Princeton, 1969.

9. Walter C. Clemens, Jr., "The Impact of Détente on Chinese and Soviet Communism," *Journal of International Affairs*, 28, no. 2 (1974), 141 .

general accord unthinkable a decade earlier, whereby the two powers pledged themselves to peaceful coexistence and promised to avoid tension-producing situations, to resolve differences amicably, not to seek advantages at the expense of each other, to recognize mutual security interests, to exchange opinions and hold meetings of leaders, to promote scientific, technical, and cultural exchanges and tourism, and so forth. Perhaps never have two adversaries, fearful of being enemies, promised so much to try to be friends. A *Pravda* commentator wrote, "In the history of international relations it is difficult to find another example of such fruitful results achieved through negotiation." [10]

Exchanges of many other kinds prospered—in sports, culture, science, medicine, and space and environmental studies; a Soviet passenger liner began regular service out of New York. But the chief Soviet need and interest was economic. In this area, the turnaround was striking. It had been the American feeling that trade with the cold war enemy was immoral or certainly more likely to profit the totalitarian than the free state. In 1951, as a result of the Korean War, embargo lists were drawn up, and trade between the United States and the Soviet sphere remained insignificant for many years. The United States was almost alone in seeking to restrict trade for moral or economic as well as military reasons, and from the late 1950s European countries began increasing exchanges with the East, even extending long-term credits. Businesses in the United States began complaining that it was fruitless to refuse to sell to the Soviets what they could easily buy elsewhere.

By 1971, western European nations sold sixteen times as much to the Soviet bloc as did the United States.[11] But with the war in Southeast Asia no longer a major issue, barriers crumbled in 1972. An agreement was reached whereby the Soviets would buy $750 million of subsidized grain over three years (on terms that turned out to be very favorable for the buyers), and afterward they bought a great deal more. Export controls were relaxed to permit the sale of advanced technology. Each nation agreed to establish a commercial office in the other's capital, and the Soviets would provide a center in Moscow for foreign businesses.

With the administration positively urging capitalists to do business with the communist Soviet Union, Americans hastened to offer and the Soviets moved to conclude numerous deals. Soviet delegations toured

---

10. *Pravda*, June 15, 1972, p. 5.
11. United Nations statistics.

American plants, and swarms of American businessmen trekked to Moscow, where some were personally received by the general secretary of the Communist party. American banks opened offices in the capital of world communism, and Pepsi-Cola arranged to bottle its refreshment for the Soviet thirst (for the classes, however, not the masses). United States–Soviet trade came to $1.5 billion in 1973, with American export surplus commodities totaling $1 billion. The Soviet Union, on its part, called American firms "companies" instead of "monopolies," and there was discussion of many joint ventures of American (and other Western) enterprises with Soviet organizations. Meanwhile, the Soviet Union was increasingly playing the game of world commerce, with its own investments and deals for collaboration with the capitalist world.[12]

For many years, Soviet attitudes toward the United States have been ambivalent, dislike of the leading capitalist-imperialist power being mixed with covert respect and admiration for the world's economic and technological leader. By 1973, the latter feeling seemed to have prevailed; the Soviet leadership apparently preferred, so far as was feasible, to buy from the most advanced producer and to deal with the strongest nation, evidencing more faith in the United States than this nation had in itself.

Political relations improved along with economic; criticism of the United States, long a staple item, for a time disappeared from the Soviet press. Brezhnev, visiting Washington in June 1973, spoke much of trade and cooperation and tried to ingratiate himself with senators and with the television public. The Soviet Union not only refrained from visibly taking advantage of the difficulties of President Nixon in 1973 and afterward, but supported him against his antagonists, whom it deemed reactionaries. In return, the administration was willing not only to do what it could to promote Soviet-American trade but also to restrain whatever sympathies it may have felt for repressed Soviet dissidents. At times, Brezhnev and Nixon seemed practically allied against their intellectual critics, and Nixon in Moscow in June 1974 attempted to use his good relations with Soviet leaders to check the tide of the Watergate investigation. The Soviets seemed sorry to see him forced from office shortly afterward.

The momentum of détente continued under President Gerald R. Ford. In December 1974, he seemed to feel that an encounter with

---

12. On Soviet-American trade and problems, see Goldman, *Détente and Dollars*. By 1974, the Soviets had fifty companies operating in the West (ibid., pp. 298–304).

Brezhnev was necessary to establish his presidential standing, and the Vladivostok meeting produced a (high) preliminary ceiling on the number of major nuclear weapons. United States–Soviet trade, which had slipped in 1974, resurged in 1975 with sales of industrial equipment and especially of huge quantities of grain. American attitudes were sufficiently relaxed to permit the shipment of uranium to the Soviet Union for processing.[13] In May 1975, American and Soviet warships paid courtesy calls to Leningrad and Boston, respectively, in an unprecedented gesture of amity. In July, the long-prepared link-up and joint flights of Soviet and American spaceships received much publicity in both countries. In the same month, too, President Ford, General Secretary Brezhnev, and leaders of thirty-two other countries met in Helsinki to sign a document expressing many noble intentions about European security and cooperation.

THE LIMITS OF DÉTENTE

Cordiality between the superpowers came to a height in the summer of 1973. In a sense, détente checked itself, because decreased fear of conflict permitted criticism of Soviet faults and misdeeds and a more skeptical look at dealings between the superpowers. While the rather conservative American administration continued on its path of accommodation, right-wing elements, which had never ceased to be anticommunist, raised their voices to decry giving what seemed to them too much for too little return. The labor unions continued to be stiffly anticommunist. Surprisingly, they were joined by many liberals and moderates, who felt much freer to damn Soviet repressiveness as their indignation over the Vietnam war subsided.[14]

Enthusiasm for Soviet trade wilted.[15] The lure of big orders was offset by many vexations, from Soviet red tape and secretiveness to restrictions on the movements of foreigners in the Soviet Union and the difficulties and the high cost of living and working in Moscow. Sales were only to state agencies and were usually one-shot, and prospects

---

13. *The Wall Street Journal*, April 25, 1975, p. 28.
14. For skeptical views of détente, see Gerald L. Steibel, *Détente, Promises and Pitfalls,* Crane, Russak, New York, 1975; and Vladimir Petrov, *U.S.–Soviet Détente: Past and Future,* American Enterprise Institute, Washington, D.C., 1975.
15. Goldman, *Détente and Dollars,* p. 6.

for a long-term market for any particular commodity were not good. The Soviets usually wanted help in setting up production lines, after which the foreign corporation could go home, possibly to face competition from the Soviet factory it had helped establish.[16] The Soviets showed little notion of reciprocity; it is typical that the Soviet airline, Aeroflot, had large, street-level ticket offices in New York, whereas Pan American had only a few rooms on an upper floor of a Moscow hotel.

The Soviets would like tremendous quantities of industrial equipment, but they have wanted them on credit. American imports from the Soviet Union have been chiefly mineral raw materials, petroleum, diamonds, furs, and vodka; Soviet technological specialties, such as hydroelectric equipment, are few. Big American credits to the Soviet Union have been considered out of the question, so the Europeans who were willing to sell on credit got most of the business except in foodstuffs.

Other doubts have been raised in Congress and outside. Expansion of trade on Soviet terms may support the rigidities of the Soviet system by making relaxation unnecessary for innovation. The West, by providing civilian technology, may enable the Soviets to concentrate on military development. Production techniques are sold for a small fraction of development costs. Evidently the Soviets view themselves as milking the West for their own benefit, using capitalism to overcome capitalism. Exchanges have sometimes been rather one-sided; for example, the United States gives technical agricultural assistance in return for the Soviets providing crop data, which are freely available in most countries but which the Soviets withhold, partly from general policies of secrecy and partly, it seems, to facilitate speculation on world commodity markets.

Such considerations led Congress to apply a brake to détente, particularly by means of Senator Henry Jackson's amendment to the administration's foreign trade bill. Supported not only by militant anti-communists and Jewish organizations but also by protectionists, trade unions, civil rights advocates, and many liberals, the trade bill made Most-Favored-Nation status for the Soviet Union (and other communist states) conditional upon greater freedom of emigration (Jews being understood) and severely limited export credits. It seemed possible at

---

16. Leon Zurawicki, "The Cooperation of the Socialist State with the MNCs," *Columbia Journal of World Business,* 10 (Spring 1975), p. 111.

one time that economic leverage could secure political concessions, but the Soviets were unwilling to pay the price of allowing 60,000 Jews yearly to emigrate merely to gain Most-Favored-Nation status without large credits. They proceeded in January 1975 to denounce the trade treaty reached in 1972 and to cut down severely the number of Jews permitted to emigrate.

Skepticism toward the Soviet Union also came to the fore in the American reaction to large grain purchases in 1975. That a foreign country should buy American goods is normally a subject for rejoicing, but news of Soviet purchases rather raised the fear of higher prices and the memories of the "Great Grain Robbery" of 1973. For a time the longshoremen's union even boycotted the loading of grain for the Soviet Union, and the administration felt that it had to halt grain sales after the Soviet government had bought some 10 million tons.[17] It was made clear that preference would be given to regular customers, and the Soviets had to agree to regularize their purchases in return for suspension of the embargo.

In the same spirit of suspicion that the Soviets get the better of deals, the prima facie harmless Helsinki pact was widely and bitterly criticized as a sellout and an agreement to the enslavement of eastern Europe, although by strict interpretation it would outlaw Soviet intervention in eastern Europe, and east Europeans seemed to feel that it promised them a little more freedom. Not many years earlier, it would have been considered an achievement to sit down with the Soviets and mutually promise good behavior. In 1975, for the United States to agree to the inviolability of frontiers that it had no intention of violating (peaceful change being explicitly reserved) was deprecated, principally, it seemed, because the Soviets wanted such an agreement and because of the fear that haunted American policy in the days of John Foster Dulles: that relaxation of tensions meant relaxation of defense efforts.[18] In fact, the provision for freer exchange of information and movement of persons (to which the Soviets very reluctantly agreed) was the only part of the agreement that seemed at all operative, as Western leaders and Soviet dissidents pointed to it to refute the Soviet contention that its controls were a purely domestic matter. But the supposed instrument of détente caused a worsening of feelings as the Soviets contravened its spirit.

---

17. D. Gale Johnson, "The Soviet Grain Shortage; A Case of Rising Expectations," *Current History*, 68 (June 1975), 246.

18. Cf. George W. Ball, "Capitulation at Helsinki," *Newsweek*, August 4, 1975, p. 13.

Political friction also showed that the two superpowers continued to be more rivals than comrades in the building of peace. The downfall of anticommunist governments in Indochina in April 1975 raised sensitivity to communist gains anywhere. Even President Ford blamed the Soviets for the threat of a communist power grab in Portugal in the summer of 1975, although there was more evidence of Soviet caution than of large-scale interference. The Soviets continued also to be rivals in the Near East. They showed no interest in halting the 1973 war as long as the Arabs seemed to be winning; rather, they urged Algeria, Lebanon, and Jordan to enlarge it.[19] As the ceasefire was being negotiated in October, President Nixon ordered a worldwide alert of United States forces to communicate disapproval of apparent plans to send in Soviet forces—a remarkable reflection on the shallowness of détente. After 1973, the influence of the Soviets in the Near East waned remarkably, but they vigorously opposed the interim agreements worked out between Israel and Egypt by Secretary of State Kissinger without Soviet participation. In 1975 and 1976 Soviet intervention in the Angolan civil war, directly by arms shipments and indirectly by Cuban troops, raised the fear and the anger of many Americans and generated a feeling of betrayal; the Soviets were seen as taking advantage of American goodwill or indifference in order to stake out a new sphere in Africa.

The unceasing Soviet military build-up also raised questions, as strategic ground and naval forces continued to grow. Charges of Soviet violations of the strategic arms limitation talks (SALT) agreement multiplied, and fear grew that the Soviets were driving for military superiority for political purposes. The Soviet navy particularly seemed to be offensively oriented, having outrun defensive needs and acquired the beginnings of a first-strike capacity.[20] After the Nixon visit, a statement was made by the Soviets concerning the possible use of Soviet armed forces to help national liberation movements: "Intensification and expansion of the international tasks of the Soviet armed forces also conditions objectively the need for their further strengthening." [21]

Slowdown in détente has been supported by some Soviet dissidents, who oppose in principle concessions to an oppressive government without counterconcessions in Soviet conduct. Détente, in their view, is empty without democratization. To them, détente seems to

---

19. "Reflections on the Quarter," *Orbis*, 17 (Winter 1974), 1089.

20. *The New York Times*, August 11, 1975, p. 6.

21. *Communist of the Armed Forces*, cited by Leon Goure, *The Militarization of Soviet Youth*, National Strategy Information Center, New York, 1973, p. 72.

mean only continuation, and at times even intensification, of repression. Soviet authorities take the opposite view. They emphasize the separation of trade and ideology, welcoming the former but rejecting peaceful coexistence in the latter. The Soviet people have been admonished frequently that dealings with the imperialists imply no relaxation of the struggle against capitalism and imperialism, which seems to be equivalent to a struggle to expand Soviet power. Even while the Soviet press hailed the results of the 1972 Nixon visit (concerning which the Soviet people were given little specific information), the authorities began something of an ideological clamp-down. While American businessmen trooped to Moscow, the political police became more energetic, and the media (after a brief letup) continued or at times intensified their militant output, accenting the negative about the United States. Guards isolate Americans in their foreign ghettos, and Soviet citizens are kept away from the American embassy. Soviet propagandists rather frankly concede that they cannot admit free competition of ideas, and the idea of bridge building is anathema, as ever. They tell their own citizens nothing of credits obtained in the West or the proportion of American grain in the Soviet loaf. Brezhnev reportedly reassured communist leaders that improving relations with the West was only a tactic intended to assure eventual Soviet superiority [22]—perhaps only a rationalization of his own.

In a more elaborate statement by a Soviet ideologue,

> [détente] opens up new, immeasurably more favorable prospects for the further struggle of the working class and all working people for peace and democracy, for national independence, fundamental revolutionary transformations, and socialism.
>
> Essentially the broad dissemination and forced recognition by the capitalist countries of the principle of peaceful coexistence are a new stage in the development of the world antagonism between socialism and capitalism and in the development of world revolutionary progress. A historic comparison is taking place within the framework of peaceful coexistence, that is, the advantages of socialism are being manifested increasingly fully, the economic competition between the Socialist and the capitalist countries is intensifying. . . .
>
> It is essential to stress once more that the policy of peaceful coexistence is a specific and highly effective form of the class

---

22. *The New York Times,* September 17, 1973, p. 2.

antagonism and historic rivalry between world socialism and world capitalism. This policy is an important integral part of the world revolutionary process.[23]

This and similar statements may be pro forma, arising from the Soviets' compulsion to deny the obvious fact that they are compromising their ideological position by extensive friendly dealings with theoretical class enemies. Even if they are in actuality conservative and fearful of change, their political system requires seeing the world as in struggle; this attitude cannot help having some effect on both Soviet and American conduct. It is difficult for Americans, including the best informed, to judge to what extent the Soviet Union is moving toward genuine rapprochement with the West, or whether it may be covering its flank for a showdown with China or possibly is seeking to lull the West into lethargy. Apparently, however, the Soviets are ready to support any fight that has anti-Western overtones, such as that in Angola. It must be assumed that Soviet leaders may be cynical about agreements with bourgeois states.

From the American point of view, the Soviets often are still "spoilers" in the world. Not only have they seemed reluctant to see settlement in the Near East, at least under American auspices, but they also have provided arms for Idi Amin of Uganda, the most irresponsible of African leaders. Communist parties, obedient to Soviet directives in many countries, cultivate ill will for the United States. Americans, who like to have their friendships and enmities principled and clear-cut, find qualifiedly friendly relations with an overtly hostile power difficult to understand, and see their concessions written large. In this situation, there has been some return to cold war mentality after 1973 for reasons akin to those that caused the original cold war: fear of the spread of Soviet power and a sense of a dark menace in an uncertain world. Again, as before the revulsion against the Vietnam war, more political mileage is to be found in attacking the big rival than in advocating better understanding, as alarms are sounded from time to time over communist threats here and there.

Whatever the reality of such threats or the likelihood that Soviet aid might mean Soviet control, the United States has failed adequately to recognize that for the Soviets détente itself is a concession. Close relations with the United States imply freer movement of persons and

23. A. I. Sobolev, *Working Class and Contemporary World*, reprinted by *The Wall Street Journal*, April 30, 1975, p. 20.

ideas; this development opens the way to more political demands, particularly for minorities, and brings into question the whole Soviet complex of ideology, party rule, censorship, and police control.

Really to enter the world system of the advanced industrial states would imply reconstruction, possibly dissolution of the Soviet domain in its present Russian-dominated form; the ruling elite is wholly unprepared to accept this possibility. A détente of mutual trust instead of mutual fear can come only from an evolution of attitudes conditioned by the internal evolution of the Soviet Union, aided (it is to be hoped) by the wisdom and forbearance of the United States.

EASTERN EUROPE

Marxist-Leninist communism is essentially Russia's contribution to the world. All thirteen states that joined the Soviet Union in that category from 1945 to 1961 took Soviet Russia as their pattern; most of them were actually organized, at least in their inception, by Soviet agents. However, these states have markedly different relations to the Russian motherland. China and Albania are actively hostile; North and South Vietnam, Cambodia, North Korea, Cuba, and Yugoslavia are independent but more or less friendly or allied; Poland, Czechoslovakia, East Germany, Hungary, Bulgaria, Romania, and Mongolia are to varying degrees dependent and constrained by their ties to the Soviet hegemony. None of these nations causes anxiety to the United States—the fantasies of Chinese and Cuban revolutionism having been outlived—and the chief but often unrecognized American interest is to encourage them to become independent of the Soviet Union.

The spread of communism was chiefly the result of World War II. Earlier, the Soviet state had inherited Mongolia, formerly a protectorate of tsarist Russia; aside from those nations that became communist during the disorders of the war and its aftermath, only Cuba has opted to place itself in the socialist camp. The largest number of Marxist-Leninist regimes were brought about by the westward march of the Soviet armies in 1944 and 1945, although the communist governments of Yugoslavia and Albania were the work of native communists, with secondary assistance and guidance from the Soviets. It remains the Kremlin's secret whether Stalin planned in advance to install Soviet-type governments in Soviet-occupied territories—such intentions were firmly denied at the time—but Stalin wanted reliable servants, and only properly indoctrinated communists were really reliable. Through direct and indirect pressures and especially by virtue of control of the police, by mid-1948 the governments of the Soviet sphere had been made practically carbon copies of the Soviet hegemony, with planned economies, police repression, and ideological conformity under obedient communist parties.

It is only remarkable that Stalin did not see fit to follow Leninist logic—Lenin made his revolution, after all, not just for Russia but for the world—and annex them as he did the Baltic states a few years earlier. To have done so would have been a gross affront to his former allies, who had gone to war standing for the right of states, particularly east European states, to independence. Instead, Stalin chose to exercise de facto sovereignty, to the displeasure of the United States, which viewed Soviet control over a large part of formerly independent Europe as a poor outcome of the war. Eastern Europe thus became the principal area of contention causing the cold war. But American policy was not consistent or intelligent. On the one hand, no real effort was made to use American military and economic potential to compel a Soviet retreat to acceptable borders of the Soviet Union. The United States was weary of conflict, Soviet military strength was much overrated, the image of the valorous Soviet fighters against fascism faded only gradually, and no important sector of opinion was prepared to support a crusade to rescue eastern Europe. On the other hand, many gestures were made toward challenging Soviet hegemony, with few results beyond arousing Soviet mistrust. The United States even declined, and still declines, to recognize the incorporation of the Baltic states into the Soviet Union in 1940, thereby implying the intention of, or at least a hope of, reversing that aggrandizement.

The American attitude was, in effect, that nothing was to be done concretely about the situation, but that if communist rule in eastern Europe were not recognized as legitimate it might somehow disappear—an attitude like that taken toward communist rule in China and Cuba. Since (according to cold war assumptions) a communist was a communist and a servant of the Soviet Union, there was even less point in dealing with the puppets than with the bosses. But the discontented peoples of eastern Europe might someday somehow set aside their unnatural rulers. Hence little or nothing was done to help or encourage satellites to seek more autonomy or independence of their Soviet masters, and even when they were visibly breaking away the United States was very slow to take note.

The first break in communist solidarity came from the refusal of

Marshal Tito to permit Soviet control of Yugoslav internal affairs, especially the political police. Stalin exerted all manner of pressures short of war against his rebellious disciple, but the Yugoslavs proved to be better nationalists than communist-internationalists. Tito made good his self-assertion on his own. Despite the bitterness of the dispute and the obvious desirability of a member of the bloc escaping Soviet control, the United States lent assistance only after two years and then in the face of grumbling in Congress and in conservative circles. Tito, after all, was an unrepentant communist, and the United States was fighting communism plain and simple. Yet the Yugoslavs probably hurt the Soviet cause in the cold war more as communists than they would have if they had renounced the creed, because they provided an alternative focus for dissidents within eastern Europe, a deviant model that became more attractive as the Yugoslavs introduced a little democracy into their socialism and improved their standard of living much more rapidly than the Soviets. Since Stalin's death, the Soviet Union has recognized Yugoslav independence and Soviet-Yugoslav relations have improved, while Yugoslavia has often been critical of American policies. But the existence of an independent socialist country continues to be a leaven in the Soviet bloc.[24]

To some extent Romania has also (but more quietly) pulled itself free of Soviet control, although it is gripped by a Soviet military vise, lying between the Soviet Union and its Hungarian and Bulgarian satellites, both of which have nationalistic antagonisms to Romania. After 1958, when Khrushchev was persuaded to withdraw Soviet occupying forces, Romanian leaders cautiously enlarged their autonomy, in part by playing on the Sino-Soviet split. For many years, the United States took little or no notice of Romanian stirrings for independence, although the Romanians boldly held out against the further integration of the bloc, undertook de-Russification, and adulterated their socialism with fervent nationalism. However, in 1968 President Lyndon B. Johnson, having previously indicated the disinterest of the United States in the fate of Czechoslovakia's essay into liberal communism, suggested that it would be a matter of grave concern if the Soviet Union should invade Romania as it had Czechoslovakia. Presidents Nixon (1969) and Ford (1975) visited Bucharest. While proclaiming loyalty to the Soviet alliance, Romania has gone further than most

---

24. On Yugoslav independence, see George W. Hoffman and Fred Warner Neal, *Yugoslavia and the New Communism*, Twentieth Century Fund, New York, 1962.

other communist states in commercial ties with the West, permitting
up to 49 percent foreign investment in Romanian enterprises and joining (like Yugoslavia) the World Bank and International Monetary
Fund. In 1975 Romania received Most-Favored-Nation status (already
enjoyed by Yugoslavia and Poland) and a trade treaty with the United
States like that which the Soviets declined.[25]

Where the Soviets had forces on the ground to keep control, the
United States gradually moved to acceptance of the Soviet sphere,
attachment to the status quo outweighing desire for change. The talk
of "liberation" and "rollback" of the early Eisenhower years was rhetorical; it was at best qualified, in that Soviet withdrawal was intended
to come about pacifically and through the natural growth of autonomous forces. Hence, when disturbances erupted in Czechoslovakia and
East Germany shortly after the demise of Stalin in 1953, the United
States took little note. In 1956, after Khrushchev's de-Stalinization
speech encouraged eastern European hopes, the Poles briefly defied
the Soviets before coming to a compromise; in their wake, the Hun-
garians rose in a strongly nationalistic movement for independence.
They hoped that the West (especially the United States), having expressed its interest in the freedom of the peoples of the Soviet sphere,
would help them. It is not inconceivable that the United States would
have reacted more strongly if the Western powers had not then been
embroiled in the Suez crisis, setting Britain and France against the
United States. As it was, the American response was limited to expres-
sions of sympathy, denunciations of Soviet brutality, and resolutions in
the United Nations.

By forceful action, the Soviets reasserted effective dominion over
their sphere, and it was clear to the world that no one was going to do
anything about it. In 1961, the United States again received passively
(and perhaps even with covert relief) the construction of the Berlin
Wall, which divided that city and sealed the partition of Germany, a
situation that American policy had firmly opposed in principle. Finally,
in 1968, the United States made it clear in advance that it was not
much interested in Czechoslovakia. The Soviet action there was not
merely a repression but a clear-cut invasion, because Soviet troops,
with token contingents of several satellites, entered Czechoslovak territory to deprive the Czech and Slovak peoples of their freedom of
choice. The American response was again verbal, and moves toward

---

25. On Romanian independence, see Julian Hale, *Ceausescu's Romania*, Harrap,
London, 1971.

improvement of relations with the Soviets were held up for only a few months' decent mourning for the decease of Czech freedom.

Yet there are perpetual stirrings. The desire for more trade and contacts with the West, the regrowth of national self-awareness, the decreasing effectiveness of Marxist-Leninist ideology, the unwillingness of formerly proud and independent peoples to remain permanently under the aegis of the Soviet Union (which has much less to offer economically and culturally than the West)—such feelings are always present, although more or less suppressed. The sequence since Stalin's disappearance has been several times repeated: rising expectations, more or less rebellion in some places, forcible repression, return to conformism, and renewed expectations and stirrings toward independence.

The Soviets have never been able adequately to institutionalize their dominion. Stalin relied mostly on his personal authority and the control of the armed forces and the police. Khrushchev leaned more on ideology, party contacts, and economic integration. But ideology was convincing only so long as it was successful, national communist parties pursued their own interests, and the integration of the planned economies in the Soviet-run Council for Mutual Economic Assistance (Comecon) lagged. It proved more difficult to integrate the planned economies than the market economies of western Europe. More successful was the Soviet counterpart of NATO, the Warsaw Treaty Organization (WTO); WTO was able substantially to coordinate east European military forces with the Soviet army, whose presence is the ultimate guarantee of Soviet hegemony. Despite these and sundry other unifying organizations, the bonds of the fraternal parties, and many years of intensive propaganda, eastern European countries gradually grow further away from instead of more like the Soviet model. Generally speaking, they are more open than the Soviet Union, engage in more economic experimentation, and permit more deviation from the Soviet canons of art and literature.

The United States for its part has made eastern Europe secondary to the Soviet Union in its reckonings, and relations with eastern European countries have followed in the wake of United States–Soviet détente. Trade surged in 1972 and 1973, and bankers and businessmen trekked to eastern European capitals with some of the eager anticipation with which they journeyed to Moscow. Visions of trade with eastern Europe are less exciting than those of trade with the Soviet Union because the quantities involved are much smaller. However, the obstacles are also less severe. Red tape is not quite so sticky, bureaucrats are friendlier, and the working conditions are better. Since the eastern Europeans nevertheless do not have much to sell to the United States, any big growth of trade requires credits which eastern Europeans are more eager to have than the United States is to extend.

Business has progressed mostly with Poland and Romania. These countries, like Yugoslavia, allow United States firms to own a minority interest in national enterprises, and Romania does half its trade with the West. Several American firms have established plants in Poland to manufacture goods for export to the world, including the United States (for example, Singer made-in-Poland sewing machines). Poland, like the Soviet Union, has agreed to buy United States grain on a regular basis. There has been much less progress in relations with Hungary, in part for an incomprehensibly trivial reason: the United States refusal to return to Hungary the ancient crown of St. Stephen, captured in World War II. Bulgaria has tended to hold back as the most faithful Soviet satellite, but trade with the United States grew from $5 million in 1972 to $80 million in 1975. The communist governments that feel most insecure—those of Czechoslovakia and East Germany (with which diplomatic relations were not established until 1974)—have been most truculent in propaganda and relatively cool to normalization of relations.

The fostering of trade with eastern Europe is politically very desirable. While enjoying its own rapprochement with the United States, the Soviet Union cannot well forbid satellites to go the same road, although the result can only be a loosening of bonds. The economic grip of the Soviet Union, both as market and supplier, is weakened; its protective mission is left behind as the United States and West Germany change from imperialist threats to major trade partners. Having given up the idea that the governments of eastern Europe are to be overthrown by popular discontent, the United States would seem to have even more to gain from improving political and commercial relations with them than with the Soviet Union. Not only should it be possible to increase the potential of such countries as Poland and Hungary for greater economic and political independence, but the prospects for really comfortable relations with them are much better than with the Soviets.

It seems probable that Soviet control of the countries now comprising its sphere will recede one day. It is contrary to the trends of the modern age for a great power to hold an empire of this sort, especially of peoples more productive than the people of the hegemonic power. Moreover, for the health of the world community, it is essential that this distortion should be overcome.

But this development is likely only by a slow westward drift, which the Soviet Union could at no point usefully arrest by force. It is difficult for the Soviets to retreat, or to seem to retreat, in eastern Europe, not only because of the possible economic and political losses but also for reasons of ideological standing (the modern version of oriental face). It is an essential part of the mythology that Soviet socialism is the wave of the future, carried forward by tides of history, and the sovietization of eastern Europe has been perhaps the best evidence for this thesis. The process can probably be undone only as part of the evolution of the Soviet bloc as a whole and indeed of the world state system, whereby ideology should become less important, alliances should recede, and economic and cultural relations should come to the fore.

The United States can assist this trend by offering eastern European states more incentives to open their economies to the West. Through the cold war, American policy suffered from assuming an abstraction, communism, as the enemy instead of standing simply for more positive principles: the independence of nations and the establishment of a more fruitful international order. But to assume that there is such a thing as communism, instead of a set of governments capable of diverse reactions, is to accept the Soviet rules of the game. If nations are enabled to be independent, they can in due time settle their type of government and economic system.

CASTRO'S CUBA

That an island in the Caribbean should be an economic and political dependency of the Soviet Union is an anomaly, the more ironic since it turned to communism at the very time when the standing of the Soviet Union was beginning to ebb and when the United States was setting out to save a small nonnation of Southeast Asia from communism. That a state within the closest economic, military, and political sphere of the United States should adopt alien forms and ideology and move voluntarily into the Soviet orbit reflects a monumental failure of American foreign policy. The inability of the United States, despite overwhelming material advantages, to prevent or reverse this turn is a tribute to exceptional myopia; Cuban communism, indeed, is a by-product of the anticommunism of the cold war. American administrations neither offered the Castro government inducements to friendship, nor left it alone, nor acted stoutly to topple it in the Soviet manner. On the contrary, the American policy was to annoy Castro with pinpricks and to isolate the island, thereby justifying communist mobilization in defense of the revolutionary *patria*, causing difficulties for the Cuban economy but confirming the Cuban communist view of the world; creating dependence upon the Soviet Union, and giving a satisfying excuse (imperialist blockade) for troubles mostly due to bureaucratic inefficiency. Castro needed the United States as a frightening but not dangerous enemy, and the United States responded perfectly to his need.[26]

Close contacts between states at very different economic levels do not necessarily make good friends. The United States kept a protectorate over Cuba (with right of intervention under the Platt Amendment) until 1934. Thereafter, Cuba remained a semicolony. Its sugar plantations and mills and cattle ranches were largely American-owned, its foreign trade was overwhelmingly with the United States, and its many brothels and casinos were sustained by American tourists. Democracy did not prosper, but the dictators were amenable to American interests.

Castro rebelled against the crude, corrupt, and terroristic dictatorship of Fulgencio Batista. Those who with Castro raised the standard of revolt were middle-class idealists, and they came to power at the beginning of 1959 less through successful guerrilla warfare than because of the collapse of support for the illegitimate despot and the disintegration of his army. Although Castroism had anti-American overtones from the first, the Eisenhower administration welcomed the new government. However, Castro began executing pro-Batista or anti-Castro Cubans in numbers much beyond the reprisals usually accompanying Latin American coups. Land reform and socialization hit American holdings, and Castro's rhetoric concentrated on the evils of American "imperialism." As Washington frowned, Castro turned to Communist China and the Soviet Union. Charge led to countercharge and incident led to retaliation. In January 1961, the United States, less tolerant of hostile actions in the Caribbean than it might have been of any in Africa or the Near East, broke diplomatic relations. In April the Kennedy administration gave limited help to a Cuban exile group trying to overthrow the Castro government by force. This expedition suffered disastrous defeat in landing at the Bay of Pigs, partly because

26. For accounts of the coming of Castroism, see especially Theodore Draper, *Castroism: Theory and Practice*, Praeger, New York, 1965; and Herbert L. Matthews, *Fidel Castro*, Simon and Schuster, New York, 1969.

the Cuban people did not rise as predicted by the Central Intelligence Agency (CIA), and partly because Kennedy cautiously refused to allow the American air force to participate. From pique at the Bay of Pigs failure,[27] trade with Cuba was so strictly banned that French products containing nickel were barred from the United States because France imported part of its nickel requirements from Cuba. Early in 1962, the United States persuaded the Latin Americans to join in expelling the Castro government from the Organization of American States (OAS) because of Cuba's close ties to the Soviets and its vaunted efforts to stir up communist revolutions or guerrilla movements in other countries of the Western hemisphere. Subsequently, the OAS called upon its members to cut diplomatic and trade relations. All but Mexico were persuaded to do so, although the United States was usually much more concerned about Castroite threats to Latin American governments than were the governments themselves.

There was an inconclusive debate in the American press as to whether Castro came to power as a communist or was made one by American antagonisms and misunderstanding. In 1961 he tried to settle the question by proclaiming that he was and had always been a Marxist-Leninist. But he won power by concealing such views, if he had them; the Cuban Communist party, which got along fairly well with Batista, did not support him until very late. In the first months of his rule, although he repressed anticommunism, he kept his party separate from the communists. But anti-Americanism was useful to him, and the social transformation he wished required eliminating American economic holdings in Cuba. An ambitious young man, he had hopes for hemispheric leadership as champion of the poor and deprived, which seemed realizable only in opposition to the United States. He also saw the utility of communist methods for the exercise of power. To practice a mobilizing authoritarianism, he needed a party organization and all the trappings of rule as perfected by the Soviets; the American policy of hostility made it convenient for him to designate his movement as communist and Cuba as socialist in the Soviet sense. In return the Soviet Union gave military and economic aid and half-promised to defend the island against a presumptive American attack.

Normal intercourse being cut off between Cuba and its neighboring natural economic and political partners, Cuba fell into a rut of dependence on the distant Soviets. There was occasional unpleasantness,

---

27. According to Kennedy's secretary; *Time,* August 18, 1975, p. 6.

as when Castro felt misused by Khrushchev in the missile crisis of 1962, but Castro remained a usually faithful follower. Because the Chinese could not fill his needs, he took the Soviet side in the rift with China, although his philosophy and style were closer to those of Mao Tse-tung than to those of Leonid Brezhnev. From time to time he had a glorious reception in Moscow, where a jaded society welcomed him as a full-blooded revolutionary. The Soviets valued Castro enough to keep his economy afloat at a cost of $500–$700 million yearly.

Partly for this reason, the United States felt no urgency in bridge building to Cuba while moving toward détente with the Soviet Union and China. It was easier simply to maintain the old stance of isolation and denial. The Cubans had no atomic weapons. It was necessary to deal with the Soviets and the Chinese because they were big and more or less dangerous; Cuba was small and harmless and so, like Albania and Mongolia, could be ignored. The boycott on diplomatic, commercial, and cultural relations could only be judged futile, except for the moral satisfactions afforded, but it was not to be reconsidered.[28]

By 1972, however, change appeared possible. When Nixon embraced Castro's sponsor, it seemed odd to ostracize Castro. When trade with Communist China was encouraged, it seemed perverse to ban it with Cuba. At the same time, while Castro had not confessed to giving up the professed purpose of liberating the peoples of Latin America—neither has China or the Soviet Union formally renounced aims of universalistic transformation—Cuba had shown itself incapable of much mischief. Efforts to establish revolutionary foci failed, and the Cuban revolutionary model lost allure. The adulation of Castro's quixotic colleague, Che Guevara, by extremists throughout Latin America peaked in 1970; thereafter, and especially after the fall of leftist President Salvador Allende of Chile in 1973, the Cuban message ceased to be exciting or frightening. On the one hand, the Cuban experiment was no thumping success. Although Cuba had substantial achievements in popular education, social services, full employment, and general leveling, the economy only went in circles in the decade from 1960 to 1970. On the other hand, Castro turned to cultivating normal relations with Latin American governments, which were mostly pleased to respond.

Pressure for normalization came primarily from other Latin American states, which themselves developed more anti–United States feeling in the early 1970s. More and more Latin American governments

---

28. A general account is given by Maurice Halperin, *The Rise and Decline of Fidel Castro,* University of California Press, Berkeley, 1972.

defied the United States by renewing diplomatic and commercial relations with Cuba. The United States, too, bent a little. More travel between Cuba and the United States was permitted, and in February 1973 an agreement was reached through intermediaries to prosecute hijackers. American public opinion, following the simpler logic of the situation, swung to favor reopening of relations. Meanwhile, the substantial wealth flowing to Cuba because of the increase of sugar prices made the blockade seem still more futile, and United States exporters began to press the administration to permit restoration of trade.

Through the Nixon administration, however, probably because of the president's personal aversion, it continued to be the official position that no change was on the agenda and that reconciliation would be possible only when Cuba renounced the export of revolution and cut military ties with the Soviets. In 1974, the United States did considerable damage to relations with Argentina by trying (in vain) to prevent sales of trucks to Cuba by Argentine subsidiaries of an American manufacturer.

In 1975, several small conciliatory steps were taken, much as friendly gestures were made to the People's Republic of China in advance of the announcement of Nixon's excursion to Peking. On March 1, 1974, Secretary Kissinger felt able to state the obvious: "We see no virtue in perpetual antagonism between the United States and Cuba." In July, the United States, to avoid something like isolation in the hemisphere, joined in the motion to end the OAS embargo. Permission was given for United States firms abroad to trade with Cuba. However, it remains illegal to sell American foodstuffs or medicines to Cuba, and no one seems to have suggested apologizing to Castro for the CIA's attempts to murder him.

There remain serious obstacles to normalization of relations. A large community of refugees from Cuba in the United States, especially in the Miami area, is mostly hostile to the idea. The United States, as a price of settlement with communist countries (at least, with the weaker) has regularly demanded some compensation for confiscated American properties; this policy is very difficult to implement in the Cuban case, because the amount involved ($1.8 billion) is large for the island's economy and because Castro is not prepared to admit that expropriation was not wholly justified; rather, he claims damages from the United States for the effects of economic blockade. The status of the American base at Guantanamo is also a sticking point; Cuban agitation for the independence of Puerto Rico is a minor but typical irritant, although it is difficult to see how the United States would lose if that island were cut loose. Castro, a proud character, has proclaimed that freedom to revolutionize abroad is more precious than commerce with the United States, and Cuban military intervention in Angola in 1975–1976 deeply irritated the administration. Nonetheless, no obvious useful purpose is served by continuation of the artificial barriers between Cuba and the United States, [29] they remain in place mostly because it is much easier to commit errors than to undo them.

CHINA: THE OTHER COMMUNISM

On July 15, 1971, President Nixon announced that he would visit the People's Republic of China in the near future and so turned his back on one of the strongest American policies of the preceding twenty years. There had been a few hints of change ever since disengagement from Vietnam was undertaken—some relaxation of trade and travel restrictions, the publicized tour of China by an American Ping-Pong team, and mitigation of American diplomatic opposition to Communist China. Nevertheless, this reversal was perhaps the most surprising turn ever taken by American foreign policy.

Ironically, this sudden switch by an anticommunist president to friendly relations with a long and bitterly opposed government was the most popular move that the Nixon administration ever made. The chief question was why the victory of common sense had been so delayed. Whatever reasons there had been for blanket hostility to Peking had long since been worn out. The picture of Chinese manpower added to Soviet technology to overpower the world for communism was only a chimera generated by propagandists, communist as well as anticommunist. It is true that the Chinese Communist party was originally an offshoot of the Moscow-dominated movement; but the Chinese ceased to be subservient to the Soviets after the party was nearly destroyed (1926–1928) in following the strategy dictated by the Comintern. Mao revived the party by organizing revolution in a non-Marxist fashion among the peasants.

The Japanese invasion and World War II gave the Chinese communists the means to power. Better fighters and organizers than their rivals, exponents more of a national than an international cause, they

---

29. Cf. Abraham F. Lowenthal, "Cuba: Time for a Change?," *Foreign Policy,* 20 (Fall 1975), 65–86.

won out with very little assistance from the Russians. Stalin seems to have been displeased to see the Chinese comrades win control of China in 1949, preferring a China weakly divided between Nationalists and communists, with parts under Soviet protectorate. Shortly after proclaiming his new state in 1949, Mao traveled to Moscow to settle relations with the senior communist power; he was poorly treated by Stalin but came home with a formal alliance and much show of brotherhood.

The United States naturally preferred the Nationalist side in the struggle for mastery of China, but there were no violent feelings against the communists in the years shortly after the end of World War II. When the effort of General George Marshall in 1946 to arrange a compromise failed, limited assistance was given to the Nationalists; however, when the communists were victorious, the United States was fairly ready to do business with them. It was recognized that Chinese communism, unlike east European communism, was not a Soviet imposition, and that the Chinese were in some ways less dogmatic than the Soviets. When the Nationalists abandoned their capital, Nanking, the Soviet embassy went with them to Canton; the American embassy remained provisionally in Nanking. In January 1950, it was the declared American policy not to support the Nationalists in their Taiwan refuge. It was assumed that the communists would take Taiwan in due course and that the United States would recognize the communist regime.

The Korean War, or the Chinese intervention therein, set the United States on a course of implacable hostility to Communist China. That Americans found themselves fighting Chinese forces was a result more of the blunder of carrying the war to North Korea than of Chinese aggressiveness; but the fight was bitter and American indignation was intemperate.

The Chinese communists inflicted a humiliating defeat on overextended American forces, sending them reeling back from near the Chinese border. Although the front was stabilized, there was no victory, and America was not accustomed to emerging from war with less than victory. Moreover, Americans saw China as treacherously ungrateful. Had not the United States befriended China through the Open Door policy and alone returned the indemnity paid by China after the Boxer uprising? It was recalled that thousands of American missionaries and teachers had dedicated their lives to China, and that Franklin D. Roosevelt in World War II had made a point of treating China as a great power. Tempers were raised, too, by the fact that the United States became a party, practically speaking, to the Chinese civil war because the American navy was ordered to protect the Nationalists on the island of Taiwan.

China was consequently viewed not only as a puppet of international communism but also as a danger in its own right, the aggressive power par excellence bent on indefinite conquest. There were American negotiations with the Soviets from time to time but hardly any effort to find agreement with the Chinese—the violence of whose language, to be sure, discouraged ideas of reconciliation. There were to be no contacts with the evil power; souvenirs bought by American tourists in Hong Kong were confiscated unless certified uncontaminated. So far as possible China was excluded from world affairs. Economic, disarmament, and other conferences were closed to the representatives of Peking. The United States stood as doorkeeper to the United Nations for twenty-one years, although the conduct of China was no more reprehensible than that of various other members of the world body. The rigid exclusion of the world's most populous nation (or its representation by what was practically a government in exile) used up American credits in the world body and made the United States seem narrow and dogmatic. At Geneva in 1954, Dulles snubbed the most reasonable and accessible of communist Chinese leaders, Chou En-lai, an episode Chou recalled to American visitors eighteen years later. In 1958, Dulles wanted an American air strike against China in defense of the tiny Nationalist-held islands just off the mainland.

By the early 1960s, the basis of Sino-American hostility should have been worn thin, as the Chinese had done nothing frightening for a decade and the chief bone of contention was Taiwan, a territory generally agreed to be Chinese. The fear of 700 million persons being hammered into a totalitarian instrument of power was shown to be groundless by the near-collapse of the Chinese economy in 1960 and 1961. The Sino-Soviet rift became an undeniable fact by 1963. As long as Stalin stood as symbolic leader of world communism, the two big powers had managed to cooperate fairly well, but his death set them moving apart. Mao would not bow to Khrushchev, whose policies of peaceful coexistence and de-Stalinization were contrary to Chinese revolutionary forwardness (at least to recover Taiwan) and the idolization of Mao. In 1957 the Soviets tried to placate the Chinese by promising to help them develop nuclear weapons, but they soon reneged, and the Chinese began "nuclearizing" on their own. In 1958 the Chinese asserted that they were advancing to the state of communism (the ultimate economic order in the Marxist scheme) ahead of the Soviets by instituting people's communes. The Soviets remained neutral in the

Sino-Indian border dispute; they aided bourgeois neutrals more than they aided their communist allies. In 1960 Khrushchev tried to coerce China (much as Stalin had tried to coerce Yugoslavia) by abruptly withdrawing Soviet military and civilian technicians. The Chinese predictably reacted with bitterness rather than contrition.

By 1963 the Chinese and Soviet parties were exchanging public insults, although still pretending to belong to a single movement, and there were frontier incidents along the ill-defined border in central Asia. In 1969 there were bloody clashes on the border between China and Siberia, large parts of which the Chinese claimed as heritage of the old Chinese empire. Each had come to see not the United States but the other as the biggest immediate enemy. Marxism-Leninism proved no real bond. For both Chinese and Soviets, ideology was essentially a vehicle of state power, and the two countries were much more natural rivals than allies. The Soviets even sounded out the United States in 1969 regarding a preemptive strike against China but received no encouragement.[30]

Thus, the "loss" of China to the Maoists no longer seemed the greatest victory for communism since the Russian Revolution. It divided and weakened the movement and raised up a powerful antagonist for the Soviet Union. Only such a hard-driving party as Mao's could have so reunited and disciplined China as to make it an effective counterweight for the Soviets in Asia. It should have been clear from at least the early 1960s, when the United States was beginning to become entangled in Vietnam, that there was no communist monolith, and the more the communist giants were at odds, the less menacing they were to the United States. However, the United States preferred simple pseudoverities to nuanced and responsible reactions. The American political right was uninterested in the Sino-Soviet split, which complicated the simple and satisfying view of the world torn between freedom and communist despotism. American self-confidence and scorn for power politics made playing Peking off against Moscow seem unworthy as well as unnecessary. In the mid-1960s a serious text on American foreign policy asked and found unanswerable the question of whether or not the Sino-Soviet split was useful to the United States.[31]

By the late 1960s, the United States would surely have taken reality

---

30. Harold C. Hinton, "The United States and the Sino-Soviet Confrontation," *Orbis*, 19 (Spring 1975), 44.

31. Charles O. Lerche, *Foreign Policy of the American People*, Prentice-Hall, Englewood Cliffs, N.J., 1967, p. 231.

into account (as it regularly does, albeit belatedly) if the world had been tranquil. But the war in Vietnam required a major villain, and this was a role best filled by the evil Chinese communists, although they actually gave meager assistance to North Vietnam. Recognition of the deep split between China and the Soviet Union and the unlikelihood of either nation's controlling Vietnam would have deprived intervention of what little rationale it had in cold war terms. The Chinese themselves, however, reinforced the isolation of China in the Great Proletarian Cultural Revolution of 1966–1969. This strange episode seems to have been largely a counterattack by Mao against those who were setting him on the shelf and, as he saw it, leading China down the Soviet road to decadence and bureaucratic degradation. The tone was antiforeign in general; the Chinese reviled almost everyone but the Albanians and some less developed nations and for a time nearly ceased to conduct any diplomatic relations at all. There was factional chaos in much of China.[32] It seemed unnecessary to try to improve relations with such an unpredictable and intractable power.

The turn toward better relations came in 1968 and 1969. Until March 1968 the United States was going up the ladder of escalation in Vietnam; there was talk of enlarging the war to cut off supplies to the Vietnamese communists, even of preemptively "taking out" the budding Chinese nuclear force. Fear of American attack clearly contributed to the paranoia of the Cultural Revolution.[33] But as it became clear that the United States, instead of wading deeper into the land war in Asia, was backing out, the frenzy of the Cultural Revolution began to abate. The Soviet invasion of Czechoslovakia in August 1968 and the Brezhnev Doctrine of the right and duty to intervene on behalf of socialism made the Soviet Union seem a more serious danger. With the occurrence of Sino-Soviet border clashes in 1969, there seemed to be a definite Soviet threat of war—a threat that seemingly continued for years thereafter, as large Soviet forces stood along the frontier.

For the United States, China ceased to be a great menace. Japan had become the big power of Asia by its extraordinary economic growth, while the Chinese economy lagged because of the political

---

32. Concerning the Cultural Revolution, see, for example, Stanley Karnow, *Mao and China: From Revolution to Revolution,* Viking, New York, 1972; and Edward E. Rice, *Mao's Way,* University of California Press, Berkeley, 1972.

33. William F. Dorrill, "Power, Policy, and Ideology in the Making of the Chinese Cultural Revolution," in *The Cultural Revolution in China,* ed. Thomas W. Robinson, University of California Press, Berkeley, 1971, p. 73.

disturbances. The Chinese largely gave up their never extensive efforts to propagate revolution abroad and began to support governments (such as Iran and Ethiopia) against rebels. They were markedly disinterested in the extremists in the West who idolized Chairman Mao. Chinese objectives seemed about as defensive as those of less rhetorical states. Military expenditures of China were relatively small, and the Chinese army lacked offensive capacity. On the other hand, the fact that the Chinese were putting together a nuclear force was good reason to bring them into the community of nations; disarmament negotiations could not reasonably ignore them. The United States gave up the effort to exclude Communist China from the United Nations, and the General Assembly not only accepted the delegation from Peking but excluded that from Taipei by a vote of seventy-six to thirty-five. The Chinese settled down, not only in foreign relations but internally; their motto "Better Red than Expert" was partly turned around, administrative structures were rebuilt, and the economy was set back on an upward course.

Although the reception of President Nixon in Peking in February 1972 was initially cool, the atmosphere improved as talks progressed. The Chinese, for whom the visit was an even greater ideological reversal than for the Americans, gave the affair extensive publicity; Americans found the Chinese leaders rational and approachable, less dogmatic than the Soviets. Because of Taiwan it was not yet possible to open formal diplomatic relations—mainland China refuses them with any country recognizing Nationalist China—but the issue was defused by a vague American promise of withdrawal in the area, while the Peking government indicated that it looked to peaceful reversion. A year later the Chinese bent principles by agreeing to an exchange of liaison officers, representatives who are ambassadors except in name— an innovation in diplomatic protocol.

The American people, except for a few who clung to old stereotypes, welcomed reconciliation with the most populous of nations and America's erstwhile protégé. Things Chinese suddenly became fashionable. The American intellectual community, onetime victim of McCarthyism, looked with interest if not enthusiasm on the Chinese experiment. In a remarkable turnaround made possible by revulsion against the Vietnam war, the American press showed itself eager to report the better side of the very un-American state of Maoist China. Journalists found in China much to admire: neatness, honesty, dedication, cleanliness, order, puritanism, and hard work. Businessmen also dreamed, like the Yankee traders two centuries ago, of the limitless markets of China. United States–Chinese trade soared from zero to about $700 million in 1973 and nearly $1 billion in 1974, reaching a total comparable to that of trade with the Soviet Union and making the United States China's number-two trade partner. Formerly opposed in principle to foreign indebtedness, China resorted to credit buying on a large scale. In other ways retreating from previous stiff postures, the Chinese began admitting tourists, building hotels, and even importing a few Western films.

Inevitably, the rush slowed down. China, like the Soviet Union, had rather little to sell to the American market and restricted imports to keep trade from becoming excessively unbalanced—a picture that may change as Chinese petroleum production grows. There were the same problems in dealing with the trading agencies of a communist society; American businessmen found the Chinese authorities usually inscrutable and sometimes trying. On the American side, discrimination against Chinese goods—lack of Most-Favored-Nation status—remained a barrier. There were also old claims for compensation for American properties seized by China. The Taiwan issue prevented any real rapprochement. The United States withdrew part of its small forces from that island, leaving a few thousand airmen, but it was difficult to conceive of an early peaceful settlement. Growing economically more rapidly than mainland China and highly dependent on world trade, the Republic of China (Taiwan) seems unlikely to wish to place itself in any way under Peking. Many steps were stymied by the impasse; for example, there could be no exchange of journalists with mainland China as long as Taiwan newsmen were accredited in the United States.[34]

Yet the benefits of the opening to China were overwhelming. For every barb at the United States, the Chinese hurled several at the "social imperialists" or "new tsars," as they called the Soviet Russians. On the world stage, they were fierce opponents of everything Soviet, while United States diplomats spoke mildly if at all; the Chinese did their best to push European unity and NATO strength, and they did not seem to desire American withdrawal from the Pacific area. The Chinese also did their best to minimize Soviet gains in Southeast Asia resulting from the end of the war in Indochina. The United States practically came into the enviable position of balancer between the

---

34. On recent Sino-American relations, see Steven C. Levine, "China and the Superpowers," *Political Science Quarterly*, 90 (Winter 1975–1976), 646–652.

two antagonists, both of which were desirous of American support or at least neutrality.

No important material interests set China and America at odds; neither do political interests comparable to those that unite them. For both nations the only visible potential or possible military danger is from the Soviet Union. China is no superpower and is not likely to become one within a predictable time span.[35] Its share of the world product has hardly changed over the past generation despite plans and leaps. Its relatively modest military effort is seemingly defense-oriented and has not been increased during the last several years.[36] China has made nuclear explosives and a few rockets, a fact that may have helped persuade the Soviet Union of the inadvisability of applying the Brezhnev Doctrine to the power most in need of "brotherly" assistance. Whereas the United States and the Soviet Union continue to expand their gigantic arsenals, however, the Chinese were reported in 1975 to have made no increase of nuclear weapons and missiles for a year.[37]

Consequently, there is ample reason, from the point of view of realpolitik as well as the general health of international relations, for the United States to increase and improve contacts with the Chinese. It might even be advisable to undertake military collaboration of some sort with them.[38] Far from doing so, however, the United States maintains its policy to refuse to sell goods of possible military application to China, which badly needs to modernize its forces. This restraint is a holdover, but it is true that cordial relations with China are not easily attained. As a society it is closed to a degree far beyond the Soviet Union, shrouded in exceptional secrecy, and cut off from intellectual exchanges with the outside world. It is stiffly dogmatic; possibly China cannot really be governed except in a total faith, but the faith is a serious hindrance to easy relations with the United States. For example, the American tour of a Chinese choral group was canceled because they insisted on singing political songs; the Chinese tour of a group of American mayors was canceled because the Chinese insisted on the exclusion of the mayor of San Juan, Puerto Rico, as a colonial representative.

Seeing the world through their own prisms, the Chinese seemed

35. According to the Constitution, "China will never be a superpower"; *Peking Review,* January 24, 1974, p. 13.
36. *The New York Times,* October 7, 1975, p. 13.
37. *The New York Times,* September 5, 1975, p. 3.
38. Michael Pillsbury, "U.S.–Chinese Military Ties?", *Foreign Policy,* 20 (Fall 1975), 50–64.

convinced that the operation of a Tibetan refugee organization in New York was a manifestation of hostility by the United States government.[39] For ideological reasons—they have little or nothing to gain materially—the Chinese support guerrilla movements in countries with which they have normal relations—Burma, Thailand, and Malaya. They at least verbally support terrorist movements almost anywhere and back the extremest demands of Third World nations fervently against superpower hegemony. They denounce, if they cannot impede, any relaxation of tension between the United States and the Soviet Union.

American relations with China consequently call for maximal flexibility, tact, and rationality. It is extremely important both that China should remain independent of the Soviet Union and that the 20 percent of mankind governed from Peking should find their way into the community of nations.

COMMUNISM AND WORLD ORDER

The construction of a stable and well-functioning international system requires the general assent and cooperation of all major powers. It is difficult to postulate a stable peace without shared values and a common moral order. The communist powers, however, as they would be the first to stress, do not fully share the values most esteemed in the West and cannot heartily cooperate in a world order much influenced by bourgeois powers.

In principle, the communist states do not permit any international organization to function on their territories. Citizens of the Soviet Union are posted to positions with the United Nations and other international bodies, but they remain Soviet officials and are not permitted to become (like most United Nation employees) permanent international civil servants. Communist states reject in principle the interdependence of nations of differing social structure, denying the validity of the system of sovereign states in theory and recognizing it in practice only grudgingly.[40]

---

39. *The New York Times*, October 15, 1975, p. 9.

40. Richard Pipes, "U.S.A.–U.S.S.R.: The Preconditions of Détente," *Survey*, 21 (Winter/Spring 1975), 47.

They do not acknowledge a share in responsibility for world problems. For example, Soviet and Chinese delegates at the United Nations World Food Conference in November 1974 contributed only attacks on the Western powers and capitalism as responsible for hunger in the Third World, and their peoples were told almost nothing of the business of the conference. The Soviets themselves have added to the problems of the less developed countries, impeding planning by being secretive about their own crops and then forcing up prices by buying to cover shortages. The communist contribution to the population problem has usually been to deny its reality and blame it on the customary devils. The Chinese communists in 1974 were urging less developed countries to have as many babies as possible, even while they promoted small families at home. The communist states exclude themselves from the network of unofficial organizations that covers the earth and helps to bring peoples together. The communist share of world trade remains disproportionately small, and the communist states do their best to shut out foreign cultural flow except insofar as it is considered beneficial to the state. Ironically, the countries officially dedicated to internationalist Marxism-Leninism are the most nationalistic of all. Outside their sphere (wherein sovereignty is limited by the right of intervention) the Soviets are the strongest defenders of absolute sovereignty. In the leading communist states, much is made of military heroism, and pacifism is decried. It is chiefly the communist states that have conscript armies. Only the communist states, among major powers, raise fears of armed attack; of Soviet designs on China, Romania, or Yugoslavia; and of possible Chinese designs on Burma.

Marxist-Leninist ideology, which partly expresses the barricading of the socialist society against a hostile world and partly causes the hostility, seems increasingly irrelevant and inoperative. It forms a good deal of the mental framework of the communist rulership, however, and will continue to affect the future; the younger generation knows no other philosophy. This ideology is emotional and divisive insofar as it is taken seriously. The Soviet Union and other Marxist-Leninist states make an enormous effort to deepen or at least maintain the chasm that allegedly separates socialist from capitalist societies, even while they seek to make the best of trade with the "bad" states. It remains true for the Soviet state that *alien* is practically synonymous with *dangerous*. Class conflict (or class war, as it is usually called) is at the heart of Marxism-Leninism, and to deny the possibility of peaceful coexistence between classes (as the Soviets and others insistently do)

seriously qualifies its acceptance among nations.[41] Chairman Mao calls upon the people to "oppose counter-revolutionary war with national revolutionary war, and to oppose counter-revolutionary class war with revolutionary class war." [42] But any war can be treated as class war or a war of liberation, and Marxism-Leninism is an adequate rationalization for aggression. It is the only important ideology in today's world that gives war good standing and offers the hope of profiting from it.

Relaxation is poisonous for communism, which is a creed of passion, action, and change. Yet relaxation advances, and the socialist-capitalist antithesis becomes hollow. Convergence is not a naive theory of the early end of antagonisms but a reality of the slow wearing out of the historically generated specialness of the communist states. Charles Bohlen stated a few years ago, "The only hope, and this is a fairly thin one, is that at some point the Soviet Union will begin to act like a country instead of a cause." [43] But even the best of causes become tired, and Marxist-Leninist revolutionism is hardly the best. In the communist states, even China, consumerism seems gradually to be coming back, and the old ethos of austerity and sacrifice can hardly be restored unless there is a clear threat to security. In a mere two years (1973 to 1975) the number of cars on the road doubled in the Soviet Union, auguring a different society from that of the old peasant Russia.[44]

The urge to trade partly overpowers the desire for isolation; multiple friendly contacts between increasing numbers of communist officials and foreign entrepreneurs undermine ideological controls. Soviet trade with the outside world in recent years has grown several times as rapidly as Soviet trade within the bloc. The Soviet leadership seems increasingly concerned with world opinion; fear of foreign reactions deterred reprisals against dissidents Andrei Sakharov and Alexander Solzhenitsyn, whereas Stalin would not have hesitated to send them to labor camp or execution. The police remain arbitrary and often brutal, but they apply more pressure and chicanery, rather than the forthright violence of Stalin's day. The Soviet Union has something of an uncensored literature, and large amounts of underground material reach the

41. For ideology in Soviet foreign policy, cf. Robert G. Wesson, *Soviet Foreign Policy in Perspective*, Dorsey, Homewood, Ill., 1969, Chapter 7.

42. *Peking Review*, February 21, 1975, p. 7.

43. Charles E. Bohlen, *Witness to History, 1929–1969*, W. W. Norton, New York, 1973, p. 542.

44. *The Wall Street Journal*, August 14, 1975, p. 24.

West. In theory, the ideology-bound system is unchangeable; in practice, it cannot be kept from change.

A communist movement struggling for power is likely to be enthusiastic, coherent, and effective; once installed, having no secret of eternal youth, it ages in the use of power and becomes bureaucratic and given to self-seeking. The ideology of class struggle, the proletariat and workers' revolution, has become entirely irrelevant to Soviet life. The Soviet Union, still talking of equality, knows the reality of an elite who live much more apart from the masses than comparable people in the United States, and the fixity of those in authority is much greater than in the United States. The Soviet state stands for the order and stability that the rulers enjoy—for dullness, not dynamism. Authority grows old: the men who sit changelessly on the politburo averaged 67 years of age in 1976; Soviet youth leaders are apt to be in their forties. The political system is basically anarchic and personal, without adequate ways of allocating power and replacing outworn leadership. The economic system is clumsy and becomes less effective as self-seeking goals replace Bolshevik dedication. The tenth Five-Year Plan (for 1976–1980) blueprints only modest growth by modern standards. There is no reason to suppose that the Soviet Union of 1984 will be relatively stronger in the world than it is today. It may well lag economically and technologically still further behind the more open, pluralistic, and innovative powers. The communist states are increasingly interested in Western prosperity as a means of selling their goods to pay for the imports they need.

Under these circumstances, the Soviet capacity for action in world affairs is largely military—that is, unmodern. Soviet economic influence is limited. Soviet foreign trade is less than that of Canada or Belgium. All communist foreign economic aid taken together is only one-tenth that of the Western industrialized countries, and communist terms are less generous. Neither China nor the Soviet Union exercises an important degree of leadership in the Third World; they only play up to it. The communists support Third World positions rather than vice versa. How ineffective Soviet efforts may be is shown, for example, by the defection of Egypt, in which the Soviet Union invested not only many billions of dollars in arms but also years of political support, and by the preference of Iraq (once deemed a virtual Soviet satellite) for trade with the United States.[45]

---

45. *Business Week,* August 4, 1975, pp. 34–35.

In light of the degradation of the revolution, Soviet aggression does not seem likely. If Brezhnev has associated himself with a peace program,[46] it is because Soviet leaders have more than enough problems at home without reaching out for foreign involvements. It is not impossible that the leaders may undertake foreign adventures to divert attention and legitimate their right as representatives of the victorious movement, but they may have perceived that they have little to gain from further growth of their empire. It has been of little advantage to them for states to become communist unless they are held down militarily, and eastern European countries and the Soviet minorities cause trouble enough. The danger (apart from the nuclear sword of Damocles) is less domination than troublemaking; the Soviet Union and China have the power to make agreement difficult, to cause friction, and to complicate all manner of issues.

It is difficult, indeed, for communist states to desist from making trouble for the United States and the kind of world order that the United States favors. They are likely to support virtually any movement embarrassing to the West, such as terrorists in Germany, Palestinian guerrillas, or the Irish Republican Army. Anti-Americanism, with swings of intensity, is a standard ingredient of the propaganda they pour out both internally and externally. When the Soyuz and Apollo spaceships were linking up in July 1975, the Soviet press for only a few days desisted from the regular fare of unfavorable news about the United States, from economic troubles and moral degradation to imperialistic foreign policy. Even Yugoslavia, with no material cause for antagonism toward the United States, for internal purposes pounds from time to time on Marxist themes, which specifically usually involve anti-Americanism. It is difficult for communist countries to pretend to be Marxist-Leninist if they do not attack, at least in theory, the noncommunist world and chiefly its leading representative, the United States.

Communist states also encourage and support (politically and materially) communist parties everywhere; it can hardly be claimed that communists are dedicated to the good functioning of noncommunist societies. If they were not desirous of sabotaging liberal democracy, they would have no reason to be communist. It can hardly be denied—communists would certainly not deny it—that with or without

---

46. Clemens, "The Impact of Détente on Chinese and Soviet Communism," p. 142.

reason they oppose United States influence everywhere and bring discredit, so far as they readily can, upon the United States.

Hence, it must be conceded that American anticommunism, while often exaggerated and misguided, has some rational basis. Having an interest in a livable and more or less harmonious world, the United States also has an interest in the internal affairs of communist states and in communism as a political ideology. It is necessary, however, to recognize that force and violence are seldom appropriate and usually counterproductive. The change that may be hoped for is in attitudes, and such a change can only be gradual, perhaps perceptible only over a longer period.

To hope to influence attitudes requires that the West, especially the United States, should vigorously defend its ideals, which are almost universally accepted although seldom applied. It also requires that American conduct should correspond better to the ideals. Communist propaganda, like effective propaganda in general, takes reality as its starting point; American actions, such as the intervention in Vietnam and the capers of the CIA, have furnished its basis.

The other means of influencing communist states is to bring them into closer and more friendly contact with the United States, with economic strength, technological excellence, and cultural creativity as the American political weapons. To seek to isolate communist states or to cut them off from the United States is self-defeating. This lesson seems to have been learned with regard to the communist giants, although much more might be done to make it attractive for Soviet and Chinese leaders to modify their political behavior. It still seems to be felt that something is to be gained by refusal to have dealings with Cuba, North Korea, and Vietnam. In August 1975 the communist government of South Vietnam expressed interest in a cooperative effort between governments and oil companies to search for petroleum,[47] but American corporations are prevented by law from participating. The United States has been concerned lest the Vietnamese turn Camranh Bay, once built at immense cost for the defense of the Saigon government, into a Soviet naval base; the obvious way to discourage this possibility would be to open diplomatic and trade relations with the Vietnamese government. The Vietnamese have invited the United States to do so, despite the fact that they have as much reason for bitterness over the past as does the United States.

---

47. *Business Week,* August 25, 1975, p. 36.

It is in the American interest that communist states, like other states, should be independent; treating them as such helps them to be. Marxism-Leninism is not helpful for world order in any aspect, but its significance is primarily internal, an adjunct of government. There is no reason for the United States to let communism impede good relations so far as the Marxist-Leninist state is willing. Possibly the United States will not do so where there is no bad blood and the inertia of past policies does not stand in the way. Thus in September 1975 the United States proceeded to extend prompt diplomatic recognition to the radical Marxist government of Mozambique, even while it was barring United Nations membership for the Vietnamese.[48]

---

48. On the ground, possibly logical but not acceptable to United States allies, that South Korea should be admitted at the same time.

CHAPTER EIGHT

Problems of the Poor

THE GULF

The differences between the United States and the Soviet Union are in a sense synthetic, a matter of ideology—that is, words, confrontation partly for the sake of confrontation. Across the two groups of politically defined states that are represented by these two nations, however, there cuts a division that is in some ways deeper and less bridgeable: that between the rich and the poor. A basic cause of incompatibility between Soviet Russia and China is the difference in their economic levels—the ability of the Russians to think of a modest amount of luxury against the need of the Chinese to concentrate on necessities—and the resulting differences in values. In Chinese eyes, the differences of structure between the United States and the Soviet Union fade; these two are together the hegemonic superpowers (thus, in the Chinese classification, comprising a First World, the Second World being the smaller industrial powers, from Japan to France). Differences between the United States and poorer nations are usually less antagonistic than those between the Soviet Union and China, but they are real and persistent even where no ideological issues arise. The people of India, especially intellectuals, inevitably have a very different outlook from Americans on world problems.

The category of the less developed nations (LDCs) is indistinct. A number of countries, such as Taiwan, Portugal, Greece, and Brazil, stand on the edge of the industrial world. But the group as a whole, which includes about three-fourths of the membership of the United Nations, has become increasingly self-aware and disposed to work together for common interests. Its first major conclave was the Bandung Conference of 1955. Since then the group has become more and more organized, inclusive, and assertive of its interests. Successive conclaves have brought together larger numbers of developing or less developed nations; at the conference in Algiers in 1973, there were seventy-six participants plus a swarm of observers, anticolonial movements, and sundry guests. The LDCs also have gathering places under the wing of the United Nations, particularly in the United Nations Conference on Trade and Development (UNCTAD), in which others are swamped by their voices and votes. The United Nations General Assembly itself is not far from being a caucus of the LDCs. Special meetings have been devoted to their demands and grievances, a multitude of issues likely to occupy the international arena for many years. The category of LDCs is often treated as roughly equivalent to the so-called Third World, a term applied since the 1950s to states rejecting alignment with either side in the cold war.

To some extent, the division is between north and south in the world, since most of the poorer nations are tropical. But some, such as Afghanistan, are not, and thus a geographical separation is uninformative. It is more cogent to speak of the non-Western noncommunist world as against the Western and communist worlds. (The West comprises states coming out of the European scientific and industrial revolution and their extensions overseas, including the United States. Japan, while different by race and cultural heritage, belongs economically and politically to the Western world, and others of non-Western background may likewise become "Western.") A more significant characterization is technological backwardness and poverty. A billion persons in the industrialized countries have a per capita annual income averaging around $3,000; close to 3 billion people in the LDCs average about $240 annually. Otherwise stated, one-fourth of the world's people generate four-fifths of the global product. The poorer 70 percent of the world produces 5 to 10 percent of basic industrial commodities. The per capita energy consumption of LDCs ranged from one-tenth to one-two-hundredth that of the United States.[1] The spread is, of course, enormous. The very poor, such as Afghanistan, Pakistan, Bangladesh, Haiti, and various African countries (sometimes called the Fourth World), with very little industry and no important exports, may seem nearly hopeless. Some 650 million people with per capita annual incomes under $50 are virtually outside the modern economy. On the other hand, countries such as Singapore, Brazil, and Mexico have a fair amount of modern industry and a much higher per capita income. Some Arab states, with small populations and large oil deposits, actually have the world's highest per capita incomes; however, they are like poor men who have won a lottery, and it remains to be seen whether their accidental wealth can be translated into self-sustaining prosperity.

The people of the Third World are by no means so deprived as is indicated by income figures, which refer to marketed goods and services. The poorer the country, the larger the proportion of its production outside the market economy. Especially in the countryside, people provide themselves with much nonmonetary income in food, fuel, housing, and many services. Heating is usually unnecessary, transportation is less needed, and necessities are generally much cheaper than in richer lands. But the picture is bleak. Probably two-

---

1. For statistics on the development gap, see *The U.S. and World Development: Agenda for Action,* ed. James W. Howe, Overseas Development Council, New York, 1975, pp. 254–274.

thirds of the population of the world is more or less undernourished. For most of the 600 million people of India, the possibility of hunger is the predominant fact of life. Debilitating chronic diseases—malaria, dysentery, schistosomiasis, and so forth—afflict a large majority in many countries. A large part of the adult population is illiterate. For most people of the less developed world, there is almost no hope of improvement.[2]

The absolute level of poverty is not crucial; probably most people in the LDCs have about as much material goods at their command as the people of Athens in their days of Periclean glory. But what would have been affluence a century or so ago is poverty by modern standards—that is, in relation to what people feel they might have and in relation to what others have. Those who are left behind are depressed and often bitter. Whereas the Athenians were exuberantly on top of their world, the poorer peoples of today are depressed at the bottom.

The situation of many countries is still unhappier because they tend to lag ever farther behind. A few poor countries have shown very high growth rates over the past decade; for example, Brazil and Taiwan have increased their gross national product (GNP) about 10 percent yearly for many years. But for the most part the gap remains. For the poorest billion persons, life has improved materially little or not at all in the past fifteen years, and the global slums get slummier. Unhappily, too, just as the real income of the LDCs is statistically understated, their growth is overstated. Urbanization and commercialization increase recorded income without necessarily improving well-being or even material goods; the shantytown dweller may be in many respects worse off than his country cousin who has less money. Growth of the GNP is offset or more than offset by growth of inequality, unemployment, and urban crowding.[3] The result, as the world becomes increasingly integrated economically and informationally, is rising discontent. As a Third World spokesman put it, "Once the Third World has become a mass market for the goods, products, and processes which are designed by the rich for themselves, the dis-

---

2. For a survey of problems of LDCs, see Charlotte Waterlow, *Superpowers and Victims: Outlook for World Community,* Prentice-Hall, Englewood Cliffs, N.J., 1974; for statistics, see *The U.S. and World Development: Agenda for Action, 1975,* ed. Howe.

3. Charles Paolillo, "Development Assistance: Where Next?," *The U.S. and the Developing World: Agenda for Action, 1974,* ed. James W. Howe et al., Praeger, New York, 1974, p. 109.

crepancy between the demand for these Western artifacts and the supply will increase indefinitely." [4]

It is not easy to account for such gross disparities in standards of living between peoples whose innate abilities are generally assumed to be roughly similar. Natural resources, or their lack, can hardly be blamed. Most LDCs have less land per capita than developed countries, but many have adequate space and soil, and yields per acre are low in some very impoverished countries, such as India. Mineral wealth is fairly well scattered over the globe and is not necessary for prosperity. Japan, for example, prospers with no mineral resources of consequence. It is more appealing to the LDCs and their sympathizers to blame political-economic causes, to maintain that they are poor because they have been robbed—or, in Marxist terms, exploited by the largely capitalistic Western powers. It is no doubt true that, in the jungle of international economies, the poor and the weak are disadvantaged and likely to get the worst of bargains. However, the very poor are those who have little economic contact with the outside world and produce nothing to be exploited, and these countries have shown least progress in the last two decades. The better-off LDCs, or those rising most rapidly, are among those most engaged in the world economy and hence most subject to exploitation; such nations include Hong Kong, Taiwan, and Brazil. The trouble lies more in a contrary direction: the underutilization of what the poorer countries have in abundance, human labor. In any case, the fact that the more advanced countries have used their advantages for their own benefit only explains the continuation or perhaps worsening of the situation, not how it arose in the first place. The relatively poor nations of today, generally speaking, were relatively poor fifty or one hundred years ago.

Fundamentally, the tragic situation arises because of technological change, which has produced inequality since the dawn of history. Five thousand years ago the people of Sumeria were far ahead of their neighbors in the Near East in ways of making and doing things. The Greeks of the classic age stood head and shoulders over other peoples not only in poetry and philosophy but also in material amenities and military capacity; at one time they could colonize around the Mediterranean somewhat as Europeans in the seventeenth century could establish their colonies in Asia and the Americas. Once

---

4. Ivan Ilich, in *Development, an Introductory Reader*, ed. Helen Castel, Macmillan, New York, 1971, pp. 280–281.

achieved, an advantage tends to perpetuate itself; knowledge feeds on knowledge and wealth on wealth. For some to catch up, the others would have to stand still.

The problem is general not only in time but also in space. Within western Europe, some regions (for example, southern Italy and Scotland) have lagged behind to become relatively poor. In the United States, there are Indian tribes and underprivileged racial groups suffering troubles like those of Asians, and some areas of European settlement, such as Appalachia, have become virtual LDCs. The problem is shared by the Soviet Union. Not only are rural regions far behind major cities, but much of central Asia has economic standards several times lower than those of central Russia.

The more advanced the technology of the leading centers and the faster the rate of innovation, the more those on the outside may be left behind. Inequality is peculiarly heightened in the contemporary age because of the immense quantity of knowledge and skills available for those in a position to use them and because of the extreme rapidity of development. Thus, despite unprecedented facilities for learning and even a large-scale effort to spread productive knowledge (such as never occurred in earlier generations), the gap remains or even widens. The world in a sense grows apart while transportation and communications bring it ever closer together. Ease of travel, global awareness, and improved communication encourage centralization in the most favored regions. When wealth and knowledge come together, there is better education, it is easier to invest for increased productivity, and capital is more productive. The better students and teachers go to the best universities, while talented people, especially scientists and engineers, drift from all continents to western Europe and the United States. At Western centers an Indian scientist not only can earn far more than he could at home but also enjoys superior research facilities and contacts with others in his area of interest. The loss of able people—which is difficult to halt without authoritarian controls—amounts to a substantial fraction of persons trained in some LDCs and a much larger proportion of their brighter young men who can seek an education abroad. In the LDCs, people and wealth flow to the cities; in the world, they flow to the leading centers and especially the United States.[5]

---

5. Cf. Subcommittee on National Security Policy, Committee on Foreign Affairs, U.S. House of Representatives, *Brain Drain: A Study of the Persistent Issue of International Scientific Mobility,* Government Printing Office, Washington, D.C., 1974.

In another respect, woes may be ascribed to the transfer to the LDCs of parts of the scientific-industrial revolution, making for incongruous mixtures of customs, institutions, and capacities. The Western societies have either thrust upon the Third World countries or permitted them to copy conveniences and luxuries, from automobiles to Western dress, television, bottled beverages, and modern armies. The West has created a perhaps insuperable population problem by exporting ideas of hygiene, preventive medicine, and charity; hardly any country lets famine take the cruel course of a few generations ago. An example of the insidiousness of the interaction of modern and premodern cultures is the propagation by drug companies and the acceptance by those who would be up to date of bottle feeding of babies. This practice, in unfavorable conditions, leads to malnutrition and disease in infants, needless additional expense, and a higher birthrate because of earlier conception by nonlactating mothers. But to sift out the ideas and practices that the LDCs need and to exclude those that they were better without, for the present and perhaps the future, are beyond the world's wisdom.

ECONOMIC DEVELOPMENT

Since the overall name of the troubles of the LDCs is poverty, the accepted solution is increased productivity. More productive societies should, it is hoped, be more contented and stable, possibly more democratic; raised standards of living should lead to lower birthrates in Asia and Africa just as they have in Europe; and humanity would be happily on its way to a better future.

A glance at the obstacles is sobering. The first requisite is ordinarily considered to be capital, the equipment and other investment needed to make labor productive. It is usually reckoned that about $3 of capital should give a return of $1 yearly in production; in the LDCs, however, many factors, including inflation and lack of channels for suitable investment, discourage saving, while the scarce capital on hand is drawn less to uncertain new industry than to socially rewarding land ownership. Many of the wealthy seek security by stashing funds abroad, where both government and the economy are more reliable.

Alternatively, capital may be drawn from abroad, either in direct investment or as loans. Foreign investment in the native economy injects tensions and conflicts, increases the distance between capital and labor, and is entirely insufficient. American and other investors mostly prefer safer countries in any case. Loans are very tempting; if leaders can borrow, they can at least postpone handling a problem, perhaps until their successors must deal with it. Loans, however, fall due one day and are an increasing burden on the balance of payments in the LDCs. Interest on LDC debts totaled about $10 billion yearly by 1974; with large continuing deficits on account ($38 billion in 1975), it is necessary to borrow more and more to keep afloat. As defaults become commoner, interest rates go up.

Foreign aid might theoretically come to the rescue, but its promise (as discussed later) is very limited. Simply to try to transfer capital is to invite waste and corruption and may be worse than nothing. Foreign aid tends to demoralize, since it teaches the leaders of the LDC to look abroad rather than to their own efforts and resources. Capital grants are seldom separable from selfish purposes of the donor; for example, the United States is likely to be accused, rightly or not, of financing road construction to forward the sale of automobiles and petroleum. Aid helps the ruling elite much more than the needy poor (except in emergency relief, and perhaps then also because of corruption). Alien officials, American or otherwise, seldom know very well the needs of an LDC, and projects set up under foreign auspices commonly fail in a few years.[6] Egypt's dream project, the Aswan Dam, has had nightmarish side effects, such as the loss of fisheries, decrease of soil fertility, and increase of snail-borne schistosomiasis.

In the usual parlance, *development* mostly refers to manufacturing industry, which is the obvious way to modernize, to use local labor resources, to substitute for imported goods, and even to export. In most countries, however, domestic markets are excessively small, and it is hard to break into world markets. There is a grave lack of managerial and other skills. It is usually desired and sometimes seems necessary to use modern methods and equipment that require much capital for every job produced. New industries often kill small-scale or handicraft production and so actually increase unemployment. They also increase inequality, as a small sector of the labor force, with unions demanding higher wages, becomes a lower-class elite. It might seem sounder to give more attention to the basic activity of the large

----

6. For examples, see William and Elizabeth Paddock, *We Don't Know How,* Iowa State University Press, Ames, Iowa, 1973.

majority of the population—agriculture—but results have been poor. Food production barely keeps pace with growth of population, and yields are low because of poor practices. Tropical soils are delicate, and overgrazing makes deserts, as in sub-Saharan Africa and parts of the Near East. Mechanization of agriculture increases unemployment and crowding into cities. The much-hailed green revolution, which showed that it was possible to double or triple yields of rice and wheat, has proved disappointing. The new crops need more fertilizer, herbicides, probably irrigation, and educated care; when these techniques fail or are misused, the result is disaster. Some who can take advantage of the innovations—farmers or bosses—profit, but for those who lack capital or the ability to experiment, the green revolution often has meant further impoverishment. As in the world at large, technological change in an LDC brings inequality; nearly half of the population may fail to gain from economic development at all.[7]

Capital is of little value without corresponding skills, but education in most LDCs fails to provide these skills. The illiteracy rate is around 80 percent in most of tropical Africa and not far from 50 percent even in so progressive a country as Brazil. Education at all levels is deficient in both quality and quantity and is usually directed more toward prestige diplomas (for example, in law) than toward more practical affairs, like business management. Students who are trained in advanced technologies often go abroad to work or fail to find suitable jobs at home.[8]

Ignorance is not the sole factor that holds down the productivity of labor. Nearly half of the students at the University of Calcutta (with an enrollment of more than 100,000) are said to suffer from malnutrition. Probably two-thirds of the children in the LDCs are more or less stunted physically and mentally by poor nutrition. Caloric intake, the grossest nutritional measure, is about or under 2,000 calories daily in the LDCs, compared with over 3,000 calories in the advanced countries; there has been no improvement over the last generation. American contractors building a dam in Pakistan doubled the productivity of 10,000 laborers by providing lunch for them.[9] It is not

7. Robert S. McNamara, *One Hundred Countries, Two Billion People: The Dimensions of Development*, Praeger, New York, 1973, p. 107.

8. Chandler Morse, "Making Science and Technology for LDCs," *Columbia Journal of World Business*, 10 (Spring 1975), 52.

9. Bernard Brodie, "The Impact of Technological Change in the International System: Reflections on Prediction," *Journal of International Affairs*, vol. 25, no. 2 (1971), p. 220.

unlikely that much of the otherworldliness of south Asians derives from chronic semistarvation.[10] Widespread malnutrition also contributes to the aristocrats' widespread contempt for the incapable masses and for hard, particularly physical, labor.

There are a host of other obstacles to would-be national developers. Skill in management is as crucially short as technical expertise.[11] Modern transportation and distribution technology is ill suited for LDCs and favors major commercial centers; for example, container ships are for big ports only.[12] The LDCs usually have very little access to world markets, and internal markets are discouragingly small; a majority of LDCs have populations under 5 million. A lot of free or cheap technology is available for those prepared to use it, but competitive productive technologies are valuable and have to be paid for; licenses are burdensome for feeble industries.[13] There are a host of social and political problems like those of more developed countries, but usually they are more acute in the LDCs. The disproportionate swelling of population requires a major exertion merely to keep the standard of existence from falling.

In the face of such handicaps, a few LDCs possess mineral resources to solve some or all of their financial problems, at least until the resource runs out. The riches of the scantily populated Arab states lying on lakes of oil are familiar; other countries have lesser but helpful assets: Jamaica has bauxite and Zambia has copper, for example. However, not only are these resources rather few; raised fuel prices may hurt the LDCs in general more than they do the industrialized countries. Fertilizer becomes scarce and expensive in step with petroleum; Indian farmers cannot afford gasoline for irrigation pumps. Few of the LDCs possess indispensable products, and the effect of technology broadly has been to reduce the relative share of raw materials in the value of finished goods. For example, in the electronics and computer industries, materials are an almost trivial part of input compared to design and fabrication. Modern chemistry has permitted many substitutions; formerly excellent sources of foreign

---

10. Gunnar Myrdal, *The Challenge of World Poverty*, Pantheon Books, New York, 1970, p. 83.

11. Pierre van Goethem, *The Americanization of World Business*, Herder and Herder, New York, 1974, Chapter 11.

12. Jacob D. Merriwether et al., "Distribution Efficiency and Worldwide Productivity," *Columbia Journal of World Business*, 9 (Winter 1974), 87–92.

13. Denis Goulet, "The Paradox of Technology Transfer," *The Bulletin of Atomic Scientists*, 31 (June 1975), 41.

exchange for the Third World, such as natural rubber, natural silk, nitrates, manila, and quinine, have been much reduced. Chiefly for this reason, the LDCs' share of world trade has tended to shrink, having been approximately halved from 1950 to 1970 (dropping from 30 percent to 17 percent) despite the population growth in the LDCs.

THE CROWDED EARTH

It is a tribute to the power and transmissibility of modern technology that, despite these mutually reinforcing burdens, the LDCs have not fared badly during the last decades. In fact, according to commonly accepted but unreliable statistics, they have increased gross output slightly more rapidly than the industrialized countries, having accelerated to the impressive figure of 5.9 percent yearly from 1963 to 1973, against 4.9 percent in the Western industrial countries. By historical standards, such a growth rate is phenomenal, several times higher than that of thriving European countries in the early part of the industrial revolution. This growth is made possible, of course, by the vast store of technology waiting to be applied as nations become ready. But per capita growth rate is another tale. Since the increase in population of LDCs is about 2.6 percent yearly, subtraction of population growth leaves net increase per head at about 3.3 percent, compared with a per capita rate from 1963 to 1973 of 3.8 percent in the industrialized countries. Moreover, a larger part of this statistical growth is illusory in the case of the LDCs because of the shift toward market economics; it is doubtful that many countries have experienced any real increase in material well-being, although more people have acquired some of the fripperies of modernity. Economic growth is consumed by population growth; the only achievement is that more people exist at the same near-subsistence level.

At present rates, the population of the LDCs will double in less than thirty years; that of some African and Latin American countries is doubling in twenty years, and that of some big cities in five to seven years. Such human inflation has many effects beyond dilution or nullification of economic growth. Most discussed is the pressure of more and more mouths on the food supply. Land available for cultivation does not increase and harvests barely keep up with needs, since yields per acre are very low in most LDCs. Overuse of land combines with overgrazing, deforestation, flooding, silting, salination of irrigated fields, and high costs of energy and fertilizer to reduce yields.[14] Not only food but also other resources are destroyed. For example, as forest and brush are removed to make way for crops, firewood becomes scarce; people from Pakistan to Bolivia strip remaining vegetation, exposing soil to erosion, causing flooding, and reducing fertility; dung goes into the stove instead of onto the fields.[15] Sooner or later, as Malthus pointed out two centuries ago, the result must be starvation or some other check; in the face of a surplus of births over deaths of between 2 and 3 percent, the day of reckoning is drawing visibly closer. High reproduction rates burden society with an excessive proportion of dependents and make capital accumulation much more difficult at the same time that more people need ever more schools, housing, roads, and all the infrastructure of civilized society. It is also impossible to provide useful employment for an expanding population. About a third of the labor force of the LDCs is largely or entirely unemployed, at least half in such countries as Egypt and India.[16] There are appropriate jobs for only a quarter of the semieducated university graduates of India, for whom the diploma represents the best hope of rising in life. Creating a job in industry costs several thousand dollars at a low level of technology, and the LDCs want modern technology. Industrialization can help only slightly, even assuming the unlikely possibility that there will be adequate fuels and raw materials. The world has difficulty improving the lot of the 4 billion people who now weigh on it; it can ill afford the 7.5 billion it will probably be called upon to sustain by the end of this century.

The unchecked proliferation of humanity has other unpleasant consequences. The LDCs tend to become dependent on the more advanced nations for food and thus further mortgage their economies. Many former food exporters of Latin America and southern Asia have become importers; many Third World countries buy one-half of their basic foods.[17] India's foreign exchange earnings are nearly all spent not on machinery but on food, fertilizer, and the like. The teeming shantytowns of Jakarta, Lagos, or Calcutta are already mind-numbing;

14. Lester R. Brown, "The World Food Prospect," *Science*, December 12, 1975, p. 1058.

15. Erik P. Eckholm, "The Firewood Crisis," *Natural History*, 84 (October 1975), 6–23.

16. *The New York Times*, November 8, 1973, p. 31.

17. Brown, "The World Food Prospect," pp. 1053–1059.

Bangladesh has 1,300 persons per square mile with almost no industry, and prospects of doubling its population in twenty years. The outcome can only be disease, crime, and something like a breakdown of the social order. The population explosion makes people less valuable and magnifies inequalities; the poorer classes increase themselves most rapidly while the better-educated individuals are more influenced by Western values and tend to restrict their families. Poverty thus compounds itself.

The population explosion causes bitterness within and between nations; yet ironically it results from what would at first sight be called the beneficent influence of the West, which has exported lower mortality rates without much influencing natality rates. Better water supplies, soap, elementary notions of hygiene, insecticides, smallpox vaccination, malaria control, and so forth, along with restraints on homicide, have made life perhaps not happier but certainly more secure. Even in Bangladesh, life expectancy rose from twenty-two years in 1920 to fifty years in 1968. To cope with the problem, no one proposes to restore high death rates, the course nature will take eventually if humans cannot control their own breeding. There are no ready solutions. Even if contraceptives are available, governments are unable to reach the masses that most need them. Population growth creates more poverty and ignorance, which make multiplication more uncontrollable; the longer the problem goes on, the harder it is to take in hand.

There are hints of progress. In a large majority of LDCs, birthrates are declining, although for the most part slowly. So far as they may be made available, education and social services give hope for improvement.[18] A great reason for wanting many children is for support in old age, a function the state may undertake in the better-off countries. Urbanization helps; in the cities children are usually less useful and people are more reachable. The political reason for natalist policies, to have material for bigger armies, has largely vanished; most of the LDCs at least recognize the desirability of doing something to slow population growth. The fact that 30 to 40 percent of Mexican children are retarded because of malnutrition[19] has persuaded the government that the old motto, "to govern is to populate," is outmoded; it has hence turned to the United Nations and other

---

18. A thesis of Lester R. Brown, *In the Human Interest: A Strategy to Stabilize World Population*, Praeger, New York, 1974.
19. *The New York Times*, May 27, 1974, p. 4.

agencies for assistance. India has long had an extensive birth control program, with limited results thus far; there is an effort to implement sterner measures, including even compulsory sterilization. In this respect again, the relatively more prosperous Third World nations have the best chance of success, while the very poor seem practically hopeless.

No particular interests profit from population control and some see it as harmful—landholders for economic reasons, nationalists for political causes—much as black radicals in the United States reject it.[20] Nationalists regard numbers as a means to power in the world; they have little else on which to fasten aspirations. Population is a claim on world resources and a moral lever to demand concessions of richer nations. Catholicism and Islam both frown on population control; Pope Paul in March 1974 firmly reasserted his position against birth control. In 1974 the Argentine government outlawed all contraceptives. Communists and other radicals consider population control abhorrent, perhaps because they wish to see only one answer to all problems. The Chinese communists encourage population growth in the LDCs, where they would like to see more revolutions. The Soviets encourage population growth at home, apparently for future strength, and in the LDCs Marxist students forced the closing of family-planning programs sponsored by universities in Colombia and Ecuador and refused to permit courses in demography.[21] It has been calculated that investment in birth control would be a hundred times more effective in raising income levels than investment of the same amount in capital equipment. Nevertheless, results are not immediately visible, and population control has low priority. Pressed to provide famine relief in 1973, the Indian government cut back sharply on birth control expenditures. The idea, like other new ideas, comes from the more advanced countries and is correspondingly suspect. It is resented as interference and presumably a means to prevent the less developed from growing and so becoming more powerful. A Nigerian newspaper wrote, "The idea of family planning as peddled by the Euro-American world is an attempt to keep Africa weak." [22] If the superpowers

---

20. On factors favoring and opposing reduction of birth rates in LDCs, see Michael S. Teitelbaum, "Relevance of Demographic Transition Theory for Developing Countries," *Science*, May 26, 1975, p. 420–425.

21. Benjamin Viet, "The Population Explosion," *Proceedings of the Academy of Political Science*, vol. 30, no. 4 (1972), p. 47.

22. *Nigerian Daily Times*, quoted by *Newsweek*, June 12, 1972, p. 43.

wanted to keep the less developed world as poor, impotent, and dependent as possible, they would encourage reckless breeding, but there is an almost neurotic sensitivity on the subject. A noted Brazilian economist, Josué de Castro, thus called birth control "genocide of the unborn." [23] The confidence in national destiny that is essential for development seems to imply that restricting numbers is unnecessary. A scholar can argue that in the past growth in productivity and in population have coincided, and therefore population growth is a good thing.[24]

Checking population growth seems to be an indispensable (although not sufficient) condition of economic progress or even stability. The only alternative seriously proposed is a revolution, which by redistribution should postpone the need for a short time and then by its capacities for action should take a firm grip on private behavior, as the Chinese communists seem to have done.[25] But such revolutions, useful or not, are not on the horizon.

The only predictable result is disaster. The biggest apparent threat to the survival of civilization is not nuclear war, which would hardly come unless some madman willed it, but overpopulation leading to mass starvation and misery and all manner of social and political complications, spreading from the poor to the less poor nations. Overpopulation can negate any conceivable effort of the more prosperous nations to reduce inequality in the world. It is a charge against the future that will one day have to be paid. It is not a bomb threatening to explode—the ground-down masses lack explosive energy —but an insidious cancer, which through the unchecked purposeless multiplication of cells disorganizes, sickens, and (if left untreated) eventually kills.

SOCIAL AND POLITICAL DISORDER

Problems such as inadequate growth of production or excessive growth of population are the results of human failures and should be soluble if a country is blessed with an effective social and political

---

23. *Time,* June 26, 1972, p. 40.

24. Samir Amin, "Development and Structural Change: The African Experience, 1950–1970," *Journal of International Affairs,* vol. 24, no. 2 (1970), p. 208.

25. Cf. A. Doak Barnett, *Uncertain Passage: China's Transition to the Post-Mao Era,* Brookings Institution, Washington, D.C., 1974, pp. 159–162.

order. Thus, Japan purposefully and rapidly modernized; it has ex-
changed the troubles of the LDCs for a new set of troubles—those of
the advanced industrial countries. But the LDCs generally suffer from
a lamentably defective social order; this judgment can be made not
in terms of differences from our own imperfect ways but in terms of
incapacity to achieve the goals that these countries badly want.

The productivity of a society results from a whole complex of
habits and ways beyond merely technical skills and equipment.[26]
Much of the ailment can be summarized as carelessness and corruption. One learns much about underdevelopment by sending a
telegram that arrives days later or not at all. In many places bank
checks are little used because they are so generally misused. Planning is difficult because statistics are at best hopeful guesses. Smuggling is a major business in most of the LDCs, which rely on customs
revenues because income taxes are not collectable.[27] The underpaid
employees of inflated, parasitic bureaucracies use their positions as
a license for minor and major extortion.[28] It is commonly taken for
granted that one should pay privately for official services, for special
favors, or for exemption from rules, while the mores require that
people fortunate enough to secure a place in the apparatus use it to
support their extended families. But corruption demoralizes, causes
waste, destroys the relation between productive effort and reward, discourages honest effort, and undermines the ability of the government
to carry out its programs. Governments impose all manner of controls
to promote development, but the controls not only are constrictive
and wasteful but also invite bribery and shift the emphasis from
production to political maneuvering. The poorer the country, generally
speaking, the more grasping and parasitic are the leaders; and the
worse the government, the poorer the prospects for development.

Often, governments are not only corrupt but also incompetent,
oppressive, and/or extortionist. Inflation, caused by an inability to
cover government requirements by taxation, is even worse than in
industrial countries; tax evasion is almost omnipresent. There are
usually ambitious but ineffective planning setups, and the civil service

26. Cf. Stanislav Andreski, *Parasitism and Subversion: The Case of Latin
America,* Pantheon Books, New York, 1966; idem, *The African Predicament: A
Study in the Pathology of Modernization,* Michael Joseph, London, 1968.

27. Cf. Jorge Dominguez, "Smuggling," *Foreign Policy,* 20 (Fall 1975), 87–96.

28. Cf. Ronald Wraith and Edgar Simpkins, *Corruption in Developing Countries,* W. W. Norton, New York, 1964.

often resembles charity for the privileged. In some countries as much as half the work force is on the government payroll.

Improvement is more difficult because a large number of the so-called nations, from Afghanistan to Zaire, are only nominally nations, lacking common language, tradition, or loyalties. Indonesia, for example, has over three hundred ethnic groups. In Pakistan, less than 10 percent of the population speaks the official language, Urdu; speakers of Sind, Baluch, and Punjabi clamor for recognition, while the business of the government is done in English, which is mastered by a tiny minority. The means of general understanding, especially in Africa, is the language of former colonial powers, particularly English and French. Loyalty to a tribe is much stronger than loyalty to the state; tribal clashes have killed many hundreds of thousands in Africa in the last few years. A little education seems to make people aware of differences that they previously ignored. Racism is strong where obviously different peoples come together, such as East Indians and Negroes in Guiana. Ceylon seeks to expel hundreds of thousands of Indians, and Asians have been driven out of East Africa.

Class differences are also very marked. Land, for example, is very unevenly distributed, with a few large holders and many landless or nearly landless peasants. Sharecropping and latifundia systems are a barrier to progress. Land reform is a widespread demand and probably a necessity for social health, but it usually flounders on the resistance of the possessors, who are close to the high bureaucracy and probably the military leaders as well. The inequality of the traditional society is likely to be made worse by modernization, as the newly educated elite feel themselves much further above the masses than their parents were.[29] As with the green revolution, a few are able to ride the wave of technology to wealth and status, while the majority, especially in the villages, are left behind. It is characteristic of the LDCs that they are composed of two societies with different values and little communication: the modern and relatively affluent, and the traditional and poor. While westernization has sickened native cultures, bringing insecurity, confusion, and social tension, cosmopolitan Western culture remains shallow and artificial.

Under such circumstances, democracy does not prosper. There are all degrees of authoritarianism, from arbitrary brutal despotism

---

29. Arum Shourie, "Growth, Poverty, and Inequalities," *Foreign Affairs*, 51 (January 1973), 340–352.

down, but functioning constitutional or democratic governments, in which power can be transferred by free elections, are exceptional; there are not over two dozen in the world, and few indeed among the LDCs: two or three in Latin America, probably none in black Africa, and hardly any in Asia. India, since becoming independent in 1947, rather miraculously held contested elections, although one party retained control; but dictatorial powers were invoked when Prime Minister Indira Gandhi seemed to be getting into trouble in 1975. By 1975, the seemingly unstoppable population spiral, pervasive corruption, bureaucratic strictures, inflation, and economic deterioration brought deep gloom to India. While people starved, a large part of the grain supplies was consumed by rats, and fertilizer plants worked at half their capacity. When Gandhi declared an emergency and jailed the opposition leaders in June 1975, nearly everybody seemed happy that the price of rice was concurrently reduced.

Democracy has receded generally. Uruguay, once the "Switzerland of the Americas," has become a semimilitary dictatorship, and many civilian governments have been set aside by the military in Latin America during the past decade. In Chile, a long-time showcase of constitutional democracy, a Marxist experiment was succeeded by a military dictatorship. Most embarrassing for the United States was the defection of the Philippines. The island nation, more or less an American ward since receiving independence in 1946, fell into a swamp of poverty and disorder so bad that few seemed to mind when President Ferdinand Marcos imposed martial law in September 1972.

The prestige of Western industrial civilization is such that nearly all countries, including the communist, make some bow to principles of popular sovereignty, constitutions, elections, and the like. But for numerous reasons the climate of the LDCs is withering for the kind of government that has been associated with economic progress in the West.[30] The emotional level of politics is too high. Aspirations, inflated by communications (from movies to the transistor radio), so far outrun capacities that a party could hardly promise to meet the desires of the masses. The numerical preponderance of the young is

---

30. On the politics of the LDCs, cf. *Politics in Transitional Societies,* ed. Harvey G. Kebschull, Appleton-Century-Crofts, New York, 1973; Fred R. von der Mehden, *Politics of the Developing Nations,* 2nd ed., Prentice-Hall, Englewood Cliffs, N.J., 1969.

unsettling, especially as youthful semi-intellectuals find themselves unwanted and unrewarded. Very many are becoming lawyers, for whom politics is the way to status. Wealth and status are part of the governmental apparatus or are politically conditioned. Place in the power structure is too important to be voluntarily surrendered; its loss commonly means ruin for the whole family. The bureaucracy forms the greatest vested interest; if there is some democracy, the apparatus perverts it to a means of promoting its own welfare. The press is venal, and there is little notion of impartial information. Voters are ignorant and bribable, and results are often fraudulently reported. In small, weak countries honest patriots fear that foreign powers and interests may unduly influence elections. The role of an opposition party, the health of which is essential for democracy, is unacceptable. Partisan politics inflames the already almost unbearable divisions of society; where nationhood is fragile or artificial, dissent is next to treason, and a free press is divisive. The basic consensus and general loyalty that would enable the rules of the game to prevail over personalities and passions are lacking.

American hopes for a democratic future in the Third World are thus dim, but no one has figured out a really suitable alternative. In the absence of a firm constitutional order, the holders of force are nearly everywhere at least residual holders of power, with a veto over personalities and policies, although they may not actually manage affairs. Sometimes military cliques are well motivated and more efficient than civilian leadership, but military hierarchy and training in the use of force are an unpromising basis for a stable and progressive polity. A governing political party may be an instrument of mobilization and communication; it may function well as long as it has revolutionary élan, but it easily becomes a privileged gang running affairs for its own benefit.

Usually LDCs seem to feel the need for a single boss or dictator to integrate and move the incoherent society, giving through personality the stability that institutions lack. Such leaders may be adulated beyond measure, even virtually deified, in the manner of Kwame Nkrumah of Ghana or Mobutu Sese Seko of Zaire, since they dispose of the facilities of the state to exalt their names. They may be crude or mercurial, in the manner of Idi Amin of Uganda or the youthful Muammar el-Kaddafi of Libya. The latter, a devotee of Koranic law, anti-Western and anti-Soviet at the same time, decreed the Islamic penalties of amputation of the right hand for theft and death for

independent political activity, banned strikes, abolished most newspapers, and placed the rest under strict control. Kaddafi, like many
another, seemed to search for an inspiration to reunite the Arabs by
arousing them to revolutionary greatness.

Many countries have shown a penchant for a political faith, from
Marxism and African socialism to more exotic inventions, typically
agglomerations of nationalism, socialism, ostensible equalitarianism,
pseudoscience, and populism. In Brazil, Getulio Vargas had something
called *integralismo;* Argentina's Juan Perón brought out his feebly
fascistic socialism called *justicialismo.* Nkrumah of Ghana rested his
case on *consciencism,* which began with metaphysics and went on to
syllogistic propositions about African revolutionary superiority. Another attempt to contrive values and build up the national ego is the
"authenticity" movement of the former Congo, whose President
Mobutu at the end of 1971 rebaptized the land to Zaire and made
himself the apostle of a new conscience supposedly based on au-
thentic African values.

Strong and purposeful regimes may be successful, at least for a
few years, whether or not graced with an ideological cloak. Revolutionary politics brings capable men to the top as well as any other
political process does. The new leader or leaders with a little luck
may be able to get rid of social junk, outworn institutions, and parasitic classes, give new directions, and bring the state closer to the
level of the developed world. This has been the case in varying
degrees in the states that have followed the Marxist-Leninist pattern
and ideology. It is also true of the somewhat looser rightist dictatorships, like Nationalist China, Greece, and Brazil, all of which have
registered economic growth rates near record historic highs. For
economic development it is not so important that a country have
leftist or rightist leaders as that it provide stable and purposeful
government capable of limiting consumption and putting resources
into investment.

It is by no means generally true, however, that single rulership,
dictatorial, or one-party systems are clean and efficient, in contrast to
the cumbersomeness and sloppiness of democracy. Strength of leadership degenerates into arbitrariness and abuse of power. Planning
bogs down in confusion. Mobilization of the economy multiplies opportunities for corruption and degenerates to chaotic bureaucratism,
the more suffocating since state control is complete. To maintain an
ideological picture requires censorship and thought control, which
stifle initiative and hinder correction of errors.

THE SOCIALIST MODE

Some dictatorial or authoritarian regimes are rightist, such as that of Brazil, which welcomes foreign investment (under its own conditions) and ordinarily takes an anticommunist or conservative position on world issues. Other regimes, such as that of Algeria, are much less hospitable to foreign corporations and ordinarily take near-communist or radical positions on issues. The United States naturally much prefers the former style, but the latter is the mode of the LDCs, especially in Africa and Asia. There is a strong penchant for socialism, or for attitudes and words of socialism, among the politicians of the Third World and even more among intellectuals and semi-intellectuals. India, for example, adheres ritualistically to socialist dogma, which inhibits private production, establishes a medley of economic controls, and supports an army of bureaucrats heavily armed with red tape; but it permits much private wealth and privilege and provides little social discipline or drive.[31]

Many Africans revel in Soviet or Marxist-Leninist vocabulary and symbols. One of the more extreme, the People's Republic of the Congo (capital, Brazzaville), under strongman Major Marien Ngouabi and his Labor party, is verbally dedicated to "revolutionary socialism," and the papers are full of Marxist rhetoric. The Congo's anthem is the *Internationale*, and the governing party is called the Congolese Workers' party; Marxist-Leninist principles are enshrined in the constitution. Americans are excluded, there having been no diplomatic relations since the United States was accused of plotting against the Congolese "revolution" in 1965. There are many programs of cooperation with both China and the Soviet Union, but these programs are mostly cultural-propagandistic; to keep afloat, the Congo relies on assistance from the French, who shrug off the radical phraseology as part of nation building. The economy is privately owned, mostly by the French, although growing numbers of those who have acquired education but no marketable skills call for nationalization.

One reason that Marxist ideas and attitudes are popular in the LDCs is that the Soviet Union has been doing its best to propagate them for many years. After the Russian Revolution the Bolsheviks, following the logic of Marxism, tried to ignite revolutions in the

---

31. Daniel P. Moynihan, "The United States in Opposition," *Commentary*, 59 (March 1975), 31–44, sees the Third World as intellectually conditioned by British socialism.

industrial countries. When this failed, they turned to the colonial and semicolonial world of Asia. Lenin thought to find a way to Paris and London via Delhi and Peking, and since then the poorer countries have always seemed the more promising field for Leninist penetration. Before World War II, the Comintern did its best to promote communism and anti-Western thinking in the then colonial and semicolonial countries. Immediately after the war, Stalin paid little attention to the Third World; gains nearer home were enough to occupy him. After his death, however, a strengthened Soviet state embarked on an ambitious program to win adherents by large-scale propaganda joined with political and economic assistance. The Soviet effort, coupling economic aid with military deliveries and support for Third World demands, was far from the success Khrushchev and his followers had hoped for and Western statesmen had feared; but it could not fail to make many converts for a world view strongly critical of the capitalist West.

More important, Marxism-Leninism fits the psychological needs of the LDCs like a key in its lock.[32] It gives the most satisfying possible explanation for their poverty and the wealth of the more advanced: the unscrupulous exploitation of the weak by the strong. It is easy to believe that the LDCs are victims of conspiracy and discrimination; the conviction that the "haves" are somehow responsible is almost universal. In the words of a Uruguayan scholar,

> As Toynbee and others have shown, all great empires were built by the sweat of a vast proletariat. But today, unlike what happened in earlier centuries, the proletariat that makes possible the life and prosperity of the great empires is principally external to them. . . . The fact that the proletariat that produces the great prosperity of the United States is external, living on another continent far to the south, is most important.[33]

Exports of the poorer countries are rather small in the world balance (under 2 percent of world product), and so could not enrich the Western world very much even if they were extracted gratis. But

---

32. For appeals of Communism, cf. Stanislav Andreski, *Parasitism and Subversion: The Case of Latin America*, Pantheon Books, New York, 1966, pp. 209–215; and Dick Wilson, *Asia Awakes: A Continent in Transition*, New American Library, New York, 1971, Chapter 12.

33. Juan Luis Segundo, in *Development, an Introductory Reader*, ed. Castel, pp. 122–123.

Chinese spokesmen regularly please United Nations delegates by telling them how "imperialism, colonialism, and neocolonialism" plunder weaker countries. Mexican students cheered loudly as President Allende of Chile confirmed their suspicions that Latin American poverty resulted from the greed and malice of the international corporations. Marxism-Leninism promises the presently deprived and helpless LDCs that the future belongs to them as a sort of proletarian class, destined to inaugurate the new and final stage of history. Aid from Western countries ceases to be demeaning charity; instead it is owed compensation.

To be anti-Western, as those who struggle for independence ordinarily are, is to be anticapitalist. The wealthiest, most powerful, and so most resented capitalist power receives the lion's share of disparagement; annoyance at the American presence, commercial and cultural, is the most effective argument for the Marxist philosophy. *Capitalism* is a bad word, associated not only with foreign ownership of businesses and resources but also with colonialism, landlordism, and usury. *Private enterprise* means greed and bears the burden of association with the still dominant West. *Neocolonialism* is the all-embracing neologism for the malaise of economic, cultural, military, and political weakness.

Revolution, on the other hand, is a good word because of the obvious need for deep change. *Socialism* is good partly because it is antiforeign; Burmese socialism is directed against Indian and Chinese merchants and moneylenders. Socialism is modern and bespeaks concern for the people. It seems rational because it stresses planning and intelligent guidance of the economy and all aspects of national life; it is patriotic because it offers independence of the capitalistic West. Any dictator or military clique that wishes to stress independence and dedication to improvement calls itself socialist; to be up to date, it may speak of *scientific socialism*, the Leninist term. Thus Mali and Somalia are "socialist" because the government arrogates full authority to itself and puts a few businesses in the hands of the bureaucracy.

Those for whom the appeal of Marxism-Leninism is most compelling, sometimes compulsive, are the unsettled intellectuals. Often unemployed or unemployable, torn away from traditional values and suffering anomie, unable for various reasons to internalize Western values, they clutch the answers that are offered by the elaborate and fairly sophisticated system of Marxism-Leninism. Culturally schizophrenic, only superficially educated in Western ways of thought, yet alienated from their heritage, they need the certainty of Marxism to orient themselves in their complicated and confusing world. They are modern enough in spirit to reject old religions but not the new religion of "scientific socialism." They give themselves to the creed that promises to transfer ownership to the people and control presumptively to themselves, the savants and leaders.

They are confirmed by the example of the Soviet Union, exalted as uniquely successful (ignoring Japan) in rising from backwardness to modernization, comparative wealth, and great power under the guidance of a Leninist party. The Soviets present themselves as the world-historic antagonists to Western imperialism, and very few are aware that the Soviet Union contains a large majority of the non–self-governing peoples of the world. The American loss of standing from 1965 to 1970 enfeebled the liberal democratic competitor—associated it with violence and bombs in Asia, disorders and oppression at home. For many, it seemed difficult to avoid the conclusion that the Soviet way or something like it was the road to the future.

In brief, a sort of derivative and simplified neo-Marxism—adapted to the LDCs in much the same way as Lenin once adapted Marxism to semideveloped Russia—is a powerful, sometimes seemingly dominant mode of thought in the LDCs. For them, as for the Soviet Union, it represents a means for societies suffering under the impact of Western industrial civilization to defend themselves psychologically, to reintegrate and build up power on a new basis. It thus appeals to them for reasons much the same as those which lead China to cling to Marxism despite hostility toward Soviet Russia and the utter inappropriateness of Marxism, as propounded by Marx, for the Chinese reality.

It is not remarkable that Marxist doctrines and clichés are popular among the poor nations; it is rather remarkable that their popularity is not overwhelming. But there are several reasons. One is the political reality of inequality. The people who are really very poor are practically powerless and voiceless, while the rulers are tolerably satisfied with their status and have no yen for further revolutions or sharing of the little wealth that there is. To be deprived of privileged status is far more devastating for the upper classes in poor countries than for the elite in the United States or western Europe. Another is the fact that the most successful countries are not socialistic, at least not in a Marxist sense. The Soviet Union and China cannot do very much, even if they would, for the world's poor, and the wealthy nations are more attractive models even while they are envied and disliked.

The best reason, however, for the limited appeal of socialism to the LDCs is that it has not worked very well. The countries that have ventured far into socialism (excluding those of revolutionary origin) have shown uniformly poor results. India, for example, has severely constricted private enterprise although state enterprises have functioned poorly. Nationalization of the grain trade (with low fixed prices for the sake of the poor) crimped production and led to black marketing and corruption, which continued after the controls were lifted. Burmese socialism has brought economic stagnation and made it difficult for that former large rice exporter to feed itself. The story in many other countries has been similar. In the lack of skills and weakness of public morality, politically directed enterprises function even more poorly than private ones, becoming monopolistic vested interests. Socialism has thus proved much less practical than alluring, and the usual solution is to try to regulate, not to administer, the economy, appreciating capitalists for providing jobs while denouncing them for exploiting labor.

DIFFICULT RELATIONS: ACCUSATIONS AND GUILT

The Third World is not in ferment; there are coups here and there, which usually change little, and hardly any revolutions. But the relations of the LDCs with the world's "Establishment," the industrial nations led by the United States, are usually uneasy and often bitter. In a sense, the LDCs are right to complain of neocolonialism. Whether or not there is any conscious purpose of domination or exploitation in the sense of value extracted without comparable return, they find themselves in the shadow of greater powers. Despite nationalistic talk they cannot hide from themselves that their nations are petty in the modern community.

They are militarily trivial, except perhaps at guerrilla warfare in their own territories; even for this purpose they require imported weapons. They are poor, sometimes virtually penniless, in a world of great wealth. Quality goods are imported; quality education is to be sought abroad. News, literature, and cinema and other entertainment are largely foreign; there is only a scattering of native artists, writers, or scientists of importance. Bazaars in Africa are owned by Asians. Education and business are probably carried on in an alien language. Native literary and cultural traditions decay. The LDCs see themselves deprived of a thousand things—not only the tinsel of consumer luxuries and myriad comforts and conveniences but good schools and hospitals; East and West have competed in spreading the idea that they ought to be much better off. The more integrated and educated humanity becomes, the stronger the numbing awareness of relative backwardness or deprivation, often exacerbated by the coincidence of poverty with dark skin. Ever better communications and transportation in the ever more integrated world make the leading centers in ideas, culture, science, and decision making all the more dominant, and their dominance the more irritating.

The effects of the sense of impotence on the social order are indefinable but doubtless manifold. They may include shallowness of local or national pride, lack of confidence in efforts for the present, feebleness of hope for the future, fatalism, passivity, deficiency of public spirit, a tradition of being exploited and exploiting in turn, and a gap between rulers and ruled. It is not to be expected that the traditional economic virtues of industry, careful planning, saving, punctuality, and exactness should be widely cherished; status is preferable to productive labor. This demoralization, in turn, makes more difficult or perhaps quite frustrates any efforts to catch up.

The fact of inequality infuses and shapes external relations not just with the United States but with all who somehow impinge as superiors. The Japanese, having so successfully built up their economy, find themselves spat upon in Southeast Asia. As an official remarked after Premier Tanaka's turbulent visit to Thailand, "The Asians are just envious of us. They don't mind when the farangs [Europeans and Americans] are rich. But they can't stand it when Asians like themselves have made the grade and they have not." [34] The greatest injury by the Israelis to the Arabs has been not the snatching of a small patch of the huge Arab world but the hurt to the pride of the Arabs, a people of glorious antecedents but inglorious present. That fellow Semites could modernize and especially fight so much better was an unbearable rebuke to Arab poverty and incompetence. The conflict became negotiable only when the Arab self-image was restored by initial victories in the Yom Kippur war of October 1973. It was for these psychological reasons that states with no material stake in the quarrel, such as Algeria and Iraq, became passionately involved. Black African states, too, found it easy to take an anti-Israeli stance because the strength and prosperity of Israel, a new Western-style nation in the area of the LDCs, was a threat not to material interests but to

---

34. *Newsweek,* January 21, 1974, p. 48.

self-esteem. There are even such animosities within the Third World. West Pakistan was generally held to have exploited East Pakistan and was correspondingly resented before the independence of the East showed that the Bengalis were no better off when exploiting one another; Indonesians hate Chinese merchants; and so forth.

In the past, resentment at the wealth and power of the industrial world was more subdued; weakness was part of the natural order of things. But the West has taught ideas of justice and equality and the right of all to independence and a share of the abundance of the earth. The result is bitterness. India, seat of an ancient civilization and second most populous of states, has desperately to look beyond poverty and impotence to see itself truly great in the world. One of the world's most backward countries, Chad, must flaunt its pride. When in 1974 West Germany undertook to negotiate with insurgents who had kidnapped a German citizen, the Chad government called a halt to a West German relief program. A minister explained, "It is compensated by a national sense of sovereignty. This is superior to anything they can give us." [35]

In their pride, the LDCs have to account for their condition; the easy way to do so is by blaming the rich and powerful. An Asian delegate at the United Nations asks, "Why should your standard of living be so much higher than ours?" [36] No one is so coarse as to say that it is because the LDCs manage to produce so much less. The ready answer, as noted earlier, is that they must have been bled by the greedy nations, especially the strongest and richest. In many more specific ways, the West is blamed. For example, a Panamanian newspaper accused the United States of causing the Managua earthquake in 1972 by bombing Vietnam. Hondurans and Mexicans have charged that the United States has diverted hurricanes to the detriment of their countries, a capability the United States would be very pleased to have. President Mohammed Barre of Somalia in 1972 attributed the near-war of Uganda and Tanzania to a colonial conspiracy, although no outside interest was visible.[37] The primary emotion of two-thirds of the world's nations is hatred of something vaguely called imperialism, which means the unsatisfactory distribution of power in the world.

It is practically necessary for the poor to believe that the rich are

35. Theodore Cohen, "The Sahelian Drought," *International Journal*, 30 (Summer 1975), 443.

36. *Newsweek*, April 22, 1974, p. 56.

37. *The New York Times*, October 6, 1972, p. 2.

striving to keep them down. Thus, Indian Prime Minister Indira Gandhi said, "Some affluent countries find it difficult to reconcile themselves to the idea that we can raise our head." [38] The Indian delegate at the Rome food conference faulted Secretary of State Henry Kissinger for not stressing that the food shortages of the LDCs were not of their own making.[39] Indira Gandhi spoke in the same vein: "The most relevant and revealing fact is that a tiny minority in the affluent countries is using up food, petrol, and other essential commodities out of all proportion to their needs." [40] She failed to mention that it was the shortcomings of Soviet agriculture that did most to consume the American food surplus and raise world prices. With similar logic, the representative of Dahomey in the United Nations saw the attraction of richer foreign centers for trained personnel as a continuation of the slave trade.[41] Non-Western powers are seldom to blame. Control of alien peoples by the Soviet Union or China is not imperialism, a term preferably applied to Western business in LDCs. Massacres of Africans by Africans in Burundi remain unmentioned.[42] There is no protest against the petroleum monopoly of the Organization of Petroleum Exporting Countries (OPEC), which raised prices by governmental action far beyond the dreams of the Western "monopolists." Far from feeling injured, the LDCs took satisfaction in the ability of states like their own to squeeze the rich and powerful of the earth.

The interests of the more and less developed countries also diverge. The latter are not much alarmed by communism, of course; nor, for the most part, are they greatly exercised by questions of world order, except as their security is affected. Their concern revolves naturally around their own deplorable condition. But, realizing their impotence and basic lack of autonomy in the world, they see themselves less as makers of their own destinies than as pawns of greater forces. This dependence means that, the more powerful being responsible for their situation, their way to improvement lies in securing an alteration of relations with the richer powers. Hence, their most important purpose in foreign relations is to obtain more for

38. *The New York Times*, September 27, 1974, p. 4.
39. *Time*, November 18, 1974, p. 42.
40. *The New York Times*, December 7, 1974, p. 10.
41. *Brain Drain*, p. 7.
42. Tom J. Farer, "The United States and the Third World," *Foreign Policy*, 54 (October 1975), 79–80.

themselves, however possible—better terms of trade, more aid, and more representation in world councils. The claim to redistribution is the mirror image of the complaint of exploitation.

Having no power to compel, they can only appeal on moral grounds. Hence, they have a material interest in blaming the West for their troubles, basing their claims on general, indeed largely Western-conceived, ideals of justice. They have and use the moral superiority of the poor; they fault the West for spending so many times more on instruments of destruction than on humanitarian help; they chide the West for consuming rather than giving of its abundance. They appeal and chorus indignation; the catch-phrase *imperialist exploitation*, usually without specific content, is ordinarily worth seventy to eighty votes at the United Nations. And the United States is sensitive enough that even Americans reproach their country for the sin of offering a fuller life and better professional opportunities and thereby luring brainpower from LDCs.

Those who have the major part of the earth's wealth cannot shut their ears to the cries of the less privileged, nor can they fulfill the demands or even do justice by their own standards. The favorite principle of philosophic justice is equal right to the satisfactions of life. But this tenet runs counter to the facts of the state system, the freedom of states to keep and enjoy whatever advantages they may inherit or procure, from outsize oil fields to an advanced industrial apparatus. It is impossible to abolish strength in international relations (although violence may be obsolete), and, as Thucydides observed, there can be no justice among unequals. Influence in any form, economic or cultural as well as political, is injurious to the weaker parties, but it cannot be avoided.

How the West, and particularly the United States, can relieve this crushing problem of inequality is an unsolved problem. Almost any action, paternalistic or hard-boiled, of scorn or pity, even a manifestation of virtue, may be psychologically oppressive. Any assumption of responsibility by the West tends to relieve the LDCs of responsibility. It is not clear whether charity helps more than it costs in terms of self-reliance. There is no possible means of transferring enough resources to the LDCs to help much, nor is there the will to do so. It is a nefarious delusion that the populations of the LDCs can really be fed except by their own productivity. The effective effort to improvement can come only from within.

The picture is not entirely dark. The relations of LDCs to the West are not clear-cut but rather deeply ambivalent. Should they imitate or reject? Is the United States a valued customer for raw materials and source of investment capital or a greedy glutton and exploiter? Everywhere throughout the Third World men are refighting the battles of the westernizers and Slavophiles of nineteenth-century Russia. They take over Western values while decrying Western behavior and morality. Practical and realistic considerations collide with pride and the need for self-vindication, the one being more prominent in actions, the other in words. Leaders who bitterly denounce economic exploitation and multinational corporations welcome concrete foreign enterprises.

The real conflict of interests between the LDCs and the industrialized states cannot be denied; it can only be assuaged by remembering that the deeper problem is psychological and needs to be confronted with prudent understanding.

CHAPTER NINE

The Other World: Policies

ANTICOMMUNISM

With the partial exception of the sphere covered by the Monroe Doctrine, the United States traditionally has paid little heed to the politics of the less developed part of the world. In the cold war the allegiance of these countries became an object of anxiety. In the great battle between conflicting powers and ideologies, here was a vacant field, a power vacuum to be occupied; and the side that would attract to its own sphere the majority of the less developed countries (LDCs) could well hope for ultimate victory. It was possible that their unhappy masses might opt for communism, which promised them more and appeared to many to be better adapted to their conditions. American policy makers, judging by the conformist Stalinist communist movement, feared that any nation that borrowed Soviet ideology would place itself irretrievably under Soviet protection and become part of the great "red tide."

Khrushchev did his best to stimulate such fears, anticipating the conversion of the "camp of peace" (the Third World plus the Soviet bloc) to the Soviet-led "socialist camp." In this vein, in the Congo crisis of the 1960s diplomats and journalists envisioned that that central African country would be converted into a base for Soviet control of the continent and used as a source of uranium for Soviet bombs. A leftist victory had to be thwarted by American politicking and United Nations intervention, which was of somewhat dubious legality and severely weakened that body. Yet the messy Congo situation gradually quieted and was practically forgotten. Africa remained largely indifferent to communism, and it became apparent that leftist or rightist turns in various countries were neither irreversible nor of transcendental importance to the outside world.

The appeal of communism in the less developed world has turned out to be surprisingly feeble. Leaders of the LDCs have no urge to bow to new masters, including the Soviet-dominated world communist movement. Religion also stands in the way; particularly in Africa and the Near East, it has minimized communist influence in what would otherwise seem a favorable area. The Soviets want to propagate a single revolution; the many very different lands want their own particular revolution or half-revolution.

Since the later 1950s, Soviet growth has slowed, and that of other areas has accelerated; the Soviets themselves have lost confidence in their faith and consequently their ability to evangelize. Leaders of the Third World respect and imitate power, but Soviet capacities, especially economic, are manifestly limited. The Soviet Union becomes more like the developed West, in appearance and mentality, without having as much to offer. The Sino-Soviet split hurt Soviet influence, as Russians and Chinese gave their best efforts to combating one another.

The Soviet aid program which the United States once viewed with alarm caused more disillusionment than conversion. Soviet aid at some places and times won friends, but when the Soviets tried to turn gratitude into influence they were regularly rebuffed. In 1965 the Indonesian army used Soviet military equipment amounting to about $1 billion to suppress Indonesian communists. In the Sudan in 1971, a Soviet-supported communist coup was turned back, and the Sudanese became very critical of their former supporters. Another recipient of Soviet aid, Sri Lanka (Ceylon), resented Soviet involvement in an extremist uprising. For such reasons, what Khrushchev began as an ambitious aid program to rival American aid was cut down to insignificance by 1971.

Economic realities also dampen enthusiasm for communist revolution. The LDCs are dependent upon the Western industrial powers for both markets and supplies, and the Soviet Union can substitute only very partially. It has no use for much of the LDCs' produce and cannot pay in convertible currency. Soviet industry can only very unsatisfactorily meet the requirements of its own people; it is hopelessly incompetent to supply the range of needs of the LDCs, and these countries still find it necessary or desirable, despite frequent ideological distaste, to turn to the West for modern technology.

Many governments call themselves socialistic, but they do not engage in violent revolutions that would destroy the upper and middle classes. Marxism, in any case, is a very mixed bag; and the revolutionary tendencies in the world, which seemed close to Sovietism in the 1950s, have moved away as the Soviet state has itself become staid and its doctrines stale.

The feeling that something called communism had to be denied further victories was still strong enough in the 1960s to seduce the United States into intervention in Vietnam; but unhappiness in this effort made possible the perception of the simple and obvious fact that American efforts to guide the politics of weaker nations are probably unnecessary and unproductive. It no longer seemed necessary to become nervous over every political crisis; typically, the civil war which tore apart the Sudan for a decade up to 1973 was hardly noticed. When Chile in 1970 elected a Marxist president, Salvador

Allende, by a scant plurality of votes, the State Department was displeased, and the Central Intelligence Agency (CIA) injected itself
into the situation; but the hemispheric defection caused nothing like
the panic reaction it would have aroused a decade earlier. American
commentators have assumed that India was firmly in the Soviet orbit.
The Soviet Union, in fact, has long courted India, perhaps mostly as
an offset to China; in the Indo-Pakistani war of December 1971, when
the United States for no good reason supported Pakistan, India
seemed to be a close ally of the Soviets. However, Washington failed
to become alarmed at the idea of 600 million communized Indians
attacking the world, and relations continued normally. Only when
communist (Cuban) troops were actually sent into the Angolan civil
war did the administration become disturbed; even then, the Congress
remained more fearful of a new Vietnam than concerned about the
outcome of the Angolan conflict.

The shallowness of Soviet political gains in the Third World is
best demonstrated by the Soviet experience in the Near East. In 1955
and afterward, as a consequence of American gaffes, the Soviet Union
gained entree into the Near East as arms supplier and chief political
support against Israel. The American anxiety was great enough that
the marines were sent to Lebanon in 1958 on the official finding (not
supported by a United Nations observer group) that there was
danger of a victory of forces allied with Nasser's Egypt and controlled by international communism. The Soviet presence grew year
by year, especially after the Arabs, badly defeated in the 1967 war,
broke relations with the United States and turned to the Soviets as
their friends and potential saviors. In Egypt and Syria, and to some
degree in Iraq and Algeria, the Soviets appeared to be making themselves at home, garnering the political benefits of a multibillion dollar
investment.

Yet in Egypt, for example, where Soviet contingents were largest,
they never made much ideological progress; the small Egyptian Communist party was kept repressed. The Soviets complained that the
Arabs were nationalistic, the Arabs that the Soviets wanted to promote
their foreign ideology. There was friction over trade and the Soviet
use of Egypt for espionage. Soviet advisers aroused the hatred of
Egyptian officers by their demands, if not by their overbearing manners and contempt. Russians lived in fenced-off compounds, and large
areas were closed to Egyptians. Even President Anwar el-Sadat was
once excluded from the Marsa Matruh naval station.

Egyptian President Gamal Abdel Nasser, who had brought the Russians in, died in 1970 and was succeeded by the more pragmatic Sadat. The latter, in June 1972, gave the Soviets an ultimatum to furnish more modern offensive weapons. Presumably wary of complications with the United States, the Soviets ignored the demand; thereupon Sadat ordered the withdrawal of the 15,000 Soviet personnel. The Russians, for whom withdrawal of power is a breach of historical principle, left quietly, diplomatically explaining, "Mission accomplished."

The Egyptians continued, however, to receive some materiel from the Soviet Union; in the 1973 renewal of conflict with Israel the Soviets aided and encouraged the Arabs as much as they felt able to do without serious risk of confrontation with the United States. In the aftermath of the war, however, as it became apparent that the Soviet Union could not greatly help its clients to achieve their victory over Israel, the Arabs moved sharply away from the Soviet embrace. Egypt resumed diplomatic relations with the United States, accepted American mediation in negotiations with Israel, and undid much of the socialization of the economy undertaken during the years of close friendship with the Soviets. The United States, not the Soviet Union, was invited to help in clearing the Suez Canal. More reluctantly, Syria, despite Soviet blandishments, began looking to the West to end its isolation and lessen its dependency on Soviet arms. Iraq, which had at times almost seemed to be a member of the Soviet bloc, likewise evinced a desire for broader contacts. Unless there should be a resurgence of conflict, there seems no reason to foresee any permanent Soviet domination in the Near East.

The United States will probably remain, as it has been, the whipping boy of more or less radical regimes. Third World governments, calling themselves anti-imperialistic, confiscate American properties and abuse the United States for many real or alleged sins, from CIA subversion to the immorality of the Peace Corps. In Calcutta, two Americans were held on dubious charges because, according to an Indian lawyer, "it might be useful to show that the Americans are doing harm to India." [1] Idi Amin of Uganda frequently insulted the United States, made his country uncomfortable for Americans, and in July 1973 jailed a Peace Corps group in transit as imperialist agents.

---

1. *The New York Times*, August 6, 1974, p. 10.

Libyan President Muammar el-Kadaffy often lashed out at the United States and racked up victories by expropriating the American oil companies.

However, the idea of a grand duel for the allegiance of humanity is obsolete. If the United States believes in good relations with Moscow and Peking, it cannot matter greatly who rules in Saigon. It is not even very important for the prestige of democracy whether the LDCs are democratic, pseudodemocratic, or outright authoritarian, as long as democracy remains the form of the economically and culturally advanced countries and dictatorship is associated with backwardness. It is not apparent that the United States should even try seriously to encourage democracy in the Third World; it may be counterproductive to promote an unsuitable model.

It would be unfortunate for the United States, though probably not disastrous, if the LDCs should turn en masse to the disciplined radicalism called communism, but this development seems less and less likely as the world communist movement loses coherence and dynamism. It no longer appears that the problems of dealing with the LDCs have much to do with a world struggle for power; they are rather part of the problem of building a world order.

THE SPHERE OF THE UNITED STATES: LATIN AMERICA

One part of the less developed world—Latin America—has a special relationship to the United States because of geography, a slightly sentimental "neighborhood" tradition, and the expectations of the world. If things go ill in Latin America, it is still seen to some extent as a responsibility of the United States.

Happily, the lands of the Latin part of the Americas are relatively promising. There are areas of dire poverty, but Latin American incomes and levels of energy consumption average about three times those of Africans. At least Brazil, Mexico, and Venezuela may be close to entering the ranks of the developed nations. Agricultural resources are fairly ample in relation to population and in some areas—for example, the Argentine pampas—positively bountiful. Latin American countries have little enough national cement, but they have much more than many Asian and African countries. With the exception of Amerindian enclaves, Latin America is culturally closer to the West than is the Near East, not to mention black Africa.

The special interest of the United States in Latin America dates from the wars of independence (1810–1828) when the nations of the southern part of the Western Hemisphere seemed to be following the glorious example of the United States, the leader in the New World. But there was much more neglect and indifference than influence until the continental expansion of the United States was completed, and that country became a great industrial power looking for engagements in the wider world. Only with the advent of the Spanish-American War in 1898 and the acquisition of a Spanish territory (Puerto Rico) and a protectorate over Cuba did the United States make a significant impact on Latin American affairs. Since then, the overriding foreign power for all the republics has been the United States, although the United States has been physically interventionist only in the area nearest itself, the Caribbean basin, which it considered vital to its security. Early in this century, such countries as Brazil and Argentina were nations with world standing, ambitious for leadership on their continent; but such aspirations gradually yielded to growing United States power.

The benign Good Neighbor policy of Franklin Roosevelt involved a retreat from the crasser aspects of intervention and brought more respect for the dignity of other states in the Americas. The principle was formally accepted that "no state has the right to intervene in the domestic or foreign affairs of any other state." Nevertheless, United States penetration of Latin American economies and culture advanced through the 1930s. World War II brought American supremacy in the Western Hemisphere to its height. Two powers that had offered some challenge, Germany and Italy, were eliminated and discredited. France and Britain were also effectively removed. The high degree of cooperation achieved by the United States in Latin America during World War II—much higher than that during World War I—was a testimonial not only to the popularity of the allied cause and moral repugnance for the fascist powers but to the loss of effective autonomy by the Latin countries.

But World War II was the high point of cooperation between the United States and Latin America. The United States became preoccupied with the contest with the Soviet Union, containment of communism, and the cold war, causes for which few Latins had much zest. In 1954, Secretary of State John Foster Dulles was able to secure acquiescence for the isolation of the leftist government of Guatemala but not collective sanction for its overthrow. Nationalism and resentment against United States economic penetration gradually came to the surface, while the American government paid little attention to its Latin neighbors. The attack and stoning by hostile crowds of Vice President Richard M. Nixon, who was on a supposed goodwill tour of South America in May 1958, and the victory in Cuba on January 1, 1959, of a dynamic revolutionary, Fidel Castro, jolted the United States. Castro soon began turning Cuba away from traditionally close ties with the United States and undertook to incite the hemisphere to revolution against Yankee hegemony. The idea of communist uprisings in the Americas was much more an affront to the United States than was such an aberration in the Old World. But time ran out on the Eisenhower administration, which bequeathed to John F. Kennedy an effort by Cuban exiles to settle the Cuban trouble with American logistic support, in the same manner that a leftist government of Guatemala had been overthrown in 1954. This effort failed at the Bay of Pigs in April 1961.

To counter the revolutionary threat more appropriately, President Kennedy proposed the felicitously named Alliance for Progress, an idealistic democratic alternative to bring rapid economic improvement and thus political stability to the hemisphere. The objectives of this ambitious program included a much increased capital flow ($20 billion in ten years—half private, half public funds) to Latin America, promotion of political democracy and social justice, and Latin American economic integration. The North American giant was seemingly proposing something like a Marshall Plan for its less fortunate neighbor republics, and equally excellent results might be hoped for. But the Alliance foundered on lack of common purpose, nationalist-leftist distrust, weakness of the Latin American middle classes, shortage of capital, scarcity of Latin American managers, North American bureaucratic muddles, and the inability of the United States to shape alien societies politically.

The hemispheric community supported the United States in the Cuban missile crisis in October 1962, giving a legal basis of sorts for the quarantining of Cuba. But the successful resolution of the crisis, the blow to Castro's prestige, and decreased fear of communism in the hemisphere lowered the priority of the Alliance for Progress. With the war in Vietnam, the United States government had still less attention left over for the Latin Americans. The Johnson administration, succeeding Kennedy in November 1963, no longer actively promoted democratic liberalism; Lyndon Johnson felt that the United States should give more attention to the promotion of its own and its citizens' interests in Latin America. After 1968, the Nixon approach of the "lowered profile" was applied particularly in Latin America; the Latin Americans, formerly critical of intervention, had even more occasion to complain of neglect. In 1973 and 1974 Secretary of State Henry Kissinger began to push for a "new dialogue" and sought to assuage discontent by opening negotiations about such irritants as the status of the Panama Canal and the price of Latin American commodities. However, he indicated to the Latin Americans the fact that they were not very important by repeatedly postponing until February 1976 his travel south, meanwhile spending a large part of his time flitting east and west.

Diplomacy, or lack of it, may have had little to do with the fact that relations of the United States to its southern neighbors changed fundamentally and perhaps permanently. United States predominance was diluted by increasing trade and contacts with western Europe, Japan, communist countries, and others. The big power of the north was no longer acceptable as a patron; the Latin American republics considered that they belonged, rather, to the increasingly organized and vocal Third World, with many interests in conflict with those of the major industrial powers. The Organization of American States (OAS), set up in 1948 to promote hemispheric solidarity under the United States aegis, was often a forum for flagellation of "Yankee imperialism." With Soviet rocket-carrying ships cruising the seas or anchoring freely in Cuban harbors, the ideal of hemispheric unity lost strategic cogency. Special economic relations in the Western Hemisphere have always clashed with the broad goal of a nondiscriminatory world trading system. Several Latin American nations joined the Organization of Petroleum Exporting Countries (OPEC) oil cartel, and they all protested as economic imperialism the 1975 American trade bill, which excluded from its benefits nations that expropriated American properties without "adequate" compensation or joined cartels to raise raw materials prices, OPEC being intended as a target of the bill.

In this spirit of standing up to the colossus of the north, Panama raised with growing stridency an issue of which Americans had been totally unaware: the status of the Panama Canal and the Canal Zone. What had been taken for granted as a piece of United States property was held up as a symbol of Yankee imperialism, not only in Panama but throughout Latin America. The canal was irritating to Latin Americans not because it does any material harm to Panama but because it is there, it is rich, and it stands for the superiority of the United States. In a sense, the Panama Canal had for Latin Americans the same meaning as the Israeli occupation of Arab lands had for the Arabs. The Panamanians have been cautious, calling only for reversion to Panama over many years; but the issue is difficult because the United States Congress has seemed very loath to surrender anything of consequence. This type of conflict is a new experience for Americans, who have looked on loftily as the French wrestled with Algeria and the British with Suez. It is not easy to admit that the United States occupies a colonial position; in fact, the canal represents about the last remaining example of the rule of a powerful state on the territory of a weak one. Theodore Roosevelt's manner of acquisition of the Canal Zone was disreputable by modern standards; the canal is no longer of great strategic value; big tankers and aircraft carriers cannot use it; and it is subject to Panamanian violence. For all these reasons the United States would evidently be well advised to clear the ledger.[2]

The old sphere of influence sometimes seems to be a sphere of confrontation; with reason, in 1974 an advisory group to the president advocated that the special relationship with Latin America be abandoned.[3] Yet withdrawal is not easily accomplished. One reason is economic; investment has been relatively heavy south of the border,[4] although the proportionate stake in Latin America has been shrinking for several decades. In 1960 Latin American investments constituted 26 percent of United States foreign holdings; by 1972, they were 14.5 percent;[5] and they continue to decline as other areas become more attractive. Propinquity, traditions, and the shared name of "America" assure the republics to the south a special place in United States foreign policy. Even if other areas, such as the Near East, should be materially more important, however, it is not easy to shed paternalistic feelings for the weaker states that have so long been under the United States shield, many of which copied the United States Constitution. Most Latin Americans seem to share the feeling that the United States

---

2. The argument for stepping out of a colonial-imperialist position is presented by Stephen S. Rosenfeld, "The Panama Negotiations—A Close-Run Thing," *Foreign Affairs,* 54 (October 1975), 1–13; and Thomas M. Franck and Edward Weisband, "Panama Paralysis," *Foreign Policy,* 21 (Winter 1975–1976), 168–187.

3. *Business Week,* November 9, 1974, pp. 71–72.

4. On United States exploitation of Latin America, cf. Raymond Aron, *The Imperial Republic,* Prentice-Hall, Englewood Cliffs, N.J., 1974, pp. 231–251.

5. *Statistical Abstract of the United States 1974,* Government Printing Office, Washington, D.C., 1974, p. 781.

still has a special responsibility toward them; when a State Department official early in 1973 broached the idea that the United States might withdraw to observer status in the OAS to free that body from United States domination, this suggestion was roundly protested by those desirous of assistance. Because of multiple links, the United States still is more influential in Latin America than in other sectors of the Third World.

Influence and responsibility raise a recurrent dilemma: whether to intervene (by nonviolent pressure) or to stand aside, whether to promote change in desired directions or to favor stability. In either case, the United States is likely to be blamed. In a sense, either to give aid or to deny it is intervention. To cultivate friendly relations with military dictatorships is immoral according to the United States' liberal mode of thought; to attempt to democratize is a dubious exercise. Even to make information available may be resented; the propagandizing of birth control, for example, has been denounced as an imperialist imposition by both Catholics and communists, an insidious device for eluding responsibility for economic aid. To fail to pay attention is neglect, while efforts to exert leadership are offensive to some and earn the gratitude of few.

In no other quarter of the world is there so much anti–United States feeling as in Latin America. Life would be easier for the United States if it could further detach itself from Latin America, treating it simply as another part of the Third World and renouncing responsibilities along with privileges. Such a move would be a blow to tradition, but it might be wise explicitly to drop the Monroe Doctrine.[6]

This change in policy would doubtless be healthy for the Latin Americans, also. They have stood too long in the shadow of a single, overwhelming power, a shadow that blighted them because it was there. The United States has been in effect oppressive toward Latin America even while believing itself beneficent. For the Latin Americans it would—or perhaps will, since this is the direction of the world —represent a considerable degree of freedom to be able to deal with western Europe, Japan, and the Soviet Union on approximately the same terms as with the colossus of the north.

---

6. As suggested by Zbigniew Brzezinski, *Between Two Ages: America's Role in the Technotronic Era*, Viking, New York, 1970, p. 288.

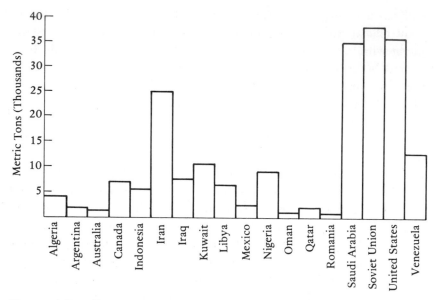

Figure 4 Petroleum Production per Month in Selected Countries, 1974.
(United Nations statistics, 1975.)

OIL AND ISRAEL

Oil is the most important single commodity for modern industry, the most valuable item of world trade, and overwhelmingly the most important product the United States must get from the less developed world. It is indispensable for transportation; no practicable substitute is on the horizon. It is also exceptionally concentrated; 60 percent of the world's reserves lie in the Near East, and over half of the Near Eastern resources are concentrated in Saudi Arabia. Formerly, this situation was of no great concern to the United States, once a major exporter. But in recent years American production has ebbed while consumption has mounted ever higher, and the United States, like almost all industrial countries, has become increasingly dependent on imports. Petroleum is consequently a natural subject of contention between the West and some of the LDCs.

Until the 1970s, however, the business of the international oil companies seemed fairly immune to politics. Holdings of Gulf Oil in Kuwait were regarded as almost as secure as its fields in Texas. But pressures in the Middle East began to rise, with the growth of self-assertiveness and leftist sentiment in the Third World and encouragement from the Soviets to squeeze Western interests. One of the side effects of the antagonism between Israel and its Arab neighbors was the Arabs' determination to take control of their oil resources. The percentage of profits taken as royalties was raised step by step, and moves were made toward nationalization. What one country got others demanded. After September 1973, when Libya effectively completed nationalization of foreign petroleum properties, it was clear that foreign ownership of oil production had no future.[7]

A sharp confrontation began ten days after the beginning of the October 1973 (Yom Kippur) war. The price of petroleum was nearly doubled in one step by OPEC and in subsequent months was raised to roughly four times the pre-October level. OPEC, which had previously been able to achieve very little, was now able to increase oil prices enormously for a number of reasons. There was accumulated unhappiness at the long-term stability of oil prices, which meant a decrease in prices in real terms. The prices of other commodities (especially of grain) were soaring in the West. The OPEC nations realized that the industrial countries were prepared to pay much more for oil if they had to.[8] Most important of all, the anti-Israeli cause gave unwonted cohesion to the Arab states, which were responsible for two-thirds of world petroleum exports (the rest coming chiefly from Iran, Venezuela, and Nigeria). The Arabs also applied oil power directly, embargoing shipments to the United States (and the Netherlands) and squeezing the industrial world as a whole by cutting production 5 percent a month. Foreign holdings were taken over by degrees, with or without agreement of the companies, until the companies became little more than operating agents for the respective governments.[9]

Embargo measures were annulled after the end of hostilities, but the price increases brought about an enormous transfer of wealth and the monetary problems previously discussed. The possibility that the oil states could buy out the entire Rockefeller family fortune with six days of their income or all American foreign investments in less than two years was alarming; and there was some tendency to blame the Arabs for a mass of economic troubles probably caused more by bad fiscal policies in the West. The blow was perhaps worst for the

7. For background of relations with the Arabs, cf. William R. Polk, *The U.S. and the Arab World*, Harvard University Press, Cambridge, Mass., 1975.

8. Elizabeth Monroe and Thomas Mabro, *Oil Producers and Customers: Conflict or Cooperation*, American Universities Field Staff, New York, 1974, pp. 16–17.

9. *Daedalus*, 104 (Fall 1975), is devoted to "The Oil Crisis in Perspective."

LDCs that did not produce oil, for whom the extra cost of oil was about equal to all the economic aid they were receiving. For the United States the inflated cost of oil ultimately could mean a change in the long-term pattern of economic growth; no longer could this rich country afford to raise energy consumption 5 percent yearly.

The American reaction was to attempt, although rather feebly, to bring consuming nations together to confront the producers, an attempt that found little support, although other industrial states are much more dependent on imports. There was discussion of striving for energy independence, and a tariff was laid upon imports in the hope of weakening the cartel. Various proposals were made to reduce the impact of the dollar surplus of the oil-rich nations. There were hints of gunboat diplomacy if the Arabs should press their advantages. Secretary Kissinger urged that a floor be placed under oil prices in order to give assurance to investors in non-OPEC energy sources. The American concern seemed to be less the cost of oil than fear that renewed conflict between Israel and its neighbors might bring a new embargo and hence intense pressure on the West and the United States.

The United States also reacted by endeavoring more energetically to eliminate the strongest bond of Arab solidarity: the conflict between Israel and its Arab neighbors, a conflict that had kept up tension in the Near East for thirty years and that seemed fated to lead to a new and perhaps worse war. The American secretary of state therefore made almost superhuman efforts, much beyond those he had previously exercised, to mediate. In 1974 and 1975, Kissinger spent many weeks in a historically unprecedented "shuttle diplomacy," impossible before the jet age; he made daily or almost daily flights between Cairo or Damascus and Jerusalem, trying chiefly to give each side a better understanding of the position of the other. Despite setbacks, he was able by August 1975 to bring the parties to an agreement whereby Israeli forces evacuated part of the Sinai peninsula, including some small oil fields, with a small contingent of American civilians monitoring the ceasefire. In return, Egypt pledged not to resort to force—an agreement that would have seemed impossible a few years earlier and attested to the readiness of both sides to renounce military victory.

Antagonism remained deep, however, because it had become a way of life in the region. It went back to World War I and the Balfour Declaration of 1917, whereby the British government promised a home for the Jews in Palestine, which was then under Turkish rule. After the war, Palestine was placed under British mandate, and

Jewish immigration increased, while surrounding territories were organized as Arab states. Hitler's persecutions turned the stream of Jews into a flood and gave Zionism new passion. Friction between Jewish entrants and Arab residents troubled the British until 1947–1948, when they gave up the mandate. The United Nations then sanctioned the creation of a tiny Jewish state carved from part of Palestine. The Arabs, confident because of their superior numbers, would accept no Jewish state at all. But the resultant brief war left the Jews victorious and masters of a larger though still small territory. Armistices were reached with surrounding Arab states, but hundreds of thousands of Arabs left or were driven from Palestine to become, with their descendants, a permanent charge on international charity. There was no peace. War was renewed in 1956, 1967, and 1973. The hope of the Israelis that time would bring acceptance seemed to be an illusion; hatreds were nourished from one generation to the next.

The United States throughout was the faithful friend and supporter of Israel. There was some reluctance, particularly in the State Department, to offend the Arabs because of the economic and strategic importance of their lands. Attachment to Israel was much stronger, however, especially in the Congress. Sympathies were for the Jews, who had suffered so fearfully under the Nazis and understandably longed for a homeland of their own. American Jews who had not tasted the bitterness of the concentration camps such as Auschwitz felt especially called upon to stand by their brothers and sisters. There was admiration, too, for the small democratic state that made the desert bloom. Israel had a strong basis of American support in the Jewish 3 percent of the American electorate and in the influence of the Jews, ever prone to intellectual occupations, in the professions and the news media. The unwritten commitment to the independence of Israel was among the firmest of American engagements.

It has often been contended that the American commitment to Israel was justified by Israel's importance as a militarily strong outpost against communism and Soviet penetration in the Near East. This argument can hardly be sustained, however, because support for the Jewish state immensely complicates America's relations with the 130 million Arabs and was the most apparent factor in causing Arabs to look to the Soviet Union and to accept an otherwise disliked Soviet presence. The pro-Israeli position of the United States is not a matter of calculation but of sentiment, a result of the fact that Israel was created and enabled to survive by American support (public and private), sustained to the present by American subsidies and large-scale arms aid. It cannot be asked whether the United States might not be better advised to simplify its problems in the Near East by backing away from Israel, because to a substantial degree Israel is a projection of the United States.

Despite this fact, the firmness of American support for Israel has become somewhat more qualified since 1973. The feeling that America could and should keep out of foreign quarrels was extended from Southeast Asia to the world; wariness of a new Vietnam led to reluctance to undertake peacekeeping in the Sinai. Few were prepared to back military intervention either to chastise the oil producers or to help the Israelis. Another element is the pressure of oil. No one will admit willingness to sell Israel for Arab oil, but the fact that helping Israel may be obviously costly caused second thoughts. At the same time, there was a greater readiness to hear the Arab side of the quarrel, which is sufficiently complicated that ample facts can be assembled to make a powerful case for either side.

The United States could not fail to be touched by the opinions of the outside world. The European allies and Japan were much less sympathetic to Israel than was the United States (and hence less exercised by the Arab oil cartel). From the Arab point of view, Israel represented outright imperialism, and most of the world assented. In the general view, Israel stood for the West, the rich and technologically advanced, while the Arabs represented the poor and weaker peoples, subject to the pressures of Western power. The principle of the unacceptability of gains made by force (by a Western power, at least) dictated that Israel should give up the lands acquired in the 1967 war, which was begun by an Israeli preemptive strike. The disinclination of the Israelis to make this concession classified them, for the Third World in general, as aggressors. The anti-Israeli guerrilla groups hence became liberation fighters; although their tactics were reprehensible to the West, they were acceptable by Third World standards. So widespread was this feeling that the United Nations in 1974 invited the leader of the Palestine Liberation Organization (PLO) to address the General Assembly by a vote of 114 to 4, with only two states joining the United States and Israel in opposition; in 1975 the United States alone opposed the appearance of the PLO before the Security Council as though it were a recognized nation.

The reluctance to offend the oil suppliers figured prominently in the Western powers' leaning toward the Arab positions, but pride was doubtless more important for the LDCs. Israel was part of the problem of Western relations with the non-Western world—a power based on modern technology and Western ways that at once occupied traditional Arab lands and was a living example of Western superiority in production and warfare. The new wealth and power of the Arab states galvanized the morale of the LDCs; they might have the same good fortune if they could find oil or other strategic materials, or at least they could enjoy the discomfiture of the mighty. The increase in Arab wealth gave a new idea of power in the world. It was salutary, too, that conspicuous wealth should fall to weak lands, thereby taking away some of the onus resting upon the allegedly exploiting powers.

The high price of oil was thus by no means a complete disaster. It was not as important as it seemed; in reality, the cost of oil was not pushed much beyond the curve of world inflation, behind which it had lagged for a generation. It appeared that, at least for the industrial countries, the distortion would be ultimately manageable.[10] If the price had risen more gradually, there would have been no great problem, and necessary adjustments could have been made in due time by healthy economies. For the well-being of humanity it was perhaps as well that fuel costs should rise well in advance of the exhaustion of reserves, thereby moving the industrialized countries to take some of the measures of conservation and substitution that will one day be indispensable. It was edifying, moreover, for the United States and other countries to have to face some of the problems of worsened terms of trade and financial maladjustments that the LDCs have labored under for many decades. The monetary problem turned out to be far less than the catastrophe predicted by simple calculation; the exchange reserves of some oil producers, such as Iran and Libya, decreased, while OPEC reserves as a whole stabilized by 1976. In any event, OPEC solidarity was not likely to be eternal and could only weaken in the absence of an atmosphere of confrontation. Commodity stabilization agreements of past decades for coffee, rubber, copper, and other products regularly fell apart because countries broke ranks. However, there is a new determination, and oil, unlike coffee, is nonrenewable and can advantageously be left in the ground. But the OPEC countries are very diverse—radical Algeria, conservative Saudi Arabia, leftist Iraq, anticommunist Iran, needy Indonesia, and surfeited Kuwait. Oil is in such oversupply that some countries have cut production by half. Such sacrifice is difficult to apportion and creates considerable pressure on prices.[11]

It may be that their oil wealth will enable a few states to push

10. Cf. Hollis B. Chenery, "Restructuring the World Economy," *Foreign Affairs*, 53 (January 1975), 242–263.

11. On OPEC instability, see Leonard Waverman, "Oil and the Distribution of Power," *International Journal*, 29 (Autumn 1974), 619–635.

themselves rapidly into the ranks of the developed nations. Iran hopes
for this consummation by the late 1980s, a hope easily fulfilled if anything like the recent growth rate of 30 percent annually can be maintained. Venezuela and other countries have similar aspirations. But
the conversion of temporary wealth into permanent productivity is
not easy, and it may be that easy money will be no more salutary for
the oil states than the precious metal of the Indies was for Spain in
the seventeenth century. Oil money brought riches to only a few in
Indonesia, which overspent its new income and found itself deeper
in debt. Nigeria, flush with riches, in 1974 ordered 20 million tons of
cement when it could use only about a quarter that much. As a result,
its harbors were jammed, cement was turning to stone, ships were
being sent away, and cocoa was difficult to export.[12] Iran, too, was
glutted with merchandise it was unprepared to use, and it had no
difficulty in spending more than its multiplied revenues.

Whether or not the oil-rich countries can make their new-found
wealth a springboard to full modernization, that wealth, together with
the good showing of the Arab armies in parts of the 1973 war, have
greatly helped their self-image and self-reliance. This new independence may facilitate solution of the major political problem of
the area. It has reduced their feeling of need for Soviet support and
material aid, since the oil-rich countries can subsidize the arms purchases of other Arab countries. For example, Saudi money has enabled North Yemen, once apparently a Soviet satellite, to buy arms
from the United States.[13] It may also be that the new self-confidence
of the oil-producing nations will make it easier for the Arabs to coexist
with Israel. The more successful the Arabs are, the less reason they
have to hate the Israelis, who are, after all, fellow-Semites in tradition.
It is no longer necessary to dream of vindication by wiping out the
intruders. Thus, in 1975, the Egyptians, having had a bit of military
glory and being much beset by material problems, began on their
own to improve the conditions of living and to build new centers
along the Suez Canal. For most of the Arabs, it became more promising to catch up with Western technology than to risk military
ventures. The wealth of the Arabs also tied them more closely to the
West, where they preferred to invest their surplus and where their
purchases nearly doubled in one year. Affluence gave them an interest
in economic and monetary stability and restricted their freedom of

---

12. *The New York Times,* December 4, 1975, p. 63.
13. *Business Week,* September 15, 1975, p. 46.

action; if the Western powers were too much provoked or were ruined, the Arab stake might be expropriated or lost.

It seemed obvious that the solution of the difficulties lay not in any actions the United States might take in isolation but in the improvement of the international system. The first requisite was to eliminate or reduce as far as possible the violent confrontation in the Near East, the political condition that supports economic distortions; another Near Eastern war might be calamitous for the United States, economically as well as politically. There seems to be no question of another Arab embargo if peace is maintained. Secondly, it is essential for producers and consumers to come together to assure both a reasonable return and reliable supplies. The oil producers should have a place in the world's economic councils which corresponds to their importance in the economic system. Then they can bargain fairly and learn to act responsibly, exchanging the oil they have for the technology they want. They, too, might prefer security of return to exorbitant prices.

Thus the lamented oil crisis may mark an important step toward a new international style.

COMMODITIES AND PRICES

Trade with the Third World is profitable and important for the United States. It accounts for roughly one-third of American exports and one-fourth of imports, making a substantial contribution to the favorable merchandise balance that the United States must have in order to keep the overall balance of payments stable. Aside from petroleum, however, trade with LDCs is secondary in the United States economy. Some important materials, such as tin and bauxite (aluminum ore) are obtained primarily from the Third World, as are a number of agricultural products, such as coffee, cacao, and natural rubber. But these products are less important in the economy and are more or less substitutable, and the tendency in recent decades has been toward synthetics. Chemical factories turn out products that compete with or replace many tropical products, including quinine, rubber, vanilla, hemp, jute, and shellac.

In contrast, trade with industrial countries is of vital importance to the LDCs, and the sale of their products (primarily raw materials) is indispensable for the importation of both current necessities and equipment for development. The United States was displeased and somewhat disconcerted by the rise in petroleum prices, but many LDCs have been chronically unhappy with the return they receive for their exports. For many years it has been said and repeated that the monetary terms of trade were evolving over the long term to the detriment of the raw materials producers; striking comparisons have been made to show how many more bags of coffee or copra were required to buy a tractor in 1970 than in 1950. This shift might have been brought about by the better bargaining position of the producers of tractors in relation to the producers of coffee; it might also be attributed to a basic trend of technological civilization, that design and fabrication become more important relative to material ingredients. Science and engineering enable more to be done with less; an advanced computer requires only a tiny fraction of the materials of the clumsy early models. Moreover, the data fail to take quality into account; manufactured goods are ordinarily improved with time, whereas agricultural and other raw products are not.

Whether or not there has really been a major long-term trend against the LDCs, they have increasingly raised their voices in protest since 1973. Raw materials prices, as well as related questions of economic relations between the industrial countries and the LDCs, have become one of the hottest issues of international affairs, the dominant subject in the forums where LDCs come together—and in any general international gathering the LDCs have a large majority of votes.

The reasons that such banal issues fill the agenda of foreign ministers, who might prefer to play the game of power politics, are several. One is the subsidence of threats to security; if there were more exciting things to discuss, the world would have less patience for coffee prices. Another is the prevalence of equalitarian feeling in the contemporary world. Inequality is injustice, in the philosophy developed in the West and eagerly adopted by the intellectuals and the political leaders of the LDCs. They are ready to agree that their poverty is an inexcusable wrong, more or less blamable on the rich and powerful; the obvious means by which the poorer countries are impoverished is through the buying of their exports at indecent prices. Moreover, the LDCs have become weary of hearing talk of economic assistance for many years; no better off for all the programs but with their expectations raised, they feel like taking things into their own hands to get more for their goods. Probably most important, however, in bringing the issue to the fore has been the success of OPEC in diverting cash to the Near Eastern (and other) oil producers. The example is exhilarating, and the oil producers have been disposed to assist the movement verbally, financially, and politically. Their position is strengthened when it is copied, and they outflank attacks by insisting, as they have regularly done, that oil prices be discussed in the context of other raw materials prices.

The immediate reaction to OPEC's triumph was to move toward the formation of similar cartels for many other materials, as discussed in Chapter Three. However, despite the fillip to morale and the unprecedented backing, the efforts of the LDCs in this direction were not notably successful. Thanks mostly to circumstances external to the producers' associations, copper nearly quadrupled in price to $1.40 per pound in May 1974, but a year later, because of the recession in industrial countries, it was back to 56 cents per pound. Sugar went from 12 cents per pound in January 1974 to 70 cents in November but fell to 23 cents the following July. Banana producers tried in concert to impose an export tax of $1.00 per 100 pounds but had to settle for a fraction of that amount. The nonpetroleum cartels suffered handicaps: too many producers, the difficulty of controlling production (coffee trees cannot be turned off like oil wells), the need to keep revenues flowing (only a few oil states could cut exports almost at will without hardships), shrinking of markets in the face of high prices, and so forth.

The LDCs have consequently looked more to political action, demanding that the industrial countries cooperate with them in the transfer of wealth to the needy via better terms of trade. They have passed United Nations resolutions favoring benefits such as preferential tariffs for their manufactures, protection from rising industrial prices, international restrictions on multinational corporations, cancellation or reduction of debts, more participation in the world monetary system, and several times more foreign aid than they are now receiving. A 1974 United Nations resolution called for stockpiling of raw materials to sustain prices and, unrealistically, for an end to research on substitutes for raw materials. They want an automatic share of special drawing rights to be issued by the International Monetary Fund (IMF) and mechanisms to facilitate the flow of technology to them. They also ask for complete freedom to expropriate foreign holdings, with compensation (if any) to be decided by national authorities, contrary to United States insistence that international law requires adequate compensation. Most of all, however, the LDCs call for price supports of some kind for their exports, through hitching them to the prices of industrial goods (indexation) or cartel-monopoly price fixing. They want, in a word, more money in a new international economic order.

For all of these demands the United States has had less than no enthusiasm. There is self-interest at stake, reluctance to see American consumers and industry charged higher prices, plus fear of the negative effect on the delicate equilibria of the American economy. It is calculated that the 400 percent petroleum price increase of 1973 and 1974 reduced real growth in 1974 by $20 billion, raised the consumer price index by nearly 3 percent, and increased unemployment from 5.6 percent to 6.6 percent; in 1975, its effects continued although they were less readily measurable.[14]

There are also general considerations. Cartel pricing or commodity agreements invariably have an inflationary bias, as the pegging is regularly upward; producers want floors, not ceilings. Rigged prices are uneconomical, deflecting production according to considerations other than supply and demand, and are wasteful of resources. Marketing agreements cause bickering, as states seek to gain not by producing what is needed but by securing quotas, and they are subject to cheating. Artificial prices for materials are also damaging to the economies of the poorest countries; those that profit most are those that least need price supports. Expensive materials hurt fledgling industries in LDCs at least as much as they hurt the established industries of the West; a general increase of mineral prices would be burdensome for the LDCs as a whole.[15] There is no end to the potential demand for price supports; and if the practice becomes general, there might well be pressure to extend it to foodstuffs, in which the United States has a position quite as strong as that of the Arabs in oil. Cartel pricing would also bring substitutes into the market and would reduce foreign investment and aid. International trade could become strangled in a regulatory web, bringing its postwar growth to an unhappy end.

Despite such considerations, the moral and political pressure of the LDCs is strong, reinforced by the fear that they might resort to various forms of sabotage if they should feel excessively frustrated. Therefore Kissinger, in a major departure from previous American

---

14. *Business Week*, October 13, 1975, pp. 34–35.
15. Thierry de Montbrial, "For a New World Economic Order," *Foreign Affairs*, 51 (October 1975), 72. Commodity agreements are criticized by Peter T. Bauer, "Western Guilt and Third World Poverty," *Commentary*, 61 (January 1976), 38.

opposition, on May 13, 1975, cautiously announced, "We are prepared to discuss new arrangements in individual commodities on a case-by-case basis as circumstances warrant."[16] In an address to the United States on September 1, he recommended that "a consumer-producer forum be established for every key commodity to discuss how to promote the efficiency, growth, and stability of its market," and also announced United States adherence to the twenty-year-old tin agreement.[17]

It has thus been found necessary to open the door to international price management for political reasons, much as farm prices have been supported in the United States for social and political reasons at substantial economic cost. However, the United States hopes that the interests of consumers can be adequately protected and prefers something like the tin agreement—with buying and selling from a stockpile to smooth price fluctuations to direct price fixing. This is similar to the Lomé agreement reached by the European Economic Community (EEC) and forty-six LDCs (mostly of Africa) for a $450 million stabilization fund for twelve commodities.[18]

Third World delegates, however, welcomed this new American willingness to talk about materials and prices, less because of specific promises than because of its openness. It has seemed that the LDCs are demanding not any particular material concession so much as respect and consideration as equal members of the world community.

ONE WORLD

The Third World has little power to hurt the United States militarily or politically; the fantasy of the deprived majority exploding in wrath against the privileged few could become a possibility only if some strategy of economic development should prove unexpectedly successful. Poverty and overpopulation produce more lethargy than aggressiveness. Likewise, economically, there is reason to expect that the non-Western countries will continue to wish to sell as much as they can in exchange for industrial wares. Underdevelopment of most

---

16. *Time,* May 26, 1975, p. 71.
17. *The New York Times,* September 2, 1975, p. 20.
18. Concerning needs of LDCs and means of assistance, see de Montbrial, "For a New World Economic Order," pp. 61–78.

of the world, in other words, is no direct threat to American material interests. On the contrary, industrialization—enabling the LDCs to supply more of their own needs and to compete for more of the world's raw materials, perhaps to become politically more potent— might be quite detrimental to the material interests of the United States and other Western powers. If a collapse of civilization is in the cards, as some claim their computers tell them,[19] it will only be hastened by wider economic development.

It may be asked, then, why the United States should concern itself with the LDCs at all. Their plight may be hopeless in any case, and the United States may have more problems than it can handle at home. At best, an effort might be made to salvage the most promising —and most willing—of the LDCs, promoting effectiveness by concentrating where conditions are propitious, and writing off the wretched remainder from India to Haiti as hopeless. This approach has been given the grim name of *triage*: the battlefield practice of abandoning the desperately wounded to concentrate on the savable. It is also compared to lifeboat policy. If the lifeboat cannot carry all the passengers, it is better to save a fraction than to swamp the boat by trying to pull everyone on board. If we cannot save civilization throughout the world, we can possibly save it in the more promising lands.[20]

Such a view has a certain hardheaded logicality, but it lacks realism. The Third World or parts of it cannot be fenced off, and it has various subtle ways to avenge itself. For example, infectious diseases migrate; cholera and many other ailments endemic in the Third World from time to time slip past the border controls of the West. More serious is the drug traffic. The temptation is very strong for poor countries to help themselves by covertly pouring raw materials for heroin, hashish, and cocaine into underworld markets. Still harder to cope with is the export of poverty and social problems in the form of cheap labor, legal and illegal. Unlike European countries, especially West Germany, the United States does not bring in millions of contract workers to hold down the cost of increased industrial output, but about 370,000 persons are permitted legal entry every year, a policy which makes difficult the achievement of equilibrium population. Much worse, it is estimated that up to a million people enter

19. Denis L. and Donella H. Meadows, *Limits to Growth,* Potomac Association, Washington, D.C., 1973.
20. As argued by Garrett Hardin, *Exploring New Ethics for Survival: The Voyage of the Spaceship Beagle,* Viking Press, New York, 1972.

the United States illegally each year, mostly from Mexico; the majority of these illegal immigrants evade capture and deportation and melt into the Mexican-American communities of the Southwest. The more crowded Mexico becomes, and the more Mexicans have relatives across the border, the greater the pressure on a border that cannot be made impermeable without an army of inspectors. This accumulation of a subpopulation promises grave social troubles, aside from welfare costs and injury to the poorer sectors of the native population. Immigration adds the equivalent of an extra child to the size of families being formed. If the inflow continues and swells as the Mexican population doubles in the next generation, the United States will become a very different country.

There are other practical reasons for concern with the LDCs. While they lack strength to attack the richer lands, instability among them may complicate relations among the militarily powerful, who may not resist the temptation to involve themselves in explosive situations. The enormous and perhaps widening gap between rich and poor generates extremism and uncertainty and makes difficult a stable international order. If states become desperate enough they might well resort to nuclear blackmail or other means of exerting pressure on the affluent states.

Moreover, the world environment must be shared with all, and sooner or later various poorer states may have the capacity to wreck it. The noncooperation of a single nation might impede if not stymie international cooperation in many areas of conservation. A state might well feel itself entitled to use the oceans or atmosphere as a sewer in order to reduce costs of the industrialization that should relieve its poverty. Under the principle of free sovereignty, there would be no means of compulsion. The poor make life uncomfortable if not uncertain for the rich. Those in the lifeboat can be secure only if they are prepared to chop off the hands of those who would clamber aboard.

The most compelling reason for concern by the rich for the poor is philosophical. To waste food in a world whose masses are going hungry and are increasingly articulate and visible raises moral dilemmas; it is questionable whether we are justified in eating meat when the grain used to fatten cattle might stave off hunger pangs for ten times as many Indians or Africans. *Homo sapiens* is one species, and it is repugnant—although perhaps inevitable—that many suffer and a minority prosper for no better reason than the accident of birth in one or another of the compartments called nation-states, the boundaries of which are both artificial and permeable. It is possible that the United States might apply good organization and high technology, continue to consume ever growing amounts of energy from shale oil or nuclear reactors, and prosper materially while much of the Third World rots; but this vision is hard to sustain in the realities of modern thinking and political life. It was possible fifty years or so ago; the other world had not been brought by modern transportation and communications into the mainstream of consciousness of civilization. In all probability there will be more and more starvation on American TV news programs in coming years; if people do not become hardened to the sight and the idea, they may develop a fundamental change of attitudes.

This sense of responsibility, often of guilt, for the unhappiness of distant fellow-humans is a distinctive quality of the advanced nations. The Soviet leadership apparently has very little idea of any obligation to help; in its comfortable ideological view, the troubles are due to capitalism and so are no concern of the socialist state. The Soviet press takes virtually no notice of the poverty of the LDCs, except occasionally to attribute it to imperialist exploitation. Individuals of the LDCs may be assumed to be humanitarian (although the cheapness of human life is widely accepted), but broad humanitarianism is the specialty of the most educated and informed peoples. Syria and Egypt were able to use prisoners as bargaining pawns after the October War, although Israel held about twenty times as many Arab prisoners as they held Israelis. The oil-rich states have pledged large amounts to less fortunate states injured by petroleum costs, but they have delivered little except arms subsidies for fellow Arabs.[21]

Possibly a generalized humane outlook is inherent in the truly civilized condition; such peoples as the Swedes are especially disposed to castigate themselves for making merry at Christmas while life is bleak for Pakistanis or Malians. Concern for fellow humans is inherent in the democratic order as understood at present. It has been an American thesis since the Declaration of Independence that all men are endowed with equal rights. This principle has been neglected in practice, but democracy rests upon a general view of the worth of the individual and a sense of basic equality. Equalitarianism is the ethical fashion of our age, and logic decrees that equality should not stop anywhere; people within the democratic state must enjoy

---

21. Maurice J. Williams, "The Aid Program of the OPEC Countries," *Foreign Affairs*, 54 (January 1976), 308–324.

equal rights, the sovereign states must be respected as equal in attributes, and something of equality of all peoples follows. It can hardly be said that all persons eligible for American passports are entitled to share in the good life while noncitizens are entitled only to starve. Principles do not come to an end at national borders. It is especially difficult that they should do so in the case of the United States, which forms no very distinct nation but is a conglomerate of races and cultures, among which those related to Third World peoples are conceded an equal place. Concern for the underprivileged at home implies some feeling for the much more underprivileged of the world.[22] There is responsibility also because the West, usually without malice, has invaded the lives of the rest of the world and made it impossible for them to continue in traditional modes of life. It is then difficult to say that the poorer countries are to be left entirely to their own devices because their efforts to assimilate Western technology are not fully successful.

Morally speaking, the world becomes more like a single community; starvation in Africa is as real as starvation in America. Political theories that would divide the world—racism and exclusive nationalism—are backward-looking and are ill regarded in modern intellectual circles. The newer dimensions of international relations are concerned less with power as understood by our ancestors and more with the needs of humanity. The enormous material disparity between the less and the more fortunate states is hence a challenge to the democratic-humanitarian ethos of the advanced world with its open societies, and it is also a contradiction to the postulate of free and sovereign units, each looking to its own well-being. Hence the richer nations have all accepted in theory some obligation to raise the well-being of the poorer, whether or not their power-political interests are served thereby.

FOREIGN AID

That the richer and stronger nations should help out those denied the benefits of their superior civilization is an old idea. It was alloyed with crasser motives in the imperialism of the late nineteenth century. At that time, many Americans, like contemporaneous Britons, were

---

22. The egalitarian ethos is discussed by Robert W. Tucker, "A New International Order," *Commentary*, 59 (February 1975), 38–50, and "Egalitarianism and International Politics," *Commentary*, 60 (September 1975), 27–40.

ready to take up the "white man's burden" and envisioned Anglo-Saxon institutions reforming the world. Theodore Roosevelt was deeply convinced that the white or Anglo-Saxon peoples must undertake to improve the inferior peoples. Senator Albert Beveridge, embracing the need to civilize the barbarian and indolent Filipinos, promised, "We will not renounce our part in the mission of our race, trustee, under God, of the civilization of the world." [23] President William McKinley felt this call of duty to assist the Filipinos, just as President Gerald R. Ford felt morally driven to aid the threatened peoples of Indochina.

In its modern and less imperialistic form, the idea of the responsibility of the richer to improve the lot of the poorer is an outgrowth of World War II: help for allies and relief for the victims of hostilities. Then the Marshall Plan undertook the reconstruction of war-torn societies. Where infrastructure and technical and managerial skills were available, the United States injected capital—about $6 billion yearly for several years. Production rose rapidly, the many governments worked well together, and a strong Europe was restored in friendly association with the United States. This extremely successful program encouraged a similar endeavor in the cold war to strengthen allied states or to fortify needy nations potentially subject to the lure of communism, and foreign aid became a permanent part of American foreign policy.

But while the feeling has grown stronger throughout the Western world that the industrialized nations must act to alleviate the misery of the Third World, American official policy has evolved in the contrary direction. The United States furnished 2.8 percent of the gross national product as foreign aid in 1949, but only a tenth as much relatively in the period 1974–1976 (somewhat over $3 billion yearly, less than a quarter the amount spent on tobacco products). In Marshall Plan days, the United States furnished almost all development aid given by the West; prior to the Vietnam escalation the American share was two-thirds; recently it has been under one third. Thirteen countries in 1974 gave a larger share of their national product to foreign aid than the United States did.

A major reason for the decrease was the war in Vietnam. Not only did the war turn popular sentiment away from involvement in

---

23. *Readings in World Politics*, ed. Robert A. Goldwin and Tony Pearce, Oxford University Press, New York, 1970, p. 377.

general, but it also discredited foreign aid specifically. The program of assistance to South Vietnam appeared as a major factor in the entanglement. For years Vietnam received the lion's share of American aid with no beneficial results. Even after the withdrawal in early 1973 of American forces, South Vietnam and Cambodia were the recipients of the greatest share of economic as well as military aid. Over half of the food allotted to alleviate hunger in 1974 went to Indochina, essentially as military support. Weariness with Vietnam was consequently closely related to weariness with foreign aid.

At the same time, Americans were distracted by multiple concerns closer to home. The balance-of-payments deficit suggested trimming expenditures abroad. Inflation and recession took priority in the minds of the people, the Congress, and the president. No longer seeing themselves automatically growing richer, Americans were less conscience-troubled by their riches. Resentment at the oil cartel partly neutralized sympathies for other LDCs. If anyone were called upon to furnish charity to them, it might well be the oil moguls who were drowning in money. The fading of interest in saving nations from communism also deprived the aid program of its politically most effective rationale.

More basic was the nonsuccess of the program. Just as the North Atlantic Treaty Organization (NATO) flourished but the Southeast Asia Treaty Organization (SEATO) failed, the ideas of the Marshall Plan transferred (on a smaller scale) to the Third World brought disillusionment. From 1950 onward, $3 to $4 billion yearly were laid out as a regular part of American foreign policy, but the poorer countries showed few signs either of gratitude or of catching up. It was like poverty at home: the more money spent on welfare, the more unmanageable the problem seemed to become. In postwar Europe, only capital was missing; in most of the LDCs, everything was missing. It was necessary to build up industry, increase agricultural production, educate the population, and foster better government; this task was excessively complex and incomprehensible.

Since the United States, like other industrial nations, has more money than understanding, it was easily and widely assumed that the chief problem was the transfer of more capital to the poorer countries. This approach had numerous drawbacks. The new capital benefited those in charge of the government much more than the people in general, and it put the United States on the side of the "ins." Since aid is handled by those in power, governments are all in favor of it, but it is likely to increase inequality and corruption and to promote official interference in the recipient economy.[24] Much may be wasted; when storms and flooding made hundreds of thousands in East Pakistan homeless in 1970, the millions of dollars of relief sent by world charity went to private profit or rotted on the wharves. In 1972, when the United States sent grain to Afghanistan to succor a famine-stricken area, the Afghan army refused to permit its trucks to carry the relief supplies.[25] Yet if the donor injects himself into the picture and tries to dictate how assistance is to be used or tries to administer it directly, the result is irritation and irresponsibility. The donor may be incapable, too. The inspector general of foreign assistance said, after an African tour, "I have found them [aid programs] universally strangled in bureaucratic red tape. AID [the State Department's Agency for Industrial Development], as presently constituted, cannot succeed in its mission. It is too fat, it is too inflexible, and it is drowned in rationalizations that prevent accurate assessment of its effectiveness." [26] It is certain that aid elicits little gratitude. It is not certain that it really fosters economic growth; there has not been impressive correlation between amounts of aid and growth rates.[27] According to a study, "Foreign aid is not associated with progress and, indeed, may deter it." [28] Since 1948, Venezuela has received half or more of the profits of the oil companies operating there; the golden river disappeared with little return except in luxury goods.[29] According to former President Alfonso Lopez of Colombia, "We have concluded that foreign aid breeds an unhealthy economic dependency and delays or undermines measures that should be taken for development." [30]

Foreign aid, which covers two-thirds of the imports of Bangladesh, seems to relieve that country of any pressure to tackle seriously either

---

24. Bauer, "Western Guilt and Third World Poverty," p. 36.

25. *The New York Times,* January 24, 1972, p. 53.

26. *The New York Times,* September 18, 1975, p. 1.

27. Cf. Lawrence Whitehead, "Aid to Latin America," *Journal of International Affairs,* 24 (February 1970), 198–199; also Charles R. Frank, Jr. and Mary Baird, "Foreign Aid: Its Speckled Past and Future Prospects," *International Organization,* 29 (Winter 1975), 145. For a negative view see Peter T. Bauer, *Dissent or Development,* Weidenfeld and Nicolson, London, 1971, pp. 95–135.

28. Thomas P. Melady and R. B. Suhartono, *Development: Lessons for the Future,* Orbis Books, Maryknoll, N.Y., 1973, p. 70.

29. Normel Gall, "Oil and Democracy in Venezuela," *Common Ground,* 1 (January 1975), 58.

30. *The Wall Street Journal,* October 30, 1975.

agricultural productivity or population control.[31] It is conceivable that food relief may in the long run cause more starvation than would have existed without aid. A golden shower without initiative and responsibility on the part of the receiver is education for dependence. It makes it easier to blame others for the nation's troubles; no doctrine could be more mischievous for the poor countries than the expectation of salvation from abroad. It may distort investment patterns, encourage less efficient use of capital, decrease domestic saving, and possibly facilitate the flight of domestic capital. The most successful non-Western industrializer, Japan, deliberately excluded foreign capital while zealously promoting the importation of technology.

Excellent intentions may have poor results, partly because donors are more eager to appear to be helping than to assess long-term impact.[32] Showy projects, easily undertaken on credit, are often burdensome. Famine in the Sahel has been worsened by helpful Westerners who drilled deep wells. These wells enabled the pastoral peoples to water more cattle and thus to overgraze the land and increase the area of the desert. Governmental programs that operate even in the United States not infrequently become boondoggles; far out of sight, with the handicaps of language and alien culture, it is very hard for them to be efficient. From the bureaucratic point of view, the first objective is to get the money spent. The objectives, moreover, are confused; economic growth and the putative building of stable democratic societies compete with the urge to win friends, to promote diplomatic objectives, or to promote American business. The only sure effect of the touted goal of transferring 1 percent of the product of the industrial nations to the LDCs would be to salve Western consciences.

Differences of economic level, values, and culture cause a multitude of complications if one society tries to do something to or for another. However well intentioned, aid is interference. Motives are always suspect; the recipients, taught by experience to be skeptical, doubt the altruism of strangers' actions; if the big and distant United States has a project in Ruritania, it must be for its own benefit and so presumably to the detriment of Ruritania. Noting that aid failed to benefit the needier sectors of the world, Robert McNamara, president

31. *The New York Times*, December 15, 1975, p. 3.
32. P. T. Bauer, "Foreign Aid Forever? A Myth of Our Time," *Encounter*, 62 (March 1974), 15–30.

of the World Bank, inaugurated a policy of concentrating on projects
to help the poor. This approach replaces the at least clear-cut task of
raising production with the complexities of bringing about social
justice or changing societies. It was interpreted as an American ploy
to prevent revolution while postponing the economic development
needed to raise the poorer countries' industrial level.[33] Reasonable
demands may be ill received; Turkish opium farmers in 1971 roundly
damned the United States for the agreement whereby the United
States paid the Turkish government to restrict areas of opium growing. Leaders of the LDCs talk of the environmental movement as
"only the latest weapon in the wealthy nations' conspiracy to keep
ahead of the rest of the world." [34]

Aid underlines inferiority and implies a sort of vassalage. It is
almost impossible, perhaps hypocritical, for givers or supervisors of
aid to avoid feeling deeply superior, and they are likely to seem to
be putting on superior airs because they belong to the Western culture
and are of the Caucasian race. The "ugly American" is a weak helper
for the CIA in creating antagonism against the United States; but
his intervention is seen as neocolonialism, which in a sense it is, even
though he may profit materially not at all. Few are prepared to see
even Peace Corps workers or Christian missionaries as motivated by
idealism. "We aren't fooled, we see through your pretended altruism,"
say the less favored to salve their pride.

Foreign aid expresses dominance, and inequality turns almost anything into a source of friction. Panamanians are rankled not only by
the American flag over the Panama Canal but also by the manicured
lawns of the Canal Zone. Even where there is community of traditions
and economic levels are similar, the presence of the stronger power
is irritating. It is hardly contended that American corporations deal
unjustly with Canadians, but the corporations are there and are associated with the stronger United States, which is not so attentive to
Canadian feelings as it might be. Canadian nationalists hence react
not only by cutting down American TV programs but by fantasizing
American military invasion.[35] It is understandable thus that Indians
regard the $10 billion of aid given by the United States as a humilia-
tion and a form of imperialism.[36] In virtual paranoia, Indians have

---

33. *The New York Times,* June 25, 1974, p. 29.
34. *Newsweek,* June 12, 1972, p. 40.
35. *Time,* December 10, 1974, p. 48.
36. *The New York Times,* March 24, 1974, Section IV, p. 4.

denounced a malaria research project by the World Health Organization with no American participation except the contribution of some blocked rupees. An official news agency insinuated that this project was a plot for American germ warfare against the Indian people.[37] Yet about this time the Indian government was quietly letting it be known that a renewal of the humiliating aid would be welcome.

In view of these difficulties, foreign aid might well be used for frankly national purposes. When Japan invests in foreign countries for cooperative programs to increase the production of materials needed in Japanese industry, both sides profit. And foreign aid is a legitimate and useful accessory of diplomacy. It has thus served adequately to glue alliances which might otherwise break up. The ability to promise munificent assistance to both sides, especially Israel, greatly helped Secretary Kissinger to get disengagement agreements on the Israeli-Egyptian and Israeli-Syrian fronts in 1974 and 1975. The ability to give food aid to the hungry peoples has likewise helped to sustain a fairly good image of the United States in the darker days of Watergate and sundry revelations of unseemly activities by the intelligence community.

Another answer to problems of development aid is to turn it over to multilateral organizations. This transfer is strongly desired by the LDCs, which periodically demand the enlargement or adoption of big development programs under United Nations auspices—that is, more or less under their own control. Such a shift would remove from the United States the onus of interference, make foreign advice more acceptable, and separate political from humanitarian motives; this step is generally supported by the experts.[38] In Congress, however, the idea persists that any foreign program financed by the United States should be plainly in the national interest and should be under American control; only in 1975, in the face of the clamor of the LDCs against putative exploitation, did the Congress show much inclination to yield. Still, close to nine-tenths of United States aid is bilateral. The Congress has been very slow to appropriate funds even for loans to poor nations through the World Bank and related institutions, which are strongly under United States influence. Distrust of international agencies is not entirely chauvinistic; they may be even more

---

37. *The New York Times*, July 31, 1974, p. 9.
38. Frank and Baird, "Foreign Aid," p. 163.

bureaucratic than American agencies and more openhanded about passing out funds to the LDCs represented in them.

There may be cause to turn more of the administration of aid over to private or semiprivate organizations. They are smaller than government departments, less rigid, more adaptable, very likely better motivated and therefore would be less resented. Food relief is probably more efficiently administered, at least on a modest scale, by such organizations as the Cooperative for American Remittances Everywhere (CARE) or Catholic Relief Services; in fact, an increasing amount of food aid has been channeled through these groups. Private foundations can often best manage such services as educational assistance, agricultural demonstration projects, and health care.[39]

If foreign aid in the sense of government-to-government transfer of resources is thus unpromising, it would seem only a perversity of politics that less is done to make it easier for LDCs to earn their way, the obvious alternative. This method would generally be simpler and probably more effective than an administered program of artificial capital transfer in any practicable dimensions, although it is less appealing to those who enjoy the sense of power that comes from managing and doing. It requires less sacrifice on the part of the peoples of the industrial nations, in many cases none at all. Independence should generate self-respect and a will to improvement that is withered by charity. Administration, wherein aid often goes sour, is hardly a problem. Exports by LDCs put money in the hands of the producers rather than the often parasitic political elites who benefit now from foreign aid.

International price regulation may be found to be undesirable, except as an effort to stabilize the disconcerting gyrations of such products as sugar, cacao, and copper by stockpiling. Much might be done to maintain or to open markets, in accordance with American principles of economic freedom and competition. Most tropical products enter the United States dutyfree, but a mass of protective restrictions discourages the LDCs from trying to export anything competitive with American agriculture. Markets might well be enlarged for particular commodities. For example, it would be economically advantageous for the United States and Europe to give up expensive

---

39. Cf. Kenneth W. Thompson, *Foreign Assistance: A View of the Private Sector,* University of Notre Dame Press, Notre Dame, Ind., 1972; William and Elizabeth Paddock, *We Don't Know How,* Iowa State University Press, Ames, Iowa, 1973.

beet sugar production in favor of more cheaply producible cane sugar.[40] Exports needed by LDCs might also be facilitated. How little attention was paid to this aspect of assistance for the needy was shown in 1973, when the United States temporarily embargoed fertilizer exports, although a pound of fertilizer will probably produce much more on an undermanured field in Asia than on an Iowa farm. There might be a case for stronger measures, such as restrictions on nonessential fertilizer use in the United States.

It would be still more promising to encourage processing and manufacturing. Most industrial nations grant tariff concessions to LDCs, but the United States did not do so until 1976, and then only with many restrictions.[41] Duties are generally nil or trivial on crude products, but they rise with the degree of fabrication, penalizing the effort to industrialize. The manufactured exports of LDCs are limited, and American consumers could only gain if these products were admitted freely. Allowing access to the American market would also represent consistency in policy, encouraging the economically open world that the United States advocates. However, with the inconsistency that Americans understand more easily than do foreigners, the general principle is forgotten when political interests complain of injury. Exports of the LDCs are likely to be in labor-intensive products and thus may threaten jobs in ailing United States industries, such as shoes and textiles. But some adjustment assistance could be written off as foreign aid, to the benefit of the economies of both the United States and the Third World. The sacrifice in any case would not be large; manufactured exports of the LDCs are only about 5 percent of the manufactured imports of the industrial nations.

Some of the LDCs have shown an encouraging ability to enter new lines of production. The most striking have been the lands of the Confucian tradition, from Korea to Singapore. Brazil also has become an industrial state, capable of exporting automobiles and color televisions. More remarkable is the success of the Republic of the Ivory Coast in promoting an export agricultural economy based on cash crops such as coffee, cocoa, pineapple, and bananas. It has begun processing and selling canned fruit and juices and is establishing small-scale industrial plants for export as well as for the local market; it has maintained a growth rate of 7 percent yearly since 1960. These

---

40. As suggested by Robert S. McNamara, *One Hundred Countries, Two Billion People*, Praeger, New York, 1973, p. 78.

41. For details, see *The New York Times*, November 25, 1975, p. 51.

countries are exceptional, but they provide hope; if markets were better assured, other LDCs would doubtless be better able to follow.

There is much to be said for concentrating attention on the transfer of technology, which is probably the direction of the future for foreign aid as it is for the multinational corporations in the Third World. Making technology available to other countries has been on the American agenda since President Harry S. Truman made his Point Four proposal in 1949, but only with the September 1, 1975 address of Secretary Kissinger did the United States seem to be moving very seriously in this direction. He advocated, among many measures, an international energy institute, an international industrialization institute, and an international center for the exchange of ideas. However, it has become increasingly evident that it is not sufficient, and frequently not very helpful, simply to make existing technology available to nations in very different circumstances, particularly with labor surplus and capital shortage. Leaders of LDCs often want the last word in technology and regard anything less as an imputation of inferiority. But it is becoming clear that more is to be gained by fostering middle-level technology—much of which does not exist but can well be developed by the recipient countries with some assistance from outside. Relatively simple and inexpensive machines that consume little fuel and are easily handled and repaired can be manufactured in LDCs. Small, perhaps hand-powered, agricultural equipment instead of big tractors, cheap transportation instead of automobiles, and windmills instead of nuclear reactors will increase the productivity of labor many fold. It is only logical that technology should be very different where a tractor costs not a year's income but a hundred years'.

In many areas, such as management and marketing, the ways developed in the West are presumably poorly adapted to the very different economies of the Third World, but little study has been given to the question. Increasing attention has gone to tropical agriculture, but it is still the poor stepchild of agricultural research. The United States spends $400 million yearly on the fight against cancer, but the world spends less than $25 million a year on the health problems of the less affluent majority.[42]

Hardly anything would seem more urgent than population control, and the United States does furnish appropriate advice to scores

---

42. *The New York Times,* April 14, 1975, p. 25.

of countries; yet there has been no crash program for the development of more reliable, easily used, and inexpensive contraceptives. Indeed, contraceptive research in the United States, looking to domestic needs, has been practically strangled by regulations. The problem, however, is less the means of contraception than the attitudes toward reproduction. Much research and social engineering in this vital area remain to be done.

Educational and cultural assistance, as thus far conducted on a trivial scale, arouses less animosity than economic assistance and should in the long run be more fruitful. Schools in LDCs are often inadequate and poorly geared to practical needs. American support for more vocationally oriented institutions at secondary and higher levels would on the one hand increase the prestige of vocational training, and on the other, provide a channel for the transfer of technology. In brief, although foreign aid has not produced many cures, there is much that could with a prudent will be tried.

DEALING WITH THE LESS DEVELOPED COUNTRIES

Whatever the United States may achieve in promoting the spread of technology and what is commonly called development in the Third World is likely to be marginal. The Third World is too big, too complex, and too alien for outsiders to do much about it, even if they are gifted with more wisdom than is to be expected. At best, they can give some assistance in what the LDCs are doing for themselves. India's future rests on the ability of Indians to manage better, to eliminate corruption, and to make labor more effective in the hundreds of thousands of villages.

The lands of the other world must make their own way, and it cannot be the way of the United States. It is probably a grave error to think simply in terms of raising the gross national product. This is a false hope; the distance to be traversed is too great, and by the time an LDC traverses it, the American way may have become unsustainable. The earth's resources, atmosphere, and waters cannot support an automated, throw-away civilization for the mass of humanity. The United States consumes an inordinate share of the world production of raw materials—in the opinion of many, an ecological sin. For all the world to have a diet as rich in animal protein as the American diet would require a severalfold increase of basic food production, more arable land than exists, and energy inputs that would exhaust petroleum reserves in thirteen years.[43] Much of modernization, from packaged and processed foods to bigger, smoggier cities, may be positively undesirable in human terms, while the effort to follow an impossible model produces frustrations in individuals and social tensions in society. The less developed world needs saner goals than some of America's achievements, such as the hypertrophy of the automobile. But there is no reason, with existing technology, that the people of the world, unless the population increases inordinately, should not enjoy decent nourishment, housing, basic services, and cultural opportunities. This improvement can be achieved only by placing the quality of life ahead of the quantity of goods.

It is difficult for America to serve as a guide for the LDCs if the future cannot much resemble America's present. It is also difficult because many of their troubles are political—ineffective, parasitic, disorganizing government, which can turn to ashes the noblest enterprise. The problem is illustrated by the decline of Uruguay and Argentina, which fifty years ago seemed to have all the advantages that a developing country might desire—ample resources, homogeneous population, a high literacy rate, representative institutions, excellent climate, and freedom from external threats. That they have deteriorated to something between anarchy and dictatorship with stagnant economies seems an obvious political failure. But neither the United States nor any other power knows how to influence another country to political virtue—even if it knows what political virtue is.

The difficulty of doing much to reshape the less developed world is further increased for the United States by the fact that international relations suffer from the burden of inequality, the impact of political, economic, and cultural dominance—which, it may be argued, is a major factor in the political sickness of the parts of the world chronically subjected to it. Superior power is injurious even without intent of injury, and to assume responsibility for uplifting others is the ultimate expression of superiority. Belief in the special value of one's own people and culture is perhaps essential for social health and is inevitable; Western nations would not be true to themselves if they did not believe in their own worth. Yet true self-respect requires no imposition but implies some modesty; the irritations of inequality that can be exacerbated by haughtiness can be salved by tact.

To a large extent, Third World nations in their attitude toward

---

43. David Pimentel et al., "Energy and Land Constraints in Food Protein Production," *Science,* November 21, 1975, pp. 754–760.

the West and the United States are reacting to the arrogance of the past and present; the shrill voices of Guinea, Algeria, Cuba, and many other Third World nations are the result of hurt pride, a demand to be respected more than a demand for material benefits, "a collective cry of defiance." [44] Since the objects of the outcry are rich, the club of the LDCs is leftist; Taiwan and South Korea are excluded. The clamor is unconcerned with injustices committed by the communist states or LDCs because these powers do not challenge their self-respect.

It is not easy to deal with this injured outcry. An angry rebuttal is likely only to be turned back by hostile votes in an international forum. However, American business has been compelled to learn to deal more suavely with sensitive foreigners than it did a few decades ago. The American government, chastened by Vietnam, has similarly adopted a lowered profile. It was a marked improvement when Secretary Kissinger went to a conclave of American ministers not to tell them what they must do but to listen; he promised nothing that could not be fulfilled and tried to remove or reduce specific irritants. The LDCs may seem at times to be unreasonable, at least in terms of Yankee business sense, but they are not unreachable. The Arabs have been influenced by United States policies more responsive to their feelings, and the expulsion of Israel from the United Nations, for which there seemed to be the votes early in 1975, was quietly dropped. The United Nations also declined to offend the United States by placing the alleged colonial status of Puerto Rico on the agenda. In his September 1 address already referred to, Kissinger actually promised nothing that would cost the American taxpayer much, but he indicated a readiness to consider sympathetically the needs and ideas of the LDCs. The response was a remarkable improvement of the atmosphere. These countries have basically a deep respect for the West and the United States.

Improvement of relations with the LDCs requires, perhaps above all, respect for them as fellow-members of the species and regard for their peoples and cultures. Encouraging their self-esteem, however, does not include propagation of the fashionable idea that they are poor simply because they are exploited or robbed. This assumption is in a sense insulting, implying that they are only helpless pawns. It is injurious because emphasis on supposed or real injustices does not

---

44. Tom J. Farer, "The United States and the Third World: A Basis for Accomodation," *Foreign Affairs*, 54 (October 1975), 84.

stimulate improvement but promotes the idea that betterment is to be achieved primarily by squeezing something from the West, an idea that is both demeaning and misleading.[45] It is no favor to the LDCs to encourage them to look everywhere but at home for the sources of their woes. It is much sounder for the United States to uphold its moral position, rejecting claims for compensatory transfers of wealth,[46] while assuming a posture of understanding toward the needs of the Third World.

It is desirable to work with, not for the LDCs. It would also be well to emphasize reciprocity; the supplicants must expect not only to receive but also to give. If the rich have a broad responsibility to the poor, the poor must equally have a responsibility to world order. This obligation is obvious in such areas as terrorism; it is likewise clear in economic affairs. Although the poor have a claim on food supplies, they have none on indefinite breeding. If they desire to be respected as equals, they must behave as responsible sovereignties.

Another condition for satisfactory relations with the Third World and its development is an international climate of nonviolence and rationality in which economic problems would be less aggravated by political and ideological strife and hence more solvable in terms of long-term human needs. A tranquil and prosperous world permits attention to nonpolitical questions, and the crucial questions of today are or should be nonpolitical. A world threatened by clashes of power fixes its attention on essentially irrelevant questions of prestige, power, and ideology, such as the threat of communism or the control of the Sinai peninsula—questions of who is on top rather than how problems are to be handled.

If the evolution of the LDCs can be separated from rivalries of world power that need not concern them, it should be easier for the United States to refrain from direct interference in their politics. The instinct of people who have power is to use it, but good relations with the LDCs require abstinence from direct or indirect meddling, no support for particular parties, and no social engineering, but treatment of all with respect and detachment.[47] The United States has

---

45. As pointed out by P. T. Bauer in a letter to *Commentary*, 60 (August 1975), 9.

46. Farer, "The U.S. and the Third World," p. 87.

47. M. Singer and A. Wildavsky, "A Third-World Averaging Strategy," in *After Vietnam, The Future of American Foreign Policy*, ed. Robert W. Gregg and Charles W. Kegley, Jr., Doubleday, New York, 1971, p. 86.

largely given up the effort to promote democracy in its own image in the LDCs, in the style that was traditional from the marines' intervention in the Caribbean early in this century down to the grandest of interventions in the Third World in Vietnam. Efforts to implant American institutions (for example, in South Korea and the Philippines) have rarely proved helpful or lasting. Even lecturing about democracy, a legitimate exercise of free speech, seems to do little good. Indira Gandhi, criticized for crushing Indian democracy, reacted with a hot response. But the United States is learning to deal in a friendly fashion with a variety of regimes, from monarchies, such as Iran, to states led by socialistic parties, such as Sri Lanka (Ceylon).

In fear of violence and revolution, America has tended to stand with the elites and by supporting them has made them less responsive to their own people, as occurred most notoriously in Vietnam but also to some extent in many other countries, from the colonels' Greece to semifascist Spain and the Latin American military dictatorships. In the future the United States may be prepared to regard more radical approaches benignly, in the awareness that the institutions of the West are neither perfect nor probably the most suitable for the poorer lands. Conceivably, for example, it might appear that something like the Chinese commune system is the best way at a certain level to confront the major scourges of the LDCs' excess population growth, chronic disease, and unemployment, areas in which the Chinese seem to have made notable progress. It may be indispensable to resort to a political order that deemphasizes material incentives in favor of some kind of social justice, however contrary this point of view may be to the traditional American attitude.

It is possible, even predictable, that such an approach will be less discordant with future American attitudes. Rapid economic growth for the industrial nations is apparently becoming a thing of the past. If America becomes less materially spendthrift, its mentality will come closer to that necessary for the LDCs; the gap should begin to close both materially and psychologically. Increasingly for both the richer and poorer worlds, the greatest questions are those of social integration and purpose.[48]

It may be that the problems of the LDCs are unsolvable, but this supposition is not yet proved. If it is true, the problems of the more

---

48. On basic problems, see K. H. Holsti, "Underdevelopment and the 'Gap' Theory of International Conflict," *American Political Science Review*, 69 (September 1975), 827–839.

advanced countries are probably also beyond solution. On the other hand, if the more advanced nations, and above all the United States, can get the better of their own mounting troubles and reach an outlook appropriate for the postindustrial age, it may be possible that they can show the way toward relieving the troubles of the less fortunate peoples.

CHAPTER TEN

The Evolving
State System

INTERNATIONAL PLURALISM

In the weariness and frustration of nonsuccess in Vietnam, the United States began groping for a more satisfactory philosophy of international relations. The chief theory brought forward was a revival of the old balance of power concept, an idea which came naturally to Henry Kissinger, a student of nineteenth-century European diplomacy. The balance of power—that is, the mutual counterbalancing of a plurality of great powers—could reasonably be credited with having kept the peace of Europe (except for a few rather nondestructive wars) for the century from 1815 to 1914. Hence it might reasonably be hoped that a new balance of power might preserve the peace in the nuclear age.[1] Specifically, President Richard M. Nixon proposed a five-sided world, the corners of the pentagon being held by the United States, the Soviet Union, western Europe, Japan, and China.[2]

The scheme was attractive. The standoff between two superpowers was blamable for the tensions and dangers of the cold war.[3] Certainly, the idea of a fear-ridden superpower launching a preemptive nuclear strike belongs to a two-part world. There is something to be said for the two-front world; it is simple and clear-cut, and it avoided major conflict through the postwar era. It has also been comforting that only two powers were in a position to apply major force in the world.[4] But bipolarity is a tense and dangerous international geometry, characterized by a narrow range of stability and a concentration of hostilities, in which each side fears that any change may lead to a decisive, possibly fatal gain for the other. It entails an absolutist mentality in which any disturbance seems threatening and any adjustment becomes a dangerous concession, any gain for one side is an inadmissible loss for the other.

---

1. For models of the international system, see Morton A. Kaplan, "Variants on Six Models of the International System," in *International Politics and Foreign Policy*, 2nd ed., ed. James N. Rosenau, Free Press, New York, 1969, pp. 291–303; also, Morton A. Kaplan, *System and Process in International Politics*, John Wiley, New York, 1962.

2. For the Nixon concept, see Louis R. Beres, *Transforming World Politics: The National Roots of World Peace*, University of Denver Press, Denver, 1974, pp. 21–25.

3. On the meaning of bipolarity, see Joseph L. Nogee, "Polarity: An Ambiguous Concept," *Orbis*, 18 (Winter 1975), 1193–1124.

4. Cf. John Spanier, *American Foreign Policy since World War II*, 6th ed., Praeger, New York, 1973, pp. 229–230.

The balance of power idea, however, also has serious weaknesses.[5] One is that the world continues to be essentially bipolar in strategic power.[6] Japan is militarily insignificant, Europe does not exist as a political entity, and China is a superpower only in human numbers. Moreover, the balance of power represents an outmoded way of thinking, with little relevance to the present-day world. The maneuvers of the old system, centered around war or the threat of war, no longer avail. The old balance-of-power concept rested upon a rating of the military strength of the powers. Regiments or warships could be added up and probabilities of victory could be estimated, as cannot be done with nuclear missiles. Traditional foreign policy was made by professionals, who could act upon their calculations with little attention to public opinion. In this age, foreign policy is less amenable to the old kind of calculation. There is no particular reason, either, to treat the present world as subject to five powers only; many other nations, from India and Brazil to the oil giants, have an important role.

It is true that the world system has become much too complicated to be explained in terms of the confrontation of the two genuine superpowers. Soviet armies on its borders moved China to openness toward the United States, and the Soviet Union reacted in the proper balance-of-power (not the ideological) manner to the American rapprochement with China. The Soviets have shown apprehension at any sign of improved understanding between western European capitals (like Paris and Bonn) and Peking. It was even reported [7] that the Soviets wish the United States to remain strong in Europe, a desire that would have been an absurdity a few years earlier. For their part, the Chinese want Europe strong and united; they have evinced the wish to see American forces remain in Europe, and probably in Southeast Asia, in order to check the Russians. They were very hostile to the German-Soviet treaty of 1970 and looked askance at the Soviet-sponsored European security conference, desiring no détente that would permit more Soviet pressure on themselves. China, Japan, and the Soviet Union form one power triangle; China, India, and the Soviet Union another. Soviets and Japanese, Japanese and Chinese, or Soviets and Europeans may

---

5. Stanley Hoffman, "Weighing the Balance of Power," *Foreign Affairs,* 50 (July 1972), 618–643.

6. Kenneth M. Waltz, "International Structure, National Force, and the Balance of World Power," in *International Politics and Foreign Policy,* pp. 304–314.

7. *The New York Times,* May 19, 1973, p. 37.

find common interests contrary to American desires; it seems certain, as the world goes, that they must do so.

Standoff has changed, in large part at least, to kaleidoscope. If there are several truly independent powers, the ideological dichotomy dissolves along with the political. China long ago made Maoism an autonomous inspiration. Japan and Europe differ considerably from the United States in their emphases. The modern mentality demands ideal justifications for violent actions, but events can no longer be fitted into a simple black and white picture. Total commitment gives way to maneuver. Ideological truculence becomes a positive handicap, because its claims of universal validity are offensive to other major powers and it impedes possibly advantageous dealings with potential partners. The decline of ideology as a factor in international politics is proportional to the strengthening of multipolarity.

In a world of blurred polarity, changes can be absorbed by relatively painless realignments. The domino theory does not operate, nor is it necessary to see any area not under superpower influence as a vacuum to be filled. If Vietnam "falls" it does not fall to either China or the Soviet Union. The contest for power is less desperate, because diplomacy, insofar as it still deals with power, seeks not the destruction of a rival but a relative betterment of position. In the present complex situation, with its currents and countercurrents, it may become difficult even to expand spheres of influence, because the gain of one nation means a loss for all the others. Before World War I, powers could make such deals as the division of Manchuria by Japan and Russia, and France and Britain could accommodate each other's interests in Africa, but such procedure is difficult today.

The ebbing of bipolarity has various implications. The poorer nations may have suffered in that the superpowers have become less concerned with courting them. The poor countries can no longer hope to achieve much by open or implied threat of turning to the other side. An alleged communist menace no longer suffices to guarantee an aid program for Zaire; the United States finds it more important to work out its relations with Japan, Europe, China, and Russia. But this decrease in the ability to exert pressure would seem to be more than compensated for by an increase in the freedom to maneuver. In the emerging world, weak countries such as Algeria, the Sudan, Peru, or Guyana defy the United States or the Soviet Union with impunity. The United States has ceased to command even where its position is strongest, as in Panama, the Philippines, or South Korea. A State Department official commented on a Korean coup: "The secretary's attitude was one of acknowledgment that the United States no longer has the means or desire to exercise its former powers over a client state." [8] In the multipolar world, the powerless are still powerless, but they are freer.

For the Soviet Union, a pluralistic world further downgrades ideology and encourages the opening of Soviet society, the better to participate in international exchanges. A thoroughly Leninist Soviet state cannot have allies or independent friends. Multipolarity raises the specter or, from the American viewpoint, offers the best hope for the awaited liberal evolution of Soviet society. For the pluralistic United States, on the other hand, a multipolar world is more attractive than the alternatives: a world state (of which there is no prospect), hegemony by a single center, or the bipolarity of the cold war. America has little to lose and much to gain from the elimination of ideology from foreign relations; it can welcome a variety of outlooks, none of which need be feared. The troubles of American foreign policy will be lessened insofar as the United States shares leadership (and the odium that comes with it), reducing commitments and political involvement. It is no longer possible, as it seemed before the world wars, for this nation to sit back and enjoy the security of the balance of power from the sidelines. Neither does it seem necessary to carry the burden that corresponded to the American share of global industrial production after World War II.

THE POST-POSTWAR ERA

The international system is an anarchy of one hundred fifty sovereign states uncontrolled by any effective peacekeeping machinery, with endless points of friction between the many outwardly irrational or irreconcilable regimes. Yet although the world on TV may seem to be dissolving in chaos, there is phenomenally little warring. History records no comparably low ratio of conflicts to independent states. The world may be moving into a tranquil period, as old tensions are eased or disappear and are not replaced by new ones. Not only has civil conflict in Indochina burned out; the inflammable Near East has wavered between guns and diplomacy. The superpowers talk of peace,

---

8. *Newsweek*, October 30, 1972, p. 56.

and a Holiday Inn is built not far from Stalin's grave for the convenience of American business people. The two once utterly hostile Germanies have come to mannerly coexistence and mutual recognition. Berlin, a bone of contention for decades, has almost disappeared from the news. The Sino-American confrontation belongs to the past, and it is assumed that somehow the Taiwan problem can be pacifically resolved.

This settling down of the world is more understandable if it is recalled that the troublesome political issues of the past generation have virtually all come out of the disruption of the world wars, with the accompanying and largely consequent decline of European power and the breakup of colonial empires. The Korean and Vietnam wars, the German problem, and chronic friction over Berlin all resulted from the inability of the powers to draw acceptable lines between Soviet and Western spheres of influence in the power vacuums caused by World War II. The cold war and the contest between America and China in Asia amounted to a sorting out of the results of World War II. The Soviets did not know how much they could achieve from their spectacular victory or how much they could hold; hence their push into eastern Europe and their probes toward Turkey, Iran, even Libya, to lay claim to whatever was claimable. There followed decades of crisis, but by now the limits seem to have been fairly well fixed and accepted.

The United States likewise sought in Vietnam to retain an untenable position arising from the breakup of the French empire during the war. It might be said that World War II ended on April 30, 1975 in Vietnam. The problem of Israel in the Arab world was also engendered by the wars. Britain in World War I promised the Jews a homeland in Palestine, and the sufferings of European Jews in World War II led them to resolve to have their own state in the historic territory. The decline of international tension may be in large part understood as the world's convalescence from the sickness of the world wars—really a single conflict broken by a twenty-year armistice. In 1914, the British foreign secretary, Sir Edward Grey, said, "The lamps are going out all over Europe; we shall not see them lit again in our lifetime." It was not until nearly sixty years later that one could believe that the political darkness was on the way to being dissipated.

The great conflicts generated a violent spirit, which has through the postwar decades slowly come unwound. The wars were felt as crusades against hostile systems, and for the victors it became natural to think of force or the threat of force as the remedy for political troubles. It was in this spirit that the United States continued wartime programs into the postwar period; lend-lease became foreign aid, and psychological warfare became the selling of American policies by the United States Information Agency (USIA). Wartime intelligence engendered the Central Intelligence Agency (CIA). The cold war was inaugurated by men who had been shaped in the great war.[9] The entire cast of American (and Soviet) foreign policy became somewhat militarized; the cold war continued the basic tasks of the hot war, repelling enemy forces, and securing the safety of the world. The wars likewise battered international law almost to extinction and made civil dealings with foreign governments conditional upon ideological agreement with them.

The grinding, bitter, and bootless grappling of the European nations in World War I, when millions were sent to their death perhaps for less reason than ever before or since, shook the foundations of Western civilization and opened the world to violent and extremist thought. The disturbance and desperation of the war lifted Bolshevism to power in Russia. Although Russia had been uncomfortable in its westernization and troubled by an unhappy intelligentsia, Lenin's party could come to power only because the war broke the old regime and its instrument of order, the army, and made a desperate people willing to clutch at far-out panaceas. Fascism and Nazism likewise showed how the fury of the war had generated political fever. World War II ended fascism as a respectable doctrine, but it regenerated the confidence and expansiveness of Soviet communism and brought communism to power in China with an even more revolutionary and anti-Western mentality. Then in the first postwar years communist governments were installed in eastern Europe and Korea under Soviet auspices, and Leninist communism was partially imitated in various countries emerging from a different kind of struggle, that against colonial domination.

The passions engendered by war wear out, and the overturning of the old order ceases. Generations grow up farther from the great struggle and know the operative war system only as history. The boundaries achieved, even when laid down as temporary, become accepted and permanent. The revolutions turn old and stale, and no really new ones are in prospect—there has never been a social revolution in any moderately democratic or fairly advanced country. The Soviet Union, as an authoritarian state, becomes stiff and cautious, repeating slogans of equality and social change only from habit and internal political needs

---

9. George F. Kennan, *Memoirs, 1950–1963*, Little, Brown, Boston, 1972, p. 321.

and reverting toward the basic conservatism of tsarist Russia. In China, Mao tried to rerevolutionize the country through the Great Proletarian Cultural Revolution of 1966–1969; but it was possible only to break down institutions, not to rekindle the revolutionary fire. China has become more concerned with its quarrel with the Soviet Union than with the propagation of revolution. The present Soviet elite lacks direct awareness of Lenin's revolution, and it will be difficult to sustain Maoism in China without Mao. As those who officered the cold war in the United States left the scene and as the Soviet Union and China lost radical self-assertiveness, it became easier for the United States to take a relaxed view of change in the world. With the subsidence of ideology, the ideal of revolution—impractical in the modern state—fades into indifference or reliance on growth and technology to bring change.

The wars also ushered in the transformation of the state system, not only by sapping the strength and vitality of the European powers that formerly dominated it but also by raising expectations of freedom and equality. The democratic powers made the rights of weaker nations and self-determination of peoples their slogan, largely through Woodrow Wilson's prodding, in order to mobilize world opinion against the Germanic powers. Britain and France, holders of the world's largest empires, did not intend that these principles should apply to their own dominions. But the idea that all peoples, not merely Europeans, should decide their own destinies was not to be smothered; Africa and Asia begun stirring even where a surface calm was maintained. In 1917 the British promised eventual self-rule to India, which comprised the bulk of the population of the British empire, and in 1919 Mohandas Gandhi organized his first passive resistance campaign, which marked the end of tranquil rulership. World War II completed the work of World War I. France, the Netherlands, and Belgium were entirely cut off from their colonies, and Britain was weakened. War aims being again and more strongly the democratic ethos and human rights, the idea that equality applied to all became accepted. The process of dissolution of empires led to complications and conflicts, as in the Congo (Zaire), Cyprus, and the Indian subcontinent. By the 1970s, however, not only the traumas but also the excitement of liberation had been dissipated. With only trivial remnants of the old colonial empires remaining, the number of sovereign states tripled, all theoretically equal in rights.

There are still many areas of potential conflict, including uneasy eastern Europe, the Near East, and the Sino-Soviet border. But none of today's major powers, with the possible exception of Communist China,

claims any important territory held by another. Territorial squabbles
are for the less developed countries and are remarkably few.

New eras of international relations are not easily, quickly, or pacifically born; they are like new continents taking shape in earthquakes
and volcanism. The transition from a European state system to a world
state system has cost two cataclysmic wars and more than half a century of crises, uncertainty, and tension, but the outlines of a new system
seem to be emerging, for better or worse.

THE OUTMODING OF FORCE

A salient fact of international relations of recent decades is that the
utility of brute force (by which is meant, practically speaking, the
ability to kill people) decreases as the amount of armaments potentially available increases. Yet force still plays a role and may decide
major issues. The retention of Czechoslovakia in the Soviet domain
was the work of armored columns prepared to shoot. The separation of
Bangladesh from Pakistan and the formation and enlargement of Israel
came about because certain armed forces could destroy other armed
forces. If the Soviet Union or any other state should decide to impose
its will on a neighbor, it could ultimately be restrained not by the dis-
approbation of the world community or even by economic sanctions
but only by counterforce.

This reality is the excuse for the existence of armed forces in a
world where everyone knows that war is desperately dangerous. However, there are many other reasons for nations to expend their substance
on military power beyond their apparent defense needs or their likelihood of being able to employ force for political purposes. Powers of
the second rank that can hardly gain anything by threatening their
neighbors spend far too much on armaments, although they are faced
with no military danger except possibly from a superpower, a threat
that they could not contain by their own resources in any case. Such
countries as Peru or Brazil love to have jet squadrons, modern tanks,
and cruisers. It is easy to equate the supreme interest of national self-
preservation with the most dramatic and incontestable form of
strength. The capacity for self-defense was historically the basis of
sovereignty; presumably for this reason the interacting states are called
powers in English and the equivalent in other European languages.

International relations have been, and to some extent still are, practically equated with questions of war and peace; even in the 1970s, international relations theory may be stated in such terms, distant as they are from the normal intercourse of states.[10] The theorists, it seems, like to view the world scene as an endless contest for dominion, like a complex chess game, although there are no longer any winners.[11] National security is still high politics, alongside which less threatening aspects of the interaction of peoples lack interest. As recent scholars put it, "Depend entirely on threat and punishment, and the ordering of society will be based entirely on coercion. International politics tends toward the latter condition. Since Thucydides in Greece and Kautilya in India, the use of force and the possibility of controlling it have been the preoccupation of international political studies. They still preoccupy the men who are responsible for the military and foreign policies of their nations," nuclear weaponry being only another form of force.[12] The media revel in war and violence on the international scene, much as they make the most of crime at home, while quiet growth is seldom mentioned.

Power and danger are interesting. The military is a way of life, with vested interests, tradition, and glamor, color, and pageantry (the United States armed services spent $48 million for brass bands in 1973). Heads of state are treated to military honors. Military men believe in the importance of their profession and are in a position to press the point, as professionals of national strength and security. To some extent, nations consequently develop foreign policies that justify or utilize their cherished and expensive armed forces. Vanity of leaders plays some part. Frederick the Great of Prussia (1712–1786) frankly wanted to see his name emblazoned in history for soldierly glory, and Adolf Hitler daydreamed of grandiose victory monuments. Modern presidents and dictators may not be entirely immune to the disease. It may be [13] that elder statesmen play the game of foreign policy in the spirit of small boys playing soldier or making model battleships, or of

---

10. Cf. Raymond Aron, *Peace and War: A Theory of International Relations,* Anchor Books, Garden City, N.Y., 1973.

11. Texts are: John Spanier, *Games Nations Play: Analyzing International Politics,* Praeger, New York, 1972; and Miles Copeland, *The Game of Nations,* College Notes and Texts, New York, 1969.

12. Robert J. Art and Kenneth N. Waltz, *The Use of Force: International Politics and Foreign Policy,* Little, Brown, Boston, 1971, p. 4.

13. As remarked by Charles W. Yost, *The Conduct and Misconduct of Foreign Affairs,* Random House, New York, 1972, p. 21.

juvenile gangs fighting for turf, or of the thousands who vie for permits to shoot bears.

For states that have to create nationhood or bind up an incoherent society, pride of power is tonic; hence half-starving India goes nuclear. In a world where not everyone is trained to higher philosophy, armaments appeal to visceral and primitive feelings and to red-blooded sporting instincts beyond calculations of gain. National prestige, whatever it may really signify, is equivalent to the prestige of the leaders, and the nearest measure is military power. Great nations must have glory in somewhat the same way that addicts must have narcotics. Historians take it for granted that power means involvement, which requires a backing of strength. The great feel that they have a duty to play a bold role.[14] The temptation is catching; one nation must do because others do, or may, and the expectation of conflict is self-fulfilling.

For such reasons, war is among the hoariest of human traditions;[15] probably bands of early *Homo* were scrapping long before they had earned the right to be called *sapiens.* Sometimes men have fought for little apparent purpose, as though from boredom or aggressive instincts. War has fixed status and title to territory; practically every nation of Europe owes its contours to battle. In ancient times, war was gainful for the victor, who could plunder, enslave, and impose tribute. Sovereigns were morally free to attack one another unless bound by a treaty of peace, which was usually made for a specific period. Neighbors were traditionally enemies, because each represented an enduring threat to the other; the way to greatness was territorial aggrandizement. Prolonged peace was possible, before the industrial revolution, only where a single power succeeded in imposing uncontested dominion, as did the Roman or Chinese empires.

War was perfectly respectable in early modern Europe; as Francis Bacon wrote in the seventeenth century, "No body can be healthy without exercise, neither natural body nor politic; and certainly to a kingdom or estate, a just and honorable war is the true exercise. A civil war, indeed, is like the heat of a fever; but a foreign war is like the heat of exercise, and serveth to keep the body in health; for in a slothful peace, both courages will effeminate and manners corrupt." [16] For

---

14. As remarked by J. William Fulbright, *The Crippled Giant: Foreign Policy and Its Domestic Consequences,* Random House, New York, 1973, p. 267.

15. Cf. Kenneth N. Waltz, *Man, the State, and War: A Theoretical Analysis,* Columbia University Press, New York, 1959.

16. Francis Bacon, "Of the True Greatness of Kingdoms," in *Essays,* Heritage Press, New York, 1944.

Clausewitz in the 1820s, "war is nothing but a continuation of political intercourse with the admixture of different means." As he saw it, the wars of civilized peoples were less cruel and destructive than those of savages and were certainly not reprehensible; his views were less bellicose than those of most of his fellow-officers. Theodore Roosevelt believed an occasional little war was a jolly fine thing.

The experience of the nineteenth century generally supported such attitudes. The minor wars neither bled the people significantly nor threatened to shatter the social system. Intelligent men—especially in a rising, semiauthoritarian country like Germany, but elsewhere, too, including the United States—glorified war as an instrument of greatness and a maker of the character of the nation. By three brief and relatively bloodless wars (successively with Denmark, Austria, and France) Bismarck forged his Reich—a small sacrifice for a grand purpose. The decision for war could be taken lightly, as, for example, when French Emperor Napoleon III in 1870 seized upon a trivial slight implied by Bismarck's doctored telegram as an excuse for war against Prussia. The United States, likewise, rather casually but with better reason for confidence, entered an unnecessary war with Spain. In the colonial wars between 1870 and 1914, glory and real estate were purchased for little bloodshed.

Bismarck himself, however, was wise enough to turn pacific after he had won his game, renouncing further expansion with the remark that "Herzegovina is not worth the bones of a Pomeranian grenadier." The modernizing and industrializing nineteenth century experienced a substantial evolution of attitudes. For several centuries, the perfection of the means of firepower had been making war more destructive, less heroic, and less attractive as a sport, while the growth of nationalistic and democratic sentiments made it seem to be more outrageous. Conquest of weaker states by their stronger neighbors was already ill regarded in nineteenth-century Europe. There was widespread resentment even of Prussia's taking Alsace-Lorraine from France, although the territory had been German and was largely German-speaking, and its loss could be regarded as the penalty for France's having declared war. Being inhibited from expansion in Europe, the various nations transferred their self-assertiveness into colonizing backward lands overseas. Even overseas, however, the ethos of empire was more restrained than in earlier centuries, and aggression was limited for the most part to lands without well-organized national governments, as in Africa. India became a European possession in the eighteenth century; in the nineteenth, the powers sought in China not colonial dominion but concessions and bases.

On the eve of World War I, Norman Angell overestimated the capacity of humans to assimilate reality and argued that war between modern nations was obsolete.[17] He became subject to facile ridicule, but he was not entirely wrong. There were no profound antagonisms among the leading powers in 1914 and no real reason for them to fight. World War I was begun by relatively backward states: Austria, Serbia, and Russia; the other nations allowed themselves to be pulled in. However, the general ignorance of the reality of war permitted complacency. Despite some hand wringing and gloom, as in the case of Sir Edward Grey, few people doubted that the fighting would be over in a few weeks or at most months, that some provinces might be lost or gained, but that life would go on approximately as before.

The four years of carnage showed that the powers could not count on fighting in a civilized manner and convinced most people that they should not fight at all. In the peace settlement, the League of Nations consecrated the sovereign equality of weak states and strong, and the Allies received overseas territory not as property (colonies) but as wards (mandates), theoretically temporary and subject to the international community. The United States, the chief victor, set an unprecedented example by taking nothing. Something of the new temper was shown by the condemnation of United States intervention in Nicaragua in 1926; in 1912, indifference had been the reaction.[18] The Kellogg-Briand Pact of 1928 declared war making a crime, and all states nominally agreed. Little was achieved except the mode of undeclared war, but eighteenth-century monarchs would never have pretended to renounce a favorite instrument of national policy. When Japan acted contrary to its obligations by taking Manchuria, the American Stimson Doctrine proclaimed an end to the custom of the ages by refusing to recognize forcible conquest.

The fear and repugnance of war among civilized peoples ironically contributed to the outbreak of World War II. The French, British, and Americans were so eager to avoid a new catastrophe that they were paralyzed in responding to successive aggressive thrusts and encouraged the appetites of the dictators. The Germans, too, feared war; the

---

17. Norman Angell, *The Great Illusion*, Wm. Heinemann, London, 1914.
18. Cited by Louis J. Halle, "Does War Have a Future?," *Foreign Affairs*, 52 (October 1973), 23.

generals repeatedly tried to restrain the dictator, and there were no cheers as German troops marched away to battle. World War I was everywhere greeted with enthusiasm, World War II with apprehension. Even Hitler was prepared to start the war only by attacking a second-class power, Poland; the Western powers thought that they might avoid fighting by blockading instead.

When war showed itself in 1914–1918 to be not an extension of politics but a catastrophe, it came to be regarded as a criminal enterprise on the part of the enemy. After World War II, political and military leaders were accused of the newly recognized crime of "planning aggressive war," and some Germans and Japanese were executed for their share in starting hostilities, quite apart from their guilt for unusual cruelties, such as the murder of civilians or the maltreatment of prisoners. Of old, a king who lost a war would be considered punished by the humiliation of defeat and probably would have to give up a province or a colony. Nowadays, any leader of a great power contemplating serious war must be aware that in case of defeat his life would be forfeit—somewhat like the defeated chieftains who were sacrificed to the gods of the victors in pre-Spanish Mexico.

Despite much publicized violence, the postwar world has shown unprecedented reluctance to engage in war—especially war with the most effective weapons. The United Nations, like the League of Nations, outlawed war; unlike the League, the United Nations has become an important repository of hopes for peacekeeping. There have been ample occasions for beginning World War III many times over in central Europe, east Asia, and the Near East, tensions being compounded by revolutionary ideologies; but the powers have shied away. In terms of historical precedent, it is almost incomprehensible that the United States did not use its overwhelming superiority in weaponry at the end of World War II to achieve what seemed an important and justifiable goal: the withdrawal of Soviet troops to ensure self-determination for the countries of eastern Europe. The Korean War was a remarkable innovation—a war between the armed forces of two big powers who restricted their fighting to a single area.

The prewar diplomacy of threat and land grabbing as carried on by Adolf Hitler and Joseph Stalin belongs to a dead age. For many reasons, the acquisition of territories has ceased to seem to be the sign of, or the way to, national greatness. Imperialism, formerly considered very grand, has come to be synonymous with international crime. Talk now turns to "economic imperialism" and "cultural imperialism," but coercion by bankroll or television serial is very different from gunboat imperialism. The old idea of the power vacuum, implying that a great power must be an overlord everywhere, still appears in print but has little meaning. Even nonmilitary coercion is a serious accusation in the new international system.

The use of force in the Third World by industrial states—by France in Indochina and Algeria, by Britain and France against Egypt in 1956, by the United States in Cuba (indirectly) and Vietnam—has been unrewarding, partly because ruthlessness has been inhibited by responsiveness to world opinion, partly because the people at home have withheld support. A few decades earlier, the actions of the stronger and more advanced powers would have been thought wholly proper, but Vietnam turned into a phenomenal display of the ineffectiveness of technological violence.

Gunboat diplomacy was pronounced dead in 1974 when Western states could not muster a half-way credible threat against militarily powerless nations that attacked Western economies by withholding oil and quadrupling prices. If the industrialized nations made no real threat, it was because it would obviously have been ineffective; mutterings of the possibility of intervention only served to irritate the oil producers. Comparison with the heated Anglo-French reaction to a much less serious blow, the nationalization of the Suez canal, showed something of how the world had changed in eighteen years.

Warring in the postwar period has occurred in the Third World— India-Pakistan, Arab-Israeli, civil wars in the Sudan, Nigeria, Angola, and so forth. Even there, however, the incidence has been low. Latin America, which once had wars with some frequency, since 1935 has experienced only trivial clashes. The territorial wars that have occurred among the less developed countries (LDCs) have all been brief, and no nation has tried to occupy the heartland of the enemy. Even the "wars of liberation" that preoccupied the 1960s have largely faded away. Except in the Arab-Israeli case, the idea of further altering boundaries by force seems to have been given up, and even the embittered Arabs seek to win back lost lands by economic or political pressure more than by military pressure. In 1971, India soundly trounced Pakistan but acquired no real estate. Numerous disputed or uncertain boundaries in the Third World have failed to generate the armed conflict expectable in earlier generations. A clash like that of Greece and Turkey over Cyprus in August 1974 in another age would certainly have led to war. Even if they would like to fight, small states cannot readily do so because the rest of the world wants to get into the act of stopping the violence. The superpowers, and nearly all other nations, strongly want stability.

The new respect for the legitimacy of states is very striking. Recognition of the equal rights of persons in a democratic society has been extended to the collective persons of the world community. Of more than a hundred sovereign entities, not a single one has been extinguished during the postwar period; in very few cases has territory been lost. The unwillingness of the world to recognize the legitimacy of expansion achieved by force cost Israel most of its diplomatic support after 1967. All states claim to uphold the principles of international law, sovereignty, and independence. No political leaders treat poor and backward countries with the scorn that was taken for granted in the nineteenth century; today when an artificial state with a largely stone-age, unsophisticated people is created, as in the granting of independence to Australian New Guinea, the new member of the international community is immediately accorded full rights. With the principal exceptions of states of the Soviet sphere, nations have practically complete freedom of action within their own territory; no matter how they may insult big powers or nationalize foreign property, they have little reason to fear armed assault. Respect for the territorial status quo and a general desire for security has extended to resistance to splitting states, despite claims of ethnic minorities, as in the Sudan, Nigeria, and the former Belgian Congo (Zaire). The United States opposed the separation of even such a geographic monstrosity as the two Pakistans because it feared the unsettling effects of the division.

After the Cuban crisis, "a world in which nations threatened each other with nuclear weapons now seemed to [John Kennedy] not just an irrational but an intolerable and impossible world." [19] There is still ample violence in the world, but the violence of state against state has largely lost its meaning; current international problems are singularly unamenable to solution by military strength.[20] If, in fact, force were considered unusable in international relations even when important interests are at stake—and hardly any interest can be called absolutely vital except the integrity of a state—this change would be a fundamental alteration in the nature of the state system. If it becomes reality,

---

19. Arthur M. Schlesinger, Jr., *A Thousand Days: John Kennedy in the White House,* Houghton Mifflin, Boston, 1965, p. 893.

20. Paul C. Warnke, "Apes on a Treadmill," *Foreign Policy,* 18 (Spring 1975), 24.

this change could be only slowly assimilated into political thinking, but it would promise revolutionary consequences for the human condition.[21]

THE NUCLEAR SHADOW

Nuclear technology has brought a revolution in international relations much more profound than the introduction of chemical explosives many centuries ago. If it is possible that "the history of usable combat may at last be reaching its end," [22] most credit must go to the perfection of the engines of destruction, especially through nuclear explosives. Gunpowder and cannon killed the sport of jousting in the sixteenth century, and Alfred Nobel believed that the high explosives he invented would eliminate war as irrational. They would have done so but for blindness and self-deception. Such self-deception is no longer possible; probably no one in high authority has illusions of victory in nuclear war. No less important, the danger is immediate and dramatic, with hardly any way to avoid tremendous losses. Scientists have concluded optimistically that a few members of the human species would survive the detonation of 10,000 megatons of nuclear bombs—about half of what is available[23]—but the target nations might well be left lifeless. Without this threat hanging over them, the superpowers might well have been unable to restrain themselves during the cold war from escalations that would have led to a grinding struggle of land and air forces. It is not necessary that nuclear war should mean inevitable suicide; the uncertainty is enough.

Since the atomic threshold is so frightening and the possibilities of accident or escalation are ever ominous, the nuclear powers endeavor to stay well clear of nuclear confrontation. The only safety lies in keeping tension within bounds, and the Soviet Union and the United States seem to have come to a degree of understanding on the management of crises. Statesmen know that they have to communicate and to avoid provocation, even though they despise their opponents and what they

---

21. As pointed out by Robert W. Tucker, "Oil: The Issue of American Intervention," *Commentary*, 59 (January 1975), 23.

22. Russell F. Weigley, *The American Way of War: A History of United States Military Strategy and Policy*, Macmillan, New York, 1973, p. 477.

23. *Science*, October 17, 1975, pp. 248–250.

stand for. The atomic threat in the background, with the necessity absolutely to exclude war between major powers, is the basic motivation behind a thousand efforts to restrain violence and improve the international system. Proposals run the gamut from increasing the exchange of goods and persons down to calls for world government, which is considered ultimately essential to assure survival. Although they do not always act accordingly, all powers have an interest in stability and international order.

Paradoxically, because of their enormous offensive power, nuclear weapons are not useful for offensive purposes, except possibly as cover for a lower-level thrust. They are, however, potent deterrents—that is, defensive instruments. It is conceivable that the possession of a small missile force with atomic warheads has saved China from application of the Brezhnev Doctrine, while the French and British seem to believe that their relatively feeble nuclear forces would make an attack on them irrational. Nuclear war would be excessively unpredictable for an aggressor as well as for the victim. The positive political utility of nuclear weapons (aside from some prestige and the satisfaction of possessing the most potent instruments) is doubtful. The United States fears that strategic superiority might be used by the Soviets to extract some gain in a crisis. But this course would be hazardous, and if they did try to make such use of their nuclear arsenal, it could hardly give them more than a temporary gain. The United States would doubtless be galvanized to catch up, and it would feel that it could not permit itself to be blackmailed again. It is not clear how a nuclear superpower could profitably coerce a nonnuclear power by threat of attack; the world would certainly take a very negative view of this course of action, and the other superpower would be almost as anxious to prevent this strategy from being successful as to prevent such action against itself. Any state would be fearful of bowing to a nuclear threat lest appeasement invite more demands; it might well be judged less risky to defy the threat, in effect to challenge the nuclear aggressor to take the risk of barbaric action. Nuclear weapons are a very defective means of acquiring anything of value. They can only massively destroy; the aggressor cannot occupy and take over the direction of the target country and its economy. The Soviet Union was able to use motorized columns to "normalize" Czechoslovakia, but it could not use nuclear missiles for a similar purpose.

It is very dangerous for a superpower to engage even conventional forces in any area of interest to another superpower; the greater likelihood of nuclear war would seem to be from escalation, with one side or the other in a conflict situation raising the stakes to avoid loss of prestige or to save the investment already made and jeopardized by the stronger actions of the other superpower. There are many scenarios of how this route might lead to disaster, but the cogent fact is uncertainty, which makes it imperative to avoid escalatory situations and indeed to scale down tension in general, because of the danger of miscalculation or accident. The existence of tactical nuclear weapons (miniature nuclear devices overlapping chemical explosives in potency) makes it easier to cross the nuclear threshold. But by making any war involving the big nuclear powers very dangerous, nuclear arms further deter violence, and this deterrence is perhaps a positive gain. An encounter between two major powers has always carried the potential of escalation to massive destruction; nuclear weapons of all sorts have made the world far more aware of the perils, and less ready to march forward oblivious of consequences, than in August 1914.

Because of the danger of the potentially suicidal involvement of the strongest powers, there is great pressure against any combat at all between smaller powers. There is psychological inhibition for them, too, in the overweening presence of the inconceivably potent nuclear arsenals; it therefore is hard for nonnuclear powers to take military actions of their own very seriously except for local objectives, such as the protection of the Turkish community on Cyprus in 1974. There is also a powerful deterrent against a smaller nuclear power using its weaponry. Even if it could use nuclear force against a weaker power, it would have to be afraid that the far more powerful nuclear superpowers would deny it the fruits of victory, if not punish its temerity. It would be a dubious gamble. Hence, many nations that could easily construct a nuclear force have desisted from doing so. In an earlier age it would have been inconceivable that nations would have denied themselves the most potent weapon for their armories.

The fear of general destruction, with radioactive clouds carrying death around the world, is the new legitimacy of states, sheltering the independence of all because no one knows what might occur if violence were allowed to prevail anywhere. The result is that the politics of high power—of the potential of turning the globe into an inferno— is divorced from the ordinary affairs of the human universe. There is no continuity between the thought universe of nuclear war and the humdrum life of states. In the nightmarish realm of potential nuclear force, there is no tradition, no law, no humanity, no realism except the phantasmagoric specter of technology destroying its maker. Nuclear theorists necessarily treat the powers as paranoid. While the ultimate issues of security move in this miasmic atmosphere, the ordinary relations of states are left to proceed on a level of concrete reality, dealing not with hypothetical madness but with material benefits and human needs.

MODERN INTERNATIONAL RELATIONS

The idea of war improving the human stock or national character has been set aside not merely because of the hyperbolic weapons explosion, however. There are many other reasons why international violence becomes increasingly inconsonant with modern civilization.

Not only has the cost of violence increased; the rewards have decreased. Before the nineteenth century, there was hardly any thought that a nation could strengthen itself or better its standing in the world except by polishing its weapons or acquiring territory. These goals were achieved by diplomacy backed by force or by the employment of force; wars were primarily for territorial stakes. This mentality persisted, despite the importance of industrialization, through the nineteenth century and into the twentieth. Rulers hoped to get more land with more subjects to be conscripted or taxed for the benefit of the national grandeur; secondarily, they hoped for colonies overseas to increase the national wealth. Germany seemed to prove the validity of the territorial ideal, as Prussia grew to greatness and became the German empire by swallowing more and more small entities. World War I might have been ended by a compromise peace but for the obsession with territorial aggrandizement on both sides, especially France's determination to recover Alsace-Lorraine and Germany's resolve to have part or all of Belgium. In the 1930s, the Nazis loudly demanded African colonies, profitless as these had already shown themselves to be, and the lust for *lebensraum* grew as Hitler's easy victories expanded the Reich beyond Bismarckian dreams. So bemused were the Nazis with land grabbing that even as the shadows of unavoidable defeat lengthened they were still arguing about just how much of Europe they would annex.[24]

Yet since the growth of modern nationalism, conquests have brought little power except in uniting divided peoples. Since World War II, hardly any state has sought to increase its territories at the

---

24. *The Goebbels Diaries, 1942–1943*, ed. Louis Lochner, Greenwood Press, Westport, Conn., 1948, p. 474.

cost of bringing alien peoples under its rule. The chief exception has been the Soviet Union, which showed some hankering for various areas in the immediate aftermath of the war. But it refrained from annexing satellite states in eastern Europe. China has evinced interest in recovering lands from the Soviet Union, but it has probably raised the point about "unequal treaties" without the expectation of fulfillment. The founders of Israel wanted the Biblical lands for their home, but expansion since the founding of the state has been dictated mostly by the desire for security in hostile surroundings.

Not only has there been no empire building since the morrow of the war, but the old empires have crumbled away as unmanageable. The last was the Portuguese, outlived only by the Russian-Soviet, a somewhat different construction. Empires are for states that are essentially politically backward, Portugal long associated its large African empire with power and wealth, although Portugal was, at least in part because of the empire, the poorest country of western Europe. A long and costly war convinced the Portuguese also that they, like the French in Algeria, could no longer control, or supposedly profit from, colonial dominions.

Empire having clearly become outmoded, nations may still try to dominate spheres of influence; but this type of domination has also become increasingly difficult. The Soviets were able to profit from dominance in eastern Europe in Stalin's day; they can no longer materially do so, and the Soviet domain—with Cuba—has probably become burdensome except in terms of prestige and ideology. The United States finds it difficult to manage such formerly dependent states as Panama and the Philippines. The modern great power cannot impose overtly advantageous trade conditions. Client states become claimants. Enormous power has become largely unwieldable, at least in ordinary affairs, and there are few privileges for the super-greats of the earth. Economic coercion has little effectiveness as long as the victim has alternative sources and markets.[25] There may be American or Soviet penetration, as in Latin America or the Near East, but even small and rather backward states have learned to cope with it; outright military action is not replaced by subversion.[26] To speak of increasing the power of a modern state is mostly hollow rhetoric.

If a nation wishes to increase its power, its wealth, or its standard

25. Cf. Klaus Knorr, *Power and Wealth: The Political Economy of International Power*, Basic Books, New York, 1973, pp. 177–179.

26. Nicholas O. Berry, "The Management of Foreign Penetration," *Orbis*, 17 (Summer 1973), 599–600.

of living, influence and riches nowadays come from productivity. Although it is advantageous to control raw materials, especially oil, the most important resources are brains, skills, good organization, and willingness to work, none of which is readily to be gained by coercion. Japan has well shown how a nation can make a destiny for itself without reaching for political-military power, and it has done so with the speed of a spectacular conquest. Brazil has similarly made itself the giant of Latin America, and East Germany rose to subleadership in Soviet eastern Europe by virtue of productivity. Perhaps an even easier way for a state to improve itself would be by luring brains and talent from across the world; a small part of the ordinary military budget spent on this form of aggression could make almost any industrial country a modern Athens.

Economic development brings economic prestige and importance in the world, and there is mild competition regarding figures of output and gross national product (GNP). Economic progress is also the basis of modern military strength. Not only strategic but even conventional forces have appalling price tags. The Arab-Israeli war of 1973 ground up billions of dollars of arms in a few days, and only a rich nation (or one with a rich patron) can afford to be really armed. This development is another major innovation. It was once almost a rule that the tough barbarians were the better fighters; the nomads, tempted by wealth, would sweep down and plunder the more effete, sedentary peoples. In the eighteenth century a poor but disciplined and spartan Prussia could make itself a leading military power. Now to be strong it is necessary to be productive—that is, at least potentially rich. But a nation that is successful in the building of modern industry is unlikely to risk its prosperity and life wantonly in warfare. An agrarian society may still (foolishly) contemplate atomic war with some complacency, as Chairman Mao Tse-tung is said to have done; but the highly tuned, complexly integrated industrial society, dependent on costly infrastructure and capital-heavy facilities, must regard war as an almost unmitigated disaster.

For the modern and hence technologically capable society, force is a backward means of action, both internally and externally. Highly educated people are usually repelled by violence and narrow political causes, and violence is disruptive of the bureaucratic regularity and businesslike rationality indispensable for modern life. As the Soviet Union has become more urbanized, industrialized, and bureaucratized, it has not become notably liberal or democratic but has at least retreated from the brutality of Stalinism. It is a sign of the evolution of the mentality of the Western world that corporal punishment, even by parents, has gone out of fashion, while capital punishment has died out in nearly all modern countries. Opposition to it is so strong that in September 1975 sixteen countries withdrew ambassadors from Spain to express disapproval of the execution of five terrorists and alleged murderers. Trade unions even halted some trade for a time, all over a matter that not long ago would have been regarded as trivial and purely domestic.

Increased democratization and awareness—above all via television—have made it harder for advanced states to be warlike. Publicity favors the weaker side in quarrels and usually embarrasses the stronger. American public opinion was revolted not so much by the slaughter in Vietnam as by its visual image. Israel was much affected by its losses in the 1973 war, turning from enthusiasm for a good military performance to profound questioning. Everywhere in the Western world old-style patriotism and martial virtues have subsided; the consumer society is not bellicose. It is an age of nonheroics. Rulers may be engrossed in national prestige and power conflicts, but the people would usually rather mind their own affairs in peace. The popular interest is best served by pacific intercourse among increasingly interdependent states. The needs of states are less and less competitive, more and more shared, as it becomes necessary to cooperate for the general safety and welfare. It is a tribute to the strength of the sense of mutuality and interdependence that some obligation is felt to augment the strength of the LDCs, quite contrary to the anarchistic philosophy of international relations and the doctrine of national interest as power.[27]

Habits and institutions in foreign policy are as conservative as in any other realm of human behavior. Security has remained the dominant consideration in the foreign policy at least of the superpowers in the mid-1970s, however difficult it was to contemplate war between them. A part of the explanation must be sought in the psychology of conflict. People can hardly imagine the exploding of hundreds of megaton bombs, but they like to think and negotiate in terms of strength.[28] Leaders and writers enjoy the power game and want their country to have a gutsy, masculine stance in the world. People like the spectacle

---

27. Seen as unrealistic by Martin C. Needles, *Understanding Foreign Policy,* Holt, Rinehart and Winston, New York, 1966, p. 6.

28. Alistair Buchan, *The End of the Postwar Era,* Weidenfeld and Nicolson, London, 1974, p. 133.

and idea of violence, even if they shrink from the reality. We are in a great game; Irving Kristol, for example, compared the American world position to a chess game.[29] Political contest is interesting and invigorating, and there is a feeling that it is necessary for the health of society.

If, in fact, war has become impractical, there must be far-reaching consequences. The prime mover of the state system has been insecurity; no country has been able to take survival for granted. If survival comes to be taken for granted, there will be a new system. In the prolonged absence of conflict, the expectation of violence declines; despite the momentum of armaments, states may spend less in preparation for increasingly improbable wars or may adhere to concepts of minimal deterrence. In terms of nuclear weaponry, deterrence would require rather little. Disarmament is more likely to come by the degeneration of armed forces and a lack of will to remain battle-ready than by negotiated agreements. Over the past decades expenditures of the advanced countries on arms have been slowly shrinking as a percentage of GNP, although they continuously rise in monetary terms. Arms come to be more for show, less for the use that no one expects. With receding memories of conflict, the idea of martial glory and old-style power politics may be expected to fade. Security may be sought more in terms of a stable international order capable of discouraging violence and solving the nonmilitary problems that loom on all horizons, with vestigial armies providing colorful guards of honor.

Alliances likewise can be kept vigorous only as long as people at least half believe that a definite threat of attack exists. If the idea of a physical Soviet attack continues to recede—the fear of subversion has already gone—the Atlantic Alliance will have to look for new purposes; it will perhaps survive because it is a handy league of the likeminded. It is unlikely that new alliances will form unless new military threats are perceived; economic groupings may be in order, but they are likely to be much more ad hoc. The enfeeblement of the defensive imperative likewise weakens regional organization. Like Japan, Europe may never feel the need of its own nuclear force; the European political union is difficult to envision without external political pressures.

Power rivalry exists mostly in military or semimilitary terms; if these terms are lost to sight, relations are only mildly antagonistic and competitive, troubled by economic and cultural invasions. The diplomacy of the LDCs is already largely divorced from military considerations; these nations must depend on the world community in any case,

---

29. *The Wall Street Journal,* February 12, 1975, p. 10.

so that there is little need for them to be preoccupied with defense. Instead, they strive for recognition and material advantage—and economic issues may become sharper in a less security-conscious world. But few people become very excited over tariff negotiations, and commercial threats and reprisals are far less interesting than military démarches. If the Arabs had attacked an American naval vessel, the reaction would have been emphatic, as it was on the detention of an American freighter by Cambodians in May 1975. In contrast, putting a hundred million automobiles on short rations arouses little purple passion. Economic matters are not a question of national honor. States deal less with one another as personalities, concerned with pride and position, than as representatives of their diverse and sometimes discordant material interests.

In a civilized international community, as in a group of civilized people, fears for personal safety should not detract from attention to more complex problems. America may then be able to revert toward the earlier ideal of assured general peace guaranteed not by a balance of strength but by the reasonableness of governments and men. It is eminently in the American interest so far as possible to facilitate such an outcome, not only because of America's stake in a workable world order but also, in a narrow sense, because of national power. Soviet influence, for example, especially in the Near East, rests largely upon the idea that arms may be put to use for national advantage.

War, however, has been part of the human picture for millennia, and it has served numerous functions in the human social complex; its withdrawal, if accomplished, entails problems. War has been an adjuster among states; without force it would seem that all states, however unnatural, are to be immortal, and all frontiers, no matter how unsuitable, are to be absolute and permanent in a sanctified status quo. Throughout history, conflict has halted, or from time to time reversed, population growth, which would otherwise have long since reduced mankind to beggary; conflict thereby made progress possible. Now the near-elimination of conflict, not only among nations but also among tribes and smaller groups, has contributed, along with preventive medicine, to explosive population growth. Unless a solution can be found quickly and applied at a higher level, wastage of life must replace carnage.[30]

---

30. For semiserious speculation that war is essential, see Leonard C. Lewin's introduction to *Report from Iron Mountain on the Possibility and Desirability of Peace*, Dial Press, New York, 1962.

Less concrete are the effects of lack of competition. The traditional role of the state has been to protect its people from foreign enemies, and one reason for armaments beyond the needs of security, for the persistence of the arms race in the face of détente, is to keep up this function. If this traditional role is lost, a social cement and integrating purpose will be missed. The state that focuses on economic development, health, and equality must be fundamentally different from the defense-oriented, solidarity-building state of the past. National pride must seek a new rationale, and the legitimacy of the state will need new foundations. For some leading states with many reasons for pride, such as the United States, the problem may be less severe. Even for the United States, however, external security may permit an upsurge of disruptive internal tensions; some would contend that this phenomenon has already occurred with the decline of the energizing tensions of the cold war. The need to mobilize and muster strength for defense has seemed especially great for authoritarian societies. War and defeat have repeatedly brought renewal to imperial states in the past; nothing else would suffice to shake the consecrated apathy of self-serving cliques. Total security invites irresponsibility and indifference. Habits and attitudes derived from an age of insecurity may carry on for a few years, even decades. But the loss of the historic background of patriotism and of the stimulation of potentially dangerous competition must in the long run mean a changed type of personality and a fundamentally altered culture. This modification is another of the transitions that seem necessary for the attainment of a new level of civilization, a transition the achievement of which is unpredictable.

NEW ISSUES

Even if the potential destructiveness of modern armaments did not make it imperative to lay aside traditional conflictual modes, states are impelled to think in other terms because the world becomes more and more international or (to use the modish word) interdependent. The problems that can be solved and the opportunities that can be turned to benefit on an international scale loom ever larger relative to what an individual state can do within its borders. In some cases, the newer types of international relations present relatively few problems or can be handled fairly smoothly by general consent and through relevant organizations—for example, air traffic,[31] meteorological data gathering, or satellite communications. In other cases, there are questionable implications. Satellite observation of the earth is of much interest to all but is the prerogative of the very few; the United States has followed the enlightened policy of making photographs of Earth Resources Technology Satellites available to all interested parties. If there is developed satellite-to-viewer television—the technology for which has already existed for a decade—some form of international regulation will be necessary, if only to make it generally acceptable. Unless it is responsible to the international community in some form, worldwide TV will be too much an American show to be acceptable to many states, including the Marxist-Leninist countries, which are terrified of such a possibility.

Formerly, states were aware of threats to security only of a military-political nature, but such threats have been joined (perhaps even overshadowed) by very different ones. General Alexander Haig attests, "The most fundamental danger to NATO and Western society is the socio-economic phenomenon." [32] Retired General Maxwell Taylor sees the chief dangers to the United States in the next decade as nonmilitary.[33] Many or most such dangers have an international dimension, either because cooperation is essential to meet them or because the sovereign states acquire an increasing capacity to cause trouble in the world at large if they are careless, selfish, or ill-humored.

The volume and rapidity of travel make disease control an international concern. Poorer countries may be tempted to exercise their sovereign right to cultivate the opium poppy, the source of heroin and other narcotics; the Turkish government is more responsive to pressure by its farmers than to pressure and blandishments by the United States. The Turks say that addiction is an American problem that they are not called upon to solve, and the $36 million paid by the United States under a 1971 agreement to assist in ending opium cultivation was not enough. Even if the traffic from Turkey is partially limited, Pakistan, Laos, or Mexico can enter the market.

The sheltering of terrorists is also a prerogative of sovereignty. As

---

31. On the need for a new international regimen in aviation, see Andres F. Lowenfeld, "A New Takeoff for International Air Transport," *Foreign Affairs*, 54 (October 1975), 36–50.

32. *Time*, June 9, 1975, p. 13.

33. Maxwell Taylor, "The Exposed Flank of National Security," *Orbis*, 18 (Winter 1975), 1013.

long as there are any struggles that may be called wars of liberation against "Western imperialism," some LDCs are likely to be sympathetic to terrorism or to encourage hijackers and brigands who claim a political purpose and who regularly take hostages and demand transportation abroad. Even when captured in Western countries, Arab terrorists have been handled with extreme leniency, and international action has been blocked by Arab and African states. In terms of life lost, terrorism is not a major problem; 520 persons were killed between 1968 and 1974—fewer than the number of murders in any major American city. Terrorist action is nevertheless a potential danger. The United Nations can do nothing about the problem, because the poor nations view terrorism as a sort of retribution against the rich. It seems a low-grade surrogate for war, the revenge of the alienated against the world order, unpunishable within the rules of the international system; no remedy is in sight, short of improvement of the international atmosphere.

Less exciting is the danger to the earth's commons—assets that cannot be held by individual states. It was a workable hypothesis to regard the high seas as available to all nations as long as technology permitted only scratching the surface of its potentialities. Until after World War II, nations claimed territorial waters of only three miles; beyond this narrow zone, the seas were open to all. Now fishing has become scientific; fleets of factory ships equipped with electronic gear sweep up the desirable fish; in a hungry world, if the fish are to be the booty of whoever grabs them first, exhaustion of the supply is not far behind. The same is true of whales, several species of which have been hunted nearly to extinction. The product of world fisheries peaked in 1970; management and restraint will be necessary to reattain that level.

To assure their share many countries, especially those of Latin America, unilaterally proclaimed zones of up to two hundred miles of coastal waters as their preserve; the United States, the Soviet Union, and other leading industrial nations objected, but the two hundred-mile limit is on the way to general acceptance. In that event, territorial waters will take in 36 percent of the oceans and 95 percent of fisheries, with the United States acquiring the most area—over 2 million square miles.[34] The International Whaling Commission has attempted to preserve whale fishing (as well as whales) by restricting catches. It has

---

34. Lewis M. Alexander, "The Extended Economic Zone and U.S. Ocean Interests." *Columbia Journal of World Business,* 10 (Spring 1975), 35.

encountered much resistance from Japan and the Soviet Union, but these states seem to have bowed rather reluctantly to the pressure of world opinion and the realization that, if there is no restraint, there will be no more whales.

The minerals of the sea bed also present difficult questions. The United States led the way in 1945 by proclaiming ownership of the continental shelf (which is not clearly defined), a move that Chile, Ecuador, and Peru cited in 1952 as justification for their claims to a two hundred-mile fishing zone.[35] A very large part of the still unexploited resources of gas and petroleum is deep underwater, and clashes of claims are numerous. Moreover, there are huge amounts of manganese, nickel, copper, and other minerals on the floor of the oceans; these become more valuable as land deposits are worked out. There is some agreement that the international community has rights to this potential wealth, as stated by a 1967 United Nations resolution. The LDCs, unable to exploit the ocean bottom for themselves, would like an international organization (in which they would have a majority) to take charge and use its revenues for their benefit. The United States would like resources to be reasonably available, under international regulation, for exploitation by those capable of it.

There are many other maritime issues, including the width of coastal zones under absolute sovereignty, right of passage through straits, division between waters pertaining to mainlands and islands, control of pollution at sea, and freedom of scientific study of the oceans. Issues are complex and bound up with emotions of nations as well as with major economic interests. The LDCs are suspicious that scientific research may amount to scouting their resources. The United States concern has usually been to preserve as much freedom of naval and commercial passage as possible and to make riparian control as unrestrictive as possible. Several conferences bringing together thousands of delegates have failed to achieve agreement. The world may have to get along without any ocean law, except as it evolves from successive understandings over time.[36]

Closely parallel to the right to exploit the seas is the sovereign right, in the present state of international law, to use the seas or the atmosphere as dumping ground for wastes. A little progress has been

35. Warren G. Magnusson, "U.S. Ocean Policy," *Columbia Journal of World Business*, 10 (Spring 1975), 24.

36. H. Gary Knight, "Jurisdictional Issues in Ocean Management," *Columbia Journal of World Business*, 10 (Spring 1975), 5.

made; in November 1972, ninety-one nations agreed to ban the release of certain poisonous wastes into the ocean. However, enforcement is up to each nation, and there is no agreement on responsibility in such a probable case as the breakup of tankers carrying hundreds of thousands of tons of oil and causing immense damage to seacoasts, or the dumping of insecticide into the Rhine by a German barge, rendering the water supply of the Netherlands unpotable. Some nations ban DDT; others continue to use it, although it spreads throughout the biosphere, even to Antarctica. American spray cans are accused of endangering the vital ozone layer, but the fluorocarbons involved are manufactured in many countries. One nation's sulfurous smoke becomes another's acid rain. Human action is probably modifying climates inadvertently, to the detriment of some people and perhaps the benefit of others. Weather modification is on the agenda; the American military tried rainmaking to slow down communist resupply in Vietnam. The United States and the Soviet Union have agreed on a pact outlawing manipulation of weather or other modifications of the environment for military purposes.[37]

The Soviets—and the British and French—propose to build as many supersonic planes as possible; if they insist on operating at economically high altitudes, their discharges may have damaging effects on the stratosphere. The Soviets have also boasted of grandiose schemes for turning Siberian rivers south to water central Asia; if this is done, it might modify the climate of the Arctic and hence of much of the Northern Hemisphere. If the LDCs cut down tropical rain forests to clear land for crops, the global climate might be severely affected. But no one, except an unidentifiable and often incoherent world opinion, could call upon them to desist.

Environmental issues, like questions of control of ocean resources, tend to set the less against the more developed nations. Pollution in the industrial countries is twenty to fifty times as much per capita as in the LDCs,[38] but the richer countries are much better able to control it. If rules are to be applied effectively, all must cooperate. The LDCs have increasing power to damage the world environment, but they resent the idea that they should not be as free to grow as Western countries were in an earlier generation. Pollution standards seem to

37. On this problem, see Gordon J. F. MacDonald, "Weather Modification as a Weapon," *Technology Review,* 78 (October–November 1975), 57–63.

38. Eugene B. Skolnikoff, *The International Imperatives of Technology,* University of California International Studies Center, Berkeley, 1972, p. 181.

them to be a device for holding them back, while most waste and pollution is the fault of the advanced countries. Radical nationalists and Marxists, with the encouragement of the Chinese, treat the whole affair as an imperialist plot. Advanced nations may be forced to discriminate against goods produced under lowered environmental standards in order to prevent the migration of highly polluting industries to complacent, industry-hungry countries.

Somewhat different is the question of the rational use of resources. There is no global policy, but the world will run short of many readily available resources in the not distant future.[39] The United States uses an inordinate percentage—nearly a third—of world fuels and minerals; the suppliers are glad to sell, but the world can point an accusing finger at the United States as chief villain in the depletion of resources. Energy is the key to industrialization; the United States uses 250 times as much energy per capita as typical black African states, but if fuels and minerals become scarce, the LDCs will suffer more than the richer nations, because their more modest imports will be priced above their capacity to pay. The LDCs are also driven to using inferior products; smog from low-grade coal choked Ankara beyond American nightmares. The size of American cars thus becomes relevant for foreign policy. To make the best use of the finite stores of earth, it seems essential that buyers and sellers get together both for commercial purposes (stable prices and markets) and for rational exploitation for the general benefit.

Food is also becoming a scarce resource, renewable only in limited quantity and subject to indefinitely expanding demand. By 1985 the LDCs alone will probably want to import more grain than the United States can export. The food shortage is increasingly to be treated as a global problem, since high costs of food and fertilizer are felt everywhere.[40] The American position in this area is very strong, and food is a powerful diplomatic weapon as population rises faster than agricultural productivity. Philosophical and moral questions may well turn into political ones: how much obligation does America have to furnish food to the starving, or to sell abroad when there is a demand at home (as in the 1973 embargo of many agricultural exports)? Are Americans obligated to eat less meat in order to leave more grain for the needy? Must they try to maintain a grain reserve for the bad years

---

39. Yuan-li Wu, *Raw Material Supply in a Multipolar World*, Crane, Russak, New York, 1973.

40. Cf. Lester R. Brown, *By Bread Alone*, Praeger, New York, 1974.

that are sure to come? It has become an international issue that the United States consumes (because of animal feeding) five times as much grain per capita as the average LDC. Perhaps such obligations may be balanced against the obligations of other nations to provide fuel or minerals at reasonable prices—but the large majority of the peoples of the Third World are short of both food and fuel.

Excessive increase of population is usually regarded as the affair of the country concerned, and efforts to intervene in any way are dismissed as necessarily self-interested—that is, imperialist. But insofar as borders are permeable and the world cherishes a democratic-humanitarian ethos, it is an international concern if any country swells its numbers unreasonably.[41] For equity, restrictions of the birthrate should be universal; if some nations freely burden the world and the future while others limit themselves, it may at least be contended that those that increase their needs biologically have little claim for the charity that would enable them to increase still more. Overreproduction in even a few nations adds seriously to the general problems of understanding and international cooperation, perpetuates or intensifies inequality, and adds to social problems. Unless a high fence of controls can be built between the developed or truly developing nations and the hopelessly poor, there must be achieved, formally or informally, a restriction on the numbers of all. It may ultimately be necessary to reduce world population. Humanity can continue to exist comfortably for a very long time on this planet, it would seem, only if the number of people is substantially cut back. It has been suggested that the suitable ecological carrying capacity of our planet might be about 500 million—the number reached about 1600, and only an eighth of present multitudes.[42]

A very different danger is the misuse of nuclear energy, not only in the arms race of the superpowers but also in the spread of nuclear materials to an ever larger number of powers.[43] The nuclear club was limited to five—coincidentally the permanent members of the Security

---

41. As argued by Mary E. Coldwell, "Population," in *The Future of the International Legal Order* (IV: *The Structure of the International Environment*), ed. Cyril E. Black and Richard A. Falk, Princeton University Press, Princeton, N.J., 1974, pp. 32–67.

42. Lorus and Margery Milne, *The Arena of Life*, Doubleday, Garden City, N.Y., 1971, p. 137.

43. Cf. George Quester, *The Politics of Nuclear Proliferation*, Johns Hopkins Press, Baltimore, 1973; William Epstein, "The Proliferation of Nuclear Weapons," *Scientific American*, 232 (April 1975), 18–33.

Council—from 1968, when the Chinese exploded their first atomic bomb, until May 1974, when India carried out an underground test. A dozen or more other countries could make A-bombs quickly if they desired. Sweden, Argentina, Iran, Rumania, and Japan are among the candidates that have not ratified the Nuclear Nonproliferation Treaty. Israel already reportedly has secretly stockpiled a few nuclear bombs. Brazilian politicians have spoken of the need for atomic explosives for their great country. The Indians excused their spending on nuclear explosives when millions go hungry on the implausible grounds that they were interested only in experimenting with peaceful nuclear explosives, which both the United States and the Soviet Union have found to be of very little utility. But India was rather obviously moved by pride and the desire to keep pace with China. As an Indian minister remarked, "A poor man takes pride in a nation's prestige." [44] To acquire a delivery system is not excessively difficult; cruise missiles are a cheap substitute for intercontinental ballistic missiles (ICBMs).[45] Since nuclear weapons are hardly usable in any case, the mere possession of a few A-bombs or potential A-bombs may be a sufficient psychological boost for a poor nation. There is not much international disapproval; if the United States is entitled to keep adding to its huge arsenal, it cannot very well object to India's humble bid for nuclear status. The obligation not to acquire nuclear weapons in the Nuclear Nonproliferation Treaty was conditional upon movement toward disarmament by the nuclear powers; this effort has been singularly absent. The United States has never modified a weapons program in order to discourage other powers from desiring nuclear arms.[46] On the contrary, the United States rewards the possession of nuclear armaments; this factor was a major reason for the 1971 turn to détente with China.

The spread of nuclear weapons is very dimly regarded by the United States, but the American attitude is not totally negative.[47] India's explosion, although of no immediate military significance, makes that country feel a bit more independent; its nuclear capability may also have some effect in discouraging hypothetical Chinese designs

---

44. *The New York Times*, May 23, 1974, p. 6.

45. Kosta Tsipis, "The Long-Range Cruise Missile, *The Bulletin of Atomic Scientists*, 31 (April 1975), 24.

46. F. A. Long, "Arms Control from the Perspective of the 1970's," *Daedalus*, 104 (Summer 1975), 10.

47. Cf. Spanier, *Games Nations Play*, pp. 254–260; for views of various nationalities, see *Nuclear Proliferation Phase II*, ed. Robert M. Lawrence and Joel Larus, University Press of Kansas, Lawrence, Kans., 1974.

against India. A Chinese second-strike capacity should much reduce or perhaps eliminate the likelihood of Sino-Soviet war. If Romania had a few nuclear rockets secreted in the mountains, it would be less subject to the Brezhnev Doctrine. More broadly, the danger of nuclear war might be least if there were four or five strong nuclear powers. Fear would be diluted by being spread over several potential enemies, and there would be little temptation to seek to destroy a nuclear opponent, because real victory would require destroying all nuclear rivals. For lesser powers, too, the possession of nuclear weapons might conceivably be sobering. Small nuclear arsenals are no real threat to the superpowers and might conceivably contribute to the stabilization of relations among weaker powers. There might be more hesitation—there is already a great deal—to engage in armed conflict. If Israel and Egypt had nuclear weapons targeted upon each other, there might be a stronger inclination to adjure hostilities.[48]

It is the general view, however, that multiplication of nuclear arsenals is dangerous. If many, perhaps irresponsible states have nuclear arms, the chances are greater that a bomb will one day explode because of malfunction, miscalculation, or irrational behavior on the part of leaders or military personnel. There is no certainty that other powers would take such precautions as have the American forces, which have provided, for example, that missiles can be started only if two launch centers and two men in each center act together. Increase of the number of nuclear powers would certainly complicate the arms race; Soviet measures to keep up with China may seem to require a response by the United States. Sane rulers will do anything possible to avoid nuclear risks, but there may be less than fully sane dictators. It cannot be dismissed as an impossibility that a fanatical or disturbed leader of a desperate Third World state might surreptitiously send a rocket against one of the big powers to start a war among them. Or he might frankly engage in nuclear blackmail, like zealots who, to make a point, do not mind blowing themselves up at the same time that they blow up an airliner.

However, as long as the superpowers, and especially the United States, make themselves examples of armament, there is every reason to expect a long-term proliferation of nuclear weapons. The necessary technology is becoming ever more accessible, and nuclear energy is

---

48. For a skeptical view, see Hadley Bull, "Rethinking Non-Proliferation," *International Affairs* (London), 51 (April 1975), 175–189.

increasingly useful because of the high cost of fossil fuels. Uranium used for the generation of electricity produces plutonium; a single reactor may yield 200–500 kg per year, sufficient for fifty to one hundred smallish A-bombs. If controls are 99.9 percent effective, the plutonium escaping controls by 1980 would suffice for one atomic bomb per week.[49] In a few years, civilian reactors in dozens of countries will probably be yielding enough plutonium for several thousand A-bombs or cores of H-bombs annually. Nuclear reactors are modish—although somewhat disappointing in the United States and poorly suited to the LDCs—and states want them even if there is no present economic need. Egypt, for example, wants its reactor although there are ample supplies of cheap natural gas in the neighborhood, and the United States has also promised nuclear reactors to fuel-rich Iran. The industrial powers compete: When the United States declined to permit the export to Brazil of plutonium separation technology (which is not needed for power production but is useful for making explosives), West Germany stepped in with a contract for up to eight reactors costing upwards of $4 billion and including plutonium separation.

Even if all states are virtuous and wish only to contain the nuclear jinni, the perils are still enormous. Security has been lax even in the United States; much less can be expected of poorer, less advanced countries less cognizant of dangers. There are no real safeguards.[50] Radioactive discharges must be expected. The disposal of poisonous wastes presents severe problems in the United States, but it does so much more in other countries. It seems inevitable that unauthorized persons will be able to acquire enough plutonium to menace the world. Not only is plutonium among the worst of poisons—an invisible grain being potentially fatal—but it is not difficult with a bit of learning, some chemical explosives, and a few kilos of plutonium to make a portable A-bomb. Terrorists might then threaten to kill not a few dozen hostages but tens of thousands.[51]

In brief, the potentialities of nuclear fission, like other aspects of the hypertrophy of technology, make it imperative that humanity

---

49. Stockholm International Peace Research Institute, *The Nuclear Age*, MIT Press, Cambridge, Mass., 1975, p. 81.

50. Cf. Adlai E. Stevenson III, "Nuclear Reactors: America Must Act," *Foreign Affairs*, 53 (October 1974), 64–77.

51. Mason Willrich, "Terrorist Keep Out," *The Bulletin of Atomic Scientists*, 31 (May 1975), 12–16; David Krieger, "Terrorists and Nuclear Technology," *The Bulletin of Atomic Scientists*, 31 (June 1975), 28–34.

assure social and political stability with a high degree of responsibility within a sound and harmonious international order.[52] The minimal precaution would seem to be a strengthening of the International Atomic Energy Authority, which in 1975 had all of sixty-seven inspectors.[53] More realistic but less achievable would be the full internationalization of nuclear fuel.[54] The nations can no longer afford to act—no longer do act—as antagonists in a perennial free-for-all for power, the chief interest of each being to get ahead of other nations. Cooperation is essential for prosperity and survival on an ever more integrated "spaceship earth."

STATE AND COMMUNITY

The historical nation-state is outmoded. It can no longer pretend to assure the safety of its citizens or to fill their needs by itself. Its war-making function is obsolete.[55] The sovereign selfishness of the nation-state is contradictory to the requirements of humanity for the management of trade and a monetary system that maximizes the utility of exchanges. The nation-state is incompetent in arresting nuclear danger, controlling pollution, utilizing the oceans, restraining population growth, conserving natural resources, and operating worldwide communications systems. It is superseded by the internationalization of the economy and the international corporation, whose resources may be greater than those of all but the biggest states. The nation-state may endanger or trouble the world community in many ways, from harboring hijackers and producing narcotics to spewing radioactivity into the atmosphere and breeding recklessly. It is doubtful that it can be consonant with a modern integrated world.

The nation-state has lost reality as it has lost its principal functions. The classic nation-states of postmedieval Europe, such as France,

---

52. Bernard T. Feld, "The Menace of a Fission Power Economy," *Science and Public Affairs*, 30 (April 1974), 32, considers the dissemination of nuclear weapons to be the gravest security problem of coming decades.

53. *Newsweek*, July 7, 1975, p. 27.

54. As proposed by Lincoln P. Bloomfield, "Nuclear Spread and World Order," *Foreign Affairs*, 53 (July 1975), 741–755.

55. John H. Herz, "The Rise and Decline of the Territorial State," in *International Politics and Foreign Policy*, 1st ed., ed. James N. Rosenau, Free Press, New York, 1961, pp. 84–85.

Hungary, or Sweden, were cultural entities, with their own languages and literary traditions, created and endowed by history. Today only a few nations (chiefly the United States, the Soviet Union, and China) have much culture that they can properly call their own. Most are bathed in a cosmopolitan industrial culture, mixed with more or less of their shrinking special heritage. A large majority of states lack a functional language of their own; most have only an insignificant historical tradition and a feeble spiritual identity. Even if they desire and have the police power, they cannot shut out the ways and ideas of the advanced world. As much as the huge Soviet Union strives to do so, it cannot exclude "bourgeois" vices, and many millions of Russians listen to foreign radio. The integrity of nationhood is also infringed upon by the satellites that circle unchallenged above all nations. It has become hard to keep secrets, since satellites can photograph anything larger than a few inches across and can show more about natural conditions than the countries concerned can learn. In the homogenized world, the external ceases to be foreign; cultural and political differences narrow; attitudes become worldwide;[56] and foreign policy merges into domestic policy.

The internationalization of society has proceeded apace for many years: the number of persons studying outside their own country, the amount of foreign mail and telecommunications, tourism, and international trade and investment have grown since World War II at rates of 6 to 10 percent yearly.[57] In the world as seen from the window of a jet plane, not to speak of the beautiful globe visible to a spaceship, it is ridiculous to think of states attacking one another in so-called national interest.

With the increased prominence of economic issues, the once clear-cut line between foreign and domestic issues is blurred. Because of interdependence and the instant replay of events anywhere through the world media, every state claims the right to criticize the doings of other states. Many Americans would require that better trade relations with the Soviet Union be conditional on civil rights for Soviet dissidents and freedom of emigration. The response of the Ford administration—that what the Soviet Union does internally is its own business—may have been diplomatic, but it is outdated. Spain has been penalized

---

56. Alex Inkeles, "The Emerging Social Structure of the World," *World Politics,* 27 (July 1975), 492.
57. Ibid., pp. 477–479.

by the European Economic Community (EEC) because of its repression of domestic terrorists.

A more marked example of insistence on the internationalization of what were formerly held to be purely domestic questions is the attack on white rule over black majorities in Africa. Rhodesia and South Africa have for years been principal objects of passionate speeches and many resolutions in the United Nations. In theory, the United Nations is entitled to take an interest on the ground that racial oppression is a threat to the peace; in practice, the nations concern themselves with what they regard as a contravention of the world moral code, and the United States has strongly supported this position. The racial question also crosses national boundaries when American blacks support guerrilla movements in Africa and African embassies maintain contact with black organizations in the United States.

The nation-state is thus obsolete, its foundations undercut, its secular role negated. Yet we live in the age of the sovereign state par excellence. The number of nations has tripled in thirty years, and nations are sacrosanct as never before; since World War II hardly any nation has been subject to a clear-cut attack. Since the weaker states are morally shielded from force, it is increasingly difficult for the powerful states to coerce them by economic or political pressure, and they show themselves to be correspondingly willful on the world stage. The sovereign state is obviously the basis of the international order, and it has a role as essential as ever.

One reason is that the modern nation-state, having partly or entirely lost defensive capabilities, has taken on a wide range of new functions of economic regulation and social guidance, education, and welfare. If there were a perfect world security authority, it would still be necessary to have local administrative agencies. The nation-state is increasingly the expression of organized society when family, tribal, or village controls recede. It is not necessary for this purpose to have any particular set of states with any particular boundaries; but once such states and boundaries exist, they represent the largest single vested interest in modern society, by far the largest employer and perhaps the organization with the greatest stake in stability. As such, they are self-sustaining and are vulnerable only to external violence. With its variety of economic, cultural, and social functions, the modern state also serves as a focus of morale and self-identity while other bonds weaken. The nation-state is something to which people necessarily belong in an age of eroding loyalties; in an increasingly homogeneous world of many ideas but little faith, it is still of some comfort to feel with or fight (nonviolently) for Denmark or Panama. Nationalism is still very real, especially in the Third World, which feels more strongly the need for a banner to hold the people together in the face of the cultural and economic onslaught of the West. Independent sovereignty provides a bit of dignity for those who do not have much else to show.

The greater reason, however, that the sovereign state is as sacrosanct as it is outmoded is that it represents the regnant principle of order. If there were no fixed states, there could be no stability; to ban violence is to decree respect for the various entities that constitute the international system, even while removing the sovereign right of making war. If the principle of nonaggression is to be valid, it must be general; if the rights of one are to be upheld, so must the rights of all be. There can be no coercion—not even economic coercion, according to a United Nations General Assembly resolution, and there is no higher law-making body.

In a slightly different sense, the freedom of sovereign states is the ultimate freedom for people. The fundamental liberty of independent states makes possible other liberties. As long as there is a multiplicity of sovereignties, there will be variety and choice; no despotism can extend indefinitely and no tyranny can be absolute unless it can absolutely seal its borders. Books forbidden in one place can be published in another, and at least a few people everywhere have access to deviant ideas. When there are numerous sovereignties, no universal solutions can simply be decreed. Solutions must come through confrontatation of different views to arrive at consensus.

It is part of the price of this freedom that decisions of any kind may be difficult to reach; a sort of liberum veto in international affairs hinders proceeding against the opposition of any major power. Big powers can do little to coerce small ones if the latter are resolute, although their leaders may be uneducated and irresponsible. There may be a conflict with democratic-humanitarian considerations; it is surely wrong to let the welfare of Mauritius, Malta, or Bahrein weigh seriously against the welfare of a thousand times more people in China, the Soviet Union, or India. The interests of the weak may prevail over those of the strong; for example, it was small Latin American powers that pioneered the idea of a two hundred-mile limit of sovereignty over the oceans. All of the major industrial powers were opposed, yet the poor could prevail because of the general respect for statehood even when stretched over the oceans.

In practice, the rights of sovereignty usually correspond to the interests of the weak and the poor, as, for example, in their power to confiscate great-power assets that fall under their jurisdiction. It is the weak states that most vociferously denounce as imperialistic anything that may appear to trespass on sovereign independence. Since nationalism and sovereignty are the defense of those who lack other defenses, the paradoxical situation arises that it is more acceptable for weak states to be vocally self-assertive, even chauvinistic, than for powerful ones. Guinea or Panama can berate great powers, make demands, and assert claims in a manner that would be deemed outrageous on the part of a rich industrial state.

This problem is overriding: the many states are free, in their sublime sovereignty, to despoil the commons of the world or to endanger or hurt other states, directly or indirectly. No law stands over them, except insofar as they see fit to accept it, and force is practically unusable to discipline them. It is an anomalous situation, yet it could be worse. No alternative is in sight, and it has traditionally been and remains American policy to preserve an open, pluralistic system of independent states.[58] The compartmentalized world permits a variety of approaches, elastic and experimental, with security for diversity. This is the kind of world in which the United States can most comfortably act.

----

58. Frank Tannebaum, *The American Tradition in Foreign Policy*, University of Oklahoma Press, Norman, Okla., 1955.

CHAPTER ELEVEN

World Order

SUPRANATIONAL ORGANIZATION: THE INADEQUACIES OF THE UNITED NATIONS

The obvious way to bridge the gap between the sovereignty of nations and the needs of the community is to join the states in a political association. Such a union has been a long-time dream of civilized humanity, weary of the self-destructive quarrels of free states. It was partially realized in the informal Concert of Europe, which contributed, with many congresses and conferences, to the maintenance of peace in post-Napoleonic Europe.[1] The idea comes naturally to Americans, who successfully fitted the thirteen squabbling colonies into a federal government. Woodrow Wilson and Franklin Roosevelt were typically American in their idealistic universalism.

The establishment of a world body to prevent war and advance the peaceful cooperation of nations was a major American objective in World War II. The United States made concessions to the Russians to secure their cooperation in the United Nations and greeted its founding with typical enthusiasm. It quickly became apparent that the United Nations was not the big answer to world problems, but for a few years it was very useful for American diplomacy. It regularly took a pro-American, anti-Soviet position because the Soviet bloc had only five or six votes and most members of the United Nations were dependent on the United States. Thus the United Nations was helpful in pressing the Soviets to withdraw from Iran in 1946. In the cold war, the United States worked primarily outside of the United Nations to avoid complications of the Soviet veto in the Security Council, but the United Nations was a forum wherein communist purposes were condemned before the delegates of the world. A United Nations commission certified that communist rebels in Greece were being helped from abroad. The Security Council endorsed the defense of South Korea. At this time, it seemed possible to turn the United Nations into a competent peacekeeper and instrument for containment by stretching the charter under the still-born "uniting for peace" resolution of November 1950, which provided that the General Assembly could take over if the Security Council showed itself unable to act in a dispute.

Soon after this cooperation reached its peak in the Korean War,

---

1. For the history of international organizations, see Inis L. Claude, Jr., *Swords into Plowshares: The Problems and Progress of the International Organization*, 4th ed., Random House, New York, 1971.

however, alienation of the United States began. The membership of the United Nations gradually became less amenable to American direction. From 1945 to 1955 only nine states were admitted, but in the post-Stalin relaxation the bars were let down and the organization was flooded with new members: Soviet satellites, neutralist states, and many less developed countries (LDCs) with little interest in American anticommunist purposes. During the Congo crisis in 1960 and afterward, the United Nations fairly closely followed American wishes, although it was no longer feasible to put American troops under the United Nations flag and influence was exerted primarily through the secretariat. But the United Nations was helpless in the India-Pakistan conflicts. The United States firmly steered the world body away from controversies in the Western Hemisphere, such as the Guatamala crisis of 1954 and the crisis in the Dominican Republic in 1965; this avoidance stemmed not only from a desire to keep other powers out of an American sphere but also from an awareness that the United Nations would undoubtedly be unsympathetic. In many other situations, such as the Biafran civil war in Nigeria, the Soviet occupation of Czechoslovakia, and the Cyprus quarrel of 1974, the United Nations showed itself a pitiful non-giant. In 1964, it was in effect decided that the United Nations could take no measures not authorized by the veto-bound Security Council except on the basis of voluntary contributions. In other words, it could in practice undertake peacekeeping operations only when the United States and the Soviet Union were in agreement. It could at best mediate and conciliate. It could not even do this much in the biggest conflict of the postwar period, the Vietnam war, partly because communist China and North Vietnam were not members of the United Nations, partly because other nations were reluctant to become involved. Furthermore, the United States government saw no reason to associate the United Nations with the 1973 settlement in Vietnam.

In the American view, the United Nations lost value because it was increasingly divorced from the realities of power and responsibility under the numerical domination of new, mostly weak, and sometimes irresponsible members. The biggest bloc in the mushrooming General Assembly consisted of the forty-odd black African states; the topics of greatest interest to the assembly became anticolonialism in various aspects and the status of blacks in Rhodesia and South Africa, subjects of secondary concern to the United States. The United States found itself in a minority, sometimes almost alone, in a large number of matters voted on in the United Nations. As the LDCs, supported vociferously by the communists, became more self-assertive in the 1970s, American disenchantment grew. In 1973 the General Assembly affirmed by a vote of 104 to 5 (with 19 abstentions) the "inalienable right to self-determination and independence" of Puerto Rico, despite lack of evidence that the people of that island were dissatisfied with their association with the United States. Sundry resolutions approved any form of violence in the struggle for national liberation, virtually sanctioning terrorism. In that same year, only fifteen states voted with the United States on several important issues. In 1974 South Africa was suspended (perhaps illegally) from the General Assembly over the protests of the Western powers. The Algerian president of the assembly, abandoning conventional neutrality, treated the leader of the Palestine Liberation Organization as a head of state and limited the Israeli right of reply. Israel was subjected to discrimination in the supposedly nonpolitical United Nations cultural body, UNESCO (United Nations Educational, Scientific, and Cultural Organization), to the widespread disgust of intellectuals. Further convincing the United States of the disutility of the United Nations, the assembly in 1974 adopted a declaration on "the establishment of a new international economic order," including the right of expropriation without compensation and the right to form cartels to impose monopoly prices. On November 10, 1975, the Arab bloc secured the passage of a resolution condemning Zionism as a form of racism, by a majority of 72 to 35 with 32 abstentions; this position was regarded by the United States government and American public opinion generally as a travesty of United Nations ideals. On December 5, 1975, a resolution calling for the end of assistance to Israel was passed by a vote of 87 to 1 (the United States) with 17 abstentions. The United Nations had come far from the days of the early 1950s, when the United States hoped to make the General Assembly a sort of world parliament.

The United States made no move to withdraw from the United Nations, since it recognized the necessity for that organization, but the world organization lost much of the American support without which it could be only a hollow sounding board. Formerly, successive presidents rhetorically called the United Nations a pillar of American foreign policy, but it has lost nearly all the importance it once had for Washington. The Congress reduced the American share of the general budget ($253.7 million in 1974) to 25 percent and in some minor ways defaulted on specific obligations to the United Nations. In 1974 the American delegate, in a considered statement (to a nearly empty hall), warned against a "tyranny of the majority" adopting "one-sided, unrealistic resolutions that cannot be implemented"[2] and thereby eroding American support. Third World delegates immediately took on the mantle of democracy, cited the will of the majority, and pointed to the automatic majorities the United States could once summon; it was forgotten that those majorities corresponded to political and economic power. In 1975, Ambassador Daniel P. Moynihan envisioned the dictatorial states, which form a large majority, using the United Nations as a forum to attack the democratic minority.

The United Nations has other serious defects. It has no means of compelling nations to pay dues on assessments. The Soviet Union and its satellites declined to pay their share of the costs of peacekeeping operations after 1956, and other nations joined in default. Now more than a score of nations of varied political complexion are behind in their payments. The only penalty for those who do not pay is that they are not entitled to put their nationals onto the United Nations staff. Places on the United Nations payroll, the world's best-paying civil service jobs, are allotted according to contributions and are highly coveted, especially by persons from poorer countries. The secretariat has little ability to resist political pressures, and the competence of its bureaucracy is at best middling.[3]

More basic is the unreality of representation, the one nation, one vote policy in the General Assembly for states that vary in population by a ratio of as much as 10,000 to 1 and in economic capabilities by an even larger disparity. Half the members pay the minimal dues of 0.02 percent of the budget, and states together paying only 3 percent and comprising 5 percent of the total population of the member states have a two-thirds majority of the vote. The fact that a numerical majority in the United Nations can represent so little deprives that body of much of its authority and leads to many proposals for schemes for other nations to finance, resolutions of more rhetorical than practical significance, and uninhibited use of the world forum for propaganda. The indignation of the United Nations majority is only anti-Western, however; the United Nations takes no position on repressions of minorities by the Soviet Union, China, or Third World dictatorships. A relatively harmless example of the effect of voting strength was the location of the United Nations Environmental Program in Nairobi, a pleasant but inaccessible and expensive city, lacking in facilities and potential staff.

---

2. *Time*, December 16, 1974, p. 45.

3. Seymour M. Finger and John F. Mugna, "The Politics of Staffing the United Nations Secretariat," *Orbis*, 19 (Spring 1975), 117–145.

When meaningless majorities can make big decisions, the major powers are naturally unwilling to confer authority on the world organization. There is no way of altering the situation, because charter revision requires the assent of two-thirds of the members and the five permanent members of the Security Council, and the smaller nations are firmly wedded to the pseudodemocratic principle of "one nation, one vote."

The United Nations is a symbol, not a force. Its peacekeeping role is limited to furnishing a framework for implementation of United States–Soviet agreements. Thus, the United Nations helped implement the resolution of the 1962 missile crisis, and the United Nations presence on Cyprus was helpful although it could not prevent hostilities. It has provided a prestigious and unobjectionable presence for local pacification in Kashmir, the Near East, and sundry lesser trouble spots. When the superpowers were prepared to stop the Yom Kippur war of October 1973, a United Nations resolution called for ending hostilities, and eventually a small United Nations force—not a fighting army but a dissuasive presence, a moral and stabilizing force—separated the belligerents. But when the United States and the Soviet Union were in disaccord, the United Nations was not even notified, and the United States trumpeted its warning by the alert of strategic forces. Disengagement was eventually negotiated not in the United Nations or even under United Nations auspices, but by the shuttle diplomacy of Secretary of State Henry Kissinger.

The judicial arm of the United Nations, the International Court of Justice (successor of the Permanent Court of International Justice, which the United States rejected in the 1920s), suffers from even greater futility. Although all members of the United Nations automatically belong, the Soviet Union is opposed to any such derogation of sovereignty, and the United States in 1946 reserved the right to determine which matters were of a domestic nature and hence outside the court's purview. Hardly anyone calls upon the court to adjudicate anything; it has a case or two, usually minor, every year or so; it has decided on fourteen cases since 1946. In 1973 it was called upon to halt French nuclear tests in the South Pacific, but the French paid no attention to its embargo.

It is not to be taken for granted that the United Nations reduces antagonisms. It can be argued that it rather contributes to acrimony, as the main focal point of the confrontation of the Third World against the industrialized West, and that it is not so much a forum for settling disputes as for attacking the opponents (diplomacy by demagoguery). The delegates take propagandistic positions to gain attention, and extremists set the tone. In one opinion, "use of the United Nations as a battleground, like other hostile acts, contributes to the intensity of disputes and diminishes possibilities for peace." [4] Such use of the United Nations may, however, sublimate quarrels from bullets to rhetoric.

In some ways, nevertheless, the United Nations is a great success. The membership includes almost every functioning state except the divided ones (Vietnam, Korea, and Taiwan). It represents the conscience of the world far more than any other body. It is the chief world forum, and many of its decisions are reached by consensus, not by votes. The result is not specific action but the mobilization of world opinion. [5] The United Nations is a handy root under which numerous special, voluntary organizations operate. It is potentially at least a means of American access to world opinion; more than a hundred foreign ministers may meet in New York, making that city the nearest thing to the capital of the world.

The obvious beneficiaries of the United Nations are the LDCs; in the General Assembly and committees their voices are heard as nowhere else and acquire prestige from the world body. The resolutions they pass are heard, even if frequently not concretely obeyed. Many of its agencies are designed to serve the LDCs. UNCTAD (United Nations Conference on Trade and Development) particularly functions as caucus for the LDCs, with its own staff and committees. The United Nations gives technical assistance that enables the LDCs to bargain more effectively with multinational corporations and serves as a catalyst for policy agreement in this and other areas. [6]

The chief utility of the United Nations lies in its incarnation of the principle of sovereignty. It is not a superstate, but a meeting ground where states assert their national drives. It upholds their rights and dignity and the principle of free debate and negotiation. It exposes representatives of all nations to the norms of an open society and to world expectations. It is antimilitaristic in outlook. It represents a system through which at least moral pressure can be applied against transgressors. It stands, however ineffectually, for freedom of information and human rights. Dissidents in the Soviet Union continually cite

---

4. Abraham Yoselson and Anthony Geglione, *A Dangerous Place: The United Nations as a Weapon in World Politics,* Grossman Publishers, New York, 1974, p. 157.

5. Arthur Lall, "Some Thoughts on the U.N. General Assembly," *Journal of International Affairs,* 29 (Spring 1975), 66–67.

6. Robert O. Keohane and Van Doorn Oom, "The Multinational Firm and International Regulation," *International Organization,* 29 (Winter 1975), 200.

its noble statements, especially its Universal Declaration of Human Rights, to which Soviet representatives abroad claim they adhere.

There is no likelihood that the United Nations can be improved substantially; it is more a barrier than a step to a stronger world body. There is no widely acceptable scheme for reorganizing it, nothing better than the illogical principle of equality of votes, with a few nations occupying privileged status by prerogative. Many writers find a world government of some kind indispensable for security or ecological or other needs.[7] But unless a world state is established by the victor of a nuclear war (in which one side surrenders to spare humanity), there is little prospect of any world organization that can enforce decisions against any but the weakest powers. In any event, a world superstate would be in many ways undesirable. It would probably be inefficient and, insofar as it was strong, oppressive. It would signify further undesirable centralization. It might lead to new conflicts if it infringed upon the interests of major states. The idea derives from the hypertrophy of the state, and it is in a sense backward-looking. The United Nations does not point the way to the future. There is no political means of overcoming world anarchy.

NONPOLITICAL SUPRANATIONAL ORGANIZATION

It is possible that the political approach to world order is basically misguided. The ambitious and celebrated attempt to cap the nation-state system with a security organization has had no success; the United Nations and other international political organizations have declined in use and importance.[8] But ad hoc international organization for concrete purposes has flourished; the nonpolitical side of the United Nations, which received slight attention at the time of its founding, has proved by far the more successful. Many subsidiary or affiliated organizations carry on vital labors of global improvement. These groups include the International Labor Organization; the Food and Agricultural Organization; the United Nations Educational, Scientific, and Cultural

---

7. Cf. Richard A. Falk, *A Study of Future Worlds,* Free Press, New York, 1975; Victor Ferkiss, *The Future of Technological Civilization,* George Braziller, New York, 1974; Louis R. Beres, *Transforming World Politics,* University of Denver Press, Denver, 1974.

8. Abraham Chayes, "Nuclear Arms Control after the Cold War," *Daedalus,* 104 (Summer 1975), 23.

Organization; the World Health Organization; the International Refugee Organization; the International Monetary Fund; the International Civil Aviation Organization; the United Nations Children's Emergency Fund, and about two dozen others. These agencies are all entirely voluntary and self-governing; most of them benefit the needier nations directly, and many of them have proved effective. For example, the World Health Organization has carried on a successful global war against smallpox. However, many of these agencies have suffered politicalization (and loss of vital American support) over the Palestinian question.

The United Nations makes itself nonpolitically useful in many other ways. It is the principal gatherer and publisher of global statistics; it produces hundreds of thousands of pages of reports, speeches, and sundry documents every year. A considerable amount of development assistance flows through United Nations channels, and there is pressure to increase it. United Nations agencies handle emergency relief operations and assist refugees. The United Nations Development Program spends some $300 million yearly for many projects in more than a hundred countries. If the population problem of the LDCs is to be solved, it seems that the United Nations will have to be a large factor; it is taken for granted that international action for environmental and resources management should be under United Nations auspices. In December 1972, the General Assembly decreed the establishment of a United Nations university, consisting of a network of postgraduate research and training schools working on the growing number of problems touching mankind as a whole.

While most United Nations–affiliated agencies are more or less controlled by the LDCs (with the qualification that contributions are voluntary, so the agency may have to take major donors into account), some of its agencies are dominated by the richer nations. One such agency is the World Bank, the purpose of which is to provide capital for development. Voting is by shares subscribed, so that it is representative not of the semifiction of national sovereignty but of the reality of wealth, and the United States has regularly named its president. The LDCs press either for more representation in the World Bank or for transfer of its functions to a regular United Nations body, which they could dominate. With an authorized capital of $27 billion, the World Bank makes supposedly sound loans for projects high on the recipient nation's priority list. It often tries to make its funds go further by forming consortiums of lenders, and it has a field staff to survey problems and prospects and to inspect ongoing programs. Its current president,

Robert McNamara, carried out a small revolution in Bank policy, shifting emphasis from roads and electric works to the alleviation of poverty, going more into agriculture, education, and population control; his main concern has been income distribution.[9]

Part of the World Bank complex is the International Development Association, which makes loans to countries with annual per capita incomes under $300 for long periods with no interest—that is, virtual gifts from funds subscribed by the wealthier of its one hundred members. The United States has been supplying 40 percent of the World Bank's yearly quota of $800 million. Another associate is the International Finance Corporation, which makes loans to private enterprises for purposes that should be beneficial as well as profitable. The Organization for Economic Cooperation and Development (OECD) also fosters economic development. This is the successor to the Organization for European Economic Cooperation, which was originally erected to coordinate and administer Marshall Plan aid for Europe and was broadened and transformed in 1961 as its European task was fulfilled. Including not only Europe but also the United States, Canada, and Japan, the OECD represents 20 percent of world population, 60 percent of industrial production, and 70 percent of world trade. It is a consultative-coordinating body, a sort of committee of the industrial countries, with subcommittees on environment, economic and trade policy, and development (the Development Assistance Committee). It deals with tariffs, shipping, and a multitude of technical questions. It also coordinates policies of the industrial nations toward the LDCs; for example, it supports investment insurance to encourage the flow of capital to the LDCs. Its chief means of action is the dissemination of information.

Other international organizations of the United Nations family, chiefly the International Monetary Fund (IMF) and the General Agreement on Tariffs and Trade (GATT), have the broad function of facilitating international trade. They are consequently of interest to all nations for which foreign trade is important, and they are nearly as all-embracing as the United Nations; only the majority of Marxist-Leninist nations abstain. The IMF and the GATT have contributed greatly to the liberalization and expansion of international trade in the postwar period. Before World War II there was very little effort to regulate

---

9. Andrew Boyd, "A Fresh Look at the World Bank," *Vista*, 8 (June 1973), 24–32.

international economics, and the vicious trade wars and currency instability of the 1930s visibly contributed to depression, political unrest, the growth of fascism, and the outbreak of war. Hence, shortly before the end of the war, the victorious powers, meeting at Bretton Woods, New Hampshire, set up the IMF to support currency convertibility and followed it with the GATT to foster multilateral trade. The GATT is a sort of trading club, whose members commit themselves to following rules, the heart of which is nondiscrimination. It is a framework for tariff bargaining and for the settlement of trade disputes; its main function is stability. It rarely takes votes but operates by consultation and consent of major countries. Meetings may be held once or twice yearly.[10] It has a small staff, and it sets up committees and working groups as suitable.

The IMF, a monetary fund contributed by members according to quotas based on national income, is more active. Voting power is apportioned according to investment; twenty-five industrial countries have 75 percent of the votes, the American share having declined from 35 percent to 21 percent. Major decisions require a four-fifths majority, so the United States has veto power. As is usual with such organizations, however, decisions are usually made by consultation among the major powers, particularly the so-called Group of Ten. The IMF is something of a club of the rich West, and there is pressure to admit others, both the oil-rich nations and the other LDCs, to a larger share in its governance.

The fund helped to stabilize exchange rates by permitting members in difficulty to buy needed foreign currencies for their own currency up to fixed amounts. The gold and currency assets were supplemented in 1969 by special drawing rights (SDRs) in the amount of $9.5 billion. This synthetic "paper gold" was detached from both gold and the dollar in 1974 and made a composite of sixteen leading currencies. The IMF makes part of these reserves available as loans to LDCs, which press for more drawing rights—that is, loans, preferably unconditional; this demand is widely supported because it seems to be a relatively painless (although inflationary) means of helping. The code of the IMF prohibits restrictive and discriminatory practices, and it has used its power to deny loans to emphasize its advice about many aspects of financial management, including budgetary policy and inflation control.

---

10. Robert E. Baldwin and David A. Kay, "International Trade and International Relations," *International Organization*, 29 (Winter 1975), 102.

There are also many special and ad hoc organizations, such as multinational commissions to study energy problems, raw materials, international financial needs, and the like; most of these groups are formed primarily to meet the demands of the LDCs. In addition, numerous regional organizations have been formed, especially for trade and developmental cooperation. Some, such as the European Economic Community (EEC), have been notably successful; others, such as the efforts to emulate the EEC in Central America, South America, and Africa, have been paralyzed by national animosities. Regional organizations have the advantage over international ones in that loyalties may be more easily shifted to the former. Africans have a "we" feeling about the Organization of African Unity, which encompasses all African states except Rhodesia and South Africa; the Africans have a set of concerns of their own. But nations are not much more inclined to surrender sovereignty to regional than to universal groupings, and regionalism does not seem to be the wave of the future. New groups are not coming forward, and people seem no longer to have great hope for those that were once formed in idealistic expectation. Functional international groups seem to make more sense.

The scene is also crowded with a host of nongovernmental international organizations that have no power but do have a multitude of functions. At the beginning of this century they were insignificant, but in the postwar period they have been growing in numbers at about 5 percent per annum.[11] Now they number close to three thousand, many working cooperatively with governments, some supported by governments, all in their way contributing to the internationalization of the world. The latest and possibly most important contribution to the general movement away from the nation-state is the proliferation of multinational corporations, most of them firmly based and owned in a single leading industrial nation. Labor unions, too, increasingly take on an international role.[12]

The web of interdependence becomes ever more constrictive, but nation-states are not to be coerced into joining any organizations that visibly detract from their sovereignty. They are willing to yield only bits here and there for reasons of advantage, while their power to control events is slowly eroded and boundaries become less effective.

---

11. Alex Inkeles, "The Emerging Social Structure of the World," *World Politics,* 27 (July 1975), 479.

12. Roy Godson, "American Labor's Continuing Involvement in World Affairs," *Orbis,* 19 (Spring 1975), 93–116.

There is no inclination to promote supranational agencies for their own sake or that of the international system, but rather only to accept them as seems necessary. States do not yield sovereignty in general or in principle but only for specific needs, and the concessions are always theoretically revocable.[13] The standard procedure of international organizations becomes consultation with interested parties, representation for those affected by policies, and informal decision making.

The world order is less de jure than de facto, and states cherish their ultimate rights stubbornly even if these are in practice unusable. International organization becomes a means not of overriding the nation-states but of fulfilling their requirements, and the preservation of independence is served by its practical limitation through voluntary and more or less informal arrangements that sidestep the question of sovereignty. The world thus seems to become subject by what has been called "incremental functionalism"[14] to many little "world governments" in special areas, while the sovereign states retain the powers of police and taxation, formally supreme but deprived of much of their content. This arrangement has advantages: smaller international organizations are likely to be more efficient and more responsive to their clientele,[15] and together they may make an increasingly pacific and cooperative international system.

COMMUNITY BUILDING

Conceivably there is no answer to the problem of world order, just as certain mathematical exercises like the squaring of the circle are inherently insoluble. But if there is a way to a safer international system more capable of coping with the multitude of problems confronting the nations, it would seem to lie through functional international organization and the development of better understanding and appropriate values in the intellectually integrated world. The nations cannot agree on a world constitution curtailing their freedom of action, but they can agree on many mutually and multilaterally beneficial arrangements,

13. Cf. Richard N. Gardner, "The Hard Road to World Order," *Foreign Affairs,* 52 (April 1974), 556–576.

14. Richard A. Falk, *A Study of Future Worlds,* Free Press, New York, 1975, p. 73.

15. Eugene B. Skolnikoff, *The International Imperatives of Technology,* University of California International Studies Center, Berkeley, 1972, p. 166.

the violations of which would be contrary to their interests. They cannot find security in armaments, nor can they bargain their way to disarmament by horse-trading reductions of missiles, submarines, and other weapons; they may be able to convince themselves that overkill is a poor investment. Leaders will not decide one fine day to forget about coercive power and playing the international relations game, but they may become increasingly preoccupied with commodity agreements, investments, the complexities of sharing ocean resources, worldwide epidemics, international telecasting, and the like.[16]

It may be that a new world order can best evolve elementally by countless reactions to changed circumstances. But it would be well if diplomats thought less in terms of political gain, more in terms of changing the character of relations between states.[17] Old ideas of national security are meaningless in the era of new and strange perils generated by the uncontrolled march of applied ingenuity; political ways and institutions, international as well as domestic, lag far behind new realities. As Garrett Hardin put it, the earth is a spaceship without a captain on an uncharted journey, a journey of perils for the 4 billion crew members.

Least of all are military means appropriate for the new needs of foreign policy. What is required is not unilateral disarmament but the maintenance of military strength for defense only (not for hope of political profit) and the downgrading of the military dimension of foreign policy. The reduction of armaments is desirable if only for security; the United States is probably safer in taking the lead in discouraging the arms race than in striving to maintain supremacy. It is impossible to ignore the guns in the world or to go unarmed in the lawless community, but the better hope, perhaps the only hope, for safety lies in deemphasizing arms. This change in emphasis would lessen fear and suspicion of the United States and would consequently raise American influence and make more effective whatever programs might be undertaken. It is notable that Nikita Khrushchev, in the reflective wisdom of retirement, saw this more clearly than do some American statesmen (or his successors). In his terms:

> If our enemies want to go on inflating their military budgets, spending their money right and left on all kinds of senseless things,

---

16. For a plea for a postwarfare international system, see David V. Edwards, *Creating a New World Order,* David McKay, New York, 1973.

17. As suggested by Edwards, p. 10.

then they'll be sure to lower the living standards of their own people. . . .

If we were unilaterally to curtail the accumulation of military means, we would be demonstrating that in socialist countries the interests of the people and the government are one and the same, while in capitalist countries the government represents only the interests of those who produce the means of destruction. Our good example will be noticed by the working class in capitalist countries, and it will give fighters for peace a chance to conduct mass propaganda in their countries.

By taking the initiative in scaling down the arms race, we will also appeal to the intelligentsia in the West and all over the world.[18]

The problem of world order is basically a problem of social psychology, a matter of climate of opinion or civilized consensus. It is a matter of standards of conduct, attitudes, and values, the purposes for which national leaders are driven in their dealings with other states. As former Mexican President Luis Echeverria said in a narrower context, "I do not believe that anyone, speaking objectively, can believe that an atomic equilibrium is going to insure peace indefinitely. Only a new general consciousness can do that." [19]

The international order operates, or might operate, like a band of stateless primitives, who observe norms of conduct without specific compulsion because they are taken for granted, part of the generally accepted culture.[20] In view of the unachievability of universal political organization, the impracticality of compulsion, and the extreme difficulty of legalistic solutions by agreement, voluntary cooperation is the chief hope of regulating conduct. There can be no disarmament, no control of nuclear testing, no halting of poisonous wastes or a hundred other problems unless the sovereign states so desire. The only prospective way of overcoming terrorism or stopping nuclear proliferation is through general disapproval such that it would seem unrewarding to states to be known to promote terrorism or to undertake essentially unusable nuclear programs. The only likely way of checking pollution

---

18. *Khrushchev Remembers: The Last Testament,* Little, Brown, Boston, 1974, p. 539.

19. *The New York Times,* January 8, 1975.

20. Cf. Roger D. Masters, "World Politics as a Primitive Political System," in *International Politics and Foreign Policy,* 2nd ed., ed. James N. Rosenau, Free Press, New York, 1969, pp. 104–118.

of the oceans is by the establishment of generally respected and approved international standards by agreements that no civilized state would transgress. The backing for such international law as exists is psychological, and new international law must equally have a basis in broadly accepted attitudes and expectations of proper conduct.

This view may appear utopian, but at least outwardly there is general agreement among virtually all world leaders (with the exception of some Marxist-Leninist states) on the reality of interdependence and the need for cooperation. The international order functions fairly well in some ways on the basis of general understanding. Long ago piracy and the slave trade were abolished, although both were profitable to some states. Without compulsion, trademarks are almost everywhere protected. Diplomatic amenities have been observed even in bitter wars. Territorial aggrandizement was for centuries taken for granted to be a great good, and it was still the passion of the have-not powers in the 1930s; but no major state today acknowledges any desire to seize anything. The idea, sometimes brought up, that an irresponsible regime might stir up trouble by firing a missile deceptively at an unsuspecting target seems to be one of the less real dangers. A decade elapsed between the entry of the fifth member into the atomic club and that of the sixth, despite the fact that many nations had adequate technology for the beautiful weapon. India presented its nuclear test apologetically, assuring the world of its peaceful character. The world economic order has operated rather well, with much consultation, few disruptive actions, and no trade wars or monetary maneuvers such as those that plagued the 1930s. The GATT and the IMF have played useful roles, although several states, including the United States, have unilaterally broken their rules. Even the severe disequilibria of the American balance of payments in the early 1970s and the strains of the petroleum crisis evoked very little of the old economic nationalism on the part of leading states.

What may vaguely be called world opinion or a sense of the expectations of civilized society is likely never to be the sole factor in deciding the responses of nations. It is usually only part of the atmosphere within which decisions are made—sometimes an element of calculation, more often an unconscious influence. The opinion of the global village probably had something to do, for example, with Cuba's entering into and enforcing an antihijacking convention, and with Arab states' foreswearing public encouragement for international terrorists. By 1975 it had become rather difficult for terrorists, after securing an airplane, to find any country willing to receive them. Even the minority government of South Africa, which had seemed resolved to resist any concession that might lead to the loss of status of the ruling elite, was urged to flexibility and concessions by nonviolent pressures, tried to cultivate better relations with blacks within and without the country, and asked for the world's patience while policies were gradually altered. Even such a large and self-willed state as the Soviet Union, although shielded by censorship and ideology, has seemed inclined to bend. A landmark was the commutation, because of world outcry, of death sentences against Jewish hijackers in 1970. The release of tens of thousands of emigrants yearly was also a concession to foreign (largely American) opinion that would have been unthinkable a generation earlier, although the desire for commercial advantages was probably more operative here than the urge to respectability. More striking was the Soviet retreat after bulldozing an unofficial art show in September 1974; in the face of publicity, authorities permitted what was practically the first uncensored art show in forty years, "four hours of freedom," a significant crack in the edifice of Soviet controls.

At present, none of the 140-odd states behaves in a wholly irresponsible manner. No country is prepared openly to make a business of narcotics, inviting as this might be financially. An uneducated and violent-tempered man like Idi Amin of Uganda, although happy to hurl insults at the United States, consults with and listens to fellow African presidents. The industrial nations have for decades abstained from the kind of reprisals that might start a trade war in the old style, and it indicates considerable respect for the international order that voluntary restrictions on the use of gold stocks are faithfully observed. Foreign protests have led the Japanese to apologize for whaling and to curtail it and the Finns to halt the dumping of chemical wastes in the Baltic. Influence is not always of the kind theorists might expect; it seems that the strongest pressure against apartheid in South Africa is not arms embargoes, economic sanctions, or denunciations in world forums, but ostracism from world sports.[21]

For the best use of resources, economic growth, investment, price stability, the transfer of technology, and access to markets and materials, it is necessary for the nations to accommodate their interests in the worldwide web; the rewards for belonging are equivalent to the penalties for antisocial behavior. It does not require any great degree

---

21. Neil Ulman, "South Africa's Winds of Change," *The Wall Street Journal*, August 26, 1975, p. 16.

of rationality for leaders of major countries to become convinced of the patent need for cooperation. Ideas travel fast and far, and the breadth and intensity of contact are such that a single world society may be on the way within a relatively short time.

There can be no grand policy or scheme of salvation, no crash program to solve the world's ills. There is no single necessary design for foreign policy in the complexities of the modern world but a set of many little policies, mostly multilateral and nonpolitical, to be coordinated by a general approach, an endeavor to accommodate divergent and shared interests and to achieve through agreement what an individual state cannot achieve.[22] Both leadership and consent are necessary, less to create a new comity of nations than to permit such a comity to grow up in response to the needs of the peoples. Curiously, American foreign policy operated in about this way in the halcyon days of noninvolvement in world politics.

----

22. Atlantic Council Policy Papers, *Beyond Diplomacy: Decision-Making in an Interdependent World,* Atlantic Council of the U.S., Washington, D.C., 1975.

CHAPTER TWELVE

Directions

If any power is to lead the world toward a more promising international order, it can be none other than the United States. No real competition is in sight. The Soviet Union is ideology-bound and has a narrow political system. Although some of its themes have been widely influential, it lacks the flexibility, creativity, and productive capacity to play a strong positive part. It has not done so at any time; even in the Third World, it has been a follower of trends, not a generator of movements. China is still very poor and also suffers political narrowness, while shutting itself off from the outside even more tightly than the Soviet Union. At best, it may serve as a model in some ways for the less developed countries. Japan is still a follower with little political will but may emerge as a world leader in a decade or two. If western Europe could find political unity, it might recover much of the longtime eminence of Europe in world affairs; however, an organization capable of making and pursuing a common foreign policy for Europe is distant, if not a mirage.

The economic and political preeminence of the United States has declined rather steadily ever since 1945, when the United States manufactured the bulk of the world's industrial production. The United States can no longer act as unchallengeable economic and political leader—at one time it almost seemed the sole authority—of the noncommunist world. It must increasingly consult and take others into account, especially in economic affairs. Militarily, too, the Soviet Union has come gradually closer to parity. The United States remains, however, by far the largest economic power. If there are to be amendments to the world trade and monetary system, they must probably come from American initiative; it is impossible for them to come without the backing of the United States. Militarily, the United States stands about as far above other powers (except the Soviet Union) as it did a decade or two ago, and it alone can make itself felt around the globe. Diplomatically, too, it stands out, having partially recovered standing lost in the Vietnam affair. Strange as it may seem to many Americans, their country is uniquely respected; still stranger, in view of voluminous revelations of misdoings in the executive branch, the United States is unique among major powers in commanding general confidence. As Secretary of State Henry Kissinger said after the 1975 Israeli-Egyptian accord, "Only the United States is trusted by both parties." [1] The pact was possible only because both sides had confidence

---

1. *Newsweek*, September 15, 1975, p. 32.

in the integrity of the United States and its representatives, its good purposes, and its faithfulness to commitments.

Not only has the United States exercised political leadership; for better or worse, it is the world's great trend setter. It is the center of action and world attention, the most admired as well as the most envied and resented of nations. It holds the lead on the frontiers of change and innovation, the truly revolutionary power in the world.[2] The United States is not only in the vanguard of technical innovation, introducing new products and new ways of production; it is also the biggest source of intellectual innovation. It is the center of the world informational nervous system. It sets the intellectual trends of the world, with Europe and Japan following the American lead and the Soviet Union well behind. Concern with population growth, with pollution and environmental protection, and with other preoccupations of the new age came from America, as did the new left and hippyism. Americans might prefer tranquility and stability; but America is the world's great stirrer, the prototype of the postindustrial nation, the potential chief mover of the modernization of the international system. The idea that the United States has a special part to play came into disrepute in the 1970s for the good reason that the direction the United States was taking had led, and seemed likely in the future to lead, into counterproductive military adventures. But American leadership has not ceased to be appropriate when it is exercised in an essentially American way, stressing real cultural and economic strengths and proceeding in harmony with more specially American traditions.

Secretary Kissinger has argued ". . . that a new international system is painfully being formed, that the system that was created in the fifties is in fundamental flux, and that the seventies will be seen in retrospect as a period of an emerging new relationship among most of the power centers."[3] But the "new international system" can hardly be a new political structure; the essence of the "emerging new relationship" is the reduction of the political or power-oriented ingredient of international relations, the switch from competitive game to problem solving.

This tendency has been the dominant, although not overwhelming

---

2. A high evaluation of the American potential is given by Jean-François Revel, *Without Marx or Jesus: The New American Revolution Has Begun,* Doubleday, Garden City, New York, 1971; and by Zbigniew Brzezinski, *Between Two Ages: America's Role in the Technetronic Era,* Viking Press, New York, 1970.

3. *The New York Times,* March 22, 1974, p. 10.

one of the past few years. The State Department has become much aware of interdependence, environmental problems, and the like. But much of the militaristic cast, which came to a climax in the purposeless war in Vietnam, remains. This emphasis, which was increasingly disconsonant with modern trends and needs, was associated with a high degree of American dominance and unilateralism. It was politically easy and appealing, since diplomats, including Secretary Kissinger, thought of the world in primarily conflictual terms of allies and opponents, a contest wherein American strength gave the United States an easy win.[4]

There are many costs of power-oriented policies, and these costs grow with the erosion of United States superiority.[5] The costs include not only the obvious ones—budgetary expenses and international tensions—but many social costs at home. The time and attention of American leaders diverted from domestic needs to foreign quarrels must also be counted. There has also been a psychological burden on American efforts to act in nonsecurity areas; the use or threat of violence undermines the ability of the United States to exercise persuasion and create an atmosphere of confidence and cooperation. Every action that gives cause or excuse to view the United States as unscrupulous or imperialistic raises suspicion of other American purposes, however generous these may conceivably be; efforts to help countries stop procreating themselves deeper into poverty or to preserve some freedom for oceanography are automatically branded as imperialistic.

To turn away from old-line power politics requires little sacrifice except in the realm of machismo, because American efforts to assert the United States in power politics have seldom been very rewarding; sundry interventions, from World War I to Cambodia, were undertaken in naive optimism and have turned sour. It also becomes apparent that the United States is not prepared to sustain the role of gendarme. American society is too fragmented, and in a world where only limited wars are bearable, there is a basis of support only for wars seen as really necessary—that is, unlimited war. "Most foreign involvement does not unify the country or distract it from its problems but exacerbates [a whole series of] divisions."[6] The visceral reaction is inappropriate if not dangerous.

---

4. John D. Montgomery, "The Education of Henry Kissinger," *Journal of International Affairs,* 29 (September 1975), 55.

5. Robert Griffin, "Three Models of the Future," *International Organization,* 29 (Winter 1975), 57.

6. Earl C. Ravenal, "Who Needs It?," *Foreign Policy,* 18 (Spring 1975), 86–90.

A shift of emphasis from power and security orientation, from the old issues to the new, is easier because it would mean a reversion toward the American tradition prior to the grand interventionist excursus. This tradition has been scornful of power politics and has regarded the quarrels of states as essentially futile and insignificant in comparison with the development of the United States as a model,[7] Democratic countries are well advised not to try to operate in the ways more appropriate for authoritarian or dictatorial polities, but rather in the ways in which the democracies excel; for the United States perhaps more than any other nation this approach to foreign affairs is "consistent with the national character and traditional values of the society"[8] and promises to move with the world.

The alternative is not a definite stance toward the world, an integrated foreign policy in the traditional sense, but a set of many policies united by the need to meet global problems. There is no longer, as there was in 1940 and 1948, a single issue on which to focus.[9] There exists no positive consensus calling for drastic action in any area, only a desire for ameliorative steps. There is no clear agreement on attitudes toward the Soviet Union, toward the Arabs, or toward Europe, while the things that are to be done regarding arms, the balance of payments, the monetary system, and relations with the oil cartel, are too various to be tied together in a single framework of policy.

There may, however, be some guiding principles, including the restriction of commitments to resources that the country is prepared to invest, greater consideration for the psychological effects of actions, respect for mutuality of relations, and the eschewing of tactics that would stain the reputation of the nation if publicized, as they are nearly certain to be. The sounder aim is not to impose the American will but to create favorable conditions, not to enforce a law but to accommodate interests and satisfy needs. Leadership may be based not only on strength but also on taking into account the views and needs of others.

A forward-looking foreign policy should be easier, too, because it means turning away from the kind of endeavor in which the United States has been relatively less successful toward those fields in which

---

7. David V. Edwards, *Creating a New World Politics*, David McKay, New York, 1973, p. 11.

8. J. William Fulbright, *The Arrogance of Power*, Random House, New York, 1966, p. 265.

9. Ernest R. May, *"Lessons" of the Past: The Use and Misuse of History in American Foreign Policy*, Oxford University Press, New York, 1973, p. 147.

the nation has excelled: the economic and the cultural. As Ian Swart of the Royal Institute of International Affairs said, "The United States as a center of influence, the way in which its economy is run, the way in which it will conduct itself as a buyer and seller of resources, are of far more importance than the panoply of international negotiations and international relationships." [10] The cultural impact of the United States is, of course, incalculable but is probably even more important than its economic impact. The image that the United States projects is or could be its greatest asset. As Arthur Schlesinger, Jr. views it, "Our most abiding influence in the world has come not from arms and money, but from the intermittent sense ordinary people in other lands have had that America is on their side." [11]

The basis of American world leadership lies in productivity, science, and creativity, the areas of excellence of the open society; the American influence on the world has been and doubtless will continue to be much more the work of unofficial than official America, of business people, artists, and intellectuals rather than diplomats or generals. To exert influence the government does not have to do much or spend much. It may not be able to do much for what is essentially the work of unofficial persons and organizations. Economic policies are probably too complex and multifarious for effective coordination with or by the government, which cannot even pull together its own nonsecurity policies.[12] The state can perhaps do no more than endeavor to guide (somewhat as the Japanese government does) the activities of American firms along lines congenial to national purposes while diminishing abuses and perhaps to cooperate with the less developed countries to ensure that the multinational corporations serve the world order. It is likewise not certain that much expansion of a bureaucratic information agency is necessary or desirable—although other nations spend relatively larger amounts—but much could be done to make the more attractive and useful aspects of American culture more available by assistance to private and semiprivate enterprise. In order better to project the image of a decent, peace-loving nation concerned for the general welfare, the government need do little that it would not do in any case.

The United States cannot claim to know what is best for everyone,

---

10. *Time,* August 26, 1974, p. 13.
11. *The Wall Street Journal,* June 3, 1975, p. 22.
12. Maxwell Taylor, "The Exposed Flank of National Security," *Orbis,* 18 (Winter 1975), 1012.

but it has some ideas of the kind of world order and political outlook that gives most promise for the future. There has been a tendency to identify security interests with conservative authoritarian governments and to deal with states as entities without reference to morality.[13] This procedure has been costly in terms of the reputation of the United States, which seems hypocritical and self-serving, and in terms of the promotion of values for which America claims to stand. There is no excuse for interference in the domestic politics of other states, and it should be possible to treat and trade with all. The United States can well afford, however, to stand reasonably for its ideals and to favor those whose behavior accords with those ideals. The United States cannot, in any case, choose whether or not to influence the world; it can only choose to some extent how it brings its influence to bear.

A measured moral approach to international affairs is desirable not only because of the possibility that basic American ideals—concern for rights, legality, and a humane social order—may be relevant to world order but also because these ideals are relevant to the United States. Nothing would be more salutary for American society, the troubles of which need no elaboration, than to be able to utilize its special assets for the benefit of humanity and play a positive and inspiring role in the evolution of civilization. Some Americans seem to feel that a militant posture is necessary as a tonic for the social order, since a sense of contest helps to give direction to the national life. A recent writer on foreign policy mentioned the possible desirability of exciting "a more intense anticommunist fervor, a fervor which since World War II has been a crucial element in holding the American people together in common purpose." [14] Anticommunism has long since lost utility, but a new conception of a manifest destiny for the republic would be healthy, especially for the intellectuals alienated by long deviations from what were supposedly American ideals, and for the youths educated to cynicism about the national purpose.

There is still ample need for pacific American intervention. The disorderly international order that has grown up spontaneously patently requires reshaping through the peaceful means that are possible and appropriate and that the United States is by capability and background best equipped to employ. Not only is American national

13. Laurence Stern, "How We Failed in Cyprus," *Foreign Policy*, 19 (Summer 1975), 77.

14. James R. Cobbledick, *Choice in American Foreign Policy: Options for the Future*, Thomas Y. Crowell, New York, 1970, p. 84.

interest bound to the well-being of the world, in that America must suffer if humanity as a whole suffers and very likely must fail if mankind fails; there is also some moral obligation on the part of the world's most powerful nation, which makes its presence felt everywhere (in neocolonialism, according to the less developed countries), to take the lead through the modern crisis. The many dangers to the prosperity of the human species must overwhelm their frail makers unless people can solve the prior problem of order with freedom on the world level.

It would be an error to expect too much. The United States will probably continue to lumber unsteadily into the future, usually trying to do little better than to avoid falling into a pit. But in a world that is largely impoverished, where freedom of information and real political rights survive in only a small minority of countries, the United States should have as special a destiny as when it inspired the world's reformers, two centuries ago, with its vision of a new order. It is more difficult now than it was then to imagine how the world's problems can be solved unless the United States takes the lead in building the future.

Bibliography

There are several bibliographies on American foreign policy, including Samuel F. Bennis and Grace G. Griffin, *Guide to the Diplomatic History of the United States, 1775–1921* (Government Printing Office, Washington, D.C. 1935) and Elmer Plischke, *American Foreign Relations: A Bibliography of Official Sources* (Johnson Reprint Co., New York, 1966, 1955). Significant more recent works are to be found in *American Defense Policy since 1945: A Preliminary Bibliography*, compiled by John Greenwood, ed. Geoffrey Kemp, Clark Murdock, and Frank L. Simonie, University Press of Kansas, Lawrence, 1973, and *The Foreign Affairs 50-Year Bibliography: New Evaluations of Significant Books on International Relations, 1920–1970*, ed. Byron Dexter, Bowker, New York, 1972. The Council on Foreign Relations has also published bibliographies covering 1919–1932, 1932–1942, 1942–1952, 1952–1962, and 1962–1972. Various American foreign policy textbooks also include bibliographies; that of Cecil V. Crabb, Jr., *American Foreign Policy in the Nuclear Age*, 3rd ed., Harper and Row, New York, 1972, is especially extensive. Note is consequently taken here only of books published since 1970; of course, only a minor fraction of the many works potentially useful to the student of foreign relations can be included. This listing also omits many works cited in the text.

Journal articles are also omitted, although much of the most interesting writing appears in this form. The most useful, indeed quite indispensable, are *Foreign Affairs* and *Foreign Policy*, both many times cited in the text. Others that are frequently very helpful include *Orbis, Journal of International Affairs, World Politics, International Studies Quarterly*, and *Stanford Journal of International Studies. International Organization, International Security*, and *Columbia Journal of World Business* are excellent in the areas indicated by their titles. *Atlas* handily brings together statements of foreign leaders and press. For the world from other points of view, the student may look to *International Journal* (Canadian), *International Affairs*

(British), *International Affairs* (Soviet), *Politique Étrangère* (French), and *Aussenpolitik* (German, published in English).

CHAPTER ONE   FROM ISOLATION TO INTERVENTIONISM

Alexander, Charles C. *Holding the Line: The Eisenhower Era, 1952–1961.* Indiana University Press, Bloomington, 1975.

Armstrong, Hamilton Fish, ed. *Fifty Years of Foreign Affairs.* Praeger, New York, 1972. Outstanding articles from *Foreign Affairs.*

Aron, Raymond. *The Imperial Republic: The United States and the World, 1945–1973.* Winthrop, Cambridge, Mass., 1974. The rise and fall of the United States as the dominant political-military power and the course of dollar diplomacy from the cold war years to the early 1970s.

Asprey, Robert B. *War in the Shadows: The Guerrilla in History.* Doubleday, New York, 1975. Vietnam conflict in terms of guerrilla warfare.

Barnet, Richard J. *Roots of War.* Atheneum, New York, 1972. Sees the cold war and Vietnam as products of capitalism and a manipulating leadership.

Bartlett, C. J. *The Rise and Fall of Pax Americana: U.S. Foreign Policy in the Twentieth Century.* Elek Books, London, 1974. A condensed general history.

Brown, Weldon A. *Prelude to Disaster: The American Role in Vietnam 1940–1963.* Kennikat Press, Port Washington, N.Y., 1975. A review of inovlvement in Vietnam before it became a war, exceptionally tending to justify the American actions.

Caridi, Ronald J. *Twentieth-Century American Foreign Policy: Security and Self-Interest.* Prentice-Hall, Englewood Cliffs, N.J., 1974. Relates internal political pressures to the formation of foreign policy.

Chayes, Abram. *The Cuban Missile Crisis: International Crises and the Role of Law.* Oxford University Press, New York, 1974. Uses the crisis as a case study for an inquiry into international law.

Davis, Lynn Etheridge. *The Cold War Begins: Soviet-American Conflict over Eastern Europe.* Princeton University Press, Princeton, N.J., 1974. How the Atlantic Charter principles in 1941 developed into explicit confrontation between the United States and the Soviet Union over eastern Europe.

Donovan, John C. *The Cold Warriors: A Policy-Making Elite.* D. C. Heath, Lexington, Mass., 1974. An analysis of backgrounds and assumptions of leaders who shaped national security policy from 1945 onward.

Fitzgerald, Frances. *Fire in the Lake: The Vietnamese and the Americans in Vietnam.* Little, Brown, Boston, 1972. Sees intervention as ineffective because of the cultural gap between East and West.

Fulbright, J. William. *The Crippled Giant: American Foreign Policy and Its Domestic Consequences.* Random House, New York, 1972. A senator's ruminations on postwar United States history.

Gaddis, John L. *The United States and the Origins of the Cold War, 1941–1947.* Columbia University Press, New York, 1972. A detailed and balanced but antirevisionist analysis.

Gallucci, Robert L. *Neither Peace nor Honor: The Politics of American Military Power in Viet-Nam.* Johns Hopkins Press, Baltimore, 1975. A study of American involvement, laying blame mostly on bureaucratic politics, especially of the military.

Gamson, William A., and Andre Modigliani. *Untangling the Cold War: A Strategy for Testing Rival Theories.* Little, Brown, Boston, 1971. Attempts to develop a new research strategy for the cold war.

Gardner, Lloyd C., ed. *American Foreign Policy, Present to Past: A Narrative with Readings and Documents.* Free Press, New York, 1974. Viewing United States cold war diplomacy from the present back into history, from President Nixon's foreign policy outline of February 1972 to Secretary of State Bryan's recommendation to President Wilson concerning Haiti.

Guhin, Michael. *John Foster Dulles.* Columbia University Press, New York, 1972. Suggests that Dulles was more a realist than usually reputed.

Jones, Alan M., Jr., ed. *U.S. Foreign Policy in a Changing World: The Nixon Administration, 1969–1973.* David McKay, New York, 1973. A collection of essays offering detailed analysis of internal and external forces in six geographic areas.

Kalb, Marvin, and Elie Abel. *Roots of Involvement: The U.S. in Asia, 1784–1971.* W. W. Norton, New York, 1971. Background for the Vietnam war.

Kendrick, Alexander. *The Wound Within: America in the Vietnam Years, 1945–1974.* Little, Brown, Boston, 1974. A chronicle of American life since World War II, relating the Vietnamese experience to its effect on foreign and domestic policy.

Kolko, Joyce, and Gabriel Kolko. *The Limits of Power: The World and United States Foreign Policy, 1945–1954.* Harper and Row, New York, 1972. A revisionist view of the beginnings of the cold war.

Kuklick, Bruce. *American Policy and the Division of Germany: The Clash with Russia over Reparations.* Cornell University Press, Ithaca, N.Y., 1972.

Liska, George. *Beyond Kissinger: Ways of Conservative Statecraft.* Johns Hopkins Press, Baltimore, 1975. A somewhat convoluted analysis finding the Kissinger policies basically shortsighted.

Merli, F. J., and Theodore A. Wilson, eds. *Makers of American Diplomacy: From Benjamin Franklin to Henry Kissinger.* Charles Scribner's Sons, New York, 1974. Twenty-five essays on personalities.

Middleton, Drew. *Retreat from Victory: A Critical Appraisal of American Foreign and Military Policy fom 1920 to the 1970s.* Hawthorn, New York, 1973. A plea to take up the burdens of world leadership.

Miller, Lynn H., and Ronald W. Pruessen, eds. *Reflections on the Cold War: A Quarter Century of American Foreign Policy.* Temple University Press, Philadelphia, 1974. Essays on various cold war topics.

Morris, Margaret F., and Sandra L. Myers, eds. *Essays on American Foreign Policy.* University of Texas Press, Austin, 1974. Articles on various topics from the 1920s to the 1970s.

Offner, Arnold A. *The Origins of the Second World War: American Foreign Policy and World Politics, 1917–1941.* Praeger, New York, 1975. An analysis of the main lines of American foreign policy between the wars.

Paterson, Thomas G. *Soviet-American Confrontation: Postwar Reconstruction and the Origins of the Cold War.* Johns Hopkins Press, Baltimore, 1974. An account of United States policy towards the Soviet Union in 1944–1950, with detailed case studies.

Poole, Peter A. *America in World Politics: Foreign Policy and Policy Makers since 1898.* Praeger, New York, 1975. An overview of American diplomatic history.

———. *The United States and Indochina, from FDR to Nixon.* Dryden Press, Hinsdale, Ill., 1973. Thirty years of United States foreign policy regarding Vietnam.

Porter, Gareth. *A Peace Denied: The United States, Vietnam, and the Paris Agreement.* Indiana University Press, Bloomington, 1976. An account blaming the United States for the failure to find an agreed peace in Vietnam.

Radosh, Ronald. *American Globalism.* Simon and Schuster, New York, 1975. Studies from the noninterventionist and anti-imperialist viewpoint.

Reynolds, Charles V. *Theory and Explanation in International Politics.* Barnes and Noble, New York, 1974. A historically oriented study on the origins of the cold war, the political consequences of nuclear weapons, the influence of economic factors on foreign policy, and international organizations.

Selden, M., ed. *Remaking Asia: Essays on the American Uses of Power.* Pantheon, New York, 1974. A search for characteristics of American imperialism in Asia since World War II.

Sherman, Martin J. *A World Destroyed: The Atomic Bomb and the Grand Alliance.* Knopf, New York, 1975. Fullest treatment of the decision to make and use the bomb.

Siracusa, Joseph M. *New Left Diplomatic Histories and Historians: The American Revisionists.* Kennikat Press, Port Washington, N.Y., 1973. A critique of the historiography of protest.

Solberg, Carl. *Riding High: America in the Cold War.* Mason and Lipscomb, New York, 1973. The impact of the cold war on American society.

Stevenson, Charles A. *The End of Nowhere: American Policy toward Laos since 1954.* Beacon Press, Boston, 1972.

Thompson, Sir Robert. *Peace Is Not at Hand: The American Position in the Post-Vietnam World and the Strategic Weakening of the West.* David McKay, New York, 1974. A warning that failure to support the noncommunist forces in the Indochina peninsula would have dire consequences for world peace.

Trivers, Howard. *Three Crises in American Foreign Affairs and a Continuing Revolution.* Southern Illinois University Press, Carbondale, 1972. Among other subjects, reflections on Vietnam.

Tucker, Robert W. *The Radical Left and American Foreign Policy.* Johns Hopkins Press, Baltimore, 1971. Cites radical change in society as the only means by which foreign policy can be changed.

Varg, Paul A. *The Closing of the Door: Sino-American Relations 1936–1946.* Michigan State University Press, East Lansing, 1973.

Whetten, Lawrence L. *Contemporary American Foreign Policy: Minimal Diplomacy, Defensive Strategy, and Détente Management.* Lexington Books, Lexington, Mass., 1974. Attempts to analyze the goals and methods of American foreign policy in nineteen essays written between 1969 and 1973.

Wu, Yuan-li. *U.S. Policy and Strategic Interests in the Western Pacific.* Crane, Russak, New York, 1975. An analysis of United States security policy in the western Pacific 1969–1974.

Zinn, Howard. *Postwar America: 1945–1971.* Bobbs-Merrill, Indianapolis, 1973. An indictment of the United States as a land of violence and repression.

CHAPTER TWO MILITARY DIMENSIONS

Ackley, Charles W. *The Modern Military in American Society.* Westminister Press, Philadelphia, 1972.

Aliano, Richard A. *American Defense Policy from Eisenhower to Kennedy: The Politics of Changing Military Requirements, 1957–1961.* Ohio University Press, Athens, 1975. Valuable account of the shift from massive retaliation to flexible response, triggered by Sputnik.

Beaufre, Andre. *Strategy for Tomorrow.* Crane, Russak, New York, 1974. Examines the directions of western European deterrence and defense and finds the NATO concept outdated.

Boskey, Bennet, and Mason Willrich, eds. *Nuclear Proliferation: Prospects for Control.* Dunellen, New York, 1970. A symposium on the Nonproliferation Treaty.

Buncher, Judith F., ed. *The CIA and the Security Debate.* Facts on File, New York, 1976. A digest of news reports related to the CIA and other members of the intelligence community, with various perspectives and opinions on the debate regarding their proper role.

Canan, James W. *The Superwarriors: The Fantastic World of Pentagon Superweapons.* Weybright and Talley, New York, 1975. An examination of the technological arms race.

Clemens, Walter C. *The Superpowers and Arms Control: From Cold War to Interdependence.* Lexington Books, Lexington, Mass., 1973. A thoughtful approach to arms-control negotiations.

Clotfelter, James. *The Military in American Politics.* Harper and Row, New York, 1973.

Cortright, David. *Soldiers in Revolt: The American Military Today.* Anchor-Doubleday, Garden City, N.Y., 1975. The effects of the Vietnam war on the army.

Donovan, J. A. *Militarism, U.S.A.* Charles Scribner's Sons, New York, 1970. A warning against the temptation to assume the role of world policeman.

Fox, J. Ronald. *Arming America: How the U.S. Buys Weapons.* Harvard

University Press, Cambridge, Mass., 1974. The management of weapons procurement in the 1960s and afterward.

George, Alexander L., and Richard Smoke. *Deterrence in American Foreign Policy: Theory and Practice*. Columbia University Press, New York, 1974. A review of the history of deterrence with eleven case studies ranging from the Berlin blockade through the Cuban missile crisis, and a sketchy foundation for a theory of substrategic deterrence.

Harkavy, Robert E. *The Arms Race and International Systems*. Ballinger, Cambridge, Mass., 1975. An analysis of the transfer of conventional arms from World War I to 1969.

Higham, Robin, ed. *Intervention or Abstention: The Dilemma of American Foreign Policy*. University of Kentucky Press, Lexington, 1975. Studies of various interventions, leading to the conclusion that abstention is rising.

Horton, Frank B., III, Anthony C. Rogerson, and Edward L. Warner, III, eds. *Comparative Defense Policy*. Johns Hopkins Press, Baltimore, 1974. A source book with chapters on the military profession or "ideology," structure and process, military doctrine, force posture, weapons acquisition, and the use of force.

Janowitz, Morris. *Military Conflict: Essays in the Institutional Analysis of War and Peace*. Sage Publications, Beverly Hills, Calif., 1975. Miscellaneous essays on political and sociological problems of armed forces in the nuclear age.

Kane, William E. *Civil Strife in Latin America: A Legal History of U.S. Involvement*. Johns Hopkins Press, Baltimore, 1972. Examines the historical evolution of United States intervention policies from the viewpoint of international law.

Kaplan, Morton A. *SALT: Problems and Prospects*. General Learning Press, Morristown, N.J., 1973. Foreign policy and political aspects of SALT I.

Kemp, Geoffrey, Robert L. Pfaltzgraff, Jr., and Uri Ra'anan. *The Other Arms Race: New Technologies and Non-Nuclear Conflict*. Lexington Books, Lexington, Mass., 1975. Discussion of the new generation of sophisticated weaponry and its implications.

Kintner, William R., and Robert L. Pfaltzgraff, eds. *SALT: Implications for Arms Control in the 1970s*. University of Pittsburgh Press, Pittsburgh, 1973. Foreign policy and political aspects of SALT I.

Kirkpatrick, Lyman B., Jr., *The U.S. Intelligence Community: Foreign Policy and Domestic Activities*. Hill and Wang, New York, 1973. A former CIA official calls for more effective control of the intelligence community.

Lawrence, Robert. *Arms Control and Disarmament*. Burgess Press, Minneapolis, 1973. A brief but sound introduction.

Legault, Albert, and George Lindsey. *The Dynamics of the Nuclear Balance*. Cornell University Press, Ithaca, N.Y., 1974. Provides a general background in the technical details of nuclear weapons and missiles, sums up the recent history of arms limitation talks, and offers a theoretical model of deterrence.

———. *The Dynamics of the Nuclear Balance*. Rev. ed. Cornell University Press, Ithaca, N.Y., 1976. A careful and comprehensive study of all aspects of the nuclear balance carried through recent negotiations.

Long, Franklin A., and George W. Rathjens, eds. *Arms, Defense Policy, and Arms Control*. W. W. Norton, New York, 1976. A collection of essays by noted authorities pointing up the great and growing complexities of arms control.

Loory, Stuart H. *Defeated: Inside America's Military Machine*. Random House, New York, 1973. How United States armed forces were affected by the Vietnam war.

McGwire, Michael, Ken Booth, and John McDonnell, eds. *Soviet Naval Policy: Objectives and Constraints*. Praeger, New York, 1975. Conference papers on many aspects of recent Soviet naval policy.

Martin, Laurence. *Arms and Strategy: The World Power Structure Today*. David McKay, New York, 1973. An overall guide to the nature of military organizations, weapons, strategies, tactics, and relationships, nonnuclear wars, arms control and disarmament, and arms trade.

Melman, Seymour. *Pentagon Capitalism: The Political Economy of War*. McGraw-Hill, New York, 1970. The expansion of the Pentagon into all aspects of American life.

———. *The Permanent War Economy: American Capitalism in Decline*. Simon and Schuster, New York, 1974. Examines the enormous investment in military spending that has allegedly led to a permanent war economy and America's decline as an industrial power.

Middleton, Drew. *Can America Win the Next War?* Charles Scribner's Sons, New York, 1975. Foresees war with the Soviet Union in and over Europe.

Moulton, Harland B. *From Superiority to Parity: The U.S. and the Strategic Arms Race 1961–1971*. Greenwood Press, Westport, Conn., 1973. A survey of strategic arms policies of a decade.

Newhouse, John. *Cold Dawn: The Story of SALT*. Holt, Rinehart and Winston, New York, 1973. A description of negotiations leading to the 1972 agreements.

Northedge, F. S., ed. *The Use of Force in International Relations*. Free Press, New York, 1974. Loosely related essays on the threat and use of force.

Paul, Roland A. *American Military Commitments Abroad*. Rutgers University Press, New Brunswick, N.J., 1973. Attempts to define a military commitment.

Prouty, L. Fletcher. *The Secret Team: The CIA and Its Allies in Control of the United States and the World*. Prentice-Hall, Englewood Cliffs, N.J., 1973. A retired CIA officer writes of CIA actions and maneuvers and their impact.

Quanbeck, Alton H., and Barry M. Clechman. *Strategic Forces: Issues for the Mid-Seventies*. Brookings Institution, Washington, D.C., 1973. An examination of doctrine, requirements, and political needs for strategic nuclear forces.

Quanbeck, Alton H., and Archie L. Wood. *Modernizing the Strategic*

Bomber Force: Why and How. Brookings Institution, Washington, D.C., 1976. An analysis of the desirability of the B-1 bomber, with negative conclusions.

Quester, George H., ed. *Sea Power in the 1970s.* Dunellen, New York, 1975. Soviet-American rivalry and naval problems.

——. *Nuclear Diplomacy: The First Twenty-Five Years.* Dunellen, New York, 1971. The Soviet-American nuclear relationship since the end of World War II.

Roberts, Chalmers M. *The Nuclear Years: The Arms Race and Arms Control, 1945–1970.* Praeger, New York, 1970. Twenty-five years of United States–Soviet nuclear relations.

Rosi, Eugene J., ed. *American Defense and Détente: Readings in National Security Policy.* Dodd, Mead, New York, 1973. Thirty-five essays by divers authors on power, values, national interest, contemporary world environment, and national security; interaction of the domestic and international environments.

Rostow, W. W. *The Diffusion of Power: An Essay in Recent History.* Macmillan, New York, 1972. An argument for an interventionist foreign policy.

Russett, Bruce M. *Power and Community in World Politics.* W. H. Freeman, San Francisco, 1974. A collection of essays from 1962–1972, on the environment of world politics, international violence, deterrence and restraint, and influence and integration.

Seitz, Frederick, and Rodney W. Nichols. *Research and Development and the Prospects for International Security.* Crane, Russak, New York, 1974. The first part surveys the post-Vietnam Nixon strategic and foreign policy framework, and the relationship of defense research and development to that framework.

Stockholm International Peace Research Institute. *Arms Trade Registers: The Arms Trade with the Third World.* MIT Press, Cambridge, Mass., 1975. A statistical survey of arms received between the mid-1950s and the end of 1973.

Ten Eyck, John C. *The Law of Diminishing War Power: From Troy to Vietnam.* Pageant Press International, New York, 1970. Case studies showing how military successes lead to overconfidence, which leads to military disaster.

Tillema, Herbert K. *Appeal to Force: American Military Intervention in the Era of Containment.* Crowell, New York, 1973. A study of occasions when the United States has and has not intervened militarily since World War II.

Walters, Robert E. *Sea Power and the Nuclear Fallacy: A Reevaluation of Global Strategy.* Holmes and Meier, New York, 1975. A critique of basic postwar strategic policy of the United States on the basis of a geopolitical approach, with a recommendation for emphasis on sea power.

Webb, James H., Jr. *Micronesia and U.S. Pacific Strategy: A Blueprint for the 1980s.* Praeger, New York, 1974. Recommends a strategy dependent on United States bases in the Mariana islands.

White, William D. *U.S. Tactical Air Power: Missions, Forces, Costs.* Brookings Institution, Washington, D.C., 1974. Argues that the policy of substituting technology for blood as far as possible can be continued at a more realistic cost level.

Willrich, Mason, and John B. Rhinelander, eds. *SALT: The Moscow Agreements and Beyond.* Free Press, New York, 1974. A survey of arms race and disarmament efforts since 1945 through SALT I and its implications.

CHAPTER THREE   ECONOMIC DIMENSIONS

Barnet, Richard J., and Ronald E. Müller. *Global Reach: The Power of the Multinational Corporations.* Simon and Schuster, New York, 1975. A provocative book that attempts to describe the problems created by the emergence of nonnational actors as a revolutionary class of social engineers.

Bergsten, C. Fred, and Lawrence B. Krause, eds. *World Politics and International Economics.* Brookings Institution, Washington, D.C., 1975. Book publication of the Winter 1975 edition of *International Organization,* relating political and economic expertise of numerous scholars on international economics.

Brooke, Michael Z., and H. L. Remmers, eds. *The Multinational Company in Europe: Some Key Problems.* University of Michigan Press, Ann Arbor, 1974. European experts concentrate on the European experience and give some comparisons with the more familiar American practices.

Bundy, William P., ed. *The World Economic Crisis.* W. W. Norton, New York, 1975. Articles from *Foreign Affairs,* 1973–1974, on world economic problems from energy to food.

Calleo, David P., and Benjamin M. Rowland. *American and the World Political Economy: Atlantic Dreams and National Realities.* Indiana University Press, Bloomington, 1973. A survey of the ideological, economic, and political concerns that have governed foreign trade policy in recent years.

Einhorn, Jessica Pernitz. *Expropriation Politics.* D. C. Heath, Lexington, Mass., 1974. Applies the bureaucratic politics model to foreign economic policy making, focusing on two cases of expropriation without compensation.

Flanagan, Robert J., and Arnold R. Weber, eds. *Bargaining without Boundaries: The Multinational Corporation and International Labor Relations.* University of Chicago Press, Chicago, 1974. Conference papers.

Gilpin, Robert. *U.S. Power and the Multinational Corporation: The Political Economy of Foreign Direct Investment.* Basic Books, New York, 1975. Contrary to many writers, Gilpin foresees a decline of the MNCs in the face of political counterattack.

Gunneman, John P., ed. *The Nation-State and Transnational Corporations in Conflict: With Special Reference to Latin America.* Praeger, New York, 1975. A conference report with negative and positive assessments.

Halilu, II. R., J. Graham Smith, and Richard W. Wright, eds. *Nationalism and the Multinational Enterprise: Legal, Economic and Managerial Aspects.* Oceana Publications, Dobbs Ferry, N.Y., 1973. Papers on laws of key countries bearing on the operation of multinational corporations (United States, Canada, Great Britain, Germany, the European Economic Community, Africa).

Hellmann, Rainer. *The Challenge to U.S. Dominance of the International Corporation.* Dunellen, New York, 1971. American investment in Europe and vice versa.

Hudson, Michael. *Super Imperialism: The Economic Strategy of American Empire.* Holt, Rinehart and Winston, New York, 1972. Revisionist view of American foreign economic policy since World War I.

Johnson, D. G., and J. A. Schnittker, eds. *U.S. Agriculture in a World Context: Policies and Approaches for the Next Decade.* Praeger, New York, 1974. An examination of policies of the United States and other countries.

Kintner, William R., and Harvey Sicherman. *Technology and International Politics: The Crisis of Wishing.* D. C. Heath, Lexington, Mass., 1975. Examines the impact of technology on national strength.

Kolko, Joyce. *America and the Crisis of World Capitalism.* Beacon Press, Boston, 1974. A statement of a radical, mostly Marxist view of the world.

Manser, W. A. P. *The Financial Role of the Multinational Enterprises.* Halsted Press, New York, 1973. A well-ordered argument that financially the multinational firms do more good than harm.

Moran, Theodore H. *Multinational Corporations and the Politics of Dependence: Copper in Chile.* Princeton University Press, Princeton, N.J., 1975. A history of copper policy in Chile from World War II through the end of the Allende regime in 1973, outlining a balance-of-power model of the relationship between foreign investor and host country.

Robinson, Stuart W., Jr. *Multinational Banking.* Sijthoff, Leyden, 1972. Focuses on American banking in France, Britain, and Switzerland.

Rosen, Steven, and James R. Kurth, eds. *Testing Theories of Economic Imperialism.* D. C. Heath, Lexington, Mass., 1974. Essays presenting an analysis of the relations between imperialism, capitalism, underdeveloped countries, and socialist systems.

Russett, Bruce M., and Elizabeth C. Hanson. *Interest and Ideology: The Foreign Policy Beliefs of American Businessmen.* W. H. Freeman, San Francisco, 1975. This study finds little or no evidence that economic interests dominate business people's foreign policy preferences or that capitalism leads to an aggressive foreign policy.

Said, Abdul A., and Luiz R. Simmons, eds. *The New Sovereigns: Multinational Corporations as World Powers.* Prentice-Hall, Englewood Cliffs, N.J., 1975.

Scheer, R. *America after Nixon: The Age of the Multinationals.* McGraw-Hill, New York, 1974. The recent role of multinational corporations.

Stephenson, Hugh. *The Coming Clash: The Impact of Multinational Corporations on National States.* Saturday Review Press, New York, 1972.

A critical view of the policies and power of the multinational corporations and their influence.

Tugendhat, Christopher. *The Multinationals*. Random House, New York, 1972. A discussion of the activities of the international companies.

Turner, Louis. *Multinational Companies in the Third World*. Hill and Wang, New York, 1973. An examination of examples throwing light on the relations of multinationals, host governments, and domestic enterprises.

United Nations Department of Economic and Social Affairs. *Multinational Corporations in World Development*. Praeger, New York, 1974. Many case studies are presented with abundant data.

Vernon, Raymond. *The Economic and Political Consequences of Multinational Enterprise*. Harvard University Graduate School of Business Administration, Division of Research, Boston, 1972. A basic treatment of the subject.

Wallace, Don, Jr., ed. *International Control of Investment: The Dusseldorf Conference on Multinational Corporations*. Praeger, New York, 1974. The result of a conference where possibilities for international control of the abuses of multinational corporations were explored, with negative results.

Wilkins, Mira. *The Maturing of Multinational Enterprise: American Business Abroad from 1914 to 1970*. Harvard University Press, Cambridge, Mass., 1974. A history of foreign investment activities of major United States firms.

CHAPTER FOUR   INTANGIBLE POWER

Hale, Julian. *Radio Power: Propaganda and International Broadcasting*. Temple University Press, Philadelphia, 1975. A study of international broadcasting as a weapon of political and ideological struggle.

Lisann, Maury. *Broadcasting to the Soviet Union: International Politics and Radio*. Praeger, New York, 1975. An examination of Soviet policies toward foreign broadcasts and the impact of broadcasts on the Soviet Union.

CHAPTER FIVE   THE AMERICAN CAPACITY

Bacchus, William I. *Foreign Policy and the Bureaucratic Process: The State Department's Country Director System*. Princeton University Press, Princeton, N.J., 1973. A review of policy making, focusing on the country director.

Batscha, Robert M. *Foreign Affairs News and the Broadcast Journalist*. Praeger, New York, 1975. Gives a good rating to television coverage.

Clark, Eric. *Diplomat: The World of International Diplomacy*. Taplinger, New York, 1974. A survey of contemporary diplomatic behavior and style.

Cohen, Bernard C. *The Public's Impact on Foreign Policy*. Little, Brown, Boston, 1973. Based on interviews with fifty policy makers.

Destler, I. M. *Presidents, Bureaucrats and Foreign Policy*. Princeton

University Press, Princeton, N.J., 1972. A critical history of attempts since 1945 to reform the conduct of foreign policy.

Esterline, John H., and Robert B. Black. *Inside Foreign Policy: The Department of State Political System and Its Subsystems.* Mayfield Publishing Co., Palo Alto, Calif., 1975. This study hardly gets "inside foreign policy," which is made by the president, but has interesting observations on the supporting bureaucracy.

Halperin, Morton H. *National Security Policy-Making: Analyses, Cases, and Proposals.* D. C. Heath, Lexington, Mass., 1975. Case studies in bureaucratic policy making.

Halperin, Morton H., with Priscilla Clapp and Arnold Kanter. *Bureaucratic Politics and Foreign Policy.* Brookings Institution, Washington, D.C., 1974. A study of bureaucratic maneuvering in the formation of national policy.

Irish, Marian D., and Elke Frank. *U.S. Foreign Policy: Context, Conduct, Content.* Harcourt, Brace, Jovanovich, New York, 1975. A mostly historical study of foreign policy making.

Janis, Irving L. *Victims of Groupthink: A Psychological Study of Foreign-Policy Decisions and Fiascoes.* Houghton Mifflin, Boston, 1973. Focuses on small-group interaction as a distortion of policy formulation.

Kahn, E. J., Jr. *The China Hands: America's Foreign Service Officers and What Befell Them.* Viking Press, New York, 1975. The misfortunes in the 1950s of thirteen military and foreign service officers who reported too honestly on China.

Spanier, John, and Eric M. Uslaner. *How American Foreign Policy Is Made.* Praeger, New York, 1974. Analyzes the presidential and congressional roles and differentiates between "rational actor" and "bureaucratic" models of policy making.

Stennis, John C., and William Fulbright. *The Role of Congress in Foreign Policy.* American Enterprise Institute for Public Policy Research, Washington, D.C., 1971. A debate on the nature of the balance between Congress and the president in foreign policy.

CHAPTER SIX   THE AFFLUENT SOCIETIES

Aitchinson, Ray. *Americans in Australia.* Charles Scribner's Sons, New York, 1973. An anecdotal history of American-Australian relations.

Auer, James E. *The Postwar Rearmament of Japanese Maritime Forces, 1945–1971.* Praeger, New York, 1973. A career naval officer details the transition from Imperial Navy to Maritime Self-Defense Force.

Burgess, W. Randolph, and James Robert Huntley. *Europe and America: The Next Ten Years.* Walker, New York, 1970. A projection of relations within the Atlantic community during the coming decade.

Calleo, David P., and Benjamin M. Rowland. *America and the World Political Economy: Atlantic Dreams and National Realities.* Indiana University Press, Bloomington, 1973. A Gaullist analysis of the last quarter-century.

Clough, Ralph N. *East Asia and U.S. Security.* Brookings Institution, Washington, D.C., 1975. An evaluation of the policy of containment in Asia and the modifications made in the American role in this region during the past several years. Sees an emerging four-power regional structure consisting of the United States, Japan, the People's Republic of China, and the Soviet Union.

Dinwiddy, Bruce. *European Development Policies: The United Kingdom, Sweden, France, EEC and Multilateral Organizations.* Praeger, for Overseas Development Institute, New York, 1973. A report on the foreign aid expenditures of European countries through 1971–1972 with useful tables and some projections.

Endicott, John E. *Japan's Nuclear Option: Political, Technical, and Strategic Factors.* Praeger, New York, 1975. Study of nuclear capabilities and prospects of America's strongest ally.

Fedder, Edwin H. *NATO: The Dynamics of Alliance in the Postwar World.* Dodd, Mead, New York, 1973. A study of the nature and functioning of alliances in general and of NATO in particular.

Foster, Richard B., Andre Beaufre, and Wynfred Joshua, eds. *Strategy for the West: American-Allied Relations in Transition.* Crane, Russak, New York, 1974. Papers on emerging United States global strategy and different views of Western security, with emphasis on strategy in regard to the Soviet Union.

Fox, William T. R., and Warner R. Schilling, eds. *European Security and the Atlantic System.* Columbia University Press, New York, 1973. Essays on arms control in Europe.

Garnet, John C., ed. *The Defence of Western Europe: Papers Presented at the National Defence College, Latimer, in September 1972.* St. Martin's Press, New York, 1974. Prominent British scholars write on relations between the United States and Europe, on European security, arms cooperation, and strategy.

Geiger, Theodore. *The Fortunes of the West: The Future of the Atlantic Nations.* Indiana University Press, Bloomington, 1973. Reflections on where technocratic capacity may be taking America and Europe.

Goodman, Elliot R. *The Fate of the Atlantic Community.* Praeger, New York, 1975. A survey of the attempt to create an Atlantic community.

Hanrieder, Wolfram F., ed. *The United States and Western Europe: Political, Economic and Strategic Perspectives.* Winthrop, Cambridge, Mass., 1974. Essays on political, economic, and strategic relations between the United States and western Europe.

Hinton, Harold C. *Three and a Half Powers: The New Balance in Asia.* Indiana University Press, Bloomington, 1975. An analysis of the balance of power in Asia from the American primacy to the period of multilateral balance, with China and Japan joining the superpowers.

Hohenberg, John. *New Era in the Pacific: An Adventure in Public Diplomacy.* Simon and Schuster, New York, 1972. A historical tour of the Pacific and South Asian horizon since World War II.

Joshua, Wynfred, and Walter Hahn. *Nuclear Politics: America, France, and Britain.* Sage Publications, Beverly Hills, Calif., 1973. Examines the question of United States nuclear reliability in Europe and of a possible western European nuclear deterrent.

Kaplan, Morton A. *The Rationale for NATO: European Collective Security*

Past and Future. American Enterprise Institution for Public Policy Research, Washington, D.C., 1973. Reviews the history of NATO strategic policies and develops "dissuasion strategy."

Kindleberger, Charles P., and Andrew Shonfield, eds. *North American and Western European Economic Policies*. St. Martin's Press, New York, 1971. Salient issues about the differences between European regionalists and American cosmopolitans.

Kohnstamm, Max, and Wolfram Hager, eds. *A Nation Writ Large? Foreign-Policy Problems before the European Community*. Halsted Press, New York, 1973. Papers analyzing the chances for European integration and its implication for the world system.

Lawrence, Richard D., and Jeffrey Record. *U.S. Force Structure in NATO: An Alternative*. Brookings Institution, Washington, D.C., 1974. An analysis of United States and Soviet military strength and tactics in Europe, with suggestions for a more efficient army structure and strategy.

Mally, Gerhard. *The European Community in Perspective: The New Europe, the United States, and the World*. D. C. Heath, Lexington, Mass., 1973. A broad study of European integration, analysis of its progress, and review of its relations to the world outside, especially the United States.

Mally, Gerhard, ed. *The New Europe and the United States*. D. C. Heath, Lexington, Mass., 1974. Speeches, essays, and pronouncements on European-American relations in various aspects.

Mayne, Richard, ed. *The New Atlantic Challenge*. John Wiley, New York, 1975. Papers of a 1973 symposium on United States–European relations.

Morgan, Roger. *The United States and West Germany, 1945–1973: A Study in Alliance Politics*. Oxford University Press, New York, 1974.

Neu, Charles E. *The Troubled Encounter: The U.S. and Japan*. Wiley, New York, 1975. A review of Japanese-American relations from Commodore Perry to the present.

Newhouse, John, et al. *U.S. Troops in Europe: Issues, Costs and Choices*. Brookings Institution, Washington, D.C., 1971.

O'Connor, Richard. *Pacific Destiny: An Informal History of the U.S. in the Far East, 1776–1968*. Little, Brown, Boston, 1969. The evolution of the United States as a Pacific power.

Piovene, Guido. *In Search of Europe: Portraits of the Non-Communist West*. St. Martin's Press, New York, 1975. Pessimistic reflections on the unhappiness of Europe.

Preeg, Ernest H. *Economic Blocs and U.S. Foreign Policy*. National Planning Association, Washington, D.C., 1974. A career Foreign Service officer writes about past, present, and future relationships among nations, focusing on North America, western Europe, and Japan.

Preston, Richard A., ed. *The Influence of the U.S. on Canadian Development: Eleven Case Studies*. Duke University Press, Durham, N.C., 1972.

Rosovsky, Henry, ed. *Discord in the Pacific: Challenges to the Japanese-*

American Alliance. Columbia Books, for the American Assembly, Washington, D.C., 1973. Articles on different aspects of Japanese-American relations.

Schaetzel, J. Robert. *The Unhinged Alliance: America and the European Community.* Harper and Row, New York, 1975. A call for a more positive American approach to European unity.

Schilling, Warner R., et al. *American Arms and a Changing Europe: Dilemmas of Deterrence and Disarmament.* Columbia University Press, New York, 1973. Deals with problems in the pursuit of European security, strategic security, and arms control.

Stairs, Denis. *The Diplomacy of Constraint: Canada, the Korean War, and the United States.* University of Toronto Press, Toronto, 1974. Traces Canada's handling of the Korean War, focusing on 1950–1951.

Stanley, Timothy W., and Darnell M. Whitt. *Détente Diplomacy: United States and European Security in the 1970s.* Dunellen, New York, 1970. A historical analysis of East-West détente in Europe.

Stockwin, J. A. A. *Japan: Divided Politics in a Growth Economy.* W. W. Norton, New York, 1975. Japanese politics in the economic setting.

Sunoo, Harold N. *Japanese Militarism: Past and Present.* Nelson Hall, Chicago, 1975. Expects Japan soon to be one of the three major military powers.

Trezise, Philip H. *The Atlantic Connection: Prospects, Problems, and Policies.* Brookings Institution, Washington, D.C., 1975. A brief exploration of military, political, and economic problems of the Atlantic alliance.

Van Alstyne, R. W. *The United States and East Asia.* W. W. Norton, New York, 1973. A concise illustrated history of a century of United States–Asian relations.

Vernon, Raymond, ed. *Big Business and the State: Changing Relations in Western Europe.* Harvard University Press, Cambridge, Mass., 1974. Explores relations between the multinational corporations and the state in Europe and the effects of the erosion of sovereignty.

Williams, Geoffrey Lee, and Alan Lee Williams. *Crisis in European Defense: The Next Ten Years.* St. Martin's Press, New York, 1974. An examination of western Europe's major defense issues over the next decade, centered on the dependence on the United States and a possible new European defense policy.

CHAPTER SEVEN THE COMMUNIST WORLD

Bender, Lynn Darrell. *The Politics of Hostility: Castro's Revolution and U.S. Policy.* Inter-American University Press, Hato Rey, P.R., 1975. Argues for review of United States–Cuban relations.

Bohlen, Charles E. *The Transformation of American Foreign Policy.* W.W. Norton, New York, 1969. Lectures on United States–Soviet relations.

Buss, Claude A. *China: The People's Republic of China and Richard Nixon.* W. H. Freeman, San Francisco, 1974. A concise survey of recent Chinese-American relations.

Cahill, Harry A. *The China Trade and U.S. Tariffs*. Praeger, New York, 1973. A detailed examination of possible American markets for Chinese goods.

Chen, King C., ed. *The Foreign Policy of China*. Seton Hall University Press, Roseland, N.J., 1972.

Confino, Michael, and Shimon Shamir, eds. *The U.S.S.R. and the Middle East*. John Wiley, New York, 1973. Conference papers by American, Israeli, and European experts.

Dulles, Foster R. *American Policy toward China, 1949–1969*. Crowell, New York, 1972. A factual introduction of the People's Republic of China.

Edmonds, Robin. *Soviet Foreign Policy 1962–1973*. Oxford University Press, New York, 1975. An illuminating study of causes of détente, especially economic needs.

Eissenstat, Bernard W., ed. *The Soviet Union: The Seventies and Beyond*. Lexington Books, Lexington, Mass., 1975. The Soviet Union in world affairs.

Goldman, Marshall I. *Détente and Dollars: Doing Business with the Soviets*. Basic Books, New York, 1975. A guidebook for diplomats and traders, with considerable insight into problems of economic cooperation.

Gouré, Leon, Foy D. Kohler, and Mose L. Harvey. *The Role of the Nuclear Forces in Current Soviet Strategy*. Center for Advanced International Studies, University of Miami, Coral Gables, Fla., 1974. A hard-line position in reviewing Soviet nuclear strategy.

Harvey, Dodd L., and Linda C. Ciccoritti. *U.S.–Soviet Cooperation in Space*. Center for Advanced International Studies, University of Miami, Coral Gables, Fla., 1974.

Hinton, Harold C. *China's Turbulent Quest: An Analysis of China's Foreign Relations since 1949*. Rev. ed. Indiana University Press, Bloomington, 1972.

Hollander, Paul. *Soviet and American Society: A Comparison*. Oxford University Press, New York, 1973. A sociologist's survey of differences and resemblances.

Hsiao, Gene T., ed. *Sino-American Détente and Its Policy Implications*. Praeger, New York, 1974. A conference report analyzing the problems and impact of Sino-American détente.

James, Peter N. *Soviet Conquest from Space*. Arlington House, New Rochelle, N.Y., 1974. An assessment of Soviet space capability designed to raise American apprehensions.

Kanet, Roger E., ed. *The Soviet Union and the Developing Nations*. Johns Hopkins Press, Baltimore, 1974. An area-by-area account of Soviet policy plus essays on the competitive United States and Chinese efforts.

Kohler, Foy D., Leon Gouré, and Mose L. Harvey. *The Soviet Union and the October 1973 Middle East War: The Implications for Détente*. Center for Advanced International Studies, University of Miami, Coral Gables, Fla., 1974. A detailed study of Soviet activities related to the Yom Kippur War.

Kohler, Foy D., Mose L. Harvey, Leon Gouré, and Richard Soll. *Soviet Strategy for the Seventies: From Cold War to Peaceful Coexistence*.

Center for Advanced International Studies, University of Miami, Coral Gables, Fla., 1973. The doctrine and practice of peaceful co-existence critically viewed.

Lach, Donald F., and Edmund S. Wehrle. *International Politics in East Asia since World War II.* Praeger, New York, 1975. Mildly revisionist interpretation centered on the People's Republic of China.

Lien, Chan, ed. *Proceedings of the Third Sino-American Conference on Mainland China.* Culture Press, Taipei, 1974. Despite its obvious viewpoint, this large book is an important source on Chinese politics, economics, and foreign policy.

Liu, Leo Yueh-Yun. *China as a Nuclear Power in World Politics.* Taplinger, New York, 1972. China's thermonuclear capacity with respect to the other superpowers.

London, Kurt. *The Soviet Impact on World Politics.* Hawthorn Books, New York, 1974. Essays by distinguished scholars rather skeptical of détente.

Lundestad, Geir. *The American Non-Policy towards Eastern Europe, 1943–1947.* Humanities Press, Atlantic Highlands, N.J., 1975. An analysis of confused American behavior.

MacFarquhar, Roderick, ed. *Sino-American Relations, 1949–1971.* Praeger, New York, 1972. A compendium of documents on postwar Sino-American relations.

McLane, Charles B. *Soviet-African Relations,* vol. 3 of *Soviet–Third World Relations, A Survey in Three Volumes.* Central Asian Research Center, London, 1975. Encyclopedic coverage of Soviet political, economic, and cultural involvements in sub-Saharan Africa from the 1950s through 1972.

———. *Soviet-Asian Relations,* vol. 2 of *Soviet–Third World Relations.* Columbia University Press, New York, 1974. A concise interpretive analysis of the role in Soviet foreign affairs of Asian nations, with chronological tables.

———. *Soviet–Middle East Relations,* vol. 1 of *Soviet–Third World Relations.* Columbia University Press, New York, 1973. Focuses on sixteen countries of the Middle East and North Africa (Israel excluded), with a detailed chronology of major events.

May, Ernest R., and James C. Thompson, Jr., eds. *American East Asian Relations: A Survey.* Harvard University Press, Cambridge, Mass., 1972. Historiographical essays with emphasis on relations with China.

Mensonides, Louis J., and James A. Kuhlman, eds. *The Future of Inter-Block Relations in Europe.* Praeger, New York, 1974. Essays on prospects for change in East-West relations in Europe with discussion of NATO and WTO military and economic capabilities, living standards, trade patterns, and energy and resource reserves.

Mesa-Lago, Carmelo. *Cuba in the 1970s: Pragmatism and Institutionalization.* University of New Mexico Press, Albuquerque, 1975. Describes the course of the Cuban revolution since 1970 as institutionalization in response to political and socioeconomic realities.

Moorsteen, Richard, and Morton Abramovitz. *Remaking China Policy:*

U.S.–China Relations and Governmental Decisionmaking. Harvard University Press, Cambridge, Mass., 1971. A plan of action for a new Asian policy.

Petrov, Vladimir. *U.S.–Soviet Détente: Past and Future.* American Enterprise Institute for Public Policy Research, Washington, D.C., 1975. A skeptical view.

Rubinstein, Alvin Z., ed. *Soviet and Chinese Influence in the Third World.* Praeger, New York, 1975. An effort to assess and describe the influence of the major communist powers.

Schwab, George, and Henry Friedlander, eds. *Détente in Historical Perspective: The First CUNY Conference on History and Politics.* Cyrco Press, New York, 1975. Papers defining and dissecting détente in the face of the continuing confrontation.

Steibel, Gerald L. *Détente: Promises and Pitfalls.* Crane, Russak, New York, 1975. A warning of the dangers of détente.

Theberge, James D., ed. *Russia in the Caribbean: Part One, Panelists' Findings, Recommendations, and Comments; Part Two, A Special Report.* Center for Strategic and International Studies, Georgetown University, Washington, D.C., 1973. These publications are the result of a 1971 conference on the Caribbean. Part One discusses Soviet activities; Part Two provides background data.

Theberge, James D. *The Soviet Presence in Latin America.* Crane, Russak, New York, 1974. A study of the relations of the Soviet Union in Latin America through the fall of the Allende government in 1973.

Ulam, Adam B. *Expansion and Coexistence: Soviet Foreign Policy, 1917–1973.* 2nd ed. Praeger, New York, 1974. The most detailed and scholarly account.

Walters, Robert S. *American and Soviet Aid: A Comparative Analysis.* University of Pittsburgh Press, Pittsburgh, 1970. An emphasis on similarities.

Wilson, Joan Hoff. *Ideology and Economics: U.S. Relations with the Soviet Union, 1918–1933.* University of Missouri Press, Columbia, 1974. A critique of the notion that the American business community opposed and then was responsible for American recognition of the Soviet Union.

CHAPTERS EIGHT AND NINE   PROBLEMS OF THE POOR AND THE OTHER WORLD: POLICIES

Alroy, Gil Carl. *The Kissinger Experience: American Policy in the Middle East.* Horizon Press, New York, 1975. An examination of Kissinger's role in Middle East diplomacy.

Arkhurst, Frederick S., ed. *U.S. Policy toward Africa.* Praeger, New York, 1975. Seminar papers critical of United States neglect.

Baklanoff, Eric N. *Expropriation of U.S. Investments in Cuba, Mexico, and Chile.* Praeger, New York, 1975. Account of philosophies and events.

Barnaby, Frank, and Ronald Huisken, for Stockholm International Peace

Research Institute. *Arms Uncontrolled.* Harvard University Press, Cambridge, Mass., 1975. A survey of modern weapons systems and critical assessment of arms race.

Bohi, Douglas R., and Milton Russel. *U.S. Energy Policy: Alternatives for Security.* Johns Hopkins Press, Baltimore, 1975. A study of United States oil import and production policies, industry structure and international marketing, with analysis of the energy crisis and OPEC policy.

Bradford, Colin I., Jr., et al. *New Directions in Development: Latin America, Export, Credit, Population Growth, and U.S. Attitudes.* Praeger, New York, 1974. Four monograph-length selections on developmental challenges in Latin America and their implications for United States policy, on development financing and export promotion credits, on population control, and on United States attitudes toward the Third World.

Brown, W. Norman. *The United States and India, Pakistan, Bangladesh.* Harvard University Press, Cambridge, Mass., 1972. Sophisticated insights into the conditions on the subcontinent

Chawla, Sudershan, Melvin Gurtov, and Alain-Gerard Marsot, eds. *Southeast Asia under the New Balance of Power.* Praeger, New York, 1974. Short essays, selected documents, and a bibliography compiled in an effort to relate Southeast Asia to the new balance of power.

Chilcote, Ronald H., and Joel C. Edelstein, eds. *Latin America: The Struggle with Dependency and Beyond.* Halsted, New York, 1974. A chronology and an analysis of United States (and other foreign) impact on selected Latin American nations within the context of the dependency thesis.

Clark, Paul G. *American Aid for Development.* Praeger, New York, 1972. Recommendations for the reshaping of American aid policies.

Cohen, Benjamin J. *The Question of Imperialism: Political Economy of Dominance and Dependence.* Basic Books, New York, 1973. Sees the cause of imperialism in the anarchic nature of the international political system rather than in capitalism.

Connell-Smith, Gordon. *The United States and Latin America: An Historical Analysis of Inter-American Relations.* Halsted, New York, 1974. A valuable background study.

Cotler, Julio, and Richard R. Fagen, eds. *Latin America and the United States: The Changing Political Realities.* Stanford University Press, Stanford, Calif., 1974. Essays by North American and Latin American scholars for a conference in Lima in 1972 on political relations between the United States and Latin America and the variety of conditions and special situations that prevail at a national level.

Davis, Harold E., et al. *Latin American Foreign Policies; An Analysis.* Johns Hopkins Press, Baltimore, 1975. Essays mostly on the foreign policy of individual countries.

Elliott, Charles. *Patterns of Poverty in the Third World: A Study of Social and Economic Stratification.* Praeger, New York, 1975. A critique of exploitation, with a statistical appendix and bibliography.

Erb, Guy F., and Valeriana Kallab, eds. *Beyond Dependency: The Develop-*

ing World Speaks Out. Overseas Development Council, Washington, D.C., 1975. A compendium by Third World scholars, useful as background for understanding their differences with and demands on the industrial nations.

Evron, Yair. *The Middle East: Nations, Superpowers and Wars*. Praeger, New York, 1973. A concise summary of diplomatic activities and strategic considerations between 1948 and 1967, with an analysis of Israel's domestic scene and United States strategic interests.

Farvar, Taghi, and John P. Milton. *Careless Technology: Ecology and International Development*. Natural History, New York, 1975. Negative findings on foreign aid projects.

Fontaine, Roger W. *Brazil and the United States: Toward a Maturing Relationship*. American Enterprise Institute for Public Policy Research, Washington, D.C., 1974. An analysis of the current relations between Brazil and the United States, suggesting that Brazil should be integrated into the developed Atlantic community.

Friedländer, Saul, and Mahmoud Hussein. *Arabs and Israelis: A Dialogue*. Holmes and Meier, New York, 1975. A debate on the fundamentals of the conflict.

Goldhamer, Herbert. *The Foreign Powers in Latin America*. Princeton University Press, Princeton, N.J., 1972. An analysis of the impact on Latin America of the important nonhemispheric powers as well as the United States.

Goodsell, Charles T. *American Corporations and Peruvian Politics*. Harvard University Press, Cambridge, Mass., 1974. An empirically based, balanced, and authoritative study.

Grunwald, Joseph, et al. *Latin American Economic Integration and U.S. Policy*. Brookings Institution, Washington, D.C., 1972. An overview of various integration schemes and United States policy toward them.

Gurtov, Melvin. *The United States against the Third World: Antinationalism and Intervention*. Praeger, New York, 1974. A detailed radical analysis of American decisions to intervene in Third World societies.

Howard, Harry N. *Turkey, the Straits and U.S. Policy*. Johns Hopkins Press, Baltimore, 1975. An analysis of United States–Turkey relations from 1830 until after World War II.

Howe, James W., ed. *The U.S. and World Development: Agenda for Action 1975*. Praeger, New York, 1975. Links the United States with the Third World in discussion of various crisis areas, such as population, ocean management, and so forth, and proposes enlightened policies.

Hunter, Robert E., et al. *The U.S. and the Developing World: Agenda for Action, 1973*. Overseas Development Council, Washington, D.C., 1973. Useful statistical appendices.

Ingram, George M. *Expropriation of U.S. Property in South America: Nationalization of Oil and Copper Companies in Peru, Bolivia, and Chile*. Macmillan, New York, 1974. Examines causes and consequences of the major nationalizations and the roles of nationalizing governments, nationalized companies, and the United States government.

Kearney, Robert W. *Politics and Modernization in South and Southeast Asia.* Halsted Press, New York, 1975. Essays on the political problems of six important countries.

Klebanoff, Shoshona. *Middle East Oil and U.S. Foreign Policy: With Special Reference to the U.S. Energy Crisis.* Praeger, New York, 1974. Discussion of the relationship between the international petroleum companies and the United States government since 1919, dependence on Middle Eastern oil, Soviet penetration, and policy implications.

Knowles, Ruth Sheldom. *America's Oil Famine: How It Happened and When It Will End.* Coward, McCann and Geoghegan, New York, 1975. A rather popular and optimistic account of the United States position.

Kristensen, Thorkil. *Development in Rich and Poor Countries: A General Theory with Statistical Analyses.* Praeger, New York, 1974. Argues that many variables associated with the development process are highest in medium-income countries, and that knowledge is replacing capital as the most important element of production.

McCann, Frank, Jr. *The Brazilian-American Alliance 1937–1945.* Princeton University Press, Princeton, N.J., 1973. An authoritative analysis of an important period.

Melady, Thomas P., and R. B. Suhartono. *Development: Lessons for the Future.* Orbis Books, Maryknoll, N.Y., 1973. Examines the growing gap between the most successful and the least successful developing countries as well as the dependency between developed and under-developed nations.

Moras, T. H. *Multinational Corporations and the Politics of Dependence.* Princeton University Press, Princeton, N.J., 1974. A study of copper investment in Chile.

Nakhleh, Emile A. *The United States and Saudi Arabia: A Policy Analysis.* American Enterprise Institute for Public Policy Research, Washington, D.C., 1975. Study of economic, political, and strategic factors in relations with the oil giant.

Negandhi, Anant R., and S. Benjamin Prasad. *The Frightening Angels: A Study of U.S. Multinationals in Developing Nations.* Kent State University Press, Kent, Ohio, 1975. Based on a study of forty-seven United States subsidiaries and comparable local firms in Argentina, Brazil, India, the Philippines, and Uruguay.

Newlon, Daniel H., and Norman V. Breckner. *The Oil Security System: An Import Strategy for Achieving Oil Security and Reducing Oil Prices.* D. C. Heath, Lexington, Mass., 1975.

Packenham, Robert A. *Liberal America and the Third World: Political Development Ideas in Foreign Aid and Social Science.* Princeton University Press, Princeton, N.J., 1973. A critical study of the underlying assumptions of United States aid programs after World War II.

Payer, Cheryl. *The Debt Trap: The International Monetary Fund and the Third World.* Monthly Review Press, New York, 1975. Contends that the rich capitalist countries exploit the helplessly dependent poor countries; has case studies of the Philippines, Indonesia, Indochina, Yugoslavia, Brazil, India, Chile, Ghana, and North Korea.

Petras, James, and Morris Morley. *The United States and Chile: Imperialism and the Overthrow of the Allende Government.* Monthly Review Press, New York, 1975. An argument that the fall of the leftist government in Chile was the result of pressures exerted by the United States through subversion and financial squeeze.

Pinello, Adalberto J. *The Multinational Corporation as a Force in Latin American Politics: A Case Study of the International Petroleum Company in Peru.* Praeger, New York, 1973.

Piotrow, Phyllis Tilson. *World Population Crisis: The United States Responds.* Praeger, New York, 1973. How the United States government changed policy on world population problems.

Poats, Rutherford M. *Technology for Developing Nations: New Directions for U.S. Technical Assistance.* Brookings Institution, Washington, D.C., 1972. An argument for substantially changed assumptions and programs of techincal assistance.

Schumacher, E. F. *Small Is Beautiful.* Harper and Row, New York, 1973. An argument for intermediate technology.

Sharp, Daniel A. *U.S. Foreign Policy and Peru.* University of Texas Press, Austin, 1972. Includes treatment of business interests and the role of the United States in international lending agencies.

Simon, Sheldon W. *Asian Neutralism and U.S. Policy.* American Enterprise Institute for Public Policy Research, Washington, D.C., 1975. An examination of consequences of détente in East and Southeast Asia.

Smith, Stewart. *U.S. Neocolonialism in Africa.* International Publishers, New York, 1974. A thesis on economic imperialism in Africa and collusion with the white-minority regimes.

Szyliowicz, Joseph S., and Bard E. O'Neill, eds. *The Energy Crisis and U.S. Foreign Policy.* Praeger, New York, 1975.

Tanzer, Michael. *The Energy Crisis: World Struggle for Power and Wealth.* Monthly Review Press, New York, 1975. Lays the blame for the fuel crisis on the oil companies.

Tendler, Judith. *Inside Foreign Aid.* Johns Hopkins Press, Baltimore, 1975. A primarily theoretical essay criticizing foreign aid from the viewpoint of organizational theory.

Thompson, W. Scott. *Unequal Partners: Philippine and Thai Relations with the United States, 1965–1975.* Lexington Books, Lexington, Mass., 1975. Strategies of small-power coexistence with the United States.

Tugwell, Franklin. *The Politics of Oil in Venezuela.* Stanford University Press, Stanford, Calif., 1975. A scholarly study of the relation of oil to political development.

Wagner, R. Harrison, *U.S. Policy toward Latin America: A Study in Domestic and International Politics.* Stanford University Press, Stanford, Calif., 1970. Covers the period from World War II to the Alliance for Progress.

Weissman, Stephen R. *American Foreign Policy in the Congo, 1960–1964.* Cornell University Press, Ithaca, N.Y., 1974.

Weissman, Stephen R., ed. *The Trojan Horse: A Radical Look at Foreign Aid.* Ramparts Press, Palo Alto, Calif., 1975. A neo-Marxist critique.

White, John. *The Politics of Foreign Aid.* St. Martin's Press, New York, 1974. A comprehensive theoretical work on foreign aid, multilateral as well as bilateral.

Wilson, Dick. *The Neutralization of Southeast Asia.* Praeger, New York, 1975. A survey of prospects for regional neutralization with focus on the ASEAN states.

CHAPTER TEN   THE EVOLVING STATE SYSTEM

Alexander, Yonah, ed. *International Terrorism: National, Regional, and Global Perspectives.* Praeger, New York, 1976. Essays by a dozen professors on nongovernmental terrorism, with a notably good bibliography.

Beitz, Charles R., and Theodore Herman, eds. *Peace and War.* W. H. Freeman, San Francisco, 1973. Essays on "The War System" and "Building a World Peace System."

Boll, J. Bower. *Transnational Terror.* Hoover Institution, Stanford, Calif., 1975. A brief introduction to the problems of international terrorism, with recommendations.

Brown, Lester R. *In the Human Interest: A Strategy to Stabilize World Population.* W. W. Norton, New York, 1974. A comprehensive and readable study of population growth and attendant problems, with a proposal for improvement.

——. *World Without Borders.* Random House, New York, 1972. An eloquent study of all aspects of interdependence.

Bruun, Kettil, Lynna Pan, and Ingemar Rexed. *The Gentlemen's Club: International Control of Drugs and Alcohol.* University of Chicago Press, Chicago, 1975. A critique of the present ineffectual international drug control system, with recommendations for improvement.

Brzezinski, Zbigniew. *Between Two Ages: America's Role in the Technetronic Era.* Viking, New York, 1970. Projects the impact of technology and electronics upon society in the United States, the Soviet Union, and other "postindustrial" states.

Buchan, Alastair. *The End of the Postwar Era: A New Balance of World Power.* Saturday Review Press, New York, 1974. An agenda of security issues.

——. *Power and Equilibrium in the 1970s.* Praeger, New York, 1973. Assesses new balances of power and presents a pentagonal structure.

Dupuy, René-Jean. *The Law of the Sea: Current Problems.* Oceana, Dobbs Ferry, N.Y., 1975.

Goodwin, Geoffrey L., and Andrew Linklater, eds. *New Dimensions of World Politics.* Wiley, New York, 1975. Essays on the nature of contemporary international society.

Hollick, Ann L., and Robert E. Osgood. *New Era of Ocean Politics.* Johns Hopkins Press, Baltimore, 1975. Policies and issues of sea law.

Johnson, D. Gale. *World Food Problems and Prospects*. American Enterprise Institute for Public Policy Research, Washington, D.C., 1975. Sees a need primarily for better political approaches.

Kay, David A., and Eugene B. Skolnikoff, eds. *World Eco-Crisis: International Organizations in Response*. University of Wisconsin Press, Madison, 1972. International aspects of ecology and economic and organizational issues.

Kemp, Geoffrey, Robert L. Pfalzgraff, Jr., and Uri Ra'anan, eds. *The Superpowers in a Multinuclear World*. D. C. Heath, Lexington, Mass., 1974. Essays on nuclear proliferation and the role of the nuclear powers.

Keohane, Robert O., and Joseph S. New, Jr. *Transnational Relations and World Politics*. Harvard University Press, Cambridge, Mass., 1972. Scholarly and forward-looking essays on transnational developments.

Kneese, Allen V., et al., eds. *Managing the Environment: International Economic Cooperation for Pollution Control*. Praeger, New York, 1971.

Levi, Werner. *International Politics: Foundations of the System*. University of Minnesota Press, Minneapolis, 1974. A discussion of the nature of international society, the role of power, modes of settlement of international conflict, and war and peace.

Liska, George. *States in Evolution: Changing Societies and Traditional Systems in World Politics*. Johns Hopkins Press, Baltimore, 1973. Posits problems in reference to regional and global balances of power in a hierarchical international system.

Midlarsky, Manus I. *On War: Political Violence in the International System*. Free Press, New York, 1975. A behaviorally oriented study of the onset and course of wars.

Nettleship, Martin A., R. Dale Givens, and Alexander Nettleship. *War: Its Causes and Correlates*. Aldine, Chicago, 1975. A thorough, scholarly, largely anthropological study of the institution of war.

Sanders, Benjamin. *Safeguards against Nuclear Proliferation*. MIT Press, Cambridge, Mass., 1975. A short monograph on the work of the International Atomic Energy Agency.

Skolnikoff, Eugene B. *The International Imperatives of Technology*. University of California Institute of International Studies, Berkeley, 1972. An analysis of the probable impact of technological advances on international political systems.

Sprout, Harold, and Margaret Sprout. *Toward a Politics of the Planet Earth*. Van Nostrand Reinhold, New York, 1971. A study of the effects of interdependence.

Stockholm International Peace Research Institute. *The Nuclear Age*. MIT Press, Cambridge, Mass., 1975. A systematic study of problems of nuclear proliferation.

Thompson, Kenneth W. *Understanding World Politics*. University of Notre Dame Press, Notre Dame, Ind., 1975. Discusses a wide range of issues with special emphasis on America's role in the world.

Utton, Albert E., and Daniel H. Henning, eds. *Environmental Policy: Concepts and International Implications*. Praeger, New York, 1973.

Emphasis on legal regulation, international management, politics, and the policy process.

CHAPTER ELEVEN   WORLD ORDER

Beaton, Leonard. *The Reform of Power: A Proposal for an International Security System.* Viking, New York, 1972. Suggestions for a structure of world order.

Bergsten, C. Fred, ed. *The Future of the International Economic Order: An Agenda for Research.* D. C. Heath, Lexington, Mass., 1973. A blueprint for systematic research.

El-Ayouti, Yassin. *The U.N. and Decolonization.* Nijhoff, The Hague, 1971 Stresses the catalytic role of the Afro-Asian states in the decolonization process.

Fabian, Larry L. *Soldiers without Enemies: Preparing the U.N. for Peacekeeping.* Brookings Institution, Washington, D.C., 1971. Survey of United Nations peacekeeping operations.

Falk, Richard A. *A Study of Future Worlds.* Free Press, New York, 1975. This study represents the North American team's model for the future world and is part of the World Order Models Project (WOMP). A desirable future world is elaborated and stages to the new global polity for the 1990s described.

Finkelstein, Lawrence S., ed. *The U.S. and International Organization: The Changing Setting.* MIT Press, Cambridge, Mass., 1969. Essays on various aspects of contemporary international organization.

Goodrich, Leland. *The United Nations in a Changing World.* Columbia University Press, New York, 1974. A study of capacities and limitations.

Hiscocks, Richard. *The Security Council: A Study in Adolescence.* Free Press, New York, 1974. A review of the achievements and failures of the Security Council, problems and prospects.

Hudec, Robert E. *The GATT Legal System and World Trade Diplomacy.* Praeger, New York, 1975. A useful history of GATT from 1947 to 1975, and a study of this area of economic diplomacy.

Mendlovitz, Saul H., ed. *On the Creation of a Just World Order: Preferred Worlds for the 1990s.* Free Press, New York, 1975. Urgent problems facing mankind are dealt with by international scholars.

Moskowitz, Moses. *International Concern with Human Rights.* Sijthoff, Leyden/Oceana Publications, Dobbs Ferry, N.Y., 1975. A plea for a new generalized respect for human rights.

Riggs, Robert E. *U.S./U.N.: Foreign Policy and International Organization.* Appleton-Century-Crofts, New York, 1971. A study on the pursuit of American policy objectives through the United Nations.

Rikhye, Indar Jit, Michael Harbottle, and Bjorn Egge. *The Thin Blue Line: International Peacekeeping and Its Future.* Yale University Press, New Haven, Conn., 1974. History plus a plea for a better organized international peacekeeping force.

Rubinstein, Alvin Z., and George Ginsburg, eds. *Soviet and American*

Policies in the U.N.: A Twenty-Five Year Perspective. New York University Press, New York, 1971. Superpower relations at the United Nations in the recent past.

Weiss, Thomas George. *International Bureaucracy: An Analysis of the Operation of Functional and Global International Secretariats.* D. C. Heath, Lexington, Mass., 1975. A useful study of the problems of international bureaucracy, using ILO and UNICEF as cases.

CHAPTER TWELVE   DIRECTIONS

Bauer, Robert A., ed. *The United States in World Affairs: Leadership, Partnership, or Disengagement.* University Press of Virginia, Charlottesville, 1975. Essays on the American role, interventionist or not.

Bloomfield, Lincoln P. *In Search of American Foreign Policy: The Human Use of Power.* Oxford University Press, New York, 1974. A critical review of American foreign policy since World War II from a liberal perspective.

Chace, James. *A World Elsewhere: The New American Foreign Policy.* Charles Scribner's Sons, New York, 1973. In the obsolescence of containment, the author examines the statist and federalist approaches.

Cobbledick, James R. *Choice in American Foreign Policy: Options for the Future.* Thomas Y. Crowell, New York, 1973. The author examines American foreign policy and presents alternatives for seven major areas of the world.

Commager, Henry Steele. *The Defeat of America: Presidential Power and the National Character.* Simon and Schuster, New York, 1975. In essays written between 1968 and 1974, Commager argues that the American tradition of mission was perverted by the cold war and the Vietnam war.

Gilbert, John H. *The New Era in American Foreign Policy.* St. Martin's Press, New York, 1974. Papers prepared for a symposium on American foreign policy in the 1970s.

Hilsman, Roger. *The Crouching Future: International Politics and U.S. Foreign Policy—A Forecast.* Doubleday, Garden City, N.Y., 1975. A prediction of the shape of the world and its implications for American foreign policy.

Kaplan, Morton A., ed. *Isolation or Interdependence? Today's Choices for Tomorrow's World.* Free Press, New York, 1975. Conference papers debating mainly the choice stated.

Kintner, William R., and Richard B. Foster, eds. *National Strategy in a Decade of Change: An Emerging U.S. Policy.* Lexington Books, Lexington, Mass., 1973. A collection of papers explaining the ambiguous Nixon doctrine.

Levy, Reynold. *Nearing the Crossroads: Contending Approaches to Contemporary American Foreign Policy.* Free Press, New York, 1975. Sees American opinion divided between an essentially domestic orientation and an international, indivisible-world orientation.

Nuechterlein, Donald E. *United States National Interest in a Changing World*. University Press of Kentucky, Lexington, 1973. An attempt to define and apply the concept of national interest.

Owen, Henry, ed. *The Next Phase in Foreign Policy*. Brookings Institution, Washington, D.C., 1973. Essays attempting to discern how the United States role will change and whether the United States can fulfill its changed role.

Index